Presented to the library
of Bowdoin College

James Charles Roy

August 3, 1999

# The Vanished Kingdom

**Also by James Charles Roy**

*The Road Wet, the Wind Close:*
*Celtic Ireland* (1986)

*Islands of Storm* (1991)

with James L. Pethica,
*"To the Land of the Free from this*
*Island of Slaves": Henry Stratford Persse's*
*Letters from Galway to America,*
*1821–1832* (1996)

# The Vanished Kingdom

## Travels Through the
## History of Prussia

⁂

## James Charles Roy

*Introduction by
Amos Elon*

Westview Press
A Member of the Perseus Books Group

Copyright © 1999 by Westview Press, A Member of the Perseus Books Group

Published in 1999 in the United States of America by Westview Press, 5500 Central Avenue, Boulder, Colorado 80301-2877, and in the United Kingdom by Westview Press, 12 Hid's Copse Road, Cumnor Hill, Oxford OX2 9JJ

*Designed by Heather Hutchison*

Library of Congress Cataloging-in-Publication Data
Roy, James Charles, 1945–
   The vanished kingdom : travels through the history of Prussia /
James Charles Roy.
      Includes bibliographical references (p.   cm.) and index.
      ISBN 0-8133-3667-8
      1. Prussia (Germany)—Historiography.   2. National
characteristics, Prussian.   3. Prussia (Germany)—History—
Philosophy.   4. Political culture—Germany—Prussia.   5. Europe,
Eastern—Politics and government—1989–.   I. Title.
DD345.R69   1999
943'.0072—dc21
                                                                99-14278
                                                                     CIP

The paper used in this publication meets the requirements of the American National Standard for Permanence of Paper for Printed Library Materials Z39.48-1984.

10   9   8   7   6   5   4   3   2   1

*This book is dedicated to*
*Francis Caswell*
*Thomas N. Brown*
*Roger Howell Jr.*
*Three schools, three historians, three mentors.*

*Ease is inimical to civilization.*
—**Arnold Toynbee**

*To have character and be a German
is the same thing.*
—**Erich Ludendorff**

**Der Spiegel:** *Besides you, only your colleague
Martin Walser is kept awake at night by the
topic of Germany. He broods: "When I think of
Königsberg, I find myself in a vortex of history
that whirls me around and swallows me up."*
**Günter Grass:** *That's too much feeling and too
little awareness.*

# Contents

List of Illustrations                                           xi


Introduction: Kaliningrad, the Nowhere City,                    1
*Amos Elon*


## Part One
## Beginnings
## The Teutonic Knights

1   Old Prussia: Finding the Way                                25

2   Marienburg: Crusades and the Birth of Prussia              43

3   Danzig: Drive to the East                                  65

4   Grünwald: The Knights Repulsed                             81

5   Frauenburg: Polish Inroads                                 93


## Part Two
## Consolidation
## The Hohenzollern Dynasty

6   Grosse Werder: The Great Elector                           105

7   Neudeck: The Soldier-King                                  115

8   Eylau: Napoleonic Disaster                                 133

# Part Three
# Blood and Iron
# Bismarck and Wilhelm

 9  Cadinen: Rush for Glory                                   163
10  Tannenberg: The Siamese Twins                             177
11  Gross Pötzdorf: Weimar Interlude                          195

# Part Four
# Extinction
# The Second World War

12  Suwalki: War                                              211
13  The River Memel: Into Russia                              231
14  Stutthof: Final Solutions                                 241
15  Rastenburg: Madness, Assassination, Honor                 253
16  Ostpreussen: Along Country Roads                          285
17  In the West: Survivors                                    313

Notes                                                         327
Select Bibliography                                           353
A Note on the Geography of East Prussia                       375
Credits                                                       377
Acknowledgments                                               379
Index                                                         381

# Illustrations

Maps and Figures

East Prussia, 1939                                                    xv
Germany, 1918                                                        xvi
Union of Ostpreussen and Brandenburg under a single
   Hohenzollern, 1618                                                109


Photos

Königsberg, 1733                                                      2
Street vendor                                                         7
Addicts in a park                                                     8
The Neue Königsthor                                                  11
House of the Soviets                                                 12
Veteran                                                              13
Countryside near Allenstein                                          17
Germania                                                             27
Hindenburg's grave                                                   30
Awaiting repair                                                      40
Kaiser Wilhelm II reviews his troops, Potsdam                        41
Bells, Potsdam garrison church                                       42
Former German estate, Stobity                                        44
German barn, Debina                                                  45
Teutonic castle, Neidenburg                                          47
Teutonic castle, Rehden                                              55
Portcullis, Marienburg                                               59
Teutonic castle, Allenstein                                          63
Danzig                                                               68
Polish war veteran, Danzig                                           70
A Danzig merchant, by Hans Holbein the Younger                       74

Effigy of Henry, earl of Derby, later Henry IV, king of England,
Canterbury Cathedral                                                76
September 1, 1939, 4:45 A.M.: The ship *Schleswig-Holstein*
and the first salvo of World War II, Danzig                         79
The Battle of Grünwald                                             82
Death of a Teutonic knight (detail from *The Battle of
Grünwald* by Jan Matejko, 1878)                                   85
Cathedral Hill, Frauenburg                                        94
Old German church and current brick quarry, near Elbing           96
Bishop's palace, Lidzbark Warmiński                               98
Polish knight of around 1500, Lidzbark Warmiński                 101
The Great Elector                                                113
Hindenburg family cemetery, Neudeck                              117
Frieze on the manor house, Finckenstein                          121
Friedrich der Grosse and hounds, Sans Souci                      127
*Frederick the Great* by J. G. Ziesenis                          131
Water tower                                                      135
*Mafiya* house                                                  137
Kant scholar Leonard Kalinnikov                                  138
Drunkard                                                        141
*Napoleon at Eylau* (detail from a painting by
Antoine Gros, 1808)                                             151
Napoleon's headquarters, Finckenstein                           153
Luftwaffe veteran at cathedral                                  156
Orthodox priest and deacon                                      157
Arrested                                                        158
Prewar military maneuvers: The kaiser instructs his
generals                                                        164
The kaiser's chapel                                             165
Klaus von Holleben with ancestor                                171
Battle standards, Tannenberg                                    178
Kaiser Wilhelm with von Hindenburg and Ludendorff               194
Weather vane, with Russian bullet holes                         196
Bernd Volprecht with trophies from his former estate,
shot since 1989                                                 199
Gross Pötzdorf                                                  200
Aronek Kierszkowski with Avery's *Reclining Woman*              215
"My parents and our employees at the fur company . . . "        220
Current tenant                                                  225
Naum Adelson, the last Jew of Suwalki                           229

Postcards of old Königsberg 232
Panzer veteran 234
"During maneuvers in East Prussia." 238
"A short way from Stalingrad. My vehicle here, all stuck." 238
"I was stationed at the academy in Potsdam. I had a class of
    reserve officers." 239
"On our way to Stalingrad. This was perfect ground for tanks." 239
"This was my class at Potsdam, reserve officers. That is me,
    the officer with the sword." 239
"My shoes are probably in there" (Aronek Kierszkowski) 246
Bormann's bunker 269
Hitler's bunker 278
Hitler's trousers, July 20, 1944 280
Nerve center of the coup, July 20, 1944: Stauffenberg's
    office and telephone, Bendlerblock, Berlin 282
Grave of Youain Mikolai Semenovich 286
Soviets storm Königsberg 288
German refugees, Königsberg, winter 1945 289
"This is my husband on his family's East Prussian estate." 291
"Otto, the foreman. He assembled all the wagons for the trek." 291
"My wedding day in 1946." 291
"This was our first home in the West." 291
German civilians flee the Soviets 296
*Awaiting the inevitable: German troops in East Prussia*, 1945,
    by A. Hierl 308
Katharina von Negenborn with recovered china 314
Marion, Countess Dönhoff 323
Count Otto William Frederick Grote and law files 326

*I was in America for a while and attended a Bible class after church. I asked everyone, "Where do you think East Prussia is?" They put it in the area of Schleswig-Holstein; they put it near Hamburg; they put it along the Rhine; they put it in Denmark—anyplace—but they never picture it the right way, up with the Baltic states. No one knows anything about Prussia, but they should. We Germans never change in our love for it.*

—**German veteran, World War II**

# EAST PRUSSIA
## 1939

N

LITHUANIA

Memel

MEMELLAND (Annexed 1939)

Memel or Niemen R.

Kurisches Haff

Tilsit

BALTIC SEA

Gulf of Danzig

Pillau  KÖNIGSBERG

Pregel R.

EAST

Insterburg

Frisches Nehrung

Frisches Haff

FREE CITY

Stutthof

Frauenburg
Cadinen

Eylau
1807

Friedland
1807

DANZIG

PRUSSIA

CORRIDOR

Gross Werder

Nogat R.  Elbing

Rastenburg

MASURIAN LAKES

Suwalki

POLISH

River

Marienburg

Finckenstein

Allenstein

Chełmno
(Kulm)

Marienwerder
Neudeck

Vistula

Grudziądz
(Graudenz)

Tannenberg
1410
1914

POLAND

Toruń
(Thorn)

0 ____ KM ____ 50
0 ____ MILES ____ 50

Jane Crosen, Mapmaker

GERMANY
1918

0 ━━━━ 50
KM
0 ━━━━ 50
MILES

Elbe R.

BRA

Magdeburg .

G E R M A

N

W                    E

S

# Introduction:
# Königsberg
# (Kaliningrad)
## The Nowhere City

IN DAYTIME THE MAIN AVENUES of Kaliningrad—wide enough to allow ten tanks abreast to pass a reviewing stand—are half deserted. Traffic is sparse. Before the Russians took it over in 1945, this ice-free Baltic seaport was the ancient German city of Königsberg, the historic capital of East Prussia and one of the more attractive towns of the German empire. Recently there has even been talk of Germany's taking the city back. But now the barren monotony and inhuman scale of Communist urban planning make Kaliningrad—the phantom of a city without any visible center—possibly one of the ugliest places in the world. Four hundred thousand inhabitants—70 percent transient sailors, fishermen, and members of the Russian armed forces—live here in squalid apartment blocks, crumbling mountain ranges of tar and cement and peeling plaster, gray on gray.

The public squares, as in most cities built by the Soviets after the war, are vast, each large enough to accommodate almost the entire population. Loudspeakers left over from the old Communist public-address system still dangle from their poles. There are no mass rallies nowadays, and the loudspeakers are rarely if ever used. But the statue of M. L. Kalinin, a former president of the Soviet Union (he is said to have sent his own wife to the gulag), is still standing in a huge square outside the railroad station. The city was named for him in 1945 after its capture by the Red Army in fierce street fighting with the Wehrmacht and its annexation by the Soviet Union. A giant statue of Lenin is

*Königsberg, 1733*

also still standing on Ploshchad Pobedy (Victory Square)—the former Adolf-Hitler-Platz.

Founded in 1255 by knights of the Teutonic Order on rising ground above the River Pregel (now called Pregolya), Königsberg was the seat of a famous Lutheran university. In the countryside nearby were some of the largest and finest estates of the Prussian military aristocracy. In this quintessentially Germanic region, the proverbial Prussian virtues of duty and discipline and austere living were cultivated in huts and manor houses, while in the city itself the dukes and the kings of Prussia were crowned. Immanuel Kant was born here in 1724, and he hardly ever left. At the university he taught not only philosophy but geography and math as well. Johann Gottfried Herder, a Lutheran minister's son who also taught here, almost single-handedly invented Pan-German nationalism as the expression of the "spirit" of language and folk song and poetry.

Königsberg was an important garrison town, where generations of Prussian officers were trained in blind, ungrudging obedience to the word of command. Yet among young graduates of its military academy

were also some of the spirited, if ineffective, aristocratic officers who conspired to launch the coup against Hitler's tyranny on July 20, 1944.

Driving through today's city, you would never guess how pretty Königsberg was. Old photographs show a scenic place, with a busy harbor, several fine churches, picturesque wharfs, and stately embankments and promenades along the river. On the hilltop stood the Prussian royal palace, with its imposing, crenellated towers. In the middle of the river was a densely built up island whose narrow lanes, lined with medieval frame houses, led to the great brick Gothic cathedral in which the Prussian kings were crowned. Its grotesque ruin survives today in the middle of the completely empty island, with Kant's relatively well preserved tombstone on the wall of the southwestern corner.

Nearly everything else has disappeared. When the Red Army stormed it in 1945, roughly a third of the old town was still standing and there were 120,000 remaining Germans. By 1947 the last of these had been deported to Germany or Kazakhstan, along with neighboring East Prussian farmers, many of whom died. Stalin ordered the old center of Prussian militarism bulldozed, leveled along the lines of a

Carthage, to be completely rebuilt as a model socialist city, a home for resettled Russians, Lithuanians, Georgians, Ukrainians, and other New Soviet Men and Women. Not all came voluntarily. Some were inmates of gulags ordered to settle in Kaliningrad after years of forced labor in the nearby swamps. The population today is still some 20 percent below its prewar level of 480,000.

The future of Kaliningrad Province, or *Oblast*, one of Russia's thirty-nine increasingly autonomous units, is currently a matter of intense debate. The sudden collapse of the Soviet empire made Kaliningrad the last bit of territory (a mere 4,200 square miles) left over from Stalin's vast gains in Eastern Europe during World War II. But Kaliningrad is now cut off from "mainland" Russia by 600 miles of newly independent Lithuanian, Latvian, and Belarus territory.

Only a few of the people I saw believe Kaliningrad should go on being governed directly from Moscow. They talk of Kaliningrad's becoming an "independent" Baltic state, of "full autonomy" within the Russian federation, of a German-Russian condominium, or of outright *Anschluss* with Germany. Like the officials of several other Russian regional governments, the local administrators here have become more independent of Moscow in recent months, and some are now actively courting virtually every prominent German businessperson, journalist, or missionary who visits the city.

"Kaliningrad must become Königsberg again," I was told by Arsenij Gulyga, a philosopher who is now the leading Russian authority on Kant. Gulyga recalls with some irony that as a young Soviet officer in 1945 he had been one of the "liberators" of the city. Now, he says, "it would be the most natural thing in the world" if the city could revert to Germany again. Geographically, it is nearer to Berlin (400 miles) than to St. Petersburg (512 miles) or Moscow (even further away). Historically, it remains a German city, he says. Gulyga would also like to see the tsarist monarchy restored.

There is a persistent rumor in Kaliningrad, as well as in the Baltic countries, that an East Prussian "government in exile" has already been formed by right-wing German politicians. At the same time, nationalists in both Warsaw and Vilnius are laying claim to parts of the Kaliningrad Autonomous Province, which they consider "historically" Polish or Lithuanian. In Warsaw in the summer of 1992, I saw leaflets calling for the return of Kaliningrad (Krolewiec) to "Mother Poland"; a few weeks later, in Vilnius, people were referring to the eastern parts of the Kaliningrad region as "Little Lithuania." The

Lithuanian ambassador to Washington provoked a minor storm last year when he announced that Little Lithuania was an empty space and could be taken over by his country immediately.

Several people I talked to speculated that Russia might sell the former Königsberg to the Germans for money—a temptation that the Moscow English-language weekly *New Times* described as possibly "too strong to resist." According to one view of German politics, past and present—which by now may be a misleading stereotype—"Prussia" and "Königsberg" are central or permanent features of the German national psyche. "Can Kohl really refuse a Russian offer to restore Königsberg?" a Polish diplomat in Warsaw asked me. He may be overestimating Germany's wealth after reunification or the true extent of its economic or strategic designs in the east. President Boris Yeltsin is thought to be sufficiently unconventional, and hard-pressed for Western currency, to entertain the idea of a sale for which there is well-known precedent—the Russian sale of Alaska to the United States in 1872.

But if Germany should reacquire East Prussia and Königsberg, this might undermine the entire postwar border pattern in Eastern Europe and revive fears of German expansionism. "Poland will strongly oppose it," a Polish diplomat says. According to a joke circulating that summer, pessimists in Kaliningrad are taking lessons in Polish and optimists lessons in German, while realists are learning how to shoot Kalashnikov submachine guns. (In fact, nearly 75 percent of the students at the state university have signed up for German courses.)

The city's economy is in a state of collapse. Average monthly pay went down from $16 a month in the summer of 1992 to an estimated $9 less than a year later, and a Russian army major makes only slightly more than twice that amount. One result is a thriving black market in military equipment. Western diplomats claim that in Kaliningrad you can buy yourself a missile ("there are more missiles here than trees") or a tank, if you so wish, and perhaps even nuclear fuel. One veteran observer told me that dozens of nuclear devices formerly located in the Kaliningrad area remain unaccounted for. On a smaller scale, petty thievery is rampant. At Lenin Prospekt I saw soldiers in uniform hawking gasoline from an army gas tank to civilian motorists.

The port's nuclear submarines have been transferred to the Arctic Sea or decommissioned, but there are many rumors, most of them ugly, about their condition and safety and of the shore-based reactors that once produced their fuel. The total amount of radioactive materials in them is said to be many times greater than that in the crippled unit at Chernobyl. In the Russian press there have been warnings of the danger of "dozens of Chernobyls" erupting in Russian naval bases in the Arctic and Baltic Seas. One morning I visited Admiral Vladimir Yegorov, the officer commanding the Russian Baltic fleet, in his office on the outskirts of Kaliningrad. I asked if there was substance to these warnings. Or was the press perhaps exaggerating? "The situation is even more serious than as reported in the press," he replied.

Early each morning, thousands line up outside the state-owned food shops, where shelves are usually bare. There are long lines for the bus, which sometimes never arrives and often has no room for more passengers when it does. Lines of a different sort form every morning at some of the main intersections: Hundreds of elderly women and men, mostly state pensioners, stand about for hours with a little something to sell—a bottle of Coke, a jar of preserved cucumbers, a handful of berries, a wilted cauliflower wrapped in a piece of torn newspaper. A dozen beautiful tulips can be had for the equivalent of twenty-five cents.

Almost every night graves are dug up and robbed by thieves who come to the cemeteries with metal detectors, looking for rings and other valuables and for gold teeth that they pry out with hammers and pliers. The police seem to do nothing to prevent this. I visited the Kaliningrad police chief, Colonel Viktor Shoshnikov, in his office. A tough-looking man with a habit of quoting Dostoevsky and Solzhenitsyn, he was sitting behind a large oak desk—before 1945 it may have served a German police chief—on which were many telephones. Keys dangled from his broad belt.

Shoshnikov began by lamenting that the crime rate in Kaliningrad had risen sharply since the beginning of glasnost and perestroika. Perestroika and the "Americanization of journalism" were inspiring permissiveness, pornography, prostitution, and capital crimes. The entire Kaliningrad region, he said, was infested by "a plague of Smerdyakovs," referring to the feebleminded, sinister half brother of the Karamazovs. People had never been afraid to go out at night, Shoshnikov said. Now they are.

At night the streets are dim. Nearly all electric power is imported from neighboring Lithuania, which is threatening to charge hard currency for it soon. In the bluish, uncertain light cast by neon and quartz street lamps, many of them damaged, the few souls still about throw

*Street vendor*

weird shadows on the ground, and the atmosphere, grim and gloomy
at best in daytime, is now even gloomier. On Prospekt Mira, outside
the rickety old Hotel Moskwa, where I was staying, drunks were hol-
lering in the dark long after midnight. I watched them stagger over the
potholes in the road, throwing bottles against the walls and shouting
obscenities at one another. Drug addicts passed the night on the scrag-

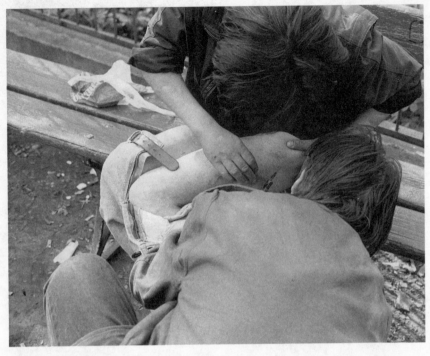

*Addicts in a park*

gly lawn nearby. According to a recent report in the liberal local
newsweekly *Mirror*, a former samizdat publication, Kaliningrad is the
"number one drug city" in the former Soviet Union. When I asked
Colonel Shoshnikov about that, he said that Kaliningrad is number
one on the list only because it is the only major city reporting true statistics; all the others were cheating.

⚜

One cannot escape an uncanny feeling of the existence of the old
Königsberg, like the negative of a damaged photograph, lying 10 to 20
feet underneath the city's surface, covered with rubble from the war
and from Stalin's bulldozers. If the huge mass of debris were cleared
away, the old topography, now flattened out, would come into view,
with its natural hills and dips, its landscaped river basins and embankments. Buried under the Lumumba and Friedrich Engels Sport Centers, under the Gamal Abdel Nasser Park and October Revolution
Housing Estates numbers 1–9, the old town has survived only in the

city's historical museum, where models of the 1945 street battles accompanied by sound effects convey an idea of the burning city's center, drowned in gunfire, at the moment of its capture by the Red Army.

Until the spring of 1991, Kaliningrad was a Soviet "security zone" known as the "Silent Swamp," since it was very difficult to visit and few people knew what was going on in the many military installations there. The region was closed to foreigners, except possibly spies, and even to most Russians except by special permit. Much of the rich farmland—before the war East Prussia was Germany's corn granary—lay fallow. Some 300 abandoned German villages that had engaged in farming before the war were never resettled. During the early 1960s, oil was found east of the city, but it was hardly developed. Nor was Kaliningrad's economic potential exploited, with its opportune geographic location at the westernmost point of the Soviet Union and its great port, as a link between Russia and central Europe. Instead, the place was turned into one of the Soviet Union's main military and naval bases.

According to a report published last spring in *Moscow News*, if war with the West had broken out, the main task of the Soviet Baltic fleet would have been to capture the Danish Straits and seal off the Baltic Sea. Between 1945 and 1991, no Western cargo ship was allowed into either Kaliningrad waters or those of nearby Baltijsk (the former Prussian Pillau). The city is still a military fiefdom, headquarters to the Eleventh Army of the Guards and seat of the admiral commanding the Russian Baltic fleet. The Baltic fleet, according to Admiral Yegorov, is expected nowadays to cover part of its maintenance costs by transporting civilian and foreign cargo and renting out ships to Western entrepreneurs and organizers of entertainments such as company anniversaries or wedding parties.

Throughout the city and its environs, the traffic on the streets is largely military. In the countryside one drives past parked tanks and camouflaged installations behind seemingly endless barbed-wire fences. Since the withdrawal of Russian troops from Germany, Poland, and the Baltic states, there is an even greater military presence. According to one Western estimate, close to a quarter million troops are now stationed here. All this, said a Western official stationed in Warsaw, may reflect not only the difficulties of absorbing the army into Russia but the extent of the Russians' self-consciousness and unease on this arch-Germanic spot.

Poland and the Soviet Union have treated the former German territories they took over after 1945 very differently. Many historic German cities in those territories suffered severe damage during the war. In the parts of Prussia (and Silesia) that fell under Polish rule (and from which 6 million Germans were expelled), the Poles made a conscious effort to absorb the German past. Claiming that in these "regained Polish historical lands" Polish merchants and peasants had always been in the majority, the Poles managed to make that past over into their own. Very carefully, even lovingly, and at great cost, they restored and in some cases rebuilt from scratch famous ancient German universities and Lutheran domed churches (they are now Catholic), castles, guildhouses, town halls, and Hanseatic burghers' mansions. The effort at rebuilding German ruins as Polish national monuments has been going on for decades; by now the brand new Gothic and baroque buildings have acquired their own patina and look genuine and old. Even that great symbol of German military colonialism in the east, the palatial castle of the grand masters of the Order of Teutonic Knights at Malbork (the former Marienburg) in East Prussia, has been restored as a major Polish historical landmark.

The Russians, apparently for ideological reasons, including their hostility to religion, and perhaps also from a sense of insecurity that the Poles did not share, systematically effaced nearly every remaining trace of German art and history in Kaliningrad. Churches, in particular, were the objects of Soviet distaste. The Lutheran Kreuzkirche, which had survived the war almost intact, served until recently as a factory for smoked fish. The main Catholic church in the city was converted into a concert hall. Other churches were blown up or dismantled. In the outskirts an old city gate—the Neue Königsthor—was left standing, a scene of long-forgotten skirmishes with the Swedes during the Seven Years' War, last restored under "the gracious reign" of Frederick William IV in 1843, according to a still legible plaque on the wall. Small-arms fire and the drunken vandalism of Soviet troops in 1945, I was told, account for the missing faces on three statues embedded in the wall that honor various kaisers from Germany's past. A few medieval forts have also survived, as have some of the stately German villas in the suburbs, which are now occupied by high-ranking Russian army officers and members of the old Communist elite. With but one exception, the major public monuments, including Kant's statue, were knocked over and melted down. Schiller alone escaped. A

*The Neue Königsthor*

Russian tank officer scrawled in chalk "Germany's Pushkin" on its pedestal, and the rank and file of victorious soldiers left it alone.

In one case, a Prussian grand elector's headless torso was turned into a Russian monument by sticking Field Marshal Mikhail Kutuzov's head on it; it can now be seen in the October Revolution Quarter. Extensive remains of the former royal palace were still standing in 1969, and according to Yuri Zabugin, a local architect, it could and should have been restored. Instead, it was bulldozed away. The bleak skeleton of a projected "House of the Soviets" has stood in its place unfinished since the mid-1980s, a monstrous eyesore twenty-two stories high, visible from nearly everywhere in the city. No trace is left of the many stone fountains that were still more or less intact after the war. "If I were dropped in this town by parachute, and asked where I was I would answer: perhaps in Irkutsk," wrote Marion, Countess Dönhoff, on the occasion of her first visit here since 1945. She had grown up on an estate a few miles outside Königsberg. "Nothing, absolutely nothing, reminds you of the old Königsberg. At no point could I have said, this was once the *Paradeplatz* [where Kant's old university stood], or here stood the *Schloss*. It is as though a picture has

*House of the Soviets*

been painted over; no one knows that underneath there had once been a different scene."

⁂

In the former *Paradeplatz*, now an open space of cement blocks, tarred walks, and a few dusty trees, I followed a group of German tourists down a flight of stairs into an underground bunker, now preserved as a war museum, where the last German commander of Festung Königsberg (Fortress Königsberg) capitulated to the Russians on April 9, 1945. Maps, photographs, and a diorama with model soldiers and flickering lights recall the savage battle in the burning streets and the heavy casualties on both sides. Hitler expected his Wehrmacht, surrounded and abandoned, to fight to the last man; walls were painted with the slogan, "We will never surrender!" But a photocopy of the capitulation agreement is on view, and it stipulates, among

*Veteran*

other things, that each German officer is allowed to take into captivity as many suitcases as he and his servant are able to carry.

The German tourists spent a few minutes in the bunker and soon climbed back up to take their seats on the bus. A few young boys crowded the exit outside and shyly tugged at their sleeves. They pulled from their shabby coat pockets little German medallions and other souvenirs dug up in the rubble, old silver spoons, combs, coins, military buttons, and rank insignia they were hoping to sell. Among several veterans hanging around, usually begging for money, there was a one-armed Russian who was offering Red Army battle medals, his own, he claimed, at thirty-five deutsche marks each. He had won one at Kiev, he said, and another in April 1945, outside Berlin.

The Hotel Moskwa was a crumbling old hostel with dusty curtains and threadbare carpets on wooden floorboards that creaked underfoot. The seedy little rooms came with small radio loudspeakers screwed to the wall that could be turned only louder or softer, never completely off, and were wired to receive but one local station that endlessly repeated the hit tunes of a local rock group named American Boys. In the long corridors, the stale air smelled of cigarette butts and cleaning fluid. On the walls were photographs of Kant's tomb and of the nearby Baltic resorts of Zelednogradsk (the former Bad Crenz) and Svetlogorsk (Rauschen), where Thomas Mann is said to have vacationed in the 1920s and where high-ranking Russian naval officers now have their summer houses.

One day, coming out of my room on the second floor of the hotel, which was reserved for foreigners, I encountered an elderly German tourist from West Berlin who called out, "Guten Morgen," and then told me in an assured tone that the Hotel Moskwa had been a German office building before the war, the headquarters of a big insurance company called Continental. This he knew for certain, he said. He himself was a Berliner, but his wife was a native of Königsberg and knew the city. We walked down the stairs together and in a more casual tone he added that there was no doubt, no doubt whatsoever, that Königsberg would soon be German again. "It is in the stars," he said. "And in the books. As Charles de Gaulle put it, everything in the world changes, except geography." The Russians themselves must be conscious of this, he continued. "They can't really believe it possible for the city of Immanuel Kant to be a Russian city. It is an absurdity."

"It's happened before," I suggested. In the eighteenth century, after the Seven Years' War, when Königsberg fell briefly to the Russians, Kant himself and the entire university faculty voluntarily took an oath of allegiance to the "illustrious and all-powerful empress of all Russians, Elizabeth Petrovna, etc." and to her heir, the future Peter III. I had just read that in a newly available English translation of Arsenij Gulyga's biography of Kant. He replied, "That doesn't count. The wars of the eighteenth century never affected ordinary people. And there was no nationalism then."

In Germany in recent years, there has been a revival of interest in Prussia and Prussianism. The bones of Frederick the Great, which the Nazis had evacuated to West Germany to keep from falling into Russian hands, were carried back to Potsdam in 1991 and in the presence of Chancellor Helmut Kohl ceremoniously reinterred next to the emperor's greyhounds in the park of Sans Souci. Prussia continues to haunt the German imagination. It figures in all sorts of German myths, both good and bad. The Prussian tradition of public service—

the plotters against Hitler had been Prussian noblemen—is pitted against Prussian worship of discipline and authoritarianism. A powerful German lobby advances the right of former Prussians to repossess the old *Heimat* or at the very least be compensated for lost property. The revival of interest in Prussia, highlighted recently by three unusually extravagant exhibitions in Berlin (on Prussia in Europe; on Bismarck, the Iron Chancellor; and on the last kaiser, Wilhelm II), has been interpreted as possibly reflecting a revival of nationalism in Germany, especially since reunification.

In Kaliningrad I was told that since the city was opened to outsiders in 1991, some 40,000 German visitors had passed through, many of them former residents of Königsberg or members of former Königsberg families who wanted to see their Prussian homeland. The traffic was increasing all the time and was known in the trade as *Heimwehtourismus*, or homesickness-tourism. To help German visitors find their way in the rebuilt city, a 1941 street plan, with its Hermann-Göring-Strasse and Adolf-Hitler-Platz, has recently been published, not by a German neo-Nazi but by an enterprising private printer in St. Petersburg.

When I joined a bus full of German visitors in Kaliningrad one morning, the Intourist guide on duty, a young woman borrowed for the day from the German Department of Kaliningrad State University, systematically called out the names of old German streets—Hansaring, Steindamm, Junkerstrasse, Reichplatz. Perhaps because the guide was so well informed, the tourists asked few questions. Like many young people in Kaliningrad today, she referred to the city by its old name, Königsberg. She had never liked Kalinin anyway, she said; Kalinin had ordered that little children caught stealing bread be shot.

For many years, she said, talk about Kaliningrad's German past had been frowned upon. As recently as 1984, the Communist Party newspaper would not publish an article, written by a colleague of hers, a philosopher, on the occasion of Kant's 260th birthday. She pointed resentfully into the empty air at long-vanished landmarks. But, she said proudly, a number of concerned citizens of Kaliningrad had been successful in at least saving the ruined dome of the cathedral, even though Leonid Brezhnev himself, on a brief visit to the city in 1980, had given instructions to tear down the "rotten tooth."

During my stay I came to know some of the *Heimweh*-tourists who stayed at the hotel. They were fairly well-to-do people, most of them past retirement age. Self-conscious, even a little cowed, they wan-

dered about the dilapidated city, complaining only of the smell everywhere of unclean lavatories and rotting food. Every morning around
nine they walked out of the hotel in smart sports clothes, living adver-
tisements for a free-market economy, armed with the latest miniature
video cameras and pocketfuls of deutsche marks in small change to
hand out as tips as they went along. Shirtless little boys ran after them
crying, "Please, please! A mark, a mark, please!" They also toured the
nearby countryside around Kaliningrad, which has changed the least.
The roads, laid out long ago in seemingly endless straight lines by
Prussian engineers, are edged with tall trees standing at exact intervals, like soldiers. Picturesque horse carts rattle on the old cobblestones and storks nest atop telegraph poles. Flocks of white geese
graze on the stubble fields. A woman from Düsseldorf said, "It's the
world of yesterday. You don't see such sights anymore in West Germany." The ancient trees that surrounded the noble estates outside
the city still stand, but the manor houses were burned down or have
collapsed.

In Kaliningrad itself word has gotten around that the *Heimweh*-
tourists are in no way anxious, as some local people had feared, to reclaim their former family houses that are now part of the squalid
housing estates of Kaliningrad. Hence encounters between former and
present-day residents of Kaliningrad are often quite friendly, and
sometimes Germans and Russians get rather emotional. The Germans
often come to visit their old houses with American cigarettes, six-
packs of German beer, Würstel cosmetics, and other small presents.
Many take small trees or shrubs from the old house back home with
them to Germany.

At the common breakfast table in the hotel, the *Heimweh*-tourists
discussed their experiences and impressions. They were hardly a
cross-section of ordinary Germans. A middle-aged lawyer from Munich said he represented an organization called the Union of Propertied Noblemen (Verband des Besitzenden Adels). But the same
*Heimat*-polemics that one hears in Germany are also heard in Kaliningrad. When a man in his sixties, who said he had escaped from the
small East Prussian town of Allenstein (today the Polish Olsztyn),
complained of Russian barbarism, another man in the group told him
not to forget that Hitler had been the principal reason for his loss and
had, at the same time, condemned all of Eastern Europe to forty-five
years of Communist tyranny. When a Berlin businessman said that
realpolitik made it imperative that Königsberg revert to Germany, a

*Countryside near Allenstein*

woman from Hanover, a retired schoolteacher, burst out, "'Realpolitik' is just a dirty German word meaning the domination of the weak by the strong."

The new self-assurance of some Germans after reunification and the collapse of Soviet power in Eastern Europe was also evident. One man said, "In 1945 we left Königsberg totally defeated. Now we come back completely victorious. We'll just buy this place. How much do you think it'll cost us in real money?" A woman said, "We saw our house. It's in terrible shape. The bathtub Father got shortly before the war is gone, too." The businessman from Berlin was the most militant. I asked him why he was so insistent that the lost territories in the east be returned to Germany. Wasn't Germany a happier and more prosperous country nowadays than ever before in its history? "You don't need East Prussia," I said. He looked at me disdainfully. Then he said solemnly, as though reciting a well-known text, "Need is not a historical category."

A woman born in the Rhineland said that in 1941, as a six-year-old child, she had been evacuated to her aunt's house in Königsberg because Königsberg was safer from air raids than Düsseldorf. When the Russians came, she escaped with her aunt over the half frozen Masurian lakes. Her aunt fell through the ice and was drowned. She said that she had visited several times with the people who now occupied her aunt's house. They felt "guilty" about living in someone else's home, she said, but they were soulful, emotional people, and she also was sentimental and got along well with them. "We agreed," she said, "that we are all losers." Her *Heimat* was elsewhere now.

But *Heimat* continues to be a charged item in the German language. Even so liberal a writer as Marion, Countess Dönhoff (editor of *Die Zeit*, Hamburg's prestigious liberal newspaper), who has devoted a lifetime to fighting right-wing romantic nationalism and to promoting responsible democratic citizenship, has cherished *Heimat* in her own way. The Federal Republic, she wrote in 1970, was well worth supporting and defending because it is a free and open society, "but it is not *Heimat*." After diplomatic relations were established between Germany and Poland, with the implied recognition of the new frontiers, Countess Dönhoff, the former proprietor and heiress of vast estates in East Prussia, wrote, "Farewell to Prussia, then? No, for the spiritual Prussia must continue to be active in this era of materialist desires, otherwise this state which we call Federal Republic of Germany will not survive."

When she publicly proposed in 1992 the establishment of a Polish-Lithuanian-Russian-German condominium in Kaliningrad, the members of the editorial board of *Die Zeit*—including former chancellor Helmut Schmidt—vehemently protested, and after reporting this reaction herself, she has not repeated her proposal in print.

"We call ourselves Russians, but we are not really Russians," the Kaliningrad writer Yuri Ivanov told me. Ivanov is the author of several books on Kaliningrad and head of the apparently well endowed Kaliningrad Cultural Foundation. He and an increasing number of Kaliningrad intellectuals would like to free the city from what they call its "historical unconscious." Ivanov was born in Leningrad in 1929. He survived the German siege and famine there and arrived in Kaliningrad in 1945 as a sixteen-year-old soldier in the Soviet army and he never left. "How could we be Russians, living where we do? I have no friends in Russia. We were never Soviets either. The so-called Soviet Man was an illusion. Our roots here are only forty-five years deep. We live in an historic German city. Those who lived here before us are our countrymen." Still, he adds, "We are not Germans either. Perhaps we are Balts."

Nevertheless he felt closer, he said, to Germans than to the highly nationalistic Lithuanians and other Balts. And he did not like Marion Dönhoff's plan of a Polish-Lithuanian-Russian-German federation. "Who needs the Lithuanians?" he exclaimed. "I fear them much more than I fear the Germans." He envied the Poles who had rebuilt Danzig in all its past splendor. "It could have been done here, too. . . . Kaliningrad ought to be an autonomous republic within the Russian federation. We must get rid of the name. Kalinin was an evil man," Ivanov said. "As in Leningrad, we must bring back the old name of the city— Königsberg. It's a historical necessity."

In the countryside German missionaries wander from town to town with mobile altars and electric organs and gift parcels from Germany. One Sunday morning, as I was passing through Chernyakhovst (the former Insterburg), a small town near the Lithuanian border, I happened upon a German Apostolic Church revivalist meeting. Outside the old German *Rathaus,* some 300 people were holding a prayer meeting. Many were young Russian soldiers in uniform. Electronic music wafted over a sea of bare heads. Banners and slogans hung between the dilapidated buildings. The service was conducted in German from the back of a truck specially converted to serve as altar and hold an electric organ, the minister pausing frequently to allow for a Russian translation. Later peopled lined up to receive small packages filled with German cookies or little plastic toys.

German Catholic missionaries are active as well. They use as their headquarters an otherwise empty lot in the center of Kaliningrad, where a priest and a dozen lay volunteers live in a few large metal boxes and prefabricated huts. Hans Schmidt, a layman from Wuppertal in West Germany, told me they do social work in the city's hospitals. Several times a week they hold services in the villages and hear confessions in three languages: Russian, Lithuanian, and German. Tens of thousands of Russians who are ethnically German live in Kaliningrad, he said. More were arriving daily from Kazakhstan, where they had been deported from their historic villages on the Volga River by Stalin during the war. They hope that Kaliningrad will soon be restored to Germany or become an autonomous region.

"We are here to reconcile Germans and Russians through Jesus Christ," said Schmidt. "If the industry of the Germans doesn't make them arrogant and if the Russians' naiveté—they are like children— doesn't lead them into mistakes, the love of God will cause the establishment here of an independent state. It will be modeled on the ancient Order of Teutonic Knights—not because the knights were German but because, like us now, they spread the word of God in the pagan darkness of Königsberg."

⚎

The new magic words in Kaliningrad are "Königsberg" and "Immanuel Kant." There are recurring calls for a referendum on going back to the city's former name. "We are all of us Kant's *Landsmänner*," Ivanov said. He spoke Russian through a translator, but he used the German word for "countrymen." One of the first things a tourist sees upon landing at Kaliningrad's newly opened international airport is a big sign, "Welcome to Kant's City."* At the tomb outside the ruined cathedral, Kant is now venerated as a local saint. Newlywed couples go directly from the municipal marriage palace to the tomb to pose for photographs. (In the past the preferred site had been the bust of Karl Marx in a nearby park.) A new monument to Kant, the copy of an original that was demolished after the war, was solemnly dedicated during the summer of 1992 in the former *Paradeplatz* by the heads of the city and regional government and a plane-load of distinguished Germans. There was some talk of renaming the city "Kantgrad," and I saw a T-shirt inscribed, "I ♥ Kant."

Königsberg and Kant are, of course, also code names for German money, German power, German influence; Yeltsin's conservative opponents in the city, many of them Russian nationalists, know this. That is why N. A. Medvedev, the university rector, who says he sided with the instigators of the 1991 coup against Mikhail Gorbachev, is against "Kantgrad" as a possible new name. "It's not pleasant to the ear," he says. Medvedev prefers a Slavic name that does not hark back to the German past, perhaps "Baltijsk."

"Young people here don't know who they are," said Yuri Zabugin, an architect and a native of the city. "Or they want to be someone else. So would you," he told me, "if you had grown up under communism in this awful place." Zabugin is restoring old churches in the city with German money. He is also the curator of an exhibition on the history of Königsberg-Kaliningrad in the local museum. Put to-

---

*Another philosopher from a local family was Hannah Arendt, who grew up in Königsberg. No one I talked to had heard of her, including Vitaly V. Shipov, mayor of Kaliningrad, and Yuri Ivanov.

gether by local arts and crafts students, it is the first independently conceived show in a museum that used to specialize in glorifying the Soviet petroleum or shoe industry. Its title is simply the number "236000," the city's postal code. "It defines the city's existence," said Zabugin. In the catalogue he described the city as a "spot on the map. Its historical name is not forgotten, nor is it still valid. The new name is irrelevant and immaterial. . . . Who are we?"

The regional Kaliningrad government issues warnings that Russia's sovereignty over Kaliningrad must not be questioned, but it is leading the efforts to form cultural and economic links with Germany. It wants Germany to open a consulate and a Goethe Institute in Kaliningrad and is soliciting German public and private funds to finance industries, tourism, mining, and transportation. It has turned to, among others, Friedrich Christians, the chairman of the powerful Deutsche Bank and the most prominent German financier currently negotiating with the Kaliningrad authorities. A German diplomat in Bonn jokingly calls Christians the *Heimweh*-banker. Christians's connections with Königsberg go back to 1945, when, as a young German soldier, he saw the Red Army's final assault on the city. If Königsberg is rebuilt, he said recently, it "would no longer be a monument to cruel destruction. Rebuilt, it will reflect the hope for peace and reconciliation in Europe."

Christians has also put forward the idea of making Kaliningrad a free economic zone between East and West, a European Hong Kong or Singapore. The Russian Federation parliament has approved the idea in principle, but arrangements for abolishing customs duties are still to be worked out. The conservative bureaucracy opposes the scheme, and the conservatives make up a majority in the regional Kaliningrad parliament. Some of them accuse Vladimir Matutshkin, the head of the regional administration who favors a free-agent zone, of being a "German agent." One of them told a local journalist recently, "If we are not careful we'll soon be governed by old SS men and Japanese samurai." The police chief, Viktor Shoshnikov, recently published an article in *Kaliningradskaya Pravda* claiming that the free-trade zone would only bring in more criminals and drugs.

The military, for its part, favors the free-trade zone, since, as Admiral Vladimir Yegorov, the officer commanding the Russian fleet in the Baltic, told me, "the free-trade zone will supply good jobs for retired officers." Few joint ventures with foreigners have been agreed upon. The most serious so far is the rebuilding of Hitler's old autobahn connecting Königsberg with Berlin. (The Poles are unhappy about this project. Work has begun so far only north of the Polish border.) On the day I met the admiral, ceremonies were taking place on Russian ships in the Baltic celebrating the reintroduction of the old tsarist banner as the official flag of the Russian navy. "Everyone in Kaliningrad is looking forward to the free-trade zone," the admiral said. "Everyone looks forward to big *bizness.*"

## Part One

# BEGINNINGS
## The Teutonic Knights

# Select Chronology

| | |
|---|---|
| 1189–1192 | Third Crusade |
| 1190 | Teutonic Order of St. Mary's formed in Acre. |
| 1229 | Order reaches agreement with Polish duke Conrad of Mazovia to seize and occupy Prussia. |
| 1231–1240 | Order conquers eastern banks of Vistula. |
| 1242 | Prussian revolt put down by the order. Another rebellion in 1260 results in virtual extinction of native Prussians. |
| 1245 | Pope Innocent IV grants indulgences to all soldiers fighting in Prussia. |
| 1254–1308 | Order engaged in Samland, Semigallia, Livonia, Lithuania. Danzig taken. |
| 1291 | Acre falls; grand master shifts to Venice. |
| 1307 | Knights Templars purged by King Philip the Fair of France, followed by show trials and executions. |
| 1309 | Grand master departs Venice, establishes order at Marienburg. |
| 1364 | War with Lithuania. |
| 1385 | Union of Poland and Lithuania under Jagiello. |
| 1390 and 1392 | Henry of Derby on crusade in Prussia. |
| 1410, July 15 | Disastrous defeat at Battle of Tannenberg. |
| 1454–1466 | Order battles Poland and revolts of Prussian towns. |
| 1466 | Order defeated, cedes half of Prussia to Poland; headquarters moved to Königsberg. |
| 1525 | Grand Master Albrecht secularizes the Teutonic Order. East Prussia a fief of the Hohenzollerns to the Polish king. |

# Old Prussia
## 1275–1995
# Finding the Way

*Our Baltic families, they seem to possess some nega-
tive sort of quality and at the very same time to assume an air of superiority, of being masters of everything. I often find it difficult to get on with them.*

*As they have for centuries been the rulers of an infe-
rior race, they are not unnaturally inclined to behave
as if the rest of humanity were composed exclusively
of Latvians.*

—Adolf Hitler

EARLY SPRING ON THE RHINE. I have taken a room in the wine village of Rüdesheim, over an hour's drive from the Frankfurt airport.
Prices, and indeed availability, of accommodations have provided my
first Germanic surprise. Expositions, business conference centers,
trade shows of enormous size (the modern equivalent, I suppose, of
Frankfurt's medieval fairs) burn up the local pool of hotel beds and
even those of modest guest houses, and I find myself paying over $100
for a garret overlooking the great river. For someone like myself, a
kind of gypsy traveler more used to sleeping by the side of the road in
tent or car, someone for whom the notion of an expense account
seems a shimmering dream from long-ago employment, this presents
a pretty substantial burden, but I consider myself lucky to find a place
at all. Jet-lagged and tired, I sleep in for the day.

Rüdesheim, as I discover walking about that evening, lacks the riverside grace that so many other Rhineland villages seem to have preserved. Garish hotels of indistinguishably "Continental" character cluster along the main avenue, targeted mostly, I am told, to the English trade, and wine bars beyond counting aggressively court the summer influx of deutsche marks. But the season is still far away, and the restaurant I eat in is empty.

The river on this blowzy, wintry night, the glorious Rhine, shrouded in mist with great hulks of barge traffic pushing upriver against a frigid, surging current, is to my romantic imagination almost larger than life. Too influenced by Wagner, I walk along the bank with wisps of *Das Rheingold* and *Die Walküre* running through my head. Trains pass by every five minutes, even late at night, horns blaring in the dark, competing noisily with the bells of red-and-white-striped barriers opening and closing the roads, and the full-throated rumble of diesel engines as idling trucks wait to proceed, all illuminated by rows of signal lights announcing a myriad of track switches—the whole commercial infrastructure of modern Germany just radiating that famous aura of strength and order.

The next morning is gray, dour, and rainy. I take a ski lift over vineyards and castle towers to the great statue *Germania*, which overlooks the Rhine here at Rüdesheim, a winged Victory built by a triumphant people in celebration of its mastery in the Franco-Prussian War of 1870. Mythologically overwrought, this immense pile features a "blood-and-iron" excess of trumpets, weaponry, drums, helmets, crowns, wreaths of laurel, and just about every martial boast invented by man. The Amazonian goddess of Germany, one hand comfortably—one might slip and even say characteristically—gripping her sword pommel, stretches the other into the sky holding the imperial crown, an archaic symbol of authority that most people today would be hard-pressed to identify. An elderly British tourist turns to his wife and utters what I expect is the most common misinterpretation to be had here. "Look at the bloody Hun," he says, "waving heads in the air. Barbarians, the lot of them."

I drive downstream as far as the Rock of Lorelei before turning inland for my appointment. This impressive wall of stone several hundred yards high falls dramatically in a more or less sheer drop straight to water's edge at a treacherous, frothy bend of the Rhine. Reputedly the haunt of river nymphs and evil spirits, many a barge from ancient times has come to grief here in fog or stormy weather, though the

*Germania*

siren calls of unworthy maidens have traditionally provided a ready excuse for the helmsman too drunk or sleepy to steer straight. The danger of accident today is more to be blamed on greed than cupidity. The summer spectacle of crowded tourist boats jostling for position under the forbidding brow of Lorelei, all the while blasting the famous song of that name by Schubert (based on Heine's poem *Die Loreley*), is about as curious an audiovisual experience as Germany has to offer. "It's a very weird scene from up here," a tour guide said to me from the observation platform, complete with mounted binoculars, at the top of Lorelei. "Sometimes I can tell von Karajan from Furtwängler, and your Chicago Symphony has a very distinctive version, but when they're all down there together, about to get plowed under by barge traffic, the whole thing sounds like a tower of symphonic babel. The tourists love it."

Further on, I stop at a roadside *Weingut* to have a glass of *Kabinett*. Without Polish workers, I am told by the housewife running the bar, there would be no wine at all. "We couldn't pay German wages and turn a profit. And the Poles make out just fine; they make plenty here, far more than they could get in their own country. They earn a wage plus enough to pay Lithuanian or border Russians to run their farms back in Poland. On top of that, from our point of view, they work harder than anyone we could hire locally. Their only problem is they tend to get morose and homesick."

Later that afternoon, in a modern bungalow in a suburban development outside a town of no particular lineage in the Palatinate, a gentleman close to eighty years of age defines for me the notion of homesick. "To plant your feet in the ground, to know it's yours and that the beautiful fields and the woods so carefully tended are only that way because your family *made* it that way—that is my idea of a homeland. And I do not mean that your father, or even your grandfather, hired a few men with a team of oxen or a tractor to clear your land, and then you farmed it. I mean ancestors you never knew about, hundreds of years ago, who first had to fight for the land and Christianize it, had to lose it perhaps, then win it back again I don't know how many times before they could truly call it their own. Always, always prepared to die for it! That's what Prussia means to me. The land out there has been a sponge for my family. It soaked our sweat and our blood and it bloomed like an oasis in the desert. I am old enough now to realize that I will never see it again as something mine in the legal sense. Because of that, I'll never go back there to visit it, though I know I could. It would be too much pain. I don't think I could trust myself from shouting, 'Get off my land!'"

"When did you last see the place?"

"In 1944. I'll never breath that air again."

I manage to reach Marburg around dusk. The trip was chaotic. All roads, no matter whether country lane or autobahn, are choked with traffic, streaking blurs of Mercedes, BMWs, Audis. I'm lucky to reach the cathedral here unscathed.

Most people come to Marburg for the Elizabethschrein from the thirteenth century, a gaudy piece of metalwork that once housed the relics of a popular saint. Its perfection justifies an entry fee, though I suppose if you came here to pray, a novel idea for this day and age, you could get in for nothing. The ticket seller says I have ten minutes until closing.

Tucked obscurely in a corner is the tomb of Paul von Hindenburg, what I came here to see. Adolf Hitler used the occasion of his death in 1934 to stage a Nuremberg-style extravaganza at burial ceremonies in

East Prussia, at the site of the old field marshal's greatest victory, the World War I battle of Tannenberg. "Dead warrior! Go now to Valhalla," Hitler reportedly intoned in mock remorse, delighted as he was to have that great senile hulk out of his way. He used the same imagery at the memorial of Erich von Ludendorff, another dinosaur from the Wilhelmite era no longer required. But Valhalla is not where Hindenburg ended up, his mortal remains at any rate. With Red Army tanks crushing through Prussia in the winter of 1945, German forces disinterred the field marshal and his wife, then destroyed the Tannenberg mausoleum. He ended up here in Marburg after various escapades in the night, temporary storage vaults, and even the forgetfulness of his guardians—a pretense, to be sure, but considered necessary when Germans realized their Allied conquerors were cremating people like Field Marshals Alfred Jodl and Wilhelm Keitel, then throwing out the ashes. Germans have a totemic obsession with grave sites, it was thought, and no one wanted old Nazi and Prussian tombs to become focal points for right-wing homage. When time and tempers had moderated to some degree, von Hindenburg was quietly reburied in this cathedral, far away from where he wanted to be.

The caretaker comes by, jangling his keys. "This is von Hindenburg," he tells me. "The shrine is over there in the transept. I will show you."

"No, this is fine," I reply, "but is there any light? I can't see a thing."

"Yes, yes, of course," and a pair of dim chandeliers cast a gloomy sheen on the dour brownstone of walls and casket. The only feature of note is the old field marshal's genealogy, row upon row of miniature coats of arms—107 in all, painted on small wooden panels—outlining the generations of von Hindenburgs who fought in the east.

"Very few people know he's buried here," says the caretaker. "I turn the lights on for ceremonies five or six times a year, but that's all. Wreaths get delivered often enough, but most tourists, well, they've never heard of him." I find this hard to fathom and say so.

"Believe what you wish. This is a new age for Germany. It used to be everyone was obsessed with the past, but now many are not, the young people mostly. You've missed the Elizabethschrein, by the way. Come back tomorrow."

Walking afterward in the university quarter of Marburg, I have a glass of beer before setting off again, this time for Berlin. Overlooking the ancient town, I can't help but consider the metaphorical signifi-

*Hindenburg's grave*

cance of von Hindenburg's poor box of bones, shuttled ignominiously
here and there in the afterglow of his country's most cataclysmic defeat: a self-professed "Old Prussian" whose birthplace today harbors
none of his race; a soldier whose lifework did not admit the possibility
of abandoning a border seven centuries old; a Junker who never owned
property on the sacred soil of his forebears until he was almost too old
to enjoy it, yet for whom the notion of land was a stigmata on his soul,
almost too holy a burden to bear.

Ever the grim, stoical military man whose inarticulate demeanor
was often caricatured as stupidity, even von Hindenburg might well
have been pressed to define exactly what Prussia was. The royal house
of Hohenzollern or the ideals and heritage of poor-though-lineaged
landowners? A piece of territory or a notion? A kingdom or the splinter of genetic memory? A piece of real estate or a Teutonic Holy Grail?
In a way, it was—and remains—all of these, and no understanding of
Germany past or present can ever be realized without coming to grips
with Prussia.

The simple word "Prussia," of course, conjures up an immediate
and sanguinary image for most people—war, and plenty of it. Spiked

helmets, jackboots, goose steps, eagles, blood, and destruction. A German of the old school might also add the word "glory," but if you were French or British or, more particularly, Russian or Polish, you might be inclined to substitute "misery." My own predilection, however hasty, would be "relentless," but again, how accurate can any of this be? The history of Prussia, and its relation to all the other Germanys that this strange but fragmented race has created, includes particles of many and seemingly contradictory elements, and the picture we end up with can remain baffling to many of us in the West. The explanation for that is geography. "Where is Germany?" the poet Schiller wrote. The same could be asked of Prussia.

Prussia today does not exist. That is a simple fact. Germany exists, but not Prussia, a territory mostly dismembered in 1945 and divided among Poles, Russians, Lithuanians. Many Germans may not seem to care, especially those from the Catholic south. For them, the heartland of Germany is easily defined, having boundaries as majestic as the Rhine and the Bavarian Alps, a heartland as historic as the old towns of Hesse, Thuringia, and Lower Saxony, a frontier as definitive as the North Sea and a frigid Atlantic beyond. Even Berlin can often seem extraneous.

To understand Prussia, however, we must avoid this southern perspective and think instead of the Roman god Janus, the two-headed deity who looked simultaneously to the past and the future, or in this case toward both east and west. Germany's destiny, or curse, lay in both directions.

Late, late into the night I am trapped in perhaps the greatest traffic snarl I have ever experienced. Cruising along north of Marburg, I had intersected the major east-west autobahn at Braunschweig, and there the character of my fellow travelers immediately changed as though by magic. Gone are the heavy sedans, outrageous sports cars, and gleaming diesel rigs driven by the comfy bourgeoisie of the Federal Republic, replaced by a plodding caravan of belching polluters from beyond the old iron curtain. Lithuanian truckers, Trabants from the former German Democratic Republic (GDR), Polish used-car and scrap dealers, all pulling the unwanted junk and refuse of democracy back home for certain profit, clog the roads to a standstill. Stopping at a rest area to clear my lungs of exhaust fumes, I ask a Pole what on earth he's going to do with a completely totaled '91 BMW. In two weeks, he tells me in perfect English, this car will be cruising downtown Warsaw with an exhilarated former Communist, probably in his fifties, behind the wheel, and he will have made $1,000. "The Germans have very little patience," he says. "They scratch something and throw it away."

"This thing looks a little more than scratched," I say.

"That depends on your perspective. As a Pole, I look at this car, or what's left of it, as an opportunity. The German looks at it as an insurance nuisance." Later he mentions that probably 15 to 20 percent of all the wrecks being hauled east are stolen. "I've seen people have an accident, they're taken off to the hospital, and when they come back to tow the car away, it's gone. I did it myself a while ago, I admit it. I was pulling a Volkswagen when I saw a smashed-up Mercedes by the side of the road, and no police. So I took a chance and made the swap."

My willpower to proceed ends at Magdeburg at about 2 A.M. The autobahn is almost completely stalled, one endless stream of brake lights stretching beyond sight toward Berlin. I pull off and enter the netherworld of East German drab, with its pockmarked, rubble-strewn streets; derelict trolleys rocking empty through the night; the usual monolithic apartment buildings that are by now the clichés of Communist progress. I turn into a side street to park, roll down the passenger seat, and slip into my sleeping bag. Inevitably, I question how safe it is to be here and promise to reread some of John le Carré's novels when I get home to see if he got the melodrama just right, but in the greasy glare of the yellow street lights fatigue overcomes concern and I go right to sleep.

A couple of hours later, World War III erupts on this trammeled, dilapidated street, devoid of life, as a beer garden 500 feet away disappears in two enormous explosions. Immediately the neighborhood is jammed with antique fire engines and police cars, the air full of sirens, flashing lights, and guttural yelling back and forth, that German tongue so aptly suited, it seems to me, to both chaos and command. I crawl as deep into my sleeping bag as I can, hoping no one notices this new and gaily painted rental car from Avis.

❧❧

Magdeburg, as it turns out, is a good place from which to review the lay of the land, though the city itself, despite a long and often romantic history, is downtrodden, as I discover touring about the next day. Nothing much seems left from the glory days of Otto the Great or Albert the Bear, great Saxon warriors who pushed and prodded their Slavic neighbors for more living space in the vast woodlands of the east; nor, for that matter, the more golden age of the Hanseatic League, when Magdeburg profited handsomely from its trading position on the River Elbe. It is equally difficult imagining Martin Luther as a young boy, singing Christmas carols in these streets to cadge a few coins. Even the Elbe seems turbid and downtrodden, no surprise given the horrific bilge of poisons that have been flushed and dumped into its flow these past fifty years. But as a benchmark, Magdeburg still has meaning.

By the year 1100 A.D., an approximate Christian frontier line stretched southward from the trading town of Lübeck on the Baltic, via the Elbe and Magdeburg, to the foothills of the Bohemian mountains. This boundary, at any given time, could be fractured or pierced by pagan Slavonic tribes going about their usual bloodthirsty business of raiding for plunder and slaves, but essentially the dynamic tension lay with their adversaries, the Christian princes of Germany, whose appetite for the same plunder and the same slaves could not be matched. Egged on by personal ambition, the desire for new lands and income, and at least the pretense of religious conversion, German rulers and petty despots pushed through forest and marsh, cleared out Slavs who stood in their way, and planted towns and villages with settlers or Cistercian monks from the homeland. A second great watery barrier, the River Oder, was reached by midcentury, with the nucleus of Brandenburg established in 1150 by a Saxon dynasty. Brandenburg, and later its capital, Berlin, would come to symbolize in modern times the kingdom of Prussia.

But in fact the heart of Prussia, its guiding ethos, lay even further east, a dominion later known as Ostpreussen, or East Prussia, the nucleus of which had been carved in the very core of pagan territories by the monastic order of Teutonic Knights. Again, the handiest physical benchmark is water, in this case the Vistula, along whose banks this military caste erected fortresses of unimaginable size and complexity both to overawe their enemies and to offer reassurance to the otherwise tentative agricultural communities established in their shadows.

By 1260 the knights held a broadly rectangular piece of territory extending from Kulm and Thorn, northward by the eastern bank of the Vistula to the Baltic Sea. From here what the bombastic nineteenth-century propagandist Heinrich von Treitschke called the *Drang nach Osten*, or "drive to the east," hit full stride as the knights embroiled themselves along the entire Baltic coast to the Gulf of Finland, at one time (about the late 1300s) controlling territory from present-day Poland, through Kaliningrad Province, all the way to Estonia via Lithuania and Latvia. They accomplished all this through daring and courage beyond estimation, ruthlessness beyond description, and a business acumen beyond the standards of efficiency commonly associated with the Germanic personality, a devastating combination unique for its time. Their ethnically diverse opponents in all of these struggles—principally Balts and Slavs—were equally vainglorious and predatory, though less single-minded and disciplined than the knights.

Like their better-known contemporaries of Norman stock, who had adventured from France all over Western Europe and the Holy Land, the Teutonic Knights feared nothing and bulled ahead no matter the odds. They welcomed the opportunity to stare death in the face.

The lands through which they lumbered back and forth were not of the best—a sandy soil on gently rolling hills, essentially lowlands running in a crescent along the southern shores of the Baltic. Generally covered with forest or inundated with marsh, it was a territory lacking in natural boundaries. Even the great rivers draining the countryside—the Oder, Vistula, Memel, and Dvina—were unpresupposing, crucial for transport and commerce but of little defensive value. Undergrowth, soggy fens, a morass of thickets and trackless scrub were the less dramatic though more formidable barriers faced by armies and settlers alike. Borders were thus shifty and delineated only with difficulty.

The one constant to keep in mind when judging the saga to come is that of separation and aloneness, the type of danger always associated with frontiers or, as they were termed by medieval writers, the Marches. For much of its history, East Prussia was divided from the rest of Germany, an isolated bastion of Teutonic language and culture surrounded on all sides by enemies bent on revenge and destruction, probably in equal measure. What Roman legionnaires felt as they patrolled Hadrian's Wall in Great Britain, what crusaders must have thought walking the ramparts of their isolated castles in Syria and Judea, so, too, the Germans as they scanned the horizon of fields just cleared or pastures just drained. Who was lurking in the woods nearby, what would nightfall bring from the shagged brambles across that stream a few hundred yards away? Of such notions and attitudes is character built.

"You had your Wild West, your cowboys and Indians," an old German friend said to me. "For us, it was the Wild East. But there was one crucial difference, I think. You won the countryside with guns and bullets, the great iron of railroads, technology, an advanced civilization. Prussia was won with the sword and battle-ax. Our knights bathed in blood, it was so highly personal a conquest, so 'up-front,' to use an American expression. Can any modern man coming from a civilized country, especially those of us who are not keen on blood sports or hunting, imagine what it must be like to skewer another human being with a sword, or cleave a man's skull down through to his neck with an ax? When you win a combat of that sort, and the prize is land—an estate and a future—your kinship with that land is intense beyond description. You didn't purchase it with money or a credit card; you killed for it and you saw who you killed for it, probably six inches away. And more often than not, you were killed for it yourself at some other place, some other time, and a hideous death most likely it was. Believe me, many Germans died! This explains, it is my belief, the devotion we have traditionally had as Germans to the idea of Prussia. It is our notion of purpose, service, steadfastness, and duty to both our race and our land. Also, to the idea of permanence. As my grandfather said to me, the Memel is a frontier that will never fall. He told me that, I need not say, before disaster struck us down in 1945."

The Memel is a river I had never heard of. It flows to the Baltic through present-day Lithuania and is more familiarly known as the Niemen. It marks the historical contraction of East Prussia when the Teutonic Knights fell apart as a military power in the fifteenth century, losing ground to Poles, Lithuanians, Russians, even Swedes, emerging from this downward spiral as possessors of a territory that more or less corresponds with its nineteenth-century borders, or what Germans past and present consider the traditional empire.

"Here you see the real Germany," a former schoolmate who works for Volkswagen said to me in his living room, reaching for the inevitable map that everyone here seems to have framed and readily accessible. "You will notice the inscription engraved below—'Map of the Empire of Germany, including all the States comprehended under that name'—that's the part I like, the 'comprehended under that name.' By that, of course, forget about Polish territories to the south! Given the date of this engraving, 1794, you have to remember that Poland by then had ceased to exist. You still had a Catholic, Polish-speaking population there, of course, but no Poland. It had been eaten up by its neighbors. Anyway, here is our northeastern border, right on the Memel, up until World War II Europe's oldest permanent border. Everything beyond that the knights had lost. To the east, a rugged, broken country of lakes and forest separated us from our enemies there. This was a no-man's-land of sorts. To the south, cleared lands and open plains, a constant battleground with Slavs, whether Polish or

Russian depends on the century. And to the west, a common border with the German provinces of Pomerania and Brandenburg, what we call West Prussia. This was joined to East Prussia by the Teutonic Knights at the height of their power in the fourteenth century, but Poland won a lot of this territory as the knights declined. Danzig in Polish hands for hundreds of years, can you believe it? But Frederick the Great, in his turn, won all this back and more during the various partitions of Poland in the late 1700s, and that's pretty much the way it stayed until World War I, when again Poland took possession of what was then called 'the Corridor,' with Danzig at the head of it, a free city on the Baltic—East Prussia *again* a satellite, separated from the motherland by territories full of Catholic Poles. If anything contributed to Hitler's hatred of the Slavs, that was it. A cancer, a challenge to Germany's geographical integrity, Poles between us and Königsberg! Then after World War II, of course, nothing. East Prussia disappears, and so it is today fifty years later, a dream and nothing else. Actually, it's not a dream anymore. It's a memory."

A memory indeed, I remember thinking to myself, but how potent a memory? What is the difference here between politics and history, between reality and mythology, between the possible and impossible? For almost half a century, East Prussia has remained the special mental preserve of a generation now dying off—the Prussian diaspora, those who abandoned everything in that frigid winter of 1945, perhaps the greatest dislocation of a civilian population at any time during World War II. A few had departed, the lucky ones anyway, by train; most others on tractors, horse-drawn carts, by automobile, on foot. They carried suitcases and backpacks and more often than not lost these along the way. An incredible number never made it far enough west to outdistance the rapid Soviet advance, which overran them with varied and often horrific results. Of the 2 million Germans who fled their homes and farms, it is possible that half died on the road. Of those who survived (followed by another million and a half later expelled by Poles and Russians), most realized within the next few years that there would be no return. East Prussia for these people drifted away into a maze of fond nostalgia, many times resolutely repressed. "For my family's sake," I heard over and over again, "I do not dwell on the past. It is so easy to become sentimental, and then bitter."

Now, and with considerable irony, at the last moments in their lives, the iron curtain crumbles and the German border, almost overnight, takes a 170-mile leap to the east. Ostpreussen is suddenly that much closer, a tantalizing few hours away by car, and no one, not any expert, can predict how the political future may look—meaning, what about Russia?

The right-wing Russian nationalist Vladimir Zhirinovsky—referred to by some in the German press as "Russia's Hitler"—recently hinted that should he replace Boris Yelstin as president, East Prussia would become a negotiable item between Berlin and Moscow, a suggestion as outrageous as it is historical, inasmuch as Poland, by tradition never consulted on matters relating to its survival, again sees itself the victim of East-West machinations.

"The Poles? I don't care about the Poles," one old refugee from Ostpreussen said to me. "No one ever has in the past, and no one ever will in the future, no matter what our politicians say today. Are they a paranoid race of people? Of course they are, as they should be. No one ever learns from history, but what happened to Poland time and time again these centuries past could well happen to it again. For the first time in four decades, I can honestly believe in the chance of East Prussia being a part of our German fatherland again. Stranger things have happened, and in just the last year or two! But for reunification to be complete, the young people must want it to happen, and for them East Prussia is a cipher, and not a very valuable one at that, something old people like myself prattle about but which the young people know nothing. Whether there is enough to unite them politically—and I don't mean skinhead rabble—to make them understand the importance of Prussia to their country, I do not know."

Marion, Countess Dönhoff, dismisses out of hand any possibility that East Prussia will be returned to the fold. "Never," she said to me derisively with a wave of her hand. "I can't take that seriously." But even she cannot understand the recent wave of interest in this ancient Germanic homeland. Her own book of childhood recollections, published in this country as *Before the Storm*, sold an astounding quarter of a million copies in Germany alone, and the countess cannot explain its success. "No one was more surprised than me," she admitted.

It is clear, however, and despite the variation in opinion, that East Prussia provides another piece in the mosaic of what is certainly a growing trend throughout Germany, the pasteurization of history, especially that of the 1930s and 1940s. Extreme examples abound, from the insidious "Auschwitz lie" to nostalgia for the Wehrmacht and even the SS. Talk of East Prussia falls more tamely into a lederhosen category of old times not forgotten, but the undertones of Teutonic

Knights, military chivalry, and territorial expansion are not far beneath the honeyed surface. This subject can and undoubtedly will be used by extremist factions as they noisily unsettle the political landscape and, even more cruelly, randomly harass and sometimes murder immigrant workers (twenty-five from 1993 to 1994). Prussia has been a war cry before; it could be again. More powerfully, it may feed into what a Polish writer recently called, in admirable understatement, "the dynamic strength of German national feeling."

The historian Jürgen Habermas summarized the situation, I think correctly, in 1993. "If you look at the German elite, it is possible to discern a powerful desire to turn Germany [again] into an independent great power in the center of Europe, with its gaze fixed on the east. The only antidote to this trend is European political unity. . . . Maastricht is necessary to restrain Germany." Margaret Thatcher, in her recent autobiography, agreed on the threat of a new and powerful Germany, at the same time reiterating her opposition to the EC as a moderating factor. "The desire among modern German politicians to merge their national identities in a wider Europe is understandable enough," she wrote, "but it presents great difficulties. . . . In effect the Germans, because they are nervous of governing themselves, want to establish a European system in which no nation will govern itself. Such a system could only be unstable in the long term, and because of Germany's size and preponderance, is bound to be lop-sided. Obsession with a European Germany risks producing a German Europe." Or as the Polish newspaper *Polityka* put it, "No one has taken [this] tendency to 'make ourselves smaller than we are' further than the Germans. They say, 'We are so insignificant, so peaceable, so harmless that there isn't anything much that we can actually do.'"

When asked by another Polish journalist, "Should we fear Germany?" Habermas had no reply other than, "I ask myself the same question." The Jewish writer Ben Hecht was even more emphatic. "Germans have not reformed," he wrote. "They are resting."

⊞⊨

From Magdeburg I take backroads to Berlin. The former GDR countryside, whether from imagination or the fact that winter is not long over, seems drained, tired, unrefreshed. I stop at Schönhausen, the site of Otto von Bismarck's ancestral estate, hundreds of flat and indistinguishable acres. A handsome memorial from the Franco-Prussian War overlooking the village square seems in perfect condition; a Soviet monument to those who fell here in 1945, a dilapidated heap of crumbling concrete, awaits the bulldozer. I take a walk through what was once the formal park in front of Bismarck's mansion, in the living room of which his favorite niece shot herself in the head as Russian troops swarmed the grounds, and ask a laborer where the former manor house had exactly stood. "Bismarck?" he replies. "Kaput, kaput."

Every dirty town I pass through has two, three, sometimes five or six great factories standing gaunt and forlorn against a quiet sky: shut down, padlocked, the huge smokestacks dormant—mercifully so, unless of course you happen to be out of work, as over 12 percent of the German labor force is.

In Potsdam I cannot find any place to eat. The enormous park surrounding Sans Souci, Frederick the Great's dream palace where the foremost warrior of them all plotted his campaigns and dallied with Voltaire, is entirely empty. A few workers haul statuary into a great pen surrounded by wire. A sign in German proclaims, "Awaiting Repair." Awaiting money, I say to myself. The palace itself is dispiriting, my guide unenthused with her party of three. No tips here, she's thinking. I had been led to expect that Sans Souci had the charm most commonly associated with some of the smaller, more refined French chateaux, but to my mind the place is suffocatingly derivative, its symmetry and famous cascading staircases so classical as to be dead.

In the tourist office nearby, once the coach house, former East Germans can glimpse a preview of what Western tourism demands, this gleaming addition to San Souci's amenities aglitter with handsome reception desks and clean toilets, sandblasted stone and gleaming brass lights, row upon row of glossy brochures and postcards, employees beautifully dressed and turned out in the latest Dracula-style lipsticks, the great swinging doors braced for a summer's load of tour buses. Unfortunately, I present my old map and ask where the site of Potsdam's garrison church had once been, and no one has ever heard of it.

The garrison church was the altar of Prussia's famous army, the place of ecclesiastical sanctification for its various aggressive wars, where preachers and divines (all Protestant) blessed German arms in much the same tradition as the Teutonic Knights (all Catholic) received the Eucharist before setting off to slaughter their enemies. Kings, princes, and field marshals were buried here; regimental flags hung from the beams; memorial tablets commemorating warriors beyond counting crowded the walls. The famous Potsdam bells rang

*Awaiting repair*

from the belfry, each named after an illustrious general or an individual battle. Here on March 21, 1933, the newly appointed chancellor Adolf Hitler officially opened the first parliamentary proceedings of the Third Reich in a ceremony as solemn as it was cynical. Few events in Hitler's career so legitimated his disorderly rise to power as this one, especially rewarding when von Hindenburg, in the full garb of a Prussian field marshal, shook the corporal's hand, an event immortalized by Goebbels's throng of photographers. Just twelve years later, on the evenings of April 14 and 15, the German armed forces paid a price for their overweening belief that they could control this madman. With the Reich crippled, reeling, virtually defenseless, wave after wave of British bombers demolished the garrison church along with entire blocks in all directions around it. Combing through the debris, "rubble women" of the reconstruction era found the bells but little else.

Many inquiries later, I discover they still exist, still tolling the hours here in Potsdam, on the more or less anonymous site of the once famous church. There will certainly be no revival of Prussian saber rattling here, no mecca in the offing for budding Nazis, monar-

*Kaiser Wilhelm II reviews his troops, Potsdam*

chists, or militarists of any stripe. Arranged in a scaffolding of dinged aluminum poles, the bells ring out nursery rhymes and hymns over-looking yet another shabby park in yet another shabby town that could be anywhere behind the former iron curtain—Poland, Hungary, the Czech Republic—anywhere. This will not be the site of a monster rally, no matter the hallowed soil.

That evening I approach the Polish border, a scene of considerable chaos. Western car rentals cannot be driven over the Oder. Theft, like death and taxes, is axiomatic once a bright new car crosses this ancient divide. Entrepreneurs, avaricious-looking salespeople, big shots of various hue and demeanor all line up to get across, seeking wealth and fortune in the fertile new markets beyond, or so they think. One cannot help regarding all of this as a more or less continuous cycle in human history, something that will never cease. Instead of the Wehrmacht, however, it's deutsche marks and dollars heading east; instead of the Teutonic Knights, it's a diesel truck hauling televisions.

This is not a vision to inspire war or revanche imperialism; the level of vulgarity is too high for that. Dreams of the east, I think, rekindle in the mind, whether in an easy chair or out on a walk it hardly matters. The wisp of music, remnants of letters and diaries, daydreams of long-dead fathers, mothers, aunts, and uncles, all buried in the sandy soil of

*Bells, Potsdam garrison church*

Ostpreussen, their graves unmarked, vandalized, obliterated—these sorts of things in former times would have been enough to spark the latent emotional fuse inside every worthy German, but today it's hard to tell. There is an unworthiness to the greed Germans see all around them. "The new instrument of torture," writes Günter Grass, "will be the market economy." That may be enough to fill a bank account yet insufficient to boil one's blood. The emotional past is there, over the border, and so, ironically, is the future. It may be a quiet, predictable, capitalistic, and safe future—that's what everyone says—but there's no guarantee.

# ❧ 2 ❧
# Marienburg
## 1275
# Crusades and
# the Birth of Prussia

*They robbed and burned wonderfully in many bands,*
*and ravaged up and down the land freely.*
**—Livländische Reimchronik**, thirteenth century

DRIVING ALONG THE RIVER VISTULA in today's Poland—through
the breadbasket of old East Prussia—I am struck by a sense of archaeo-
logical déjà vu. It is hard at times to know exactly where I am. Farm
upon farm passes by, quintessentially Slavic—tumbledown manor
houses of clearly patrician provenance but now pocked with broken
windows and missing roof shingles, their shutters hanging askew, surrounded by ramshackle wooden fences made of scrap or pallet boxes.
Chickens run loose, old plows and antiquated detritus are strewn
about the barnyard, three or four vagabond children happily careen
about, a gloomy Polish farmer comes in after work on an old jerry-
built cart with rubber wheels hauled by a sturdy draft horse. The contradiction lies in the perfectly manicured fields, the long country avenues lined with stoic trees that stretch across empty plains, and the
often enormous red brick barns, some in massive disrepair, testaments
to a sense of order and pride that belie the squalor of those who live
here now.

*Former German estate, Stobity*

This is understated country. Not overwhelmingly beautiful or lush, not cozy or conventionally picturesque, it nevertheless radiates a distinctly European flavor, an agricultural "architecture" to which the Poles seem grafted, and uneasily so. Every turn in the road brings some glimpse of Germany. A boarded-up church, an abandoned factory, a derelict power plant, all distinctively thrown up in brick, many dated "1889," "1912," "1937." Storks by the tens of dozens fill up disused chimney stacks with springtime nests.

The barns specifically are distinctive and impressive, some long and half-timbered, others three stories high with crenellations and gothic follies along their facades. A farmer angrily shoos me away from photographing his impressive specimen. He growls at me in Polish, waving his right hand up and down, gripping a pitchfork in the other. I can tell from his body language what he's saying: "You Germans come here to take our photographs. I know what you're going to tell all your rich friends back home—'Look at the dumb Pollack, shoveling cow shit by hand. Have you ever seen anything so stupid?'" He's disgusted when I try to explain how much I admire this barn. He waves contemptuously. It isn't worth a goddamned thing; the Germans built it. I take the picture anyway, my poor manners a mirror to his.

*German barn, Debina*

The level countryside saves its biggest surprise for the occasional town and village, most of which were flattened in World War II. In many such instances nothing old remains, but in a few the shell or artificial mound of a castle base still survives from days when the Teutonic Knights ruled all this land, and in several cases some enormous hulk of a fortress miraculously rears its brooding profile. The effect is usually staggering.

I have rarely seen castles as unromantic as these. Perhaps it is the ubiquitous brick construction, a material the knights originally imported from Germany and used indiscriminately in all their larger buildings; perhaps the unimposing sites, devoid of cliffs, rocky crags, sunken valleys wrapped in mist, or mountain peaks swarming with hawk or vulture. It would be hard to think of Camelot out here on the nondescript plains of East Prussia. A King Arthur would be disappointed with the regal possibilities of the landscape, to say nothing of a director from Hollywood looking for suitably dramatic sets in which to film a medieval epic.

Nevertheless, the knights had an eye for terrain. They built on rivers and streams, on slight eminences that might occasionally edge up on a strategic confluence of forest path or thoroughfare, on whatever kink in the geography an otherwise indefensible landscape might provide. They generally made up in sweat, expense, and bulk what nature did not lavish on their contemporaries in the Rhineland, who had less of a need for ingenuity in the art of castle building, given the rugged, "defensive" terrain there.

The initial fortresses that the order occupied were those of their conquered foes, overwhelmed in battle, usually mere palisades thrown up on artificial mounds of dirt, perhaps encircled by a ditch. Over time, as relative periods of stability allowed, the enormous structures we see today evolved, often surrounded by expansive walls encompassing several acres to allow for refugees from the surrounding countryside in times of raid, pillage, or rebellion. During the last, evil days of World War II as the Third Reich collapsed, ragged units of the Wehrmacht often made their last, suicidal stands amid these collapsed ruins, their decision to die fighting a direct heritage of traditions established centuries before by their hardened ancestors, the Teutonic Knights.

The territory that first occupied the knights' attention was essentially uncharted wilderness east of the River Vistula inhabited by a racially distinct clan of Balts known to us today as Prussians. A pagan people given to venerating their gods in holy groves and sacred springs, archaically isolated, essentially subsistence farmers and hunters, the Prussians left behind an alphabet of some 1,200 characters but no written records of any sort. They were not, according to contemporary sources, an overtly predatory collection of tribes, but neither did they welcome the attention of individual Christian missionaries, whom they often murdered, or the more menacing avarice of their Lithuanian and Polish neighbors. Few societal artifacts of any great interest have survived them. Occasionally, in some dilapidated country museum, a statue of Prussian origin grotesque in design or appearance may survive, but essentially their cultural legacy is one enormous blank. They appear in the historical record as those who stood in the way, their fate assimilation or, in extreme cases, death or exile.

Their tormentors were the Order of St. Mary's Hospital, better known today as the Order of Teutonic Knights, one of several quasi-monastic orders of fighting men spawned by that cataclysmic furor of medieval European history, the Crusades.

*Teutonic castle, Neidenburg*

Generally speaking, we think of these military expeditions to the Holy Land as smoothly organized and generally coherent ventures (or as much so as the times permitted), neatly encapsulated under generic labels familiar to us as the First Crusade, the Second, the Third, and so on, up through the Seventh, and spanning some 300 years from 1096 A.D. It is no surprise, in fact, to learn that these enterprises, preached with irregular degrees of vigor by vastly different popes and proclaimed haphazardly throughout the realms of Western Europe, varied widely in their makeup, aims, national leadership, and even fervor. At any single month of any single year, disparate bands of warriors, large or small, might set off for Judea, many by separate routes, to meet by surprise before the walls of some desert city other bands of errant knighthood. Some were dominated by the chivalry of France, others by lords from England; some by individual kings, others by councils; some consisted of no soldiery at all, a mob of crazed pilgrims (one made up entirely of children) led to their doom by monks or demented hermits.

Many crusades might be called—between 1157 and 1187, seven were preached by three different popes—yet not launched. Some might be launched yet ignored by important segments of the European nobility. As the Second Crusade unraveled in disaster, for example, the Germans Henry the Lion and Albert the Bear were separately hurling their might not against Saracen armies in Palestine but east of the Elbe, the heartland of Slavic tribes and their traditional enemies. But all admitted to one common belief: the remission of their sins in exchange for fighting the infidel.

Philosophically this entailed a striking deviation from the teachings of Christ in the New Testament, generally pacifist in tone and oriented toward avoiding bloodbaths, not endorsing them. Clerical spokesmen for the Crusades recognized this moral dilemma from the start but rationalized that divesting Europe of its battle-hungry population of surplus soldiery for the faraway prize of Jerusalem had a certain pragmatic appeal and was worth the sophistry required to justify it. Scouring the more fertile pages of the Old Testament, they produced ample precedent for un-Christian behavior. Jeremiah 48:40 was a popular choice: "Cursed be he who keepeth back his sword from blood." And St. Bernard of Clairvaux, clearly the most intelligent, eloquent, and relentless partisan of the crusading impulse, repeatedly offered his pagan adversaries the bleakest of choices: "Convert or be wiped out."

As far as the chivalry of Europe was concerned, few such scruples of conscience existed. Even some popes had recognized that most fighting men who took the cross were, just "a little while ago, robbers," illiterate martial men for the most part, unreflective in their desires and appetites, inured through a lifetime of brutalizing adventure from any squeamish moralizing over shedding blood or inflicting mayhem at their will. In the Holy Land, the principles at issue were so unrelievedly basic that even the dimmest intellect had no difficulty in figuring them out. The holy places where Christ lived, taught, and died had been desecrated by the infidel. The only recourse, as even the saintly Louis X of France could reason, was to push your sword right through the stomach of any Saracen you could find, "as far as it will enter."

Not surprisingly, the success of the First Crusade in taking the Holy City, along with significant portions of the surrounding countryside, ensured the necessity for all the others, since the Muslim enemy was equally cunning and resourceful, equally barred both mentally and physically from accepting defeat, and equally steeled by religious fervor to continue struggling no matter the odds. As military fortunes fluctuated, it became apparent to many leaders of Christendom that more or less permanent bodies of soldiers would be required to serve in Judea, primarily to man the fortresses, many of immense size, that had been commissioned and built by assorted European kings and princes. The two most famous orders of military monasticism were the result, the Hospital of St. John and the Knights Templar. From their modest origins as essentially protectors of pilgrims, keepers of hospitals, and frontline defenders of the holy places, both of these organizations soon prospered beyond all expectations, endowed by the aristocracy of Western Europe with valuable estates, great sums of treasure, and a steady stream of recruits. Many of these, with admirable self-restraint, eagerly assumed the strictures of poverty, chastity, and absolute obedience to their superiors, called grand masters, who directed them in both battle and life.

The international flavor of these orders was soon remarked upon, particularly by envious kings and lords who led crusades from Europe when especially dire conditions required the presence of more significant force. Once there, like it or not, they found grand masters at their sides, full of advice and prideful insider know-how that vastly irritated the royal vanities. The masters, however, were not to be trifled with, enmeshed as they proved to be in every royal court from Portugal to Germany, whether by virtue of their landed interests, their cultivation of the pious (king, queen, or powerful adviser), or most especially, their wealth. These orders were among the first international bankers of the Middle Ages, especially valued for their letters of credit and financial services that crossed all borders, rivaling in most respects the monetary capabilities of several royal houses. In the Holy Land especially, various monarchs were periodically forced to appeal for cash advances or bailouts from the monks whose dispositions, in keeping with their warlike missions, were neither meek nor submissive. When the latter balked, for whatever reason, there were generally angry scenes full of threats, recrimination, and often bloodshed, and these seeds of distrust and envy would eventually destroy the greatest order, that of the Templars.

In the shadow of these behemoths of the Holy Land, dozens of minor congregations of knights and men-at-arms sprouted here and there, many of a national or even regional character. Some evaporated in the ebb and flow of crusader hysteria; others were absorbed by larger communities; a few disappeared on the battlefield as military reversals grew apace. In 1194 a group of merchants from Lübeck, a growing German trading post on the Baltic Sea, visited Acre while doing business supplying the crusader armies and were horrified at the sight of their countrymen hacked about in holy battle but cared for by no one. They established St. Mary's Hospital in the heart of the old city, exclusively for the service of German wounded. Although no historical documentation now exists to explain the transformation of this essentially charitable enterprise into a military force devoted to the exercise of arms, it seems likely that a few former patients lingered about the place after recuperation, assisting in the treatment of their fellow Germans, and formed a brotherhood of sorts. In the everyday course of affairs, donations were sought and received, endowments created and invested, German pride put to work in matching the achievements of other semicharitable, semimilitary organizations. Records show tentative stirrings about, as the Teutonic Order joined others in building a crusader castle or embarked on a fray to the hinterlands. Eventually they were recognized by the pope as a distinct monastic order, given a rule to follow, and granted a few minor privileges. At one point the Hospitalers, noticing their presence, desired to absorb them, but the knights successfully resisted, choosing to preserve their German character.

The Hospitalers presumably did not pursue the hostile takeover very purposefully, for at no point did the Teutonic Knights appear as anything but a minor appendage to the veritable host of more illustrious and consequential personages that the Crusades produced. Richard the Lion-Hearted, Philip the Fair, Frederick Barbarossa, and Emperor Frederick II are the names generally associated with these extravagant expeditions to Jerusalem. The first grand master of the Teutonic Knights, Hermann von Salza, hardly seems a glamorous addition to this list unless you happen to be German.

The most conspicuous feature of the gloried Crusades, of course, was their gradual decline into utter failure and even disgrace. The objectives, to secure the holy places and then to maintain the various European-style city-states that evolved, mostly from material ambition and vainglory, were lost forever by 1270, date of the inglorious Eighth (and final) Crusade. The irony of all this is that peripheral crusades, the first in Spain and Portugal, the second east of Germany into Prussia and beyond, barely known of today, were immensely more successful.

The struggle for control of the Iberian Peninsula, for instance, consumed five centuries of horrific bloody struggle, but in the end the Moors were expelled and Spain and Portugal began their emergence as distinct political entities. Few details of the hundreds of battles, skirmishes, sieges, and escapades of that long-ago saga remain alive in any meaningful fashion—even in Spain and Portugal, the countries where they took place—and likewise the eastern crusades, which in the course of 200 years nearly doubled the area of Germanic hegemony and culture. The Teutonic Knights, never significant players in the politics of Asia Minor, were at the forefront of this purportedly secondary theater.

The urge to push eastward from the River Oder had not been a notion original to the knights. By the time of their transformation into a military order in about 1198, German colonization into Slavic territories had been ongoing for two centuries, and although a Christian trapping had been given the local initiatives of various German princes, the desire for new lands and kingdoms had remained the primary motive.

In 1200, however, the stirrings of an organized crusading impulse along the Baltic were clearly manifest. Remote and probably terrified missionary outposts, generally composed of Germans (whether monks, nomadic preachers, special envoys, whatever, it was certainly the time-honored blend of fervor and foolery), habitually issued calls for help as heathen reactions or predacity threatened their existence. Popes commenced a more or less continual stream of appeals for the rescue of its faithful servants, and though the major emotional call continued to focus on the Holy Land, those attending church each Sunday anywhere in Western Europe began to take notice of a diversity in choice. Many a German knight could see that a long and arduous travel to Jerusalem was no longer required for the absolution of his sins—the eastern frontier of his own people was much closer, and the spiritual rewards just as beneficial. Add to that commercial advantages and the allure was a strong one. Who wanted a kingdom of desert, sand, and blazing sun, when arable fields and bountiful forest were near at hand for the taking? "Pagans are the worst of men," one knight was related as saying, "but their land is the best."

Isolated bands of soldiery, often in groups of five or ten at a time, gradually (and anonymously) began appearing well behind the lines, as it were, in the remotest corners of Slavic territory, having leapfrogged Germany's eastern frontiers either by ship along the Baltic coast or in solitary treks through the no-man's-land of hostile wilderness. German knights were not beneath a challenge of such magnitude, no matter how foolhardy or extreme.

Around the year 1228 a Polish duke approached the grand master of the Teutonic Knights with a classically Roman offer. Wishing to con-

tinue his various military campaigns against fellow Poles and Lithuanians to the east but also aware of vulnerability along his northern
flank, peopled with the equally fierce and pagan Prussians, he proposed to position the knights as a protecting force between himself
and the Baltic. Let barbarians confront barbarians was presumably his
idea, Germans, though at least Christian, being no better than "dog
heads." The grand master, singed before on previous freelance missions, quibbled over terms. The order would face the Prussians, he
countered, but only if given a free hand. Whatever territories they won
they would keep, independent of any obligations to Poland, answer-
able only to Rome, where they owed exclusive fealty. How often history has turned on bargains as ill conceived as this, allowing the viper
to settle in one's nest. It was not a banner day for Poland as the duke
signaled his agreement.

The knights began in Kulm, on the western shore of the Vistula, utterly isolated from Germany and with no reliable allies upon whom to
count. In 1231 they crossed the river into what was largely unknown
territory.

In the span of seventy-five years, plunging first due north along the
Vistula, then careening east to Königsberg (1254) and the Memel, they
succeeded in both eradicating from the face of the earth every trace of
the stubborn Prussians and creating a monastic kingdom of some
12,000 to 14,000 square miles. They established 54 towns, each with
fortress and monastic enclosure; 890 villages; 19,000 manor-style
farms with peasant tenantries; and an entire network of roads and,
where possible, sea-lanes, along with an ambitious grid of dikes, dams,
sluices, and drainage ditches. Their strategy hinged entirely on the
castle, first to implant the cancer of their presence in the midst of enemy territory, then to offer protection to close-knit agricultural communities planted nearby (mostly with German and Flemish settlers),
finally to serve as an administrative center from which orderly rule
could emanate, the famous *Ordensstaat*.

Progress was irregular and prone to setbacks, many of a grievous nature. Insurrections by the indigenous Prussians were ghastly affairs.
Archives reveal many instances of knights being wiped out to the last
man, castles engulfed in flames, one grand master burned alive at the
stake. By the same token, these records show an inexorable advance
over time, great slaughters of the enemy, knights enjoying victory
feasts cooked on bonfires built from pagan effigies chopped up into
scrap. In 1283 the last independent Prussian clan ravaged its remain-

ing towns and fields, then fled eastward into oblivion. By this time the knights were active as far north as the Gulf of Finland.

Some ecclesiastical observers of the order, though happy with this advance of Christian borders and thankful on the knights' behalf that God had gloriously "reserved for them enemies," still voiced reservations on the propriety of bequeathing spiritual rewards on what was, at its basest level, a sanguinary campaign of secular conquest. The Prussians and Balts, it could be argued, were not the possessors of Bethlehem or Jerusalem or any other holy site where Christ had walked; indeed, they inhabited territories "where no apostle ever came." Nor had they invaded Christian lands as a provocation. The Teutonic species of religious conversion, moreover, seemed grossly inappropriate, captives (when any were taken) being offered the unappealing choice of death or taking the cross, and by taking the cross, passing into slavery. Where was the moral persuasion or charity in any of this?

Idle words. Despite the members' almost universal illiteracy, the knights were able diplomats. The grand master had a permanent representative in Rome looking out for all the order's business there, and beginning with the wily Frederick II, Germany's kings and princes lavished financial rewards on the knights. In the same span of time it took them to overwhelm Prussia, they became the wealthy proprietors of enough farmland in Germany proper to require the deployment of one hundred of their number as estate managers, ensuring a steady flow of both cash and recruits to the war zone. By the year 1300 it has been estimated that over 2,000 knights were members of the order, with another 3,000 as auxiliaries, clerks, priests, advisers, nurses, agricultural experts, armorers, and so on, all rigidly organized in a bureaucratic structure that ably churned out whatever measures various emergencies might demand, including the necessary propaganda to justify the knights' activities: *Dilatio et defensio,* the famous notion that in order to defend oneself, one had to attack. This specious line of self-justification is not necessarily unique to the German temperament, but it is a fact that similar rationalizations continually arise in Germany's long history of explaining away aggressive behavior, most particularly, of course, in both the world wars of the twentieth century. "Because of its central position," as Bismarck wrote, "Prussia [has been] forced to take the offensive in every war." These are time-honored modes of argument. To their credit, most Germans who employed them believed in what they were saying from the bottom of their hearts.

━╬━

Starting off from Kulm, as the knights did, I drift north beside the Vistula, each town passed by with some relic of the knights still apparent. Castles ruined, castles falling down, castles restored, castles ignored, castle hotels, castle prisons, castles empty and forlorn. The countryside is pretty much dead flat, the land seemingly prosperous and well tended, though strangely desolate and empty. At Rehden, one of the largest Teutonic fortresses in Prussia, I find myself almost feeling lonely walking about in the enormous forecourt at dusk, then down into the equally dead center of town, where there is no place to eat, no place to drink, no one to talk to, not a single shop still open, few if any lights signaling a welcome home in any of the dreary apartment houses nearby. If this were Western Europe, people would be flocking here to see the sights, to revel in the pseudoromanticism of medieval knights and their supposed pageantry; but it isn't. It's just another ramshackle crossroads in a Poland too poor, too distracted, too indifferent to exploit any of the natural or historical attractions that abound here. The fact that the hated Germans built it all does nothing to fuel their enthusiasm.

In Marienwerder, an early and important Teutonic stronghold, the cavernous cathedral is full of schoolchildren being led in song and catechistic instruction by a Dominican monk. As a Catholic myself, I am impressed by all this youthful exuberance, something rarely seen in the more affluent West, where Catholicism seems more an empty, degraded ritual than true belief, but later I learn that all the robust songs being practiced are aggressive paeans to mighty Poland. The nationalistic element of Polish Catholicism has frequently been remarked upon. I recall the tomb of Cardinal Wyszyński in Warsaw, devoid of any predictable quotation from biblical scripture, carved instead with the words "To Poland—Always Faithful." Walking about as the teenagers file out, I notice several saying prayers before a picture of Maximilian Kolbe, martyred at Auschwitz. "Jews died, but many, many Catholics, too," one said to me in very passable English.

"How many Catholics in proportion to Jews?" I asked.

"Many more than the Jews admit," she replied. A nun shoos them all away.

Further downriver is Graudenz, with remnants still of its Old Quarter, overlooking a Vistula crammed with wild swans if nothing else. Here evidence of the sources of Teutonic wealth is tangible: long rows of multistoried warehouses designed for the storage of grain, a primary

*Teutonic castle, Rehden*

export back to Germany and markets even more distant. Along with amber, fish, and wood, cereals such as rye, wheat, barley, and malt were the mainstay of the order's mercantile affairs, usually shipped by means of the famous cog, a broad-beamed, clumsy-looking vessel capable of loads averaging 200 tons, the common carrier of Baltic trade for centuries.* Quick to see the larger economic picture, the knights were also early proponents of the Hanseatic League, a confederation of

---

*Amber is fossilized resin, the pitch exuded from pine trees that hardens and often drops from its host after dripping down branches or trunks. In primeval times it often lay buried under layers of rotted forest and then was covered during the formation of the Baltic by seawater. Initially harvested along the coastline by simple scavenging or the dragging of nets and scoops in shallow eddies, the extraction process became something of an industry in the nineteenth century, when mines and shafts were sunk for its recovery. In Ostpreussen, amber was the monopoly first of the knights and then of the Hohenzollerns, a valuable concession that lasted right up through World War I. A 1914 Baedeker guidebook cautioned foreign tourists, for example, from souvenir hunting along the shores of the Frisches Haff: "You are not allowed to pick up fragments."

Depending on its quality—and there are many degrees—amber was highly valued both aesthetically and functionally. Jewelers from Copenhagen to St. Petersburg worked the material into decorative objects of immense beauty and value, yet thousands of pounds were also fashioned into items as mundane as pipe stems. By far the most extravagant treasure ever created from amber was the highly complicated series of panels commissioned by the Hohenzollern elector (afterward king) Frederick I, which graced his study at the royal palace of Königsberg.

independent cities dominated largely by Lübeck, the initial sponsor of
the order.

The grand masters enjoyed a reputation for hard bargaining. They
encouraged the development of town life, offering decent terms to
merchants willing to establish themselves in the often tempestuous
environment of their new domains, but nonetheless they were loath
to give away too much. The knights were not beholden to aristocrats
or any royal house in the immediate sphere of business negotiations.
They were too far away from the centers of power, too removed from
the immediate strength of kings or mighty commercial combines.
They made their deals with colonists, traders, burghers, and merchants on a straightforward business ethos of profit and loss, with the
usual arguments and tensions inherent in all such horse trading. The
later history of the order, as it declined, shows mercantile interests
chaffing under restrictions imposed by the grand masters, but during
the years of initial conquest the knights were the dominant partner.
Men of business knew full well their lives depended on the sturdy
sword arms these knights provided and realized just as keenly there
was little recourse if they didn't care for terms being put on the table.
Such is life on the frontier.

That evening I camp down by the river at Gnewin, an utterly obscure Teutonic town full of debris and the usual air of hopelessness.
The only traffic today on this majestic waterfront is poison, the
wretched effluent of countless decrepit factories, the cesspool economics of Poland's Stalinist heritage. I wouldn't stick my finger in this
water for fear it might disappear in some sulfurous combustion. Five
fishermen along the bank throw out a line or two, but nothing coming
out of this river would be fit to eat. Not a single boat, barge, ferry,
skiff, or vessel of any sort is to be seen here, a Vistula that centuries
ago was jammed with commerce.

These multiple impressions of gloom give way to appreciative good
cheer the next day as the magnificent restoration at Marienburg looms
over the horizon on an important tributary of the Vistula called the
Nogat. There is no denying the overwhelming impression this fortress
city, a multilayered monstrosity of a complex, initially provides.
Though some of the great entrance towers by the river's edge have
been defaced by graffiti and clearly important subsidiary buildings in
the surrounding town still beg for attention and repair, the sheer magnitude of all the work undertaken here to date astounds the visitor.
No one can or should doubt the capacity of Polish workmanship to do

a job of this magnitude, the scope of which is amply provided by pictures of Marienburg taken in 1945, which show much of the place in ruins. The question instead is really one of resources. Where did the Poles get the money? But the answer, after taking a tour, became very clear to me. Money didn't matter. Ego was involved; a sense of cultural bitterness and, yes, revenge, were the guiding motives here. A citadel of German arms, the capital city of Teutonic arrogance, the very center of Prussia's soul: How ironic and fitting that it be put back together again by patriotic Poles.

This concentration, this emphasis of their effort, if you will, is more or less historical, one can grant that. The knights did falter in the fifteenth century, and as they retrenched, largely because of Polish and Lithuanian pressure, they lost Marienburg and hundreds of square miles around it. For 300 years, Polish kings and princes called Marienburg their own. But it doesn't really work. "This is pathetic," a German tourist snaps at me. "If this place is Polish, then I'm a Negro!" German visitors, not surprisingly, now flock here, but this gentleman and his wife refuse to accompany the official tour. Instead they make arrangements for a German-speaking academic to guide them around that afternoon. "I will not listen to their propaganda. I want a professional, someone who knows his architecture and knows the facts. Honestly, I am willing to let the past be the past. I am willing to acknowledge that this land and this city belong to Poland now. But the Poles, they are still so angry and so chauvinistic. They built Marienburg? Nonsense!"

I, however, take the tour and read the literature passed about, along with many other Germans here today who seem less contentious than their compatriot, though the stench of urine and the sight of workmen relieving themselves over the ramparts disgusts them as typically Slav and thus unhygienic. We dutifully file through courtyards, chapels, cloister, and workshops and admire a treasure room and bakery, an armory and the obligatory torture chamber. The biggest rise of all is the monastic toilet, an immense tower called a *danzker*, its several chutes hundreds of feet above ground level, with ungainly wooden stalls built overhead to sit on. The Germans among us shake their heads in dismay, but the Poles and I are amazed at the grand simplicity of the concept, as well as the trust required to hang over such a void of suspended space and not fear that a collapse of beam or toilet seat might send one free-falling to earth below.

Until 1918 the castle was one of the kaiser's official residences. Wilhelm II is said to have stayed in it more than fifty times. In an often-

quoted speech he delivered here on May 5, 1902, he referred to Marienburg as Germany's "old bastion in the east . . . a monument that testi-
fies to Germany's task [here]: Once again Polish insolence offends Germany, and I am constrained to call upon the nation to safeguard its
national inheritance." In the very interesting museum housed off the
two-story cloister, a collection of old photographs shows the kaiser, a
vain and silly man, in various pompous attitudes, *un poseur ridicule*. A
particularly comic sequence shows Prussian guardsmen dressed up as
Teutonic Knights for a Wagnerian concert held in these halls, along
with the well-known engraving of Wilhelm, once a common image
hung in German hallways and farmhouses, himself decked out in medieval gear with helmet, sword, and shield, the word PAX inscribed over
his head. After the carnage of Verdun and other massacres along the
western front, this penny-postcard imagery went out of fashion, even
among those still committed to the monarchy.

I'm afraid the visual sequence going through my head is equally preposterous, but I can't seem to shake it as I circumnavigate the enormous outer walls, a walk of forty-five minutes. No one can study these
massive, sullen watchtowers with their almost brooding overhangs and
not be reminded of the Russian director Sergei Eisenstein's powerfully
epic film *Alexander Nevsky*, with its own equally gloomy rendition of
German knighthood. Filmed in 1937 with the prospect of war with Germany just ahead, the sunny, open-faced, jovial Slavs of Nevsky's
thirteenth-century Russian army contrast favorably, to say the least,
with the lumbering anonymity of Teutonic warriors. These beasts of
war are seen encased in heavy iron helmets, often capped with horns,
clenched fists, and other insignia of grotesque or Hunnish stripe, and
they behave as mercilessly inhuman as they look. Who can forget the
scenes where monks baptize little Slavic babies and then cast them into
the fire, burn at the stake any number of patriotic Russian soldiers, and
hang the bodies of captured foe from rampart walls? Heightened by a
deeply emotive score by Prokofiev (wrongly criticized, I think, by the
Irish critic Desmond Shawe-Taylor as merely "poster art"), the overall
impact on a poor contemporary viewer is about as grim as can be. This
is one reason I abstained from watching *Nevsky* again before coming
here (just as I avoided *Schindler's List*, for different reasons), but these
famous images, once seen, are impossible to forget.*

---

*Though *Alexander Nevsky*'s rather strident anti-German tone proved embarrassing
when the nonaggression pact between the two countries was signed in 1939, this film

*Portcullis, Marienburg*

The question really becomes, How close to the truth do any of these atmospherics ever come? What was the character of a typical Teutonic Knight of this period, and what was the true nature of their warfare? Did Eisenstein, for example, come anywhere close to approximating reality? The stagy costumes, the one-dimensional portrayal of the order as Satan incarnate, indifferent to any sort of cruelty and slaughter—did the famous director merely snatch these out of the air as stereotypical villainies unsupported by any kind of historical truth?

Chances are Eisenstein did not give the matter too much thought. It is said he figured the thirteenth century was so far removed from anyone's modern consciousness that he could make of the knights what

---

nevertheless went a long way toward the rehabilitation of Eisenstein, whose standing in Moscow during the perilous 1930s had been suspect. That most difficult-to-please patron of the arts, Joseph Stalin, put his arm around a relieved Eisenstein after the picture's successful premier and reportedly said, "Sergei Mikhailovich, you are a good Bolshevik after all!"

he wished, for whatever dramatic purposes his story required, in this instance a cardboard foil to his hero, the warrior (and later saint) Alexander Nevsky. We are so used, especially today, to reading about the vacuous lives of petty criminals and even mass murderers that we wonder, Were the knights any better, or were they simply another collection of headhunters to whom the acts of killing and assorted butchery were no different than eating a meal?

Certainly they were rough men, and the dreadful circumstances of their trade would probably nauseate any of us who happened, in some kind of supernatural flashback, to witness a customary day in the field during any given campaign.* But circumstances do exist that explain to some degree the knights' outlook and behavior, and these inevitably revolve around religion.

The early knights were monks, lay brothers for the most part who, when in the cloister, followed the ancient monastic routine of prayer, vigil, mortification, and denial. Their dress was plain, new recruits given a few shirts and rough garb, a bedroll, spoon, and prayer book. They were not allowed to lavish their shields or horse blankets with personal coats of arms that advertised far and wide the chivalric accomplishments of their bearers—only a black cross on a featureless white background. Forbidden to them were the usual daily prerogatives of the knightly class—the pleasures of the hunt, the courtship of women, the honor of tourneys. They ate sparingly, a diet of eggs and tough bread, very little meat. In battle they were bullied and cursed by their masters, often hit with clubs and knotted bullwhips to keep in line, ordered to act as a unit and not allowed the glory of individual combat. Expected to seek the loftiest goals of knighthood yet deprived of nearly every reward that generally accompanied its achievement, they sublimated all ambition to that of their order. Sustained by secret ritual, fed by the awesome power of the Eucharist, supported by the bond of comradeship that exposure to overwhelming odds most generally provides, knights of the Teutonic Order developed over time a reputation for arrogance and conceit.

Much has been said and written of how the knights grew avaricious for land and wealth, greedy for new farms and territories to exploit. Chamber accounts of grand masters have been laboriously scrutinized

---

*A typical torture of the times was to nail a man's scrotum to a wooden plank, then leave the victim a dull knife with which to extricate himself.

for expenditures grotesque to their mission, measures of self-indulgence that no one can dispute: "4 marks [about 700 grams of silver] to 2 serving men for hawks, a gift to the King of England; 3 marks for a map of the world on parchment; 1 mark for the Grand Master's fool; 3 marks for gold lace to a sable cloak; 18 marks for 4 casks of wine from Italy for the Grand Master's cellar; 12 marks for French wine," and so forth. Nor by the same token can the harsh record of their hard-fought achievements be ignored or denied.

Perhaps the grimmest insight into the mentality of these men can be found in the thirteenth-century rhyming poem *Livländische Reimchronik*, written by a Teutonic Knight who participated in the more or less incessant warfare against the pagans of Livonia. This was a struggle where life had no meaning: Prisoners rarely taken, women and children sacrificed without a thought, torture routine. Much of the fighting took place in the barren void of winter, where "undismayed heroes fall into grim death, the snow there was red with their blood." Here, in a macabre distortion of everything Christ is believed to have stood for, the knights find their God in the gore of battle. Only in the maelstrom of cleaving skulls and lopping off the arms and legs of their enemy can the essence of spiritual life be found. Mary, the Queen of Heaven and patroness of the order, is an old-fashioned pagan war goddess, demanding from her servants a merciless and single-minded devotion to the search for danger. It is not the triumph of arms that these monks must achieve, but the discovery of death. Their quest is not the Holy Grail, but martyrdom. Hence the fantastical exploits, the unhesitating obedience, the orders obeyed no matter how outrageous, the desire to charge whatever the odds, the often futile sacrifice of their lives. This was no false or vainglorious chivalry, the ethos of France and England, with its courtly etiquette and histrionic devotion to display, the better if widely witnessed. This was an elemental desire, pagan in its rough Germanic simplicity, that could often be satisfied far away from the sight of men in some squalid skirmish in bog or forest. Nietzsche wrote some of his most hyperbolic garble on this very subject, rambling on about "jubilant monsters, magnificent blond brutes . . . reverting to beasts of prey" and so on, but his rabidly anti-Christian bias blinded him to the sacred overtones that were, at least originally, the very core of belief for this often berserker knighthood. God was simple then. He was either right or he was wrong. Medieval man had no difficulty ascertaining which.

The ethos of Prussia was created single-handedly by the Teutonic Knights. Their standards became an inbred element of response and attitude for hundreds of later generations born and reared here, no matter how distant in memory the individual exploits of their predecessors became. The German general staff of the twentieth century, it is safe to say, was attitudinally a direct descendant, though attempts— some by the deranged Heinrich Himmler, others by left-wing historians—to equate the knights with SS storm troopers exaggerates the cruder similarities they seem to have shared. Many a German soldier has known nothing of the Teutonic Order, but he was brought into this world with its instincts just the same. William James considered this in 1902 when he wrote his important book *The Varieties of Religious Experience.* "The ideal of the well born man without possessions," he called it, "still dominates sentimentally the military and aristocratic view of life. We glorify the soldier as the man absolutely unencumbered. Owing nothing but his bare life, and willing to toss that up at any moment when the cause commands him, he is the representative of unhampered freedom in ideal directions." To the common eye, there was nothing "ideal" about the advance of Teutonic arms through Prussia, accompanied as it was by flame and catastrophe. But the knights needed no praise; they could take to heart the gloomy satisfaction of their own monastic chronicler: "Look at my works, ye Mighty, and despair."

⁓⌘⁓

Workmen are still busy on the Marienburg restoration, and I watch an electrical crew laying cable from the central plaza outside the main gate into the castle. This is all pick-and-shovel work—no jackhammers, compressors, or modern tools of any sort in view. Three or four men stand about in the trench with a single mattock between them. As one tires after five or six minutes of steady hacking, he passes it along to the next in line, who does his bit, and so on. I wonder if this meets even Third World standards of inefficiency, but then again, there is little to fault with the finished product, especially when seen from afar, across the Nogat in a small car park, where a handful of peddlers sell Polish sausage. The immense stratification of walls, turrets, spires, and water gates is probably the most impressive historical view in all of Poland.

That Marienburg acquired these necessarily regal trappings was the direct result of two disasters that seriously threatened the order's well-being. The first was the fall of Acre in 1291 after a siege of several months' duration, with the subsequent extinction of whatever mis-

*Teutonic castle,*
*Allenstein*

sion the knights still felt they owed in the Holy Land. The second
threat, and far more serious, presented itself in the destruction of the
Knights Templar by the avaricious king of France, Philip the Fair, in
1301.

Thoroughly strapped for funds in an age when regularized taxation
as a concept was still barely understood, this cynical monarch turned
treacherously on a man he had formerly counted as a friend (the godfather of his daughter, as a matter of fact), Jacques de Molay, grand master of the Templars. Against this, the wealthiest of all the military orders, the king succeeded in channeling a near hysteria of evil opinion.
Concocting the wildest of charges against its leadership, mastermind-
ing show trials that would have made Hitler blush, staging public hu-
miliations and executions in the square before Notre Dame, Philip
created scenes of such shocking distraction that no one noticed his ap-
propriation of all the Templars' treasure.

The German order took note of their contemporary's fate, a process that took Philip seven years to accomplish. Notions of ever returning to the Holy Land vanished in the light of these dangerous tidings, the Teutonic leadership abandoning its temporary headquarters in Venice, traditionally the departure port for crusader armies destined for Jerusalem. The grand master was not to be caught unawares, in a sumptuous palace far from his true base of power. He removed himself to Marienburg in 1309, just in time to learn that Jacques de Molay had admitted spitting on the cross and that bulls of excommunication were to be issued against all the military orders.

Unlike the Templars, however, the Teutonic Knights had a kingdom of their own. Their particularization as an exclusively Germanic brotherhood had provided them a state where the army was their army, the castles their castles, with no rival kings, men like Philip the Fair, in their midst to envy their growing horde of gold, wheat, and amber. They hunkered down in this faraway dominion of Prussia and weathered the opprobrium of Templars tortured, Templars burnt at the stake, Templars committing suicide, Templars cast to the winds. They went about their business, waited for the frosts and snows to come each year, and then, bundled in armor and fur, went out in the cold to harry eastward.

## ⇥ 3 ⇤

# Danzig
## 1375
# Drive to the East

*. . . at last*
*Far in th' Horizon to the North appear'd*
*From skirt to skirt a fiery Region, stretcht*
*In battalious aspect, and nearer view*
*Bristl'd with upright beams innumerable*
*Of rigid Spears, and Helmets throng'd, and Shields*
*Various, with boastful Argument portray'd,*
*The banded Powers of Satan hasting on*
*With furious expedition.*
                    **—John Milton, *Paradise Lost***

I LIKE TO THINK OF MYSELF as a literary traveler for the most part,
a certain village, city, province, or country providing the ready excuse
to search off the shelf some particularly appropriate book that otherwise I might never read or have forgotten since school. England, for example, is an excuse to finish off Dickens, Jane Austen having written
far too little to sustain over several visits. In Dublin I generally run
through favorite passages in *Ulysses,* and when last in Spain I managed to reach the end, finally, of *Don Quixote.* In Danzig the choice is
even clearer. I unpack an old secondhand copy of *The Tin Drum.*

It may seem odd, but Günter Grass and James Joyce have something
in common. Like *Ulysses, The Tin Drum* is literally a walk through
town, and if the uninitiated reader can overcome tumbling plots and

generally bizarre word games that perhaps only a Dubliner or a
Danziger can appreciate, specific streets, specific historical episodes,
and specific sites come barging off the page to illuminate the more
generally sterile descriptions of a Baedeker or a Michelin guide. I was
most interested to find the old Polish post office, site of Grass's most
intense scene, where he describes the earliest siege of World War II,
Oskar asleep in a laundry cart jammed with mail, and his natural father, the diffident Jan Bronski, playing skat amid the din of gunfire.

Historically speaking, Danzig defies description. Few cities in the
world have presented such a tortured mix of ethnic contradictions
(only Jerusalem comes to mind as a comparison in complexity). Established by whom, no one knows, but its position at the head of the Vis-
tulan estuary as it empties into the Baltic guaranteed the place an importance that both Slav and German recognized at once. In the
topsy-turvy ebb and flow of racial conflict, Danzig was continuously
the great prize, fought over, put to siege, pillaged, and starved, each
side assiduous in its desire to deprive the other of the bounty that this
great port oversaw and controlled.

At many periods in its long saga, this city could hold Europe almost
to its mercy. The cheap grain of the eastern European heartland fueled
the economies of Great Britain and the Continent as the West
emerged from the dark ages of subsistence agriculture, and all of it—a
virtual monopoly—flowed through Danzig to such a degree that a
frozen harbor could mean bread riots in Paris, London, or Amsterdam.
The additional streams of timber, dried fish, amber, and other commodities all were channeled through the merchant houses of Danzig.
Its importance to the rudimentary commercial life of Prussia and to
an even greater degree that of Poland cannot be exaggerated. As one
Polish historian observed, Warsaw was a mere village in comparison.

Along the great Vistula, whatever exports Poland could manage
wound their way northward to the Baltic and the countinghouses of
Danzig. In times of peace both Slav and German commingled in the
bartering and deal-making atmosphere of the marketplace, but generally speaking it was German acumen that held a wider vision and extended the reach of Danzig throughout developing Europe. Poles became the providers of a cheap and raw bounty; Germans became
wealthy loading it into ships at the famous Green Bridge.

Other than the wrath of a battlefield, Danzig provided the closest
interaction between these two peoples, though we should not, in
speaking of medieval times, think in terms of "nation-states" or "na-

tionalities." Poland did not exist as a twentieth-century country, nor did Germany. Danzigers were first and foremost Danzigers, not Germans, for example. This did not deter them from disliking Slavs, but the joys of turning profits and brokering contracts could override such inborn distaste.

Although often far from harmonious, race relations here in Danzig, though further complicated by differences in religion during the sixteenth century, still outperformed the more cantankerous confrontations that so marred the history of central and eastern Europe. The resulting quirks of cohabitation, several centuries' worth of generally compatible though often noisy relations, provided the rich vein of material through which a Günter Grass would pick and choose in 1959.*

Like every town and city along the Germanized Baltic coast, Danzig was all but razed in 1945, but as in the case of Marienburg the place has been meticulously restored, though much remains to be done. Vacant lots, piles of rubble, and streets gouged and torn apart still litter the landscape here. The old Hanseatic merchant houses, reflecting the heavy influx of Dutch traders beginning in the 1400s, are a direct transference of old Amsterdam to the Prussian fens. Business seems brisk in the many jewelry stores that quarter in these renovated mansions, their featured items being necklaces, bracelets, earrings, chess sets, even pipe stems all carved from amber, that curious and often translucent stone whose trade was monopolized by the Teutonic Knights, who took over Danzig in 1308 and reigned supreme here for 158 years, often to the despair of its mercantile class. The knights

---

*In keeping with Polish hostility toward most things Germanic, *The Tin Drum* was not translated and released in Poland for twenty-four years after its publication.

The city has been more conventionally portrayed in recent short stories by the Polish writer Pawel Huelle, though conflicts between Pole and German remain just as vivid. In "The Table" a couple protract their marital difficulties over a piece of furniture bartered from a German refugee expelled from Danzig in 1946 by vengeful Poles. Unfortunately, he left woodworm behind as well: "'Do something,' she'd say to my father. 'I can't stand it any longer! Those are German worms. Soon they'll attack the dresser, and the cupboard, because they are insatiable, like everything German,' she'd whisper in his ear." And later, the argument continues:

"Mr. Polaske's brother . . . hanged himself in the attic of their home in Zaspa."

"And why do you think he did that?" my father would ask loudly. "After all, he could have gone back to Germany like his brother."

"He hanged himself," my mother would say as she came into the room with a steaming dish, "because he was finally troubled by his conscience. If all Germans were troubled by their conscience, they'd all do the same."

*Danzig*

spent considerable treasure on this site, encircling the town with immense walls that featured sixteen gates and twenty towers. They also
developed the dockyard; built a castle, an immense cathedral dedicated to their patroness, Mary; and constructed the usual assemblage
of municipal buildings that allegorized their commitment to profit
and permanence. All in all, what remains of these ancient endeavors
from the catastrophe of 1945 exudes a weary air. Danzig has yet to re-
capture any sort of visual buoyancy. I noticed this when I saw some
French sailors from a visiting warship strolling about the town resplendent in colorful uniforms with bright red pom-poms on their
caps. All of a sudden, the drab old streets came alive.

   A free-market bustle along the main avenue of old Danzig, closed to
traffic, indicates the doctrinaire blessings commonly associated with
democracy: several score of street vendors, musicians, mimes, and ac-
robats hustling the usual assortment of belt buckles, cheap souvenirs,
postcards, pottery, and entertainment that modern tourism demands.
Scruffy art students hang out on clotheslines yesterday's assignments,
many of which are of surprisingly high quality. I inquire about a very
professional etching of Danzig's ancient skyline, punctuated with
spires and medieval towers. The price is too cheap to haggle over, and

I pay out the equivalent of $7. I watch a vendor sell videos entitled "Danzig in the 1920s—Archival Footage." In twenty minutes he sells nine, all to elderly German tourists. There seems no limit to the nostalgia business, however much the vendors detest the clientele.

St. Mary's Cathedral is the largest brick church in the world, though its history is, of course, checkered. Built by the knights as a Catholic place of prayer, it was appropriated by Protestants during the Reformation, when northern Germany became largely Lutheran. Now it is Polish and Roman Catholic, as befits the city's current lordship. The interior is cavernous and chilly. A group of Polish veterans from World War II has just unveiled a monument to their regiment, a priest sprinkling holy water over a red marble plaque. All along the wall these old soldiers pin photographs of themselves in uniform and regale each other with tall tales. One points himself out on horseback. "We non-Communist!" he tells me, meaning that he was a member of the Armia Krajowa (AK), or home army, horror stories about whom I would later hear from Polish Jews. That afternoon I wander over to the famous docks, birthplace of Solidarity, and see all the cranes and shipyards that are currently underutilized and suffering severe depression.* The water, like the old town itself, is murky and stained.

⊰⊱

Into this port on August 9, 1390, sailed three ships from England. On board were some 200 men, half of whom might properly be called professional soldiers, the retinue of Henry, earl of Derby, a "wrath kindled gentleman" according to Shakespeare, called to Prussia for the annual winter *reyse* into Lithuania.

*Reyse* is not a word familiar to most of us who speak English, nor should it be. Chaucerian scholars are probably the only people still around from whose lips it still might be heard, as it appears in the *Canterbury Tales* through one of its more famous depictions, that of the Knight, who

> *Full often time he had abroad bygonne*
> *Above all nations, to Prussia.*
> *In Lithuania had he reysed and in Russia*
> *No Christian man of his degree more often.*

---

*The shipyard finally succumbed in April 1997, a victim of free-market economics.

*Polish war veteran,*
*Danzig*

Scholars still argue over the actual personage on whom Chaucer modeled his character. Indeed, they still argue over the actual dates when various portions of the *Tales* might have been written, which crucially aid or destroy various theories of identification. But there seems enough similarity of portrait and experience to indicate that much of the Knight was fashioned on the young Derby, also known as Bolingbroke, more famous in literature as a major character in Shakespeare's *Richard II* and, to a lesser degree, *Henry IV,* the king he would later become.

In 1390 Derby was a young man of twenty-five, though already the father of three children from his arranged marriage of twelve years before. He was without question one of the premier young lords of England, heir to the house of Lancaster and all the wealth its estates could provide, his own father the famous John of Gaunt (on account of his birth in Ghent), whose career even today boggles the mind with its breadth of adventure, unremitting drama, and extravagance. In return for surrendering his rights to the throne of Castile, a pretension he could not achieve with the sword, John of Gaunt received treasure that required forty pack mules to pull away back home to England. With much of this fortune, he subsidized his son's chivalric impulses, which included two expeditions to the longest-running saga of continuous warfare in Europe, that of the Teutonic Knights and their undiminished hostility toward the Slavic peoples of Lithuania and Poland.

Since 1283 not a single year had passed without some sort of military engagement between these protagonists, nearly all of it the scorched-earth variety in a zone of operations now commonly seen, from all camps, as a rough dividing line or border area centered around the River Memel (i.e., the Niemen). Over the course of the 1300s the knights had won Pomerania, seized Danzig, and purchased Estonia, the latter financial arrangement a glowing indication of the order's wealth. This left a long and undivided strip of Baltic shoreline in their control, but its narrowest inroad to the interior was the mouth of the Memel. Just a few miles upriver, an impenetrable mass of forest, bog, hedge, and bramble obstructed all easy passage to the interior. Through this featureless wasteland ran innumerable tracks and paths, known only to guides and trappers, running from one insignificant forest clearing to another, some peopled with Lithuanian settlements, others guarded by earthen forts. This region served primarily as the point of contact, thus of conflict, in what became a tangled, bloody, and sordid experience mostly devoid of honor and chivalry, but a martial exercise just the same that taxed to the utmost the strength and perseverance of all involved.

Caesar noted of the Gauls that what they "most greatly admire is that the lands surrounding them should be devastated and laid solitary to the farthest extent." Such was the military strategy of the Teutonic Knights. Their winter *reyse* generally consisted of small raiding parties, sometimes as few as a dozen knights, carrying a week or two of provisions tied in rolls behind their saddles. Often riding through unbroken forest or along streams frozen and able to withstand the heavy weight of horses "trapped in steel," these bands would harry frontier villages and seek the booty of slaves and livestock. "He goes into the wilderness with a hundred picked men to plunder and harass the pagans," one commander wrote approvingly of a subordinate. "They dismount at the Sesupe, eat and drink, re-mount and cross the Niemen, entering four villages that were not warned of their coming and putting to the sword whoever they find beginning their night's sleep, men, women and children."

Clashes were horrible, treacherous affairs, often ambushes or surprise attacks, no fate too gruesome for the hated Lithuanian pagans,
those "pestilential enemies of Christ." Disaster, however, was never
far away from any of these intruding bands. Winter could surprise a
raiding party with blizzard or raging storm; men who knew the forest
could just as easily lose their way; supplies and fodder could trickle
away, with starvation the unhappy result. The enemy, equally fierce,
might pursue in greater strength or plan their own revenge by surging
ahead to stage an unexpected ambuscade along some well-known escape route as the knights fled, encumbered with plunder. Many times
a commander made decisions that astonish us today. In 1311 a patrol
engorged with more booty than it could handle sensed a vengeful pursuit closing in. What to leave behind: the 100 horses, the 1,000 head of
cattle, the 200 captives? Seeing more value in livestock, the knights
slaughtered their human cargo and pushed on resolutely for home.

The summer *reyse* were customarily more ambitious in scope.
Aside from mosquitoes, intense heat, and the periodic deluge of rain,
the weather was certainly more conducive to a fighting spirit, and
usually some fort or city of significant strategic appeal was targeted
for attack. This required siege equipment and considerable matériel,
usually pushed and hauled by barge or boat upriver at tremendous logistical effort and expense, to the often vast irritation of visiting
knights athirst for glory and impatient of delay.

These adventurers, as the century progressed, came from all of
Western Europe. The Teutonic Order was now in the business of promoting travel to Prussia. Their initial goal of orchestrating a universal
call to arms from the pope was achieved in 1325. Pope John XXII issued what was in effect a monster appeal for crusaders in his new en-
cyclical, which elevated the Prussian wars to a level equal in heavenly
prestige to any destined for the Holy Land itself, the draw in this case
being full remission of any sin in exchange for three years of service or
monetary donation. Bruiting the call far and wide were militant Dominican friars, great supporters of the order, who preached the crusade
from numberless pulpits. German recruits to the order—first admitted
as acolytes to convents on German soil, then shipped east to Prussia—
grew more appreciably than at any previous period in the brotherhood's history, and these were augmented by the "huge route of
knights" that signed on for the annual *reyse*, often quadrupling in size
the standing Teutonic army: Rhinelanders, Saxons, Thuringians,
Hanoverians—all stripes of Germans—joined by French, Italian, Aus-

trian, Belgian, Dutch, Hungarian, Burgundian, Scottish, and English knights, typified to some degree by Henry, earl of Derby.

Derby's two voyages to Prussia memorably survive in account books kept by his treasurer, a meticulous record of itinerary, sums paid out for the myriad supplies and equipment required, and the gifts and subsidies received in return. These ledgers, dry by nature, are vastly more informative than the various chronicles or annals of the times, which are usually bare of detail or alternately hyperbolic in the recording of victories and defeats. In Derby's case we see in the figures themselves what effort and expense were required to go on the Prussian *reyse* and thereby glean the value that important men gave to this enterprise, to say nothing of the style to which the greater lords were accustomed.

Derby left England in 1390 from the town of Boston, then the second seaport of the realm, a startling realization to anyone today who might visit the lonely coastal strip of the Lincolnshire fens. But Boston, Lynn, and Hull were all directly linked on the Hanseatic network, sheltering German merchants within their walls in the same fashion as Bremen, Lübeck, and Danzig, where English counting-houses and guild federations are all amply recorded. When Derby reached Danzig after three months at sea, he immediately authorized factors of his own nationality to buy supplies, arrange for funds, commission the purchase of thirteen carts with horse for the hauling of his immediate stores, and hire several barges to forward heavier equipment by water to Königsberg. But he lingered not at all. Hearing that the *reyse* had already begun, he dispatched the Lancaster herald ahead and set his band to the road, bypassing the splendors of the court at Marienburg to press straight for the Lithuanian frontier, entered eight days later. Catching up with the main body of invaders, he was accompanied into camp by musicians and showered with gifts: three war horses, several sheep, an ox, and two peacocks. Whether this was enough to feed his retinue is unclear.

From the account book we know of eighty-eight men in Derby's suite. Eleven knights, eighteen squires (would-be knights seeking to win their spurs in combat), ten miners and engineers, seven bowmen, four officers of Derby's household, twenty-five servants and grooms, six minstrels, five additional musicians, one herald, and one trumpeter. Historians have generally doubled this figure to account for hangers-on and those required for the menial but important tasks of cookery, baking, and washing up (Lawrence "of the kitchen and

A Danzig merchant, *by Hans Holbein the Younger*

scullery" is mentioned). Most of these men were regularly paid, some received winter gowns as a Christmas bonus, and all had to be housed and kept in essentials.

These were considerable costs, more than matched by Henry's expenditures of a more personal nature: his need for a saddle every now and then, a steed of sufficient nobility to carry him about in battle, a set of silver eating utensils, cloth for a pennon, and a deep pocket to display his own royal largesse with gifts and gratuities. In all, Henry spent 13,000 Prussian marks, calculated in the 1980s to approximate some £4,300, a considerable contribution indeed to the Teutonic war effort.

This sum, and his own energetic sword arm, certainly cleansed his soul of whatever sins he may have committed up to that point in his young life, for Henry distinguished himself in that year's *reyse*, though the siege of the important town of Vilnius, the order's objective for that year, proved ultimately unsuccessful, with only an outer fort falling to attack. In that initial triumph Henry's band and, presumably, its leader were the first to breach enemy walls and plant their standard. Chroniclers state, perhaps with exaggeration, that 2,000 of the "common souldiers" inside were then put to the sword. When the campaign broke off five weeks later—the Prussian forces "annoyed" by lack of supplies—3,000 captives were herded the 120 miles back to Prussia. Eight of these prisoners, newly Christianized, Henry took back with him to England, along with an assortment of bears, elk, a wild boar, deer, and most important, various falcons.

The Teutonic Order specialized in the breeding of these noble birds, so valued by the aristocracy of Europe as a reflection of their own brave selves. At Marienburg an aviary with full supporting cast of attendants and genealogists produced some of the finest hawks in Europe, which the grand master routinely sent as gifts to the various crowned heads whose favor he wished to curry, including Richard II (whom Henry would supplant six years later, in 1399).

Grand masters by now had become expert courtiers. Their annual campaigns, ambitious as they were expensive, grew dependent on the infusion of foreign visitors. Men like Henry, earl of Derby, who delighted to "sigh my English breath in foreign clouds," provided the indispensable manpower, however haughty and at times unruly, that bulked up the Teutonic forces. As such, the grand masters became professional hosts. Gone were the prohibitions on ostentatious food and drink, the hunting parties and tournaments that European knighthood so enjoyed. Men such as Derby did not come to Prussia to live like monks. They came to fight, and when not employed on military forays they expected to be entertained. At times, if especially important visitors happened to miss a *reyse,* a customized expedition could be arranged, as happened in 1378 with the duke of Austria. Barbara Tuchman referred to these specialty tours as "manhunts of the peasantry for sport," and Eric Christiansen, a noted expert on the order, went so far as to call them "safaris."

However callous the design, certainly by Derby's time the atmosphere was pretty straightforward. Lithuania's royal family had converted to Christianity and was making suitably appropriate gestures toward enforcing conversion throughout its realm. The Teutonic mission was thus exposed as no longer missionary at heart but temporal, a desire for new lands at the expense of traditional enemies. Derby, however motivated by religious fervor, traveled to Prussia to enjoy the

*Effigy of Henry, earl of Derby, later Henry IV, king of England, Canterbury Cathedral*

trade of war for its own sake, and the Teutonic order provided an arena where hostilities could always be, at the very least, arranged.

The order of the fourteenth century was a business entity, coolly efficient, always under control, rarely flustered into panic or despair when conditions seemed dire. The transfer of power within the order, for example, was rarely disrupted by personal ambition or feud. When a grand master died, a dispassionate sequence of bureaucratic machinery produced his successor, a Teutonic efficiency that irritated the order's enemies, who always hoped for a dynastic squabble that might distract these men from their single-minded sense of purpose.

Their celibate lives contributed to this stability: no yapping controversies between irreconcilable siblings to tear up the countryside in civil war after a state funeral, no "going native" with local women and the inevitable issue of contentious bastards all fighting one another for power. The ancient foes of these military orders in the Holy Land had seen how futile the use of their special irregular weapon—the "assassins"—could be. If a master was assassinated, according to the crusader Jean de Joinville, "another equally good would be put in his place, therefore nothing was to be gained from their death." This gave the knights a tremendous advantage as they threw themselves whole-heartedly into the dynastic squabbles of Lithuanian and Polish poli-tics, themselves immune to the same interference and cabals. During Derby's march into Lithuania, the grand master suddenly died. After mass, the invasion went forward without hesitation.

After his *reyse* of 1301, Henry dallied in Königsberg over the Christ-mas and New Year festivities. He had one of his knights to bury and two other men, captured before the walls of Vilnius, whom he tried to ransom through the good graces of Polish go-betweens. But he spent much of his time being measured for new fur coats and entering into the daily routine of a semiregal court. As Henry related to Chaucer two years later, the order had instituted a chivalric round table of sorts, called by the poet in his *Tales* the "Table of Honor," and perhaps Derby stayed hoping for admission to this select group. He was brave enough, elite enough, and certainly haughty enough for the honor, Chaucer noting that in profile "his nose was heigh," an oddity con-firmed in 1831 when, Henry's tomb having been dug up, this particu-lar vestige of his skull, with cartilage still intact, was uncovered and approvingly observed as "elevated."*

But the order did not convene the table that season, perhaps disap-pointed in the outcome of its campaign or perhaps desirous that the honor not become a formality, another excuse for another banquet. In February Derby wound his way back to Danzig and shipped home for England.

---

*The nineteenth century was a propitious time for disinterring famous men. A wood-cut from what is left of the Königsberg archives depicts the magic moment when work-men uncovered the skeleton of Kant, of particular interest for those of a scientific bent of mind who wished to measure and approximate the volume of his brain cavity as a means of ascertaining the physical manifestations of genius. This Germanic curiosity for facts and figures was grotesquely pursued during World War II by some of the more deranged personalities of the Third Reich, in medical experiments all too fulsomely recorded at the Nuremberg trials. Even today the subject fascinates some. Einstein's brain sits in a pickle jar full of formaldehyde in the Kansas apartment of a research pathologist, "next to a gas station," according to a helpful report of the *Wall Street Jour-nal*. And there is some desire among scientists to dig up Beethoven's remains for hair samples, as DNA testing might determine if this great German died of syphilis.

Before leaving the city, I have supper at a fish place outside an original medieval gate. One of the great bounties of the Baltic, not unnaturally, had been its teeming population of herring, but the inland sea has pretty much been plundered over the past several decades and catches now are thin. My Russian driver in Kaliningrad, as a matter of fact, had once been a trawler captain, but he took me down by the docks along the shoreline one afternoon where his old ship lay tied cheek by jowl with several dozen other rust buckets in various stages of disintegration. "No fish, no work, no money," he shrugged. In Danzig, my dinner of smoked eel is superb, accompanied by a glass or two of that town's excellent beer. A cartoon on the coaster shows two Teutonic Knights happily drunk with enormous steins of frothy pilsner, an uncharacteristic attempt at humor on the part of my otherwise dour and depressed Polish hosts. Certainly the waiter seems unhappy, the whole bill coming to a meager $3 or so.

I drive out to the Westerplatte to walk off my meal. The first barrage of World War II was fired here from the outmoded German warship *Schleswig-Holstein* at 4:45 A.M. on September 1, 1939. The Westerplatte is a long encircling spit of land that protects the entryway into Danzig Harbor, a natural barrier to both rough weather and military attack and thus the site of many lighthouses and many fortresses over its long history of human habitation. The anchorage here witnessed several "provocations" between the two world wars, variously referred to by the ship names of those involved—the *Wicher* incident, the *Leipzig* affair, and so on. They were all part of the supercharged war of nerves that Danzig embodied during those twenty-odd years, Germany and Poland teasing, nudging, pushing, and testing each other to the amusement of no one. The *Schleswig-Holstein*, however, was not anchored here to probe anything. Ostensibly visiting port to participate in ceremonies honoring the dead from World War I, its real mission was to soften up a few Polish marines guarding a munitions dump on the Westerplatte.

One of two buildings from that garrison post have been left standing, presumably as a monument since flower beds and shrubs are maintained along the stone walkway that winds by. These horticul-

---

*Nikita Khrushchev described the prewar policy of Poland as "a farce."

*September 1, 1939, 4:45 A.M.: The ship* Schleswig-Holstein *and the first salvo of World War II, Danzig*

tural efforts do not disguise the bullet-gouged walls, great chunks of masonry blasted away leaving craters of dusty debris and exposed supporting rods of steel. Underground bunkers, predictably odoriferous from trash and urine, have also been preserved, along with a vintage tank, unmaintained, corroding, one of its treads fallen apart.

If most people think at all of those first days of war, blitzkrieg comes to mind, German mechanized units ripping apart the primitive Polish army. Dumb Polack jokes probably originated just south of here, too, with reports of various engagements along the Corridor where Polish cavalry units supposedly attacked Wehrmacht tanks head-on, unleashing a flood of melancholic derision. In fact, the stories are untrue, based mostly on the inadvertent contact of retreating horse soldiers with advance panzer units and the sporadic exchange of blows between them. The casualty figures point to ineptitude as well: 14,000 German soldiers killed as opposed to 66,000 Poles. The treacherous Russians lost only 700 men in their campaign of surprise attack from the east. Almost a million Polish captives were taken between the two invading armies.

Neither fiction nor fact gives the true story. Though crushed by superior numbers and technology, the Poles never rolled over and ran away. In numberless stands unrecorded by any histories, they resisted to the last man in savage fighting. Here on the Westerplatte, bombarded by 11-inch naval guns and surrounded by almost 3,000 enemy soldiers, the pathetically outnumbered Poles held out for over a week. The Germans, calling this military footnote their "little Verdun," were said to be "embarrassed."

# ⊰ 4 ⊱
# Grünwald
## 1410
# The Knights Repulsed

*Our order will never lack wealth. But it will always be short of discretion and the advice of reliable people.*
**—Winrich von Kniprode, grand master, 1352–1382**

THE VILLAGE OF GRÜNWALD is a speck on the map and hardly more than that in passing, whether by foot, car, or bus. A few farmhouses off a main road, no shops, bakery, dairy, gas station, or commercial life of any kind, only a rough stone marker about 3 feet high with swords carved on either side and a date to let you know that you're somewhere special. As I get out of my car to look around, a group of kids comes out of nowhere to surround me. They are loud and rough, barrage me with questions in a good-natured sort of way, and generally impede my efforts to get a bearing on the place. I inquire, with a pack of Polish flashcards that a friend of mine back home wrote up for me, as to the whereabouts of the famous battlefield. They mock my fumbling pronunciation. I then pirouette back and forth as though brandishing a sword, but that leaves them convulsed in laughter. Finally I jot down a date in my notebook—1410—and a sheet like ice cuts all the babble short. They run off in silence en masse, tugging my sleeves to show me the way, fingers pointing, heads held high.

The figure 1410 carries weight here in Poland; it approximates in the field of heavy-duty resonance the likes of 1066, 1492, 1776, and 1812, familiar dates to those of us from the West. I would venture to

*The Battle of Grünwald*

guess that in and of itself 1410 means nothing to most people beyond this poor but undoubtedly proud land, yet nonetheless it is a watershed year in the saga of Eastern Europe.

Most historians agree that the Battle of Grünwald (known to Germans as Tannenberg) was a disaster long due the Teutonic Order. There would be many more battles to come, some ending in spectacular victory, but these merely delayed the reckoning that Grünwald foretold. Overweening ambition, arrogance beyond toleration, and an unrelenting refusal to back away from heavy odds all contributed to what was without a doubt an overwhelming military fiasco, the casualties of which will never truly be known, though numbering in the thousands to be sure. Certainly the grand master died, also his subordinate commanders, some 200 largely irreplaceable knight brothers, and foot soldiers beyond counting.

The character of their opposition is what felled the order. The Christian grand duke of Lithuania, Wladyslaw Jagiello (whose brother had died defending Vilnius from Henry, earl of Derby), had taken as wife the thirteen-year-old heiress to the throne of Poland, thereby uniting the royal houses of these former adversaries, whose antipathy to each other barely matched their hatred for Germans. Teutonic sponsorship of various rebel Slavonic pretenders drove no wedge through the heart of this alliance, and in the summer of 1410 the sandy plains of Prussia suffered a *reyse* in reverse, as a Polish and Lithuanian levy that some estimates total at 30,000 men burst through the heartland for Marienburg. The order gathered its forces and the two met at Grünwald.

My youthful guides have thinned by the wayside as I approach the battlefield. It is close to five o'clock, perhaps time for dinner or farmyard chores. The three kids still with me are clearly disappointed that all the ramshackle kiosks that serve, I suppose, ice cream or candy, have closed for the day. They are solaced to some degree as I pass out some of the dingy, overinflated paper money that passes for exchange here in Poland, but I can tell they would rather have had some sweets.

A long path over gently rolling fields leads to the primary attraction here, a tall cylindrical sculpture formed (of course) from communism's greatest contribution to world defacement, poured concrete. Two slits—or are they visors?—are supposedly representative of medieval warriors in helmets, but their only resemblance to anything I have ever seen are the statues of Easter Island, which have never struck me as particularly inspired. A rather clunky diorama of colored cobblestones spread out over a big sandpit delineates the various movements of units, but in fact Grünwald, like most medieval confrontations, featured little in the way of tactics. The grand master, eager as were all the knights for battle, evidently lost control of one of his shock battalions, easy enough in an era when to be out of range of the human voice meant you were beyond the burden of restraint. A premature charge by a third of his army diluted the usual hammering for which the knights' heavy cavalry was so famous. Instead, more lightly armed and pesky horsemen from the Polish and Lithuanian steppes were able to get between the wings of German armor to isolate, harry, surround, and exhaust them, finally to cut many down from the side or behind. Surging foot soldiers completed the slaughter.

For all its histrionic excess, an enormous painting of the battle by Jan Matejko (Poland's equivalent of Rembrandt's *Night Watch*) that hangs in Warsaw's National Museum recreates, I think more or less accurately, the monstrous confusion that a hacking, stabbing melee of this sort entailed. Granted, we can ignore the focal point of Matejko's work—the Grand Duke Jagiello, cutting a vivid swath through the red sea of German soldiery, shield and sword held high, staring straight ahead with a flat, slightly glazed look, as though stuck in traffic—but tangentially, off to the side we see the villeins at their bloody work. Slashing at the hocks of noble steeds, pulling the embroidered robes of chivalric horsemen to haul them to the ground, throwing ropes to ensnare a sword arm, giving no thought at all to ramming a pike through someone's back: All this gives the lie to any notion that knightly warfare was ever glamorous. Matejko, who specialized in these epic canvases on heroic Polish themes, finished this extravaganza in 1878. Perhaps disappointed that he had no exotic material with which to work (Tartars, boyars, Cossacks, oriental flavors), he put extra care in his depiction of the knights, particularly the grand master and his various lieutenants encumbered in heavy gear, slowly dragged from their saddles to a certain, painful death, looking just the same at these horrible scenes not in fear but plain, open-faced surprise.

The united enemies of the order dallied after their victory, losing the chance to follow up and swiftly take Marienburg, which in the end held out, heroically defended. But their hosting was a terrible scourge for the land, as were successive incursions, one lasting three years, from 1431 to 1433. A German annalist wrote of the Poles, "They conquered the town and burnt it down and they slew the young and the old, and their heathen allies committed unspeakable murders. And they besmirched the churches and cut off the breasts of young girls and women and horribly tortured them and led them away into servitude." Agriculture, trade, commerce of any sort, the development of town life and culture—all suffered grievously.

To make up their losses in manpower, grand masters resorted to the wholesale employment of mercenaries. Prussian crusades had lost their glamour in the West, where the proliferation of war between the various powers gave restless knights plenty to do in their own neighborhoods. The noble *reyse* became a thing of the past. To pay for the defense of their now clearly secular realm, the order fell back on the tried and abused methodology of extortionate taxation, thereby alienating both their townspeople and landed gentry, who complained vociferously "of a multitude of oppressions" from the order and its factors. The knights plotted wars of revenge against Poland and Lithuania. The burghers and landowners plotted with Poland, "hoping

*Death of a Teutonic knight (detail from* The Battle of Grünwald *by Jan Matejko, 1878)*

to enjoy," in the quaint phraseology of a British historian, "the practical liberty which Polish anarchy seemed to offer."

Moral rot within the order was exposed. The tradition of recruiting poor though dedicated knights, those without a noble lineage or a subsidy, had been allowed to wither over several decades, to the detriment of all that had once been worthy of the order in its earliest years. "Commanders shall only admit counts, barons, good knights and service nobleman," read one directive, and these were now expected to bring their own arms and their own mounts with them as a dowry to the order. Family lineage and financial considerations took on exaggerated importance, and some older German warriors even saw the monastic ambience as a place to spend their settled old age, an ecclesiastical retirement where the exuberance of a turbulent youth could be recalled over a glass or two of wine with collegial, aristocratic brothers. "Undress, dress once more, eat, drink, and snore" ran a contemporary jibe. Rumors of degeneracy accompanied these softening strictures, talk of women, the abduction of virgins, the murder of interfering husbands. The order required regeneration, but having a mission too mercantile (or "corporate," as one historian put it) to attract idealistic newcomers, it languished instead.

⚜

The small museum that overlooks the battlefield here has not yet opened for the season. Peering through the large glass panes, I see what seems to be an armed combat in progress—mannequins dressed in ersatz medieval gear toppled over on the floor, debris, papers, empty boxes scattered about as though a madman or two had ransacked the place. Several rather menacing axes and spears hang suspended from wall and ceiling. Walking about, I disturb a couple of teenagers in very heavy embrace and encounter the usual pair of elderly German tourists, maps and binoculars in hand, whose English, of course, is excellent.

"Quite a place, don't you agree? It could be the fifteenth century here right now. I was at the Crécy battlefield in France last year. I hadn't seen it since the war. Somewhat distracting with tractors and cars and jets overhead. But here we see the terrain exactly as it was. Poles are too poor to own tractors! Do you ride? Well, to an old horseman like myself, there could not be a more perfect environment than this. I am quite amazed that my German ancestors did not win the field that day, riding downward into the enemy. The impact must have been quite something to see."

"Do you often visit battlefields where Germans lost?"

"But of course! Since the Wall came down, I have followed my entire advance, and my entire retreat, through Russia. It's incredible how little of it has seemed to change. I was happier, I must tell you, and certainly my good wife was happier, going over what I would call the more uplifting tour of my Belgian and French career, but all that was a long time ago, and I have no regrets. I can come here and not brood. We Germans have known many defeats. The difference between us and the Poles is that we have victories, too. They single out these fields as something special, but every field in Prussia has been a battleground. There is not an inch here not soaked in blood."

How ironic, then, to contemplate the eventual fall of Marienburg, an ignominious, farcical affair where the grand master was in effect ridden out of town in tar and feathers, to the derisive hoots and profanities of Poles and assorted riffraff, after a takeover that involved no siege, violence, or death at all.

The mighty order, mourned by no one, simply crumbled apart in a forty-year span between Grünwald and the loss of Marienburg, pawned for the back pay of Czech mercenaries. Incompetence, immoderation, and sterile, empty posturing shattered forever whatever common bond German lord and German tenant had once shared here on the frontier. The squires, or Junkers, of the countryside—those knights and secular warriors who had traded land for military service over the course of two centuries—now found themselves in league with merchants and traders of the Prussian towns, all oppressed by an order crippled with bills and payments, from the wages owed their professional standing army to the enormous indemnity forced upon it after Grünwald by the victorious Poles.

Everywhere the populace felt squeezed and betrayed. The currency was debased, rents and labor fees increased, succession laws rearranged to benefit the order. To benefit the order, one commander rigged a change in title that disinherited two infant heirs. These babies were thrown into the cattle stalls, one eaten alive by dogs, the other reduced over time to harlotry. The order "will have us as serfs," the Junkers complained.

After years of acrimony highlighted by conferences, petitions, threats, kidnappings, and even the visitation of a papal legate from Portugal ("My lord should visit the unbelievers and Jews in his [own] homeland, of whom there are many," complained one opponent to the order, "and not this land"), the countryside erupted in violence, a sort of French Revolution scenario where Teutonic castles, either undefended or manned by drunken, indifferent mercenaries, were rushed and occupied by the townspeople and neighborhood Junkers in an almost spontaneous surge. The grand master himself, without a single mark to his name, threw open the chapel doors of Marienburg and invited his heretical guard, Hussites from Moravia, to take all the treasure still there: the crucifix, monstrance, prayer books with bejeweled covers, chalice, and censer. As that was not enough to cover their back wages, these ruffians roamed through the castle halls unmolested, knocking brothers down and stealing whatever they had of value. The grand master, threatened and reviled, was made a prisoner until the order's debt could be satisfied. He ate off a tin plate and was served warm beer. The insolent Czechs, opening negotiations with Poland, sold Marienburg for a fraction of the monies still owed them. The grand master, lucky to be alive, was shunted off to Königsberg.

In 1466 the order capitulated totally, signing a treaty with the Polish king that ceded half the province, including Pomerania and the cities of Danzig and Marienburg. The order held the other half, precariously, as a fief to the kingdom of Poland. Successive grand masters would send their agents, armed with bribes, through the corridors of power in Vienna, Rome, and all over the German bailiwicks, seeking to pry out some diplomatic advantage that might restore their regal position, but the order's glory days were finished.

"This is the period where you see the Junker spirit begin to emerge," a German friend said to me. "The Junkers were the tenantry of the knights, men who had come to the east to fight and to farm. The more they fought—or more accurately, perhaps, the more fighters they could provide—the larger the estate they could wrangle from the order and better the terms as well.

"At first, these were very simple leases, the order having the upper hand. There was no question as to who owned the property; it was the order. As their finances deteriorated in the fifteenth and sixteenth centuries, however, they began issuing titles and mortgages, and you see the emergence of a landowning class distinct from the order itself but—just like the order—a caste of military men for the most part, highly disciplined, highly motivated, highly attached to the soil, as the order was not. This seems a contradiction, but not so.

"The hierarchy of the order had no local genealogy. They were recruited from Germany, where their families, friends, and attachments were. They came out to do their duty in Prussia, but they never married, had issue, or left a dynastic trail there. The Junker class did, generation after generation, which is why they resented the order so greatly over time. The order was like the Bundesbank: imperious, cold, aloof, autocratic. They held the power and tightened the screws yet never deigned to share that power or their control. This is one reason the Junkers turned on them. They preferred to give their allegiance to the easygoing Poles, who mostly left them alone, which confirmed in the Junker mentality a streak of independence and, as parodied in the nineteenth century, stiff-necked arrogance. You know, the Ludendorff syndrome.

"Americans in particular confuse Prussians with Nazis. They think of Prussians goose-stepping right behind Hitler into battle. This is quite an incorrect impression. The Prussians were militarists of the first order, by which I mean they were excellent soldiers who gave and obeyed orders without question. But they were aristocrats of a provincial personality, jealous of local rights and privileges. They distrusted kings, royal courts, dictators, or Bismarckian figures all through German history because people like that, seeking to unite German interests, usually infringed on local privilege. Also, Hitler was a peasant—true Prussians always referred to him as a pig or a dog. He was also a totalitarian, anathema to a Junker on his country estate, who did not want to be told what to do. The real Prussian hated Bismarck, too, probably even more than Hitler because Bismarck was one of them, a Junker who, in order to unite Germany, betrayed his class."

The dissertation of Marion Dönhoff, based on innumerable estate records she found in the attic of Friedrichstein, her own family's East

Prussian domain, confirmed many of these details. "For each forty hides of land," she wrote, "(a hide was equal to seventeen hectares, or forty-two acres), the Order demanded heavy horseman's service: that is to say, an occupant of forty hides (about 1700 acres) was obliged to serve in full armor, equipped with heavy weapons, and 'a horse outfitted in keeping with his armor, accompanied by two additional horsemen.'"

⚜

What this humble-sounding trade-off could realize over time I saw with the count of Schulenburg in the Volkswagen company town of Wolfsburg, right on the former East German border at Lower Saxony ("If World War III had started," a VW employee said to me, "we would have seen the first tanks before breakfast"). The von Schulenburgs embody European lineage and wealth that both Hollywood (at its most garish) and the team of Merchant and Ivory (at its most reverential) seem able to parody every few years in lavish cinematic spectacles of aristocratic life. Their current princely domain of country manor and stud farm lies just a few miles outside of the town that the von Schulenburgs have dominated for some 800 years.

Two centuries' worth of descent from the *Mayflower*, you say? Pale, pale indeed to the genealogy of this regal family, its own members at times confused over the myriad positions of rank and power that so many of its illustrious forebears enjoyed. In the military sphere alone, the family could count some thirty-five generals and three field marshals. "That many?" Count von Schulenburg remarked. "Even I didn't know that."

Wolfsburg had once belonged to the von Schulenburgs in much the same way that you or I would own a table. This essentially agricultural village was appropriated by Hitler in the 1930s for the site of Volkswagen's industrial complex. The country cottage of Dr. Porsche is pointed out on the tour I'm given, bucolically situated in a town preserve full of nature walks and country paths, all of which overlook the single largest automotive plant in the universe, an enormous assemblage of factories, production lines, power plants (VW heats all of Wolfsburg through its ingenious system of recycled energy), and even the biggest sausage processor in northern Germany to feed its ravenous workers at lunchtime. I sampled some of this for lunch while strolling through the weekly "pig market," held once a month on company grounds, a little free-enterprise bazaar where VW employees sell their one- and two-year-old models for well below market prices, then turn around and buy themselves another new car at discounted cost. I remark to my guide, a VW executive who averages one or two new cars per annum, that I have been driving the same heap for thirteen years. "No one would dream of doing that here. They'd think you were crazy. But a VW can last that long. You must be pleased you bought one."

"Well, it's a Toyota actually. They're much cheaper in the U.S. than a VW."

"Whatever difference in price is more than made up for in German engineering," is his prim reply.

The von Schulenburgs ruled this estate from their magnificent castle, a multistoried affair the family gave to Wolfsburg after Hitler's eminent domain. During the boom of reconstruction after World War II, the town didn't mind lavishing princely sums on the castle's maintenance, but now that recession has hit VW hard, the millions of deutsche marks required for new roofs, repointing, rewiring, and re-plumbing have all been deferred. All the same, this stunning building remains a popular venue for weddings, art openings, and civic affairs. Particular note is always given to the stand of gnarled hardwood trees adjacent the grand entry. It was here that von Schulenburgs over the generations would sit and pass judgment on village lawsuits and petitions.

It was said to me that although the family did not care to lose this property in Wolfsburg, it didn't mind all that much. From the compensation received, they built an elaborate new manor on one of their nearby properties, "Third Reich architecture," according to an acquaintance of mine, a rather apt description I had to agree as we toured the place, now a rather shabby old-age home in the former GDR. The von Schulenburgs lost this estate, plus twenty-two others, in 1945.

"My family comes from Prussia," the count said to me in his elegant drawing room, "that is, the mark, the deutsche mark, which was Prussia. Among my forefathers were many *condottieri*, which is the Italian expression for field marshals who, on their own entrepreneurship, organized soldiers, hardware, supplies, everything, and yes, were fighting for whatever crown would pay them here or there. They took care of what was asked for. The best known in my family got famous at the retreat in the Spanish succession war, and the next step he was field marshal for the Republic of Venice and defended Corfu against the Turk. For his life, he was on the payroll of Venice, and there is a monument to him on the island of Corfu, where, as you may know, Kaiser Wilhelm had a house. The kaiser was indignant that the family would not repair the broken nose of our ancestor's statue; it was too expensive. 'What!' the kaiser said. 'You have 264,000 acres in Germany, the crown has less, something like 224,000, and you can't *afford* it!'" The count, a successful businessman, laughs at this himself.

"The other famous ancestor we have was a tutor to Frederick the Great, a lieutenant general under the soldier-king. He was a man of the cavalry, and in the Silesian War he was killed at the Battle of Mollwitz in 1741. Frederick the Great took care of his son, organized his marriage, and paid for the wedding of one of his other children, a daughter. So there is a connection between our family and the Prussian king, and it affected our fortunes—oh, there is no doubt about that.

"The whole point was to make money, and besides farming and forestry, the military was the job through which you earned it. You were rewarded in either land or money, and as for property, it was for a long time *not* their property but something we call *laise* land, very much along the lines of leasing a car today. The crown or the duke or the prince or the grand master bestowed on somebody a certain amount of acres—farming, forestry, including villages and so on—and the fellow agreed to pay one-tenth of the income to whomever had given it to him. He did not own the property, he just *had* it, and his tenure was prolonged so long as he did a good job. He had to provide for the safety of the people and take care of armed forces. He was in charge of local welfare, and he collected revenues, like a small king. It was 'his kingdom,' and my forebears were very successful. Oftentimes the *laiseherr*—the king or whatever—he borrowed monies from these captains, and if he couldn't repay them . . . they got part of the *laise* land in return, and that's really how these great estates came into being and developed. Getting property, for my family, has always meant either being successful in war or being successful in business.

"But owning property, as we say in Germany, can be 'a golden noose.' It is great in value but little income, little cash, which is why we were always soldiers, diplomats, secretaries, or whatever, to earn the additional monies. But the special thing for us is that no individual was thought to 'own' the property. You inherited it, and you have to turn it over to the next generation. You're not allowed to reduce it or to sell it; it's part of the family and not to be separated, in Prussia especially. In southern Germany it was each time divided between the children, so you have there small pieces, but in Prussia the aim was to buy more if you could, inherit it, or marry into it. So property was *kept*. You did not change your land just to get better land. What you had was part of yourself. My father always told us, 'The land we have you wouldn't rent, you wouldn't buy, you *shouldn't* rent, you *shouldn't* buy, but we have it since 800 years so, children, take care!'

"We had another expression, too: You can have our wives, but not our land!"

# ⊰ 5 ⊱
# Frauenburg
## 1543
# Polish Inroads

*And new Philosophy calls all in doubt,*
*The Element of fire is quite put out;*
*The Sun is lost, and th' earth, and no man's wit*
*Can direct him where to look for it.*
—John Donne, from the anti-Copernican poem
*The Anatomy of the World*

THE FRISCHES HAFF, called in Polish Zalew Wiślany, is a mostly landlocked lagoon running east from the Vistula and Nogat estuaries in a more or less rectangular track to Kaliningrad City, a distance of only 40 miles and at no point wider than 10. At Baltijsk a small opening to the Baltic is maintained, the point of foray for the Russian navy's now confused welter of warships and submarines, a force with no mission, no enemy, no morale. The seaside arm of sand and scrub pine is relatively undeveloped, a mecca during summer for sun worshipers staring out across the Baltic. To their backs the Frisches Haff sits in a dull and lifeless panorama, devoid of the eels for which it once was so famous, empty of the little skiffs and shallow draft barges that once plied these waters in an archaic maze of impromptu coastal trade and transport.

Standing at the harbor of Frauenburg on the mainland, I cannot get over how dead all of this feels. The fishing fleet, which I presume is the proper designation for the few dilapidated metal boats strewn

*Cathedral Hill, Frauenburg*

about these rotted pilings, is the very caricature of commercial despair. If these have been to sea anytime in recent memory, surely we'd
have read about it: "Fishing Craft from Frauenburg Disintegrate upon
Leaving Harbor—Officials Baffled"—that's a headline that would not
escape our jaded notice. I have a feeling the fishing folk hereabouts are
otherwise engaged.

From the crumbling jetty walkway, its beacon about to fall into the
lagoon, you do get an excellent view of the majestic cathedral complex
for which Frauenburg is justly known, and not only for the fact that
Nicolaus Copernicus lies buried within. This lonely, obscure, ruined
town will survive only on the travelers' checks and sturdy deutsche
marks that foreign visitors bring in their wake. The few dispirited day-
trippers from Danzig whom I pass waiting for their train home clearly
have little more than trolley fare in their otherwise empty pockets.

The allure of tourism, of course, is every poor country's dream, but a
few cultural animosities will need to be overcome if any headway is to
be made in this lucrative industry. As I drive up to the cathedral in my
bright red car, a lone boy of maybe thirteen runs downhill full tilt
from the ancient walls, stopping long enough to spit through my open
window. If this had happened in Detroit or Chicago, I would have kept

on driving, but I plunge into reverse and gun the car in his wake, following the offender into the nearby yard of an apartment house. Here, in a warren of anonymous doors and hallways, I lose the little thug, but in returning outside I hear a mocking castrati chorus taunting me in Polish, something along the lines, I would guess, of, "You dirty German pig."

Frauenburg was part of the territory the Teutonic Knights ceded to Poland in 1466. It was lost in the First Partition to Frederick the Great (1772), then regained two centuries later in the incendiary afterglow of World War II, when the entire lower town was reduced to a smoking pile of rubble, worth nothing in treasure but immeasurably valuable to the national vanity. Along with everywhere else in the former East Prussia, the Polish bulldozer obliterated all traces of Germanism, beginning with the populace. George Kennan estimated that 1.75 million people fled Ostpreussen for the West, most of them in the winter of 1945 as the Red Army, in a mood one could charitably understate as malevolent, thrust ahead for Berlin. Many East Prussians, however, too old, too infirm, too frightened to run away, hid out in the neighboring woods or remoter reaches of the countryside for the perfect quiet moment to reemerge. By 1950 all of these people had been rounded up and deported to the GDR (if they were lucky), otherwise to Siberia or some other God-forsaken wasteland of the Soviet empire. By then, their beloved homeland had been irrevocably changed.

You will not find a single memorial or forget-me-not in northern Poland left over from its German settlement. No obelisk in commemoration of soldiers who may have died in its many wars, no antique cannon or other memorabilia from the Franco-Prussian conflict to adorn town halls or plazas, certainly no village plaque listing the names of men who fought the Russian invader in 1914 or the "missing" from any other field of operations in World War I. Gravestones smashed, cemeteries flattened, churches destroyed or reconsecrated for Polish use, textbooks revised to mask any mention of the German lordship, except of course those events which dishonored it—the process was determined and thorough. Every place-name was altered, whether city or village, street or country lane, river, stream, or well, all to the nightmarish annoyance of today's visitors, who cannot travel without a geographical thesaurus in hand to know just where, historically, they might happen to be. In Frauenburg a little notation in the local museum states that the town and everything around it "has always been Polish," a ludicrous assertion to say the least but unchal-

*Old German church and current brick quarry, near Elbing*

lengeable by anyone around here, given the demographic circumstances.

German historians have at times been known to tweak the truth, of
course. Von Treitschke, self-appointed proponent of Prussian mythology, claimed Copernicus "was a German canon." How else to explain
this phenomenon, surely a product of the Teutonic gene pool? The
record, however, says otherwise. Mikolaj Kopernik was, without a
doubt, Polish.

His multifaceted career—celebrated all over this region in muse-
ums, pamphlets, posters, and schoolbooks—reached its quiet zenith
here in Frauenburg, where, as a member of the ecclesiastical entourage
of the local bishopric from about 1510 to the year of his death in 1543,
he conceived and perfected the heliocentric theory of the universe.
This described, in essence, the notion whereby all the planets in our
solar system orbit around the sun and not, as Aristotle empirically
contended, around the earth. Various towers in the cathedral close by
are pointed out as his study, and postcards of yet another heroic painting by Matejko depicting Copernicus, hair flowing wildly, arms
akimbo on a turret roof surrounded by astronomical bric-a-brac, at the
precise moment when everything came together in his mind, are for

sale in the ticket kiosk. Unfortunately, it seems that most of the time Copernicus worked at home, outside the enclosure walls. But no matter: These are but details.

The mark of Copernicus is so universalized here in Frauenburg that you cannot avoid him anywhere. An enormous statue by the Warsaw sculptor Mieczyslaw Welter overlooks the downtrodden lower marketplace, and I am relieved to notice that for once a piece of Communist-inspired idolatry actually works. There is no denying the power of this representation. Nor can one dispute the quality of exhibitions set up in various venues all over town by the government, showing this remarkably versatile man in the guise of scientist, mathematician, monetarian, medical savant, administrator, politician, soldier, and of course most preeminently, astronomer.

In keeping with Copernicus's role as a Renaissance man, it seems appropriate that the best of these collections is now housed in the former bishop's palace within the cathedral enclosure. Fifteenth-century Polish prelates, often depressed as they moved into their new domains by the gloomy Teutonic castles they were now to call home, often had a medieval wing or wall torn down to be replaced by something more opening and welcome, the kind of official residence then being favored in Italy and France. This lovely building was put up by a succession of bishops, but the underlying optimism of these cultural expressions was premature to say the least. Rampaging Swedish forces burned the place down, as did the Russians in 1945. Some of these palaces still remain in ruins; others, such as this (after a twenty-year wait), have now been rebuilt.

The exhibits themselves are technical by nature. Copernicus was not a general, and it might be argued that various editions of *De revolutionibus orbium coelestium* (*On the Revolutions of the Heavenly Spheres*) are not the draw that swords and cannon usually are. But you run with what you have. I have rarely seen so many sextants, orbs, charts, astrolabes, or other paraphernalia about which I know nothing, nor such an assemblage of learned treatises, most in Latin, from which not a visitor in a thousand could identify more than a dozen words. "Mathematics," as Copernicus noted, "are written for mathematicians." One leaves such a cornucopia of remote material a little cold in the heart, which is the problem, I suppose, with trying to display or explain a process (and a life) that was largely intellectual. It is quite a challenge to make a man's private contemplations, undertaken in the solitude of a study or on the rooftop of his house on some starry night,

*Bishop's palace, Lidzbark Warmiński*

into solid theater. This may be why the career of Copernicus has not attracted widespread biographical attention. At least Galileo, who verified Copernican theories through his use of telescopes ninety years later, was condemned by the Church and came close to losing his life at the stake or through torture. Copernicus died quietly in bed, cautious to the end over roiling clerical sensibilities too contentiously.

He did, however, live through turbulent times, and it is curious to see the trail of so many disparate personalities crisscross through the network of these Prussian towns and villages. Many of these footprints belonged to Poles, who settled (like Copernicus) in regions previously Germanic in character. Some were left by itinerant monks or preachers, tossing back and forth the arguments and rebuttals of the Reformation. Others (more likely hoofprints, as these men rarely walked) belonged to Junkers and even princes, confused as to where their allegiance lay, to whom their homage and taxes were due. One individual, Martin Luther, never left a set of prints at all, but everything he said and did weighed heavily over this land just the same.

Within these murky parameters wandered Albrecht, an unwilling, resentful, devious vassal to the king of Poland and the thirty-seventh and last grand master of the Teutonic Order, headquartered in Königsberg at the time. The order had diminished to a vestige of its former whole, chapters to the north in Livonia (present-day Latvia) having seceded in disgust over paying homage to Poles, and its German bailiwicks also severed, choosing to involve themselves in imperial politics that had little interest in faraway Prussia. Even the office of grand master had faded in allure; the order by this time was in the habit of selecting for its superior not some worthy candidate trained and schooled from within but generally a figure of the secondary nobility through whom, it was hoped, some leverage for aid and financial assistance might still be obtained from the royalty of Western Europe. In February 1511 the third and distinctly minor son of the Hohenzollern prince of Ansbach in Bavaria, twenty-one years of age and destined for an ecclesiastical career, was invited to assume the title grand master. It did not hurt that his mother was a daughter of the king of Poland.

A statue of Markgraf Albrecht stands in the outer courtyard of Marienburg Castle, a place he probably never set foot in. A Russian bullet hole decorates his right breast, a kinder fate than other notables of the order, also immortalized in bronze, suffered when the Soviets stormed the place in 1945. Herman von Salza took a few rounds in the hip, Siegfried von Feuchtwangen had a hand blown away, and Winrich von Kniprode, the greatest master of them all, had his lower rib cage punctured. Despite the mutilation, Albrecht still has an air of power and resolve about him, ill befitting a career in which he staggered from one crisis to another in sly and devious fashion. The most fundamental question about him revolves around motivation: Did he assume his new title to rescue the order or to subvert it entirely to his own family's ambitions? Given the religious and political chaos of the times and the dangers they presented, the truth of this matter will forever be obscure.

During the first ten years of his mastership, Albrecht showed no signs of spiritually reinvigorating the order, pursuing the essentially sterile strategies of plot, war, truce, and beggary that had so impoverished the Prussian countryside since Grünwald (Copernicus directed the defense of Allenstein in 1512 during a typically destructive Teutonic *reyse* through its former territories). In 1522, however, on yet another interminable mission of supplication to the court of the emperor Charles V, Albrecht had his head turned by an adherent of Lutheranism in Nuremberg, one Andreas Osiander, a former Augustinian who later took it upon himself to write an introduction for the first edition of Copernicus's *De revolutionibus*, in which he dubbed the possibly deviant theories therein "hypothetical" as opposed to "factual." (Thus a German heretic sought to soften the impact of a believing Catholic Pole whose work cast to the shadows several centuries of papal belief over the primacy of man's place in the universe, a suitably bizarre occurrence but typical of the century.)*

Albrecht moved along to the feet of the great Martin Luther himself, who was then secretly sequestered in Wittenburg after the tumultuous events of the previous year but indisputably the de facto man of the hour throughout Germany. Luther brushed aside whatever moral arguments Albrecht may tentatively have offered. Renounce the order, Luther advised, break your vows, take a wife, sire an heir, seize Prussia for yourself and your progeny to come, and above all, implant the new faith. In about every respect, Albrecht did as he was told.

Even granting that times so long ago are not often known for their subtlety of maneuver or behavior, this grab for power and riches (more of the former than the latter) cannot but strike the modern observer as crass and blatant. Henry VIII of England may well have studied Albrecht's model, if in fact he had ever heard of him, for thirty-two years later he did exactly the same thing, secularizing his kingdom, helping himself to the booty of abbots and bishops alike.

The stockpile of treasure there was to steal in East Prussia has been the subject of much scholarly debate, but the consensus seems to be: not all that much. Prussia was a poor land, too often ravaged by war and commercial uncertainty, its economic base too often reduced to that of simple barter. Horrified knights of the order expelled Albrecht from his office and honors, but they had no power and little support from the equally grasping Junkers, who endorsed the new pretender as a means of ensuring their own freedom of action. The Teutonic Order collapsed. In February 1525, only three years after meeting Luther, Albrecht kneeled before the king of Poland in the royal city of Kraków and pledged fealty to this Slavonic monarchy, a pretense that would endure for 150 years.

The East would prove to be a heterogeneous welter of peoples. Protestant German soldiers from Ostpreussen would serve the Catholic kings of Poland or the Orthodox tsars of Russia with equal

---

*Protestant theologians could be equally suspicious of Copernican theories, however. Luther remarked, "Even though astrology has been thrown into confusion, I, for my part, believe the sacred Scripture: for Joshua commanded the sun to stand still, not the earth." John Calvin, in a remark furiously questioned by some historians, allegedly called Copernicus "a fool."

*Polish knight of around
1500, Lidzbark Warmiński*

disregard for propriety. Germans and Poles would work the same fields, the same farms, the same estates over several generations, one the master, the other his employee, in a certain wary coexistence. From these decades flowed the conviction of both these haughty populations that East Prussia belonged to them.

Nothing else could bring them together, and certainly not religion. Albrecht vigorously promoted Lutheranism throughout his domain, though his confused sponsorship of the variety spewed about by Andreas Osiander landed him in serious trouble later in life. Osiander convulsed the newly established university in Königsberg (set up by Albrecht under the patronage of Sigismund, king of Poland, and not, as one would suppose from its later history, a German monarch) into theological controversy. And luckily for this renegade monk, he died before things ran out of control, a fate not shared by his equally pugnacious son-in-law, who was burned at the stake. Albrecht lived the last two years of his reign under house arrest, but the Hohenzollern line continued through his son.

# Part Two

# CONSOLIDATION
## The
## Hohenzollern Dynasty

## ⇥ Select Chronology ⇤

| | |
|---|---|
| 1594 | Elector of Brandenburg marries daughter of duke of Prussia. The two kingdoms unite under single ruler in 1618. |
| 1621–1629 | Gustavus II Adolphus campaigns in Prussia during Swedish wars with Poland. |
| 1618–1648 | Thirty Years' War. |
| 1630–1635 | Swedish phase of Thirty Years' War. |
| 1632 | Death of Gustavus; Battle of Lutzen. |
| 1640–1688 | Forty-year rule of the Great Elector. |
| 1701 | Great Elector's son assumes title "king of Prussia," is crowned in Königsberg. |
| 1756–1763 | Seven Years' War. Frederick the Great ascendant. |
| 1772 | First Partition of Poland. East Prussia geographically united with Brandenburg and Berlin. |
| 1793, 1795 | Second and Third Partitions of Poland. |
| 1804–1814 | Napoleon I, emperor of France. |
| 1805, December 2 | Battle of Austerlitz. Napoleon defeats Austrian and Russian armies. |
| 1806, October 14 | Battles of Jena and Auerstädt. Napoleon routs Prussians. |
| October 27 | French forces occupy Berlin. |
| November 7 | Blücher and Scharnhorst surrender their forces. |
| 1807, February 7–8 | Battle of Eylau. |
| June 14 | Battle of Friedland. |
| July 7 and 9 | Napoleon concludes victor's peace with Prussia and Russia at Tilsit. Prussian territories reduced by half. |
| 1812, June 22 | French invade Russia. |
| November | Retreat from Russia. Prussia deserts Napoleon. |
| 1813, February 3 | The Wars of Liberation begin. |
| 1814, March 31 | Allies enter Paris. |
| 1815 | Napoleon's Hundred Days and Waterloo. |

# ❄ 6 ❄

# Grosse Werder
## 1660
# The Great Elector

*We hold Prussia like an eel by the tail.*
—**Hohenzollern officer**

GUIDEBOOKS HAD PROMISED ME better than this. I am parked for the evening along a lovely stretch of watery fens near the Nogat, but my dinner consists of tinned fish from who knows where, a bulk of tasteless bread, a smattering of pastries too stale to eat, and a bottle of lukewarm beer—all I could get in a haphazardly stocked grocery store outside the town of Elbing. I had come to Poland expecting solid fare, hoping to sample the myriad dishes of game and bird that these people so assiduously hunt, prepare, and devour. Shooting towers and blinds are everywhere, and not a day's drive goes by that I do not see a camouflaged sportsman by the road, laden with assorted creatures ready for the pot. But out here in the country there is, predictably, no place to eat and no place to stay. The locals, in keeping with centuries of tradition, are not exactly forthcoming in their reception of strangers. Armed with my dictionary and flashcards, I have more than a few times stopped at a rural farmhouse to inquire after a meal or to ask permission for a campsite, always making certain that a few zloty are plainly visible. After a while, who needs the wariness, suspicion, and positively evil looks? There is nothing in the laws of nature that requires hostile Poles to masquerade as hospitable Irish, a conclusion I ruefully accept after a couple of weeks here.

The Grosse Werder, or Great Island, is probably the most fertile piece of land in Prussia. Triangular in shape, it borders on the Vistula, Nogat, and Baltic all together, and like the Nile it often had its fields immersed and enriched by flooding waters in the spring. Today, as always, it is assiduously cultivated, though again the affluence of its farming population varies. The elite have tractors and relatively modern accoutrements: an array of hoes, discs, spreaders, balers, and so on. The next level down may possess one of these elements, a tractor most likely, but what it drags behind is the usual assortment of ancient wooden carts, the ubiquitous *bryczka* common to all Slavic lands. The lowest rung has a horse, a flatbed trailer, and that's about it. A farmer plowing behind a mare and seeding afterward by hand is an altogether bucolic scene common everywhere in Old Prussia. That it's a hard life full of drudgery is also pretty apparent.

Archaeologists think the Grosse Werder has been inhabited since well before the time of Christ. I refrain from using the time-honored phrase "continuously inhabited" if only because few places on earth have been fought over and pillaged more frequently. These fields give substance to lines that we who peruse history books for enjoyment run across all the time—"the fields were laid waste" is the simplest variant. Another is, "Troops replenished their dwindling store of supplies from the countryside." A third might read, "The kingdom was exhausted by war"; another, "Passing armies spread typhus, scurvy, smallpox, and syphilis in their wake, stealing all before them as peasants starved and wolves ate bodies strewn on the ground."

The fragile link between life and death, bounty and poverty, happiness and despair is in many ways the legacy of these flat and (this evening, at any rate) muddy pastures. They are without any distinguishing feature; there is nothing about the soil or the water, the trees or the shrubs, the herds of cow and pig that tell us anything of events or personalities from the turbulent past. It makes no difference, to put it another way, whether corn or wheat planted here was trampled by horses or tanks, by Poles or Germans, six centuries ago or just the other day. A crop that fails, for whatever reason, is a cause for distress. When disruption comes year after year, season after season, decade after decade, it causes disaster, dislocation, wilderness. The mind does not require a ruined castle, a rusted saber, a corroded cannon, or a few spent shells to recreate an aura of past devastation. Nature does that every springtime when rain and flood make of the land a gloomy morass. This was the only wealth Prussia ever had, an agricultural capacity too easily trammeled and destroyed, yet capable all the same, given the necessary willpower, of regeneration. It is a simple tale, actually, however complicated the personalities and events, and the outcome seldom varies. Food rots in the pasture as people run for their lives without a penny to their names.

These are fields of the Thirty Years' War, a misnomer if there ever was one. Bitter fighting engulfed much of Europe before the traditionally cited starting date of hostilities, 1618, and more was to come after its concluding treaty, signed in Westphalia, 1648. Since warfare was an annual affair among the crowned heads of Europe, historians have, for simplicity's sake, isolated the German phase as a more or less separate entity, a well-intentioned though misleading distinction. The battles here on Grosse Werder, though bitter, important, and involving one of the premier figures of the day, Gustavus Adolphus, have nonetheless been generally consigned to the dustbin of irrelevance, a state of hostilities between Poland and Sweden duly recognized but barely mentioned, waged between 1621 and 1629. In fact they were part and parcel of the entire mélange that constitutes what was in fact the first European world war.

If people think that 1918 and 1945 were disastrous years for Germany, perhaps they should study the early 1600s, a stretch of conflagration whose horror many contemporary observers equated with the end of the world. The particulars are replete with names that until the nineteenth century were commonly recognized as the mightiest that ever strode the Continent—the soldiers Tilly, Pappenheim, von Arnim, Wallenstein, von Mansfeld, Turenne; the royal monarchs Ferdinand of Hapsburg, Christian of Denmark, and the Swedish Lion, Gustavus Adolphus; the diplomats Richelieu and Oxenstierna, the electors fair and foul from Maximilian of Bavaria to the Winter King, pathetic Frederick of Bohemia—an aristocratic "ant heap" in the words of the British historian C. V. Wedgwood, whose whims and stratagems, complicated beyond measure by religious, dynastic, and personal ambitions, make even the Balkan politics of today seem like child's play.

In broad terms, the struggle involved royal houses and not nations, at least as we conceive of that latter term today. Germany proper—

that is, German lands within the confines of the Holy Roman Empire—consisted of more than 300 principalities, many of the crossroads variety, lorded over by generally hapless families of degenerate knights, hoping to scratch an income from tolls, extortion, and petty thievery; others were of a more grandiose sort, such as the dukedom of Bavaria, with a court almost as regal as the emperor's. Religious turmoil, already rampant between Catholics and Lutherans, had become complicated by additional formulations, most particularly those authored by Calvin, which muddied the lines of allegiance and conscience even further.

Disputes within the confines of Germany proper attracted the attention of powers without, notably the French, Danes, and Swedes, who sought through bribery, secret treaty, and war to undermine the Hapsburg emperor. Resultant politicking produced unusual spectacles, such as that of the Catholic French king's payment to the Protestant Swedes to interject themselves on German soil as the saviors of Protestantism (against the wishes of mostly Protestant rulers) so as to cripple the Catholic emperor ruling in Vienna. Such bizarre inconsistencies were questioned by few.

The story is long, brutal, amoral, tragic, sordid, and ultimately fascinating. There was glory for some in the several major battles, fought everywhere from Schleswig-Holstein and Danzig in the north to Bavaria and Bohemia in the south. There were chests of gold and silver for many others, acquired through pillage, payoff, or subsidy. There was butchery beyond description, with entire armies completely out of control and on the rampage through city streets and country lanes. For many, the horrors were typified by the sack of Magdeburg in 1631, an event that served as a byword for blood lust in the German vocabulary for centuries to come. Simply put, there was profit for some during these tumultuous times but ruin for most everyone else.

Caught in the middle without any safe haven were the Hohenzollerns, who complicated their lot, unnecessarily it would seem, when one of their number became a Calvinist in 1613. Albert of Hohenzollern, duke of Prussia—which we must remember as an independent kingdom separated from the Holy Roman Empire by an arm of Poland—had died in 1568. His son, fond as were all the degenerate nobility of intermarriage, arranged his daughter's union with John Sigismund (as shown in the accompanying family tree), heir to the Hohen-

# Union of Ostpreussen and Brandenburg under a single Hohenzollern, 1618

Individuals of importance in this narrative have been capitalized.
Dates indicate periods of activity or rule.

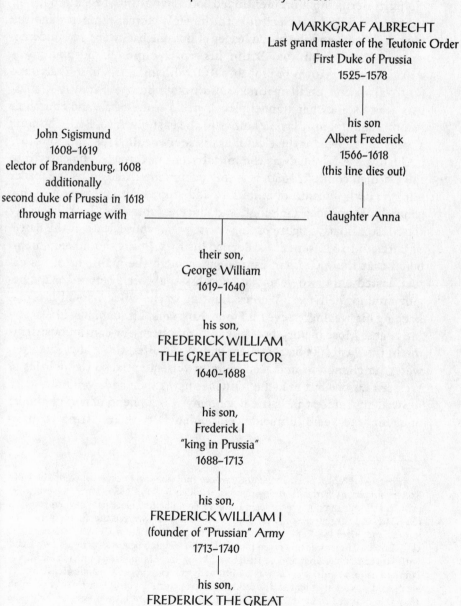

MARKGRAF ALBRECHT
Last grand master of the Teutonic Order
First Duke of Prussia
1525–1578

his son
Albert Frederick
1566–1618
(this line dies out)

John Sigismund
1608–1619
elector of Brandenburg, 1608
additionally
second duke of Prussia in 1618
through marriage with

daughter Anna

their son,
George William
1619–1640

his son,
FREDERICK WILLIAM
THE GREAT ELECTOR
1640–1688

his son,
Frederick I
"king in Prussia"
1688–1713

his son,
FREDERICK WILLIAM I
(founder of "Prussian" Army
1713–1740

his son,
FREDERICK THE GREAT
1740–1786

zollern elector of Brandenburg, probably the poorest kingdom with the poorest lands in all the empire.*

In 1618, through fortuitous death and prearranged letters of agreement, Brandenburg and Prussia were united under the rule of a single Hohenzollern, the aforementioned John, who thus became both an elector and a duke, subject of both the Holy Roman Emperor and the king of Poland, and the proud leader of not one backward and underdeveloped territory, but two. Berlin, his capital city in Brandenburg, was a wooden shantytown of probably 8,000 inhabitants, an unlikely stop for royal visitors on their itineraries through Europe. Faraway Königsberg was a somewhat grander place, with a stone castle and church to recommend it, but it lay 350 miles to the east. Even so, Berlin became a welcome refuge for the elector as disaster engulfed his kingdoms.

Gustavus Adolphus was the initial agent of carnage. His entry into the German conflict, 1630, is amply documented and stuns the reader with its dash, breadth of ambition, and stupendous success. A daring general, clearheaded diplomat, and sincere Protestant, he is probably the most attractive figure of this entire saga, whose death at the Battle of Lutzen in 1632 actually saddened his foes. But it should be remembered that these German campaigns, though the highlight of his career, lasted only two years. He won his spurs well before 1632, slogging around the Grosse Werder, fighting in the wilderness of Livonia, keeping his weathered eye on Finns, Russians, Lithuanians, Poles, and Prussians. Most history books ignore this litany of continuous fighting in the East; like battles there before and after, these are "forgotten wars," unglamorous and seemingly inconsequential to the politics of Western Europe but in fact of crucial import then and even now.

Sweden's interest in Baltic hegemony was a phenomenon of almost one hundred years' duration, coincidental with its string of enor-

---

*There were seven German electors, whose functions were established by the Holy Roman Emperor Charles IV in his famous "Golden Bull" of 1356. Three ecclesiastical princes and four temporal were technically responsible for selecting a new emperor on the death of his predecessor, who then would allegedly oversee the affairs of the disjointed and, after the Reformation, dysfunctional federation of German states. If the Holy Roman Emperor of any given moment was a singular personality in his own right, with power beyond what a mere title could bring, the throne could provide an important extension of authority, as was traditionally the case of the Catholic Hapsburgs. A weak reed was another matter altogether. The emperor's effective control over German affairs, in practice more theoretical than functional, lapsed into irrelevancy with the later rise of Prussia.

mously vigorous warrior-kings stretching from Adolphus to Charles XII. It is difficult to believe that a country as thinly populated and unblessed by natural bounty could have had the impact Sweden did on the European scene.

Poland, equally hard though it may be to acknowledge, was at this point the dominant power of Central Europe, perhaps at the very apogee of strength and influence, its borders stretching as far as Transylvania, the Caucasus Mountains, and the Black Sea to the south and only a few score miles from the insignificant capital of the tsars in Moscow to the east. In the north it had reduced the former Teutonic empire to the small enclave of Ostpreussen, surrounding it on two sides with Polish pincers, one settled on Danzig, the other on Riga in Livonia. These twin outlets to the Baltic were eyed greedily by Gustavus Adolphus, and in 1621 Sweden entered into war to seize them both.

The struggle lasted eight years and involved the entire eastern coastline of the Baltic. The battles were bitter and unrelenting, the physical resources thrown into the annual campaigns substantial and draining to both economies. The countryside—need it be said?—suffered enormously. Gustavus, for all of his attractive personality and religious conviction, was oblivious to the carnage of war, to the sufferings of those in whose domain his armies wandered. His interests were primarily those of his class, meaning the glories of war. Here on Prussian fields he perfected his martial studies—the craft of battle in the deployment of troops, the usages of mobile cannon to its most lethal effect—which he would put to devastating use later in Germany. Wounded so often that wearing a breastplate (or cuirass) of steel became too painful, he discarded all the trappings of personal armor and rode into battle in a buff coat and hat, known as the king to all, friend and foe alike, by a plume and resplendent sash. Like all the Swedish kings who followed, he ate and slept with his men in the field and never hesitated to lead a charge himself. By 1629 he had wrested Livonia from Polish control and seized most of the western corridor right up to Danzig's gate. Grosse Werder was a desolated mass of empty fields. Not a pig, horse, sheep, or cow still lived within its boundaries, nor any peasant (free or villeined made little difference) to sow or harvest crops. Disease, especially the plague, completed the detail in what was in effect one enormous Breughelian cyclorama. "I hear nothing but lamentations, nor see variety but of dead bodies," an English diplomat wrote home in despair.

These victories were unsettling to the elector of Brandenburg at that time, George William, the son of John Sigismund. This young man, by all accounts pleasant enough and handsome in a florid sort of way but indecisive and not of warlike disposition, had the misfortune to be the brother-in-law of Gustavus. He watched the bloodbaths going on in Prussia with "gloomy bewilderment" but absolutely panicked when Gustavus and 13,000 men advanced into Brandenburg proper. The Catholic emperor called for his allegiance, as did the Lutheran Swede. George William had no idea where to turn and shifted in the winds as fate and circumstance demanded. The cannon of Gustavus, trained on the paltry Hohenzollern palace in Berlin, were sufficiently convincing at one point to secure George William's allegiance to Sweden. But when the opportunity came to switch sides, he did so with alacrity.

His son, Frederick William, a man with whom the elector had little in common, followed the same prevaricating policies upon his ascension to power in 1640, though from an entirely different perspective. The father, mentally inert, reacted to events, mostly out of fear; the son, by contrast, of a far more adventuresome spirit, initiated events, quite often in cold deliberation when opponents least desired his interference. From a position of weakness, the Great Elector, as he came to be called, managed to profit, both territorially and in reputation. Prussia was still poor, still backward, still primarily agricultural, but this amoral ruler provided the necessary element required for regeneration—peace. He did so without special regard for the historical notion of a "Prussia" or a "Brandenburg," without any solicitous care, as a matter of fact, for the happiness of the people he ruled. He wanted peace because without it his Hohenzollern dynasty would be ruined. War meant poverty, especially when fought all over estates and farms from which rents and taxes were required. The Great Elector's income was a full 80 percent below that of his father's when that timid gentleman had first taken up his rule in 1619. If war must be waged, better that it be fought in someone else's domain. The Great Elector's diplomacies all revolved around extricating his lands from the devastating incursion of soldiery, both those of other powers and his own, which, to his embarrassment, were as thoroughly a rapacious gang of freebooters as any invader.

In a career spanning forty-eight years, the Great Elector brought all of these chaotic elements under control, in effect creating the substructure over which a colossal European state would later emerge. He and the Hohenzollern rulers to follow were without principles. Some-

*The Great Elector*

one else's war was an occasion for gain. Sweden, Poland, and later Russia, Hapsburg Austria, and France would find in Prussia a wavering ally and a devious foe, not averse to fleeing a cause that looked to be crumbling or to gorging on the entrails of a tottering neighbor. Few friends are to be made in such dispassionate dealings. "Politics and villainy," as Frederick the Great remarked, "are almost synonymous terms."

⊰⊱

It is difficult at times to see order in what appears to be chaos. As history books and chronological charts list battle after battle, campaign after campaign, devastation after devastation, it is understandable in a way if modern readers throw up their hands in dismay and yell, "Enough! What can all this possibly mean?" And indeed there is a body of scholarly work that fundamentally agrees, attributing much of the mayhem that litters the seventeenth and eighteenth centuries to simple human perversity. There are periods in the history of humankind when the momentum for unreasoning behavior takes on its own bloody course for no other reason than habit and boredom, an especially volatile mix when dynastic ambition, religious scruples, and purely materialist greed are folded in. But German historians (who should, after all, know best) have a better handle on all of this than anyone else, and they are correct to focus on the forty-eight-year reign of the Great Elector as crucial to the development of Prussia and its emergence as a significant European power.

Certainly the union of Ostpreussen and Brandenburg, which resulted in the creation of "Prussia," is central to our story, but in many ways the consolidation was a matter of happenstance. European aristocrats, by second nature genealogists, could spend hours poring over dynastic charts and comparing bloodlines, all with the intent of augmenting their particular family's interest in whatever minor principality, fiefdom, inheritance, or even puny farm might be available at any particular time. Marriage brokering, we must keep in mind, was a principal form of business for these people, acquiring titles and lands the primary ambition, often with disregard for their actual value in cash. Vanity for some took precedence over wealth. When John Sigismund managed to acquire both the electorship of Brandenburg and the dukedom of Prussia, he may have done so only to play the dynastic card. His purse certainly showed no surfeit.

With the Great Elector, however, the vision was different. This was a man, as vain as the next, to be sure, who primarily conspired to place his family at the center stage of European power politics. To do that required him in the first place to extricate his territories from the prevailing anarchy, then to attract the attention and respect of neighboring rulers, most of whom were more powerful than he. The elector did this in much the same fashion as a vulture—warily, carefully, prudently. He remains a favorite study for German students and academicians.

Ostpreussen seemed an afterthought to the Great Elector's maneuverings for eminence. When the French or Austrians looked at "Prussia," they looked at Berlin and Brandenburg, but Ostpreussen, this strange eastern entity, was an integral part of the mix. It would add the steel when steel was required.

## ⚜ 7 ⚜

# Neudeck
## 1760
# The Soldier-King

*In general, my subjects are hardy and brave, un-curious
as to eating, but fond of drink; tyrants on their estates,
and slaves in my service; insipid lovers, and surly husbands; of a wondrously cold, phlegmatic turn, which I
take at bottom to be rank stupidity; good civilians, little of philosophers, and still less of orators; affecting a
great plainness in their dress, but imagining themselves dressed in high taste. As to the women, they are
almost all fat and special breeders.*

—**Frederick the Great**

AT A LOCAL TOURIST OFFICE I make inquiries for Neudeck, the
ancestral estate of Paul von Hindenburg, a query accepted with distaste by the various Polish receptionists working the counter, who
profess ignorance of either name. I ask myself if it is the nature of my
interests that seems so irritating to the Poles in general or whether,
as is typical of insular peoples, they greet with suspicion any stranger
with questions. Several phone calls around town seem to confirm
that general ignorance is more likely the explanation. As hard as it
may be to fathom, it appears that no one here has ever heard of von
Hindenburg.

Wandering about later, I look for cars in the village center, usually
new ones that might have a *D* or a telltale German license plate; if the
occupants seem older than fifty, I give them a shot. On my third try I

get what I need. "We have just returned from there and will tell you everything," I am told, "but do not expect to see much."

The directions, needless to say, are precise, and as my road turns to dirt through pasture and grazing land I proceed confidently, sure that Neudeck lies ahead. I enter a Slavic hamlet with coarse, concrete houses on either side of the lane, a common well, plenty of chickens running loose, and women and children wandering about in dirty work clothes. Behind a low knoll covered with trees, several enormous barns appear still to be in use, and it becomes clear to me from the general layout that the manor house had once stood on this little hill. Poking about, I find the barest trace of its foundation.

I ask one young man if he knows where the family graveyard is, and he points it out down off to the side. It is now the farming co-op's garbage dump, where trash is burned. A few old wrought iron crucifixes and one or two sections of gate and fence are still in place, though most everything of a funereal nature has been destroyed. Von Hindenburg's parents lie here someplace, likewise his ancestors from God knows how long ago.*

Taking an inventory, then, what have we here? Another collection of empty fields, as undramatic as a crop of wheat first emerging from the soil in springtime, growing imperceptibly to our occasional gaze, then sprouting, unfolding, ready for the harvest after a long course of uneventful summer. Another mansion knocked to pieces, in this case without a trace to be seen. The several immense barns behind its crowning hill are the only evidence still left of the great estate this once was. In other words, we have nothing, not even a suitably melancholic heap of ruins where the desolated aura of a vanished nobility and its now evaporated ideals can at the very least be recalled, remembered, celebrated in some nostalgic fashion. The visitor arriving here without any prior knowledge of Prussia's long past comes for nothing but the placid view, long furrows of earth running up to woodlot or

---

*The field marshal did not himself own Neudeck until 1927, when the estate was presented to him by "a grateful nation" on the occasion of his eightieth birthday. Neudeck had been losing money for years, a combination of woeful mismanagement and the unfavorable agricultural climate of previous years. Hindenburg's sister-in-law, engulfed in debt, was prepared to sell out. Realizing how distressed the marshal would have been at the dissolution of his family's heritage, a public subscription was called and the purchase price raised. The Neudeck affair proved embarrassing to von Hindenburg in the long run, mostly due to rumors of financial scandal involving his son.

*Hindenburg family
cemetery, Neudeck*

lane. Here, however, may be the deepest clue of all, prosaic and dull perhaps, but direct and purposeful all the same.

The ethos of Prussia was that of the minor country gentry, the Junker class, who differed but little in isolation, ignorance, pretension, and courage from their counterparts in rural Ireland, England, France, Spain, or anywhere else in Western Europe. Conservative, religious, jealous of local privilege, addicted to sport and codes of honor, attuned to the ways of nature and agricultural pursuit, they enjoyed most of all their lineage of possession, which provided, among many other things, hours of tales and storytelling over a winter's fire in the kitchen.

This transcendent strain of intercourse with rural life created a knitted social fabric uniting all for miles around in a shared system of values, which did not include a very marked interest in intellectual matters. The Junkers were above all soldiers. Unlike the Anglo-Irish, unlike the Normans, in fact, the Junkers remained keenly militaristic throughout their long history. No Irish Sea or English Channel isolated them from enemies, real or imagined, or from involvement in the countless great sweeps of unrest that buffeted central Germany from all directions. In keeping with their ethos as settlers, they both intermixed with peoples of varying ethnic makeup and retained their sense of preeminence. This was not as complicated as it sounds. They were conquerors, and thus superior.

The hard life of soldier and country squire bred discipline, another genetic trait this soil may well have transferred through the food chain, but theoretically more attributable to the unrelenting *Ostkrieg,* or "war in the East." This was not some schoolboy tradition or textbook lesson learned from afar. It was taught, often with a cane or sword, by father to son, sergeant to private, commander in chief to all within earshot—*Kadavergehorsam,* literally, "cadaver obedience"—instinctive obedience, to death if so ordered.

Many Germans of the seventeenth and eighteenth centuries were as unfamiliar with their own martial history as they were with matters of courtly etiquette in faraway Versailles. Frederick the Great, for example, had little notion of (and less interest in) the Teutonic Knights or what they created in the wilderness of Ostpreussen, which in effect was the *Ordensstaat* that he himself sought to fashion.* But Frederick did not require a book to describe what he felt in his bones; it was just there, an undefinable force that could neither be ignored nor overridden.

"That's all in the past now," a German friend told me. "The striking thing about this emotional imperative, common to all sorts of phenomena in this incredible century, is to see how long it lasted and how quickly it went. Drugs, rock music, cultural immorality are fashionably identified as culprits, but actually three forces did away with it: freedom, education, no more East Prussia. They gave no quarter to these antique notions of life. You wouldn't see Germans fighting to the death over anything now."

The great cliché about the Junkers, of course, is the notion of their willing obedience to any and all the Hohenzollerns who happened to be in command at any given moment after 1640. Von Hindenburg's ponderous memoirs did more to reinforce this notion than any other

---

*His father, a man with little respect for learning, had decreed that Frederick be taught no history prior to that of the sixteenth century.

modern document, full as it was with obsequious bons mots concerning the last kaiser, "my All-Highest War Lord," a man whom neither the aged field marshal nor his chief lieutenant, Ludendorff, chose to save in the end. The Junkers obeyed their Hohenzollern masters, particularly when the cannon began their fusillades, but that is not to say they liked it.

⚔

Ostpreussen was a special preserve in the growing Hohenzollern empire, much to the annoyance of the Great Elector and his descendants. The eastern territory possessed a long history of isolation from the beck and call of impecunious monarchs, its landed class enjoying unique privileges that were not easy to dissolve. As much as honor mattered to the Junker, money jostled the inner reaches of his soul with equal persistence. Granted exemptions by the Teutonic Order, confirmed in economic privileges by the kings of Poland when they held suzerainty over the land, and further wooed by desperate Hohenzollerns attempting to secure their title to Ostpreussen, the Junkers already had a clinging memory of every hard-won concession, no matter its source. In 1660 they were a class totally exempt from taxation. The Great Elector, seeking to build a modern army that would garner some respect from the other great powers of Europe (or in his words, "to make me *considérable*"), squeezed the towns and reduced the peasantry to near slavery with onerous duties and taxes. The gentry of Brandenburg and Pomerania he did not hesitate to plunder. But in Ostpreussen he encountered formidable difficulties that took years of struggle to resolve.

The Junkers of Ostpreussen were a threadbare nobility. Their estates, though often large, were precarious for the most part, their cash flow meager. Most of the great farms were certainly self-sustaining, providing food for the table and horseflesh for entertainment, but extravagance on the scale of a French or English estate was rare. The notion of service to their state and lord was seen as ample contribution to the commonweal. Generations of Junker sons would spend their lives in genteel poverty, marching to the army's drum or managing the ever more efficient bureaucracy of the Hohenzollern dynasty. But what they did inside the confines of their own estates was a different matter altogether. They would treat the serfs as they wished and manage their private affairs in any fashion pleasing to them. The paltry flow of thalers through their account ledgers was a private affair. Bismarck, two centuries later, would be found doing the same thing as the Hohenzollerns, complaining about tightfisted Junkers. Their agendas were simply incompatible. An absolutist monarchy has no wish for independent nobles.

Frederick the Great disparaged this class; they were his "machines." He sought, as did all the Hohenzollerns, to extract the very marrow of their lives to service. "War, it is a trade," he wrote, requiring the flesh and blood of Junkers (freely given, for the most part) to man the army and money (grudgingly given, for the most part) to fund it—all this to the increase of "his interest and his glory."

⚞⚟

Just a few miles north of Neudeck, I pass through a crossroads village called Finckenstein and stumble upon what the Hohenzollerns did provide their warrior class, that is, glory. The desiccated remnants of a great mansion still remain here, much to my surprise, in a county seat of the Finckenstein family that gave this place its name. As at Neudeck, the farming complex itself, full of barns and stables, is still in use, ranging to either side in classical symmetry off the main and still charred central manor, looted and burned in 1945. Its portico, surmounted by a stork's nest, attracts my attention, for it vigorously portrays in a fanlike frieze for all to admire the full panoply of martial splendor—cannon and ball, spear and pike, flag and shako, musket and bayonet. Frederick the Great's father had the French gardens of his palace in Berlin torn up and plowed under, replaced by a drill yard. I wonder whether the field in front of this place was so used as well.

Often has it been said that Prussia was an army just waiting for a state to come by and give it direction, and such was certainly true throughout the 1700s. The Hohenzollerns, through the vanity of one of their despots, had by that time achieved the status of kingship. No longer merely an elector or a duke, Frederick I was now "king in Prussia," an elevation that nearly bankrupted the family entirely. Much influenced by the elaborate pageantry of his contemporary Louis XIV, Frederick I led a procession of over 1,000 carriages when he traveled to Königsberg for coronation, an event characterized by its "inflated grandeur," in the words of one historian. But the long trip was absolutely required for Hohenzollern self-esteem. All of Europe had to see the "king in Prussia" as a powerfully independent ruler whose domains, at least in part, lay outside the emperor's authority, beyond the

*Frieze on the manor
house, Finckenstein*

territorial confines of the Holy Roman Empire.* That East Prussia was
the least valuable of all the Hohenzollern possessions was not emphasized at the time (seven years later a quarter of East Prussia's already
thin population was carried off by plague). When Frederick the Great
took the same journey thirty-nine years later, his entourage consisted
of a single horse-drawn carriage.

---

*This resulted in the finely tuned etiquette of Frederick's new title, "king in Prussia"
as opposed to "king of Prussia," a distinction the Holy Roman Emperor thought worth
insisting upon. Many of Frederick's territories, most notably West Prussia, were still
held in semifeudal subordination to the emperor, who would not tolerate a fellow king
inside the borders of his own alleged possessions. East Prussia lay outside these formal
domains, and thus Frederick could, if he wished, be a king "in" those lands. The emperor consented to this hairsplitting arrangement in return for the use of 8,000 soldiers
in the war of the Spanish succession in 1701.

The extravagance of Frederick I was an analogy seldom repeated in that century, Prussia soon gaining for itself the morose reputation as Europe's Sparta.* Certainly the peculiar personalities of its most energetic sovereigns, Frederick William I and his son, Frederick the Great, did little to assuage this misanthropic image, which in fact was rooted in sincere self-denial.†

Frederick William I created the army and the treasury that his son would later squander to achieve a goal of "making noise in the world." The father was a crude individual, mentally deranged into the bargain, his spirit and soul warped by physical torment so severe that he often lost complete control of himself. Medical scholars seem to think his ailment was porphyria, a hereditary metabolic disorder that even today can be misdiagnosed, though one of its manifestations, blue urine, would seem to be revealing. Alan Bennett's recent play on George III, elector of Hanover and king of England, who seems to have suffered the same rare disease, illustrates for the modern audience the chaotic mood swings and excruciating physical pain that sufferers endured. Whatever the malady, it certainly affected Frederick William's powers of judgment. One moment the king might be counting money or reviewing troops; the next he could be seen beating with a cane some hapless pedestrian in the street. His powers of rationality, barely controlled during the best of times, often broke down through his regimen of hard living and harder play, the latter marked by famous all-night carousing with army cronies that often ended in beatings and sadomasochistic pranks of the most boorish character. He was once restrained with difficulty from executing his own heir to the throne over some childish prank, forcing the boy instead to watch the decapitation of a best friend who had run away with him. His hobby was collecting giants, whom he resplendently attired in the uniform of household

---

*Frederick I's most ostentatious project was the Amber Room, a series of wooden panels to which hundreds of individually carved pieces of the fossilized resin—representations of heraldic devices, garlands, reliefs, candleholders, and so on—were glued. It required ten years of mining and scavenging just to assemble the quantity of amber required for this commission, estimated at 6 tons in gross weight, and a veritable army of craftsmen and sculptors worked years to design, manufacture, and install the finished friezes. Frederick's son, the gloomy Frederick William I, despised this effete and Francophile indulgence and gave the entire room to Tsar Peter the Great in 1717, for eventual reassembly in the Catherine Palace, outside St. Petersburg.

†See genealogy in Chapter 6.

guards. Usually mentally deficient, these men were paraded continuously beneath his office windows.

In moments of clearheadedness, Frederick William was a genius of sorts, though his notions of self-sufficiency have been stripped of their integrity in the twentieth century by the xenophobia of China, North Korea, Burma, Albania, and other Third World dictatorships. Frederick William wanted a powerful Prussian army fully equipped, trained, salaried, and supported by the kingdom from which it came and was devoted to serving: no reliance on foreigners, no foreign contamination to sway the institution from complete servitude to the wishes of its king. The army became the raison d'être of the Hohenzollern state. Eighty percent of all its revenues, skillfully collected by an army of another kind, the Prussian bureaucracy, went toward military expenditure. What was left over Frederick William saved with a stinginess, it has been claimed, that bordered on mania. When he died in 1740, the army had doubled in size, from 40,000 to 80,000 men, and the treasury lay full of thalers, 7 million a year that, given Prussia's rudimentary economy and slim population base, proved "a colossal achievement."

Frederick William worshiped his own creation, however timorous he was in its use. The army was very helpful in asserting monarchical control through his mosaic of territories, overwhelming provincial objections when required or assisting recalcitrant taxpayers in making their annual contributions. Drilling, the practice of large-scale maneuvers in the field, harsh discipline and punishment—these made up the lives of Frederick William's men. But foreign adventures were kept to the minimum. The menace of this growing army was more feared in these years of relative calm than their performance.

Frederick William took to wearing soldier's garb day in and day out and all but reserved for his Junkers the role of officer in the army. Only the evolving artillery service, a science with little pedigree in the ancient call to arms, was open to the common man. (It should be noted, I suppose, that Napoleon in his youth was a commander of cannon.) Prussia, though largely at peace, was thus on a continuous footing for war, presided over by a king who, in his daily life and through the dignity of his office, merged the interests of state with those of the army. "I am the King of Prussia's Field Marshal," he was quoted as saying, a prescient remark that someone happened to jot down for posterity, luckily enough, as the king left behind few written records, being largely illiterate. A soldier, after all, had no need of learning.

His son, Frederick the Great, came to the throne in 1740 with, as is usually the case, an entirely different set of values. Learning meant a great deal to him, particularly the French variety then in vogue through the influence of Voltaire, which is one reason Frederick seldom visited his lands in East Prussia, loathing the place as a hotbed of barbarism and uncouth behavior, "the ne plus ultra of the civilized world."

Frederick aped intellectual aspects of the court of Versailles. He spoke French with his intimate circle of wits and hangers-on, wrote verse and all his correspondence in the same tongue, enjoyed art and collected assiduously, played the flute and composed several pieces himself—all to the more or less scornful amusement of Francophiles, who derided most of these efforts as second rate.* In the field of war and bloody battle, however, Frederick was universally regarded as without peer.

Certainly no man has ever had more psychological effect on the German people. His example, his career, his extraordinary resilience and devotion to duty have for two centuries been held as the very perfection of soldierly conduct. Carl von Clausewitz, theoretician of the Prussian military spirit, referred to Frederick simply as "the King," no other identification being necessary. Generations of schoolboys, cadets, colonels, staff officers, field marshals, and even kaisers studied every facet of his campaigns, seeking to emulate, when their turn came to lead the troops, some of the eternally inventive stratagems with which Frederick outfoxed his usually superior foes. Even Adolf Hitler, whose detestation of aristocrats and hereditary monarchs was famous, gained strength from Frederick's refusal to accept defeat no matter the overwhelming odds. As the eastern front collapsed in 1944, Joseph Goebbels took to soothing the Führer's jangled nerves by reading aloud to him from Frederick's memoirs, full as they were with fortitude and resolution: "In the face of storm and the threat of shipwreck, I must think, live and die like a king!" That Frederick disdained his generals and never heeded their advice no doubt further

*His detractors included Voltaire, whom the king invited to Berlin in 1751 for an extended stay that eventually pleased neither. As Macaulay wrote, "Never had there met two persons so exquisitely fitted to plague each other." Frederick was adept at extracting what he wanted from people, whether subjects or illustrious visitors mattered little. He is said to have remarked of Voltaire that "I have sucked the fruit and shall now throw away the skin." Voltaire departed Potsdam in March 1753, entering France four months later after a series of semicomic adventures.

endeared him to Hitler, though it is unclear whether the Führer ever knew that Frederick was homosexual.

Von Clausewitz admired every facet of Frederick's military skill. In his famous work *Vom Kriege* (*On War*), he wrote most admiringly of Frederick's boldness, a "creative power" that even when abused through reckless maneuver (a recourse often forced upon Frederick the Great by dire circumstance) could not be faulted as anything less than a "fine failure." Von Clausewitz cited as an excellent example Frederick's initiation of hostilities in 1756, a conflict later known as the Seven Years' War that, but for the madness of a Russian tsar, very nearly destroyed the kingdom. Sensing that a coalition of opponents was stirring to attack him, Frederick dispensed with the princely practice of declaring war and struck first without warning, a Germanic tradition dating back to the Teutonic Knights and twice repeated in the twentieth century. Frederick, completely amoral in such matters, was simply exercising the natural prerogative of a superior military mind. Looking over the political terrain, seeing the inevitability of conflict, what other course of action than to be "beforehand with his enemies"? Warfare, after all, in von Clausewitz's most famous postulation, "is only a part of political intercourse, and by no means an independent thing in itself."

The warfare that Frederick perfected was essentially one of maneuver. Tactics of the day were rigidly conceived and often played out as though by rote. Opposing armies searched for superior positions on any given terrain, which, if denied them, often discouraged the development of battle, an old German axiom having it that not to lose should be counted as a victory. Armies were expected to perform mechanically, their deployment amid the actual din of combat to be identical to their actions in annual maneuvers. It was still possible for a single commander to more or less control his entire front and to see, if he had the proper vantage point, just what was going on. Though armies were bigger and battles more complicated than those of the Thirty Years' War, they could still turn on the single order of a single individual. An opportune charge, in other words, could still carry the day.

Frederick dared to go against the grain. Endowed with a masterful appreciation for terrain, expert in the "miracles of execution," he could confound the opposition by unorthodox feints and parries, plunging ahead at the strongest point of a line or appearing in force where or when least expected. His generals were predictably aghast and often paid the penalty for obeying his many arbitrary decisions—

120 died under Frederick's command, a proportion not seen in any other European army. Whenever asked for orders, he could simply reply, "Attack, as do I!" His courage was legendary, the number of horses killed beneath him beyond counting, his uniform a collection of bullet holes, nicks, and creases. Whereas Napoleon outgrew the martial exuberance of youth, best exemplified by his charge over the bridge at Arcole in 1796, Frederick never did. Napoleon declined to die on the field at Waterloo or to lead his old guard in its last desperate attack. During the Battle of Zorndorf in 1758, Frederick leapt from his horse, grabbed a standard of the Fusilier Regiment von Bülow, and strode toward the Russian enemy, shouting to his men, "Dogs! Would you live forever?" It is edifying to note that histrionics of this sort were not always effective. At Zorndorf, the king remarked afterward, his men ran away like tarts.

And why not? Warfare was a deadly enterprise, the casualty figures far higher than any customarily seen. Frederick routinely might lose 10,000 or 15,000 men in any given battle.* The fine army inherited from his father disappeared over time, replaced by the end of his career with a force over twice the size but bloated by inferior soldiery. War, always sanguinary, had become a lethal business indeed. When Frederick died in 1786, there were few friends from his youthful cadet days still alive to mourn him.

The Seven Years' War, through chance and tactical brilliance a victory for Frederick (who then reaped innumerable benefits from the peace conference that followed), proved an unmitigated disaster for Ostpreussen. Fighting Austrian, French, imperial, and Russian troops all at the same moment, the king was helpless to protect his eastern borders in 1756 when a Russian horde crossed the Memel and wasted everything in its path. Königsberg fell, the town burghers pledging their allegiance to the Russian tsar, as did Immanuel Kant a few months later in a particularly obsequious submission to Catherine the Great, who had succeeded to the throne after ordering her deranged husband strangled.

It is said that Frederick held a grudge against his faraway province from that year on. He certainly never visited it again after its recovery from Russia and paid no heed to the growing fame of its resident intellectuals, such as Kant, who was frequently snubbed by the academi-

---

*In the single year of 1759, Frederick's army shrunk by 60,000 men.

*Friedrich der Grosse and
hounds, Sans Souci*

cians of Berlin with no doubt royal assent.* Frederick's lifelong bias
against most things German never wavered. The language he scorned
as a mishmash of local dialects that prevented the emergence of a national literature. The food and drink were unbearable—at public functions "it is my German cook that dresses my dinner; but when I am
snug in my little private apartments, I have a French cook who does
his best to humor my palate which, I must confess, is rather of the
nicest." As for manners and fostership of the arts, these he considered
provincial at best and nonexistent anywhere off the beaten path. Culturally, the whole place was "a desert." He tried reading Shakespeare
but agreed with Voltaire that it was hardly worth the effort. Why
spend time wading through "that vast manure heap" when the delica-
cies of Molière brought more enlightened insight?

Like his father before him, he nurtured the material development of
his territories, inviting Protestant refugees (noted for their thrift and

---

*Nietzsche, for different reasons, also thought little of Kant, considering his philoso-
phy tepid and unmanly. "Kant is a scarecrow," he noted in his journal.

business acumen) to resettle in Prussia from wherever they had been persecuted. He built canals, fostered agriculture, encouraged trade and the stirring of industry, reformed the judiciary, and relieved some of the cruder oppressions under which the peasantry toiled—but all with the coldly impersonal objective of funneling thalers into the treasury to increase the might of his military posture. Curiously enough, however, he achieved his greatest coup without firing a shot, which validated to some degree the Hohenzollern premise of maintaining a full-time standing army, no matter the cost. "Make boldly your approach to crime," as Frederick once wrote his nephew. "Never ask anything feebly." .

⚔

The River Vistula, a few miles west of both Neudeck and Fincken-stein, formed the western border of Ostpreussen. Across its waters was an arm of the Polish kingdom, ending at the city of Danzig, that in the twentieth century we have come to call "the Corridor." These had been Polish lands since 1466 and showed it: few estates of any measure, acres upon acres of unimproved land, much of it waste or under water, worked by an abject class of serfdom whose status was no better than helotry. Their masters, often nearly as poor, were the distinctly minor nobility of Poland, of ancient lineage to be sure but little else. Haughty, given to airs and temper, but numerous beyond the capacity of their ragged little farms to support, they had effectively crippled Poland's potential to emerge as either a great or modern society. Its dynastic politics were equally undermined by surrounding powers (notably Russia), who routinely interfered in the appointment of kings and even ministers. Having no defensible borders, Poland was easy prey to avaricious neighbors whose passion for maps, bloodlines, and treaties of alliance proved almost a disease. As Catherine the Great helpfully remarked to Frederick's brother, "It would seem that in Poland one has nothing to do but stoop to pick up whatever one pleases."

In 1772, taking advantage of internal crises, the three eastern powers of Russia, Austria, and Prussia unilaterally divided 30 percent of Poland among them. Without Frederick's reputation and army, the feast might well have been a restricted affair, but no one in Vienna or Moscow cared for another war with Prussia.*

---

*The king's nemesis, Maria Theresa, archduchess of Austria and wife to the Holy Roman Emperor, was genuinely aghast when her ministers proposed the First Partition. "She weeps," said Frederick, "but she takes."

Though the smallest piece of territory went to Frederick, it could well be judged the most important. Brandenburg and Ostpreussen were now united by a wide, rectangular swath of land of approximately 6,000 square miles, running northward from Thorn to the Baltic coastline and Danzig (the latter two cities still left for Poland, though the Second Partition twenty-one years later granted these as well to Prussia). "Such a unification of territories can only be compared with the [Berlin] Wall coming down," a German acquaintance said to me, "and if you think about it, both were bloodless coups. Geographically, they made from various parts an integral whole. A marvelous piece of statecraft to be sure, however coldly executed, though one could have predicted that the Poles would never learn to accept it. Their trade to the outside world via Danzig, for instance, was strangled. They have very long memories when it comes to injustice."

It may seem difficult to imagine today, driving west over the Vistula and passing by farms no different than those I just visited at Neudeck and Finckenstein, that 200 years ago the same trip would have been a culture warp of stupendous proportion. Frederick himself couldn't believe it when he toured the area the next year. "These provinces cannot be compared with any European country," he wrote Voltaire. "The only parallel would be Canada." Wretched barefoot peasants, no schools, police, courts, hospitals, town life, or industry of any sort, his new possessions were sunk in poverty, ignorance, and tyranny. "It is not reasonable that the country which produced Copernicus should be allowed to molder in [such] barbarism."

But even Frederick saw the potential of what was now being called West Prussia. New farms were planned, new towns established, new estates carved up, new settlers brought in, many of whom retained Polish workers as their cheap labor. These natives were often joined by hundreds of their compatriots from the south during harvest time. Conditions, immeasurably improved by German administrators, made the lot of farmhands far superior to that endured at home. It also confirmed in German minds that Poles were an inferior race fit only for the harshest labor.

Although this enlargement of Prussia's dominions had at least a certain political justification, the land grab of 1796, known as the Third Partition, was nothing less than basic plunder, and it would be callous not to admit the wrong of what happened. The primary villain of this piece was imperial Russia, tired of the constitutional process being explored by Polish liberals and angered by their eventual eruption into revolt. Subtlety has never been a Russian virtue, and after a few minor setbacks they crushed Polish forces and eradicated the name of Poland from European maps. Prussia, a willing and equally greedy partner, picked up significant pieces of leftover territories far greater in square mileage than that obtained in the First Partition. The long agony of Poland really began during those evil days of repression.

Reconstructed Warsaw never lets you forget it. From the ghetto memorials to sidewalk plaques to execution sites along the medieval walls, marked by flowers and memorials, you cannot take a step without some reminder of how nothing has gone right for this wretched land in over two centuries. An important exhibition in 1994 at the restored Krasiński Palace, commemorating the 200th anniversary of Tadeusz Kościuszko's hapless rebellion, ratchets up the pressure. The elegant foyer of the palace library, with Renaissance statuary and ornate plaster molding, is overwhelmed by an enormous gibbet on center stage, noose dangling in the fresh breeze from outside, reproduction death notices in Polish tacked all over the room. The only thing that's missing is the dangling body of Bishop Ignacy Massalki, executed by the Russians for his role in the uprising. The Polish curse has been geographical by nature, the result of its vulnerable position between two immeasurably arrogant powers. Polish intemperance, by turn, has always invited dangerous reaction. Even today the Polish scene is riven with angst—fearful of a united Germany, fearful of a crumbling Russia, spurned and then resentfully accepted into NATO, haunted by its history, still buried in poverty. It fears the kick of a dog.

✥

Frederick the Great remains a revered figure in Germany. Unlike more recent Teutonic warlords, the memories of whose carnage remains a sore point both here and abroad, the soldier-king is far enough removed in time that some of his more genteel possessions—his flute, his library and paintings, Sans Souci—somehow soften the career we know to have been both selfish and sanguinary. Germans with whom I spoke had nothing ill to say of him.

That Frederick brought verve to the political table is without question. In that sense he was a worthy descendant of the Great Elector, able to see beyond his own borders to greater Continental horizons. And the creation of a united Prussia—the linkage of Brandenburg to Ostpreussen—was a logical objective and masterfully won, though at a cost that even the king suspected might prove to be too high.

Frederick the Great *by*
*J. G. Ziesenis*

Frederick's triumphs certainly "internationalized" the image of Prussia and, by extension, his own, and this was deemed worthy of any amount of treasure. Everyone had come to know who Frederick was, where Berlin lay on the map, the mettle of Prussia's ferocious army. Europeans may not have realized that Frederick left his kingdom nearly bankrupt or that his success, vast by any measure, could just as easily have been catastrophe, but such are the vagaries of life. Prussia had now achieved the plateau of greatness. This proved both a blessing and a curse.

Frederick had gone too far on too little, which of course had been a Prussian tradition since 1286, when the knights began inviting challenges that were fundamentally too immense for such a poor and relatively modest territory to embrace. From the eighteenth century on, however, the gambles had grown in size and were thus larger in potential consequence. Military triumphs, especially when they come in a rush, one after the other, tend to create the notion of invincibility.

From 1780 on, the arrogance that so many opponents found particularly galling in the Prussian character became the permanent fixture of their perceived personality. Prussian soldiers had been fighting in central and eastern Europe anonymously for nearly 500 years, but Frederick's brilliant military career had suddenly brought them out of the shadows. Ostpreussen continued to churn out officers and soldiers, many of very narrow and provincial vision, which fresh military laurels did little to alter—with one essential difference: An aura of invincibility now infected the Prussian mindset. A case could be made that the disastrous two-front wars that Germany embarked upon in the twentieth century—enterprises that seem in retrospect akin to madness—found their inspiration in the often insouciant example of Frederick the Great. The glare of his fame would spark danger for generations of Prussian soldiers to come.

# ⊰ 8 ⊱
# Eylau
## 1807
# Napoleonic Disaster

*A day of bloody memory.*
—**French officer at the Battle of Eylau**

FOUR OTHER PASSENGERS stand on a train platform in the old Prussian town of Braunsberg, now a part of Poland and called Braniewo. On this Easter Sunday morning, we are all awaiting the Kaliningrad Express, an allegedly direct and straightforward connection to the capital city of Russia's most peculiar component, a province without identity, purpose, future, or even nationality.

Kaliningrad, the former Königsberg, harbors but a handful of the people who want it most. Few Germans, Poles, Lithuanians, or foreigners of any sort have much to do with the place. It is an outpost for displaced Russians told to live there, many by Stalin himself, who with the megalomania common to dictators of the twentieth century habitually uprooted enormous segments of his country's population and simply moved them off to a different address, whether by whim or design few dared to question. Kaliningrad is a foreign legion outpost, separated from Russia by hundreds of miles and absolutely extraneous to much of importance going on today in that turbulent country. The train, an ancient diesel of antediluvian origin, lumbers in, and the four of us embark.

At no time in the three and a half scheduled hours of this trip does the Express exceed 35 mph, and at several junctures it stops altogether

for ten or fifteen inexplicable minutes. At the border with Russia, passengers and coaches alike are totally ransacked. Heavily armed soldiers remove ceiling panels and disassemble seats, comb every piece of
luggage, and use mirrors to examine the underside of all the carriages.
Dogs bark and sniff packages. A female officer carrying a wrench to
take toilets apart checks the pipes. She then orders me, alone of all the
passengers, to leave the train.

The is not a happy experience. My bag and cameras are pointedly
left on board, my passport taken away and given to someone else. I follow her along the cinder railbed to a small shack, inside of which five
heavily smoking officials interrogate me in Russian. They ask for my
wallet and meticulously count out the $1,000 I'm carrying in tens and
twenties. They are impressed, as I can tell from the animated discus-
sion. It is pretty clear that Western visitors are few and far between on
the Kaliningrad Express. The woman who rousted me from the train is
particularly voluble and unfriendly. If looks could kill, I'd be hanging
from a lamppost. She motions me to wait outside. After twenty minutes and much conversation, overheard but not understood, my wallet
is returned and I am marched back to the train. As we lurch on toward
Kaliningrad, I lock myself in the WC and count my money. It's all
there.

The train is an hour late. It has taken over four hours to cover some
45 miles. The city has no appreciable charm as we crawl into the main
station. The only feature of note is a tall steeple standing alone in an
industrial complex, clearly a remnant of German times, when Kaliningrad was dotted with monumental architecture. A solitary tree
grows from its roof. Later I searched it out by car and discovered not a
church but a pockmarked, beaten-up water tower, used as an observation post during the city's defense in 1945 and thus heavily racked by
Russian fire. Like everything else in this place, it has been left to disintegrate.

During my stay I make arrangements to lodge with my driver's family, consisting of his wife, son, and teenage daughter. None of them
speaks English, but sign language enables us all to coexist with little
difficulty. Despite my protestations, the two children are deprived of
their small bedroom on my account. Each morning we all queue up for
the single water closet.

The view from their tiny terrace fifteen floors up, crowded with pot-
ted herbs, great multigalloned jugs of pickled eggs and pigs' feet, and
drying racks of underwear and socks, is immense, stretching from the

*Water tower*

former *Altstadt,* or Old City, with only the ruined cathedral left standing, down the River Pregel past an array of dreary apartment towers. Though early in the morning, groups of street people are draining quart bottles of cheap vodka in the barren park land of what was once a riverside promenade, and I watch as they divide, like the river current round a boulder, between two of their number locked in a lurching fistfight.

This entire panorama seems devoid of hope, a destination Lyndon Johnson probably had in mind when he told people of my generation to "love it or leave it." But then again, my driver is irrepressibly happy. We have had an enormous bounty for breakfast, followed by a *"salud"* of vodka; his daughter, drenched in a pleasing perfume, is buried in *Vogue;* his son is playing with Ninja Turtles; and his wife is the very picture of a contented homemaker. There seems nothing wrong with his life at all, other than having haphazard employment at best, driving a few foreigners around.

Before setting off for the countryside, we pick up my interpreter on the other side of the city, a university student, the daughter of an army colonel who resigned on account of poverty. He couldn't support himself and his wife on an officer's salary and is now trying his luck in the free-market economy as an entrepreneur. "Does that mean he's in the black market?" I ask.

"Certainly not! We wouldn't be living here"—waving at yet another monolithic apartment building—"if my father was dishonest. I wish to see your eyes protrude. Take him to the *mafiya* houses," she says to the driver, and a few dangerous minutes later, after navigating some potholes big enough to swallow a Fifth Avenue bus, we see several examples of ill-gotten gain, mansions of incredible size and extravagance cheek to cheek with ramshackle hovels far from their Hohenzollern prime. Curiously enough, many of these nouveau riche displays are copies, in the German style, of ancient castles, what in architectural parlance might be called "mock Teutonic" or "ersatz grand master."

"This is all profiteering," my interpreter tells me, her earnest voice trembling with anger. "My father works so long and so hard, but he is a patriot. These people are scum."

❦

On our way to Kaliningrad University, we see the new statue of Kant that replaced the original, destroyed by Red Army troops in 1945. Kant was born here in Königsberg in 1724 and never, it appears, traveled more than a few score miles from its walls in the eighty years of his lifetime. This seems to me an extraordinary circumspection considering the breadth of his philosophical inquiries, which seemed at times to transcend the boundaries of mere existence. His famous epitaph, "The starry heavens above me and the moral law within me," summarize, if such is possible in just a few words, the dilemma Kant sought to solve, the ceaseless friction we human beings endure to fathom the world around us. Do we trust our senses—what we see and hear—or do we rely on our common sense and rational thought, how we think? Easy questions to ask but immensely difficult to solve. Where, for example, does God fit in?

Scholars are amazed that an eighteenth-century Königsberg could have produced Immanuel Kant. The city was a cultural hinterland, its university "barely more than a glorified high school" through whose corridors Kant hustled for students to attend (and pay for) his lectures. He did not secure a tenured appointment there until he was forty-six,

Mafiya *house*

when he at last could abandon, like Jonathan Swift, the tedious financial necessity of tutoring the children of clergymen and provincial
Junkers. For the next decade, he published nothing, but between 1781
and 1796 he authored a major philosophical treatise or revision nearly
every year, an astonishing output that began with his *Kritik des
reinen Vernunft (Critique of Pure Reason)*, one of the most influential
books ever written.

"The history of philosophy," says Leonard Kalinnikov of Kaliningrad University, "can be divided into two periods, pre-Kant and post-
Kant. He was the colossus who dominated both eras, the equal to
Plato from the past and the equivalent to Columbus in the future as
he charted territories that no one knew existed. He was an absolutely
unique personage, so very new, so extraordinary, whose own students
and peers had no idea what he was saying, only inklings. By the time
of his death in 1804, you had several thousand printed analyses of his
philosophy already in print and all over the place in terms of how people interpreted his work. Surveying the intellectual wreckage left in
his wake, the Jewish philosopher Mendelssohn referred to him as 'the
all-shattering Kant.' In many ways it was total confusion. I do not

*Kant scholar
Leonard Kalinnikov*

think Kant meant to replace God himself, but he came very close. His portrayal of God is certainly very modern, the detached, isolated being. A far cry from what we read in the Bible, which got him into some trouble with Prussian authorities."

Professor Kalinnikov and I examine some of the university's Kantian memorabilia. "*Kritik des reinen Vernunft* came out in eight editions, and we have three. You must realize that we Russians are extremely interested in Kant. We were the first to translate his works from the German and Latin, as a matter of fact, in the nineteenth century. And the French thought Voltaire was smart! But with communism our natural ambition to study him went into retreat. For example, I am the first and only Kant scholar here at the university, and even now we haven't a Kant chair. In 1974 we tried to organize a festival, it was the 250th anniversary of his birth, and UNESCO had proclaimed it 'the Year of Kant.' The old rector was a Stalinist of the first order and he said no, Kant is strictly forbidden, nothing German is allowed. Well, Moscow intervened, and we had the conference, and each year we make microscopic advances. Someday we will have an international institute of Kant here, so that researchers can come and have a special building just for Kant studies, to breathe Kant's air."

"The old university, I take it, was destroyed in the war?"

"Oh, completely so. The miracle is that the cathedral and his grave survived. Everything was burning, an extraordinary situation of complete mass destruction, and yet Kant's tomb survived as if by magic. That was a lesson, I think, for Kantians everywhere. Though our senses and our rationalism both indicated utter ruination, still something of beauty can avoid disappearing. People think Kant is dry and academic, no life force, but the fate of his grave indicates mystery at work."

"Do you think Kant has any meaning today?"

"Without doubt, yes. As a famous German professor said, 'To go back to Kant means to go forward.' Take for my meaning three examples in current affairs. Marxism considers community as the major purpose for a human being's existence; in other words you involve yourself in society's goals to further the purpose of the state. Kant said just the reverse, that a human being has his own role and destiny to achieve in the moral order of things which lie beyond what the state should interfere with. This is a good idea for the times we live in.

"Secondly, Kant's notion of absolute moral laws transcend the narrow, ethnic, and nationalistic limits that governments or schools of thought such as communism insist upon. Kant felt no borders could prevent a person the freedom to live without restraint where he wanted, both physically and spiritually. This idea is modern and important for us as Russian society begins to open.

"And third, Kant said—or implied, I should say—that if we seek to secure peace for ourselves by resorting to armies and weaponry, then we guarantee a permanent peace: underground, all in the cemetery together. True security can be provided only by collective agreements, signing treaties as in the United Nations. This idea is related to Kant's on human nature, the possibilities of human attitudes. As I say to my students, I want to demonstrate how the ideas of Kant are not just thoughts of the eighteenth century, a collection of antiques. Kant managed to penetrate into the ethos of our own times. His ideas are universal."

⊱⊰

We are headed for Eylau at the Polish border, but on the way out of the city I am first shown a controversial highway project that is intended to link Kaliningrad with Berlin. The Russians have started their share of this enterprise, but the Poles have not, for obvious historical reasons. "Why build a road for Germans to use the next time they invade us?" a student in Warsaw said to me. From the look of things, this ambitious undertaking (in Eastern European terms, that is) will never be completed. A few miles are ready to drive on, and a new bridge is finished over the Pregel right alongside its dynamited predecessor from World War II. But other than that, little progress or activity can be seen. A single earthmoving machine and a single truck sit abandoned on the roadwork, no construction people visible anywhere. My driver shrugs, and soon we are lurching along the thinly maintained "grand route" south to the border, stopping occasionally to view what remaining sights there might be left to visit.

At Nordenburg we pull over to see a ruined German church. In the crow-infested chancel, amid cow dung, broken bottles, and piles of partially burned garbage from home and farm, a single commemorative slab dating from the early seventeenth century lies still embedded in the wall. I cannot help pointing out this remarkable relic to my interpreter, who couldn't care less. "That is the past," she says. "It is of no value to me or to anyone else. What the vandals began, let them finish. In a year this stone will all be in pieces, and no one will care." Clearly bored, she returns to the car to wait until I'm finished.

Coming out of the church in a few minutes, I am greeted by a scene straight from the silent cinema of Charlie Chaplin. A decrepit old truck, weaving back and forth over the road, sideswipes a utility pole, entangling a welter of wires in its bumper and ancient headlights. Like some game fish taking a lure, it continues a few hundred veering yards, the air full of pings as cables snap from their moorings, hissing and sparking when they hit the ground or anything metal. I take off, fearing electrocution, but passersby don't miss a step. The drunken originator of this municipal chaos staggers out from his wire-entangled cab and miraculously dances with death in a tango of sidesteps and pirouettes before reaching the sidewalk. I take his picture as he vomits by a pole. My driver says it will take a year to restore service to this village. "Repairs take time," he says, "and no one is important enough here to demand attention." We finally reach Eylau and eat a sandwich while parked by the ruined barns of an old Cistercian monastery. "These are still in use," my interpreter tells me. I would never have guessed.

*Drunkard*

We have come here, at my insistence, to tour the battlefield of Eylau. For many reasons, this horrific engagement from the winter of 1807 has always enthralled me. Perhaps it is Antoine Gros's famous painting, now in the Louvre, showing the emperor Napoleon, shivering in a silver, fur-lined coat, riding over the corpse-strewn field, his skin a ghastly greenish pale, those conquering eyes bereft, it seems, of satisfaction; or perhaps it is mere perversity on my part, seeking to explore an action, a campaign, about which most people know very little—"Who remembers Eylau?" as even a French historian admitted. Actually, the answer is quite simple. Eylau should be seen as a portent of what was to face the emperor five years later when he launched what many commentators have called the most ambitious military expedition ever yet attempted, the invasion of Russia. If Napoleon, not a reflective man perhaps, but capable all the same of intense concentration, had stopped for a minute to recall what actually happened on that seventh of February in 1807, he may well have entirely reconsidered the Russian adventure, which, in the end, precipitated his downfall. He could have seen the bloody future sprawled across the freshly fallen snows of Ostpreussen.

⫚⫚⫚

It is Russia, of course, that provides dramatic background to this terrain; whether we're speaking here of Prussian history or Napoleon's makes little difference. The Russian state, though primitive, ill organized, still a cipher to the Europe of London, Paris, and Vienna, nonetheless could then be seen emerging from its antiquated past. The immensity of landscape, stoicism of character, volume of population and resources were as yet of a scale unappreciated in the West. Relatively meager societies like Sweden thought nothing of declaring war on Russia, just as the Teutonic Knights, Lithuanians, and Poles before them had for centuries, a boldness that we of modern times, given our cold-war perception of Russia as colossus, must think of as near insanity. In primitive and medieval times, the great bulk of Russian strength was beyond the puny powers of tsars, courts, and boyars to organize, but the Napoleonic era sets for us a benchmark. Slow and lumbering Russia remained a heavy sledge, brought to bear on military and economic issues only with difficulty and considerable effort, but its power, when applied, began to arouse the attention of those on whom it was aimed. Napoleon could be excused, perhaps, for failing to see this in time. Whether Hitler had the same excuse is rather more open to question.

Russia bore the brunt of Napoleon's 1807 campaign because it was the only power left standing on the field of hostilities, save Britain, which hardly counted out here on the eastern borders. Prussia, the mighty Prussia of Frederick the Great, had utterly dissolved in a single battle, the calamitous engagements at Jena and Auerstädt in 1806, followed as it was by a succession of surrenders (many without a fight) of key fortresses stocked with a bounty of arms and munitions. These debacles astonished a European audience brought up for years on the dictum of Prussian invincibility. Napoleon himself could hardly believe it. As the queen of Prussia remarked, "We fell asleep in the shadow of Frederick the Great," and few could dispute her statement as French troops marched into Berlin. Parvenu that he was, Napoleon and his generals bantered in the crypt beneath Potsdam's garrison church at the foot of Frederick's tomb, the plainness of which amazed the garish French. Napoleon helped himself to several souvenirs. It is said he unsheathed Frederick's jewel-encrusted sword and waved it in the air.

Stagnation was not the special preserve of Prussia. What spelled its doom, along with that of monarchial Europe in general, were the incendiary proceedings of revolutionary France, spilling outward beyond its border with notions both bizarre and alien, to say nothing of dangerous. Fanning the conflagration were French bayonets in a revolutionary army that numbered an astonishing 1 million men by 1794, all eager for foreign adventure, whatever the guise or slogan. "The French require a prince to be active, enterprising and courageous, and above all to take them robbing abroad," said Napoleon, who managed in his military career of twenty-three years to fight some sixty battles from Spain to Moscow, from Egypt to the northern Prussian plains of Eylau.

Napoleon's transformation from Corsican adventurer to self-proclaimed emperor of France is one of those few sagas in human history about which many ordinary people know a great deal, not a happenstance common to this era of universal ignorance. More books, articles, plays, analyses, sketches, and dramas have been written about this singular personality than probably anyone other than Christ himself, and his mercurial personality of a thousand shades is no doubt the partial explanation.*

The French themselves were always doubtful of his sincerity. Was he committed to the revolution or personal gain? Did his love of France outshine his love of self? Were his soldiers of any regard to him or only the cannon fodder required by destiny? Did he have a mission guiding his path—the regeneration of Europe—or was he heart and soul but another Wallenstein, an unscrupulous freebooter like so many others who have trooped across the European landscape? Was he a military genius or just a lucky man? And if France was confused, what about everyone else in Europe?

On one facet of his personality, there was certainly universal agreement. "Boney," as Wellington coldly put him down, "is not a gentleman." But by 1807, gentleman or no, he was certainly at the height of his prowess, managing with enormous political skill to subvert riot

*A biographer in 1933 estimated that over 30,000 titles concerning Napoleon had been written, based not only on the events of his career witnessed and commented upon by numberless contemporary observers but also the output of his own pen. Napoleon is said to have dashed off some 60,000 letters, memos, and orders, of which over 40,000 are in print.

and social disorder into a self-serving force that essentially positioned him at the pinnacle of power within a changing France. That he was a victorious general was of enormous importance to this rise, a common attribute to the run-of-the-mill strongman who happens to seize power through coup d'état, but Napoleon added several components unique to himself that separated his career from the ordinary. Courageous, disciplined, organized, eloquent, master of the grand gesture, possessed of vision and altruistic principle when necessary, he was a man who had a sliver of himself to give every stratum of society no matter how contradictory his character or behavior. No other gesture so became him than his coronation of 1804, just a few short years after anyone with a title or an ounce of royal blood was liable to the guillotine. He was at once the common man placing a crown on his own head yet also a majesty in his own right, worthy of all the silly pomp he had himself mocked earlier in life. If he had not appealed so meaningfully to so many, he never could have sullied the great cathedral of Notre Dame with a performance so glorious and yet so vacuous. Europe was a harlot, he had declared. In that case Notre Dame was surely a brothel, an opinion no one seemed to share on that happy afternoon of 1804.

Though not particularly innovative as a strategist or field commander, he was without question the quickest thinker of any contemporary, a master of assessment and rapid decision. Often outmaneuvered conceptually, he had the uncanny ability to turn a crumbling situation to his own favor. His mobility doomed many an opponent's advantaged position or preconceived plan of battle. Napoleon's greatest weapon could often be the rigidity of his enemy's mind. Opportunism was a quality he possessed in abundance.

The Prussian army, by contrast, was a moribund, creaking vehicle waiting for the blow that might splinter it. Whereas the energetic armies of France were now filled with a free people running amuck with glorious slogans of *Liberté, égalité, et fraternité,* Prussian forces remained a "penal institution" noted for the perfection of its field maneuvers, usually achieved through faultless discipline and obedience to orders. Exactitude of performance, however, was guaranteed only by the most primitive of methods—the club, the knot, the swagger stick, the running of a gauntlet. Recruits were routinely beaten and brutalized; independent thought was treated as anathema. The command of the army grew top-heavy with aristocrats and Junker sons whose contempt for the common man was legendary.

As has always been the case, however, warfare was changing. Frederick the Great's marvelous riposte of maneuver and counterfeint was no match for an opponent who demanded resolution, who would give battle regardless of terrain—"You engage," as Napoleon said, "then you wait and see." And no longer could the military mind focus on the narrow front before him, hoping to master the destiny of a campaign by mastering the few hundred yards of his left or right wings. Students of the art of war could examine the ancient battles of Caesar and Hannibal all they wished, hoping to apply past tactics to current circumstance. But to manage a classic envelopment as was the case at Cannae now required an arena of operations that simply dwarfed those of the classical past. A typical battlefield of the Napoleonic era could well be 60 miles in length and involve 200,000 men, statistics that would have rocked Frederick the Great (or, with his personality, might well have excited him). Napoleon's "line" of 1814 stretched across the Continent as the crow flies from Hamburg to the Bohemian foothills south of Dresden, in effect from sea to mountain, where no flank could theoretically be turned. Ingenuity and spatial conception were now required of the Hohenzollern kings and their generals, and these were commodities in very short supply.

The successors to Frederick the Great were men of modest abilities. Frederick's immediate heir, in fact (a nephew—Frederick had not visited the bed of his wife since 1740, or forty-six years before he died), was so overwhelmed by the military burden that he relinquished it to his generals, aides, mistresses—whomever he felt he could trust. This of course gave rise to cabals, jealousies, and aristocratic squabbles over rank and precedence, all to the general neglect of strategic analysis.* This is not to say the army did not march and maneuver. It did, with precision. But at Jena the rigidity of thought and inherent conservatism of the officer corps threw away whatever chance of success Prussia might have had there.

Jena was the twin of Austerlitz, Napoleon's magnificent triumph of the previous year, 1805. In the latter engagement Napoleon annihi-

---

*Prussian forces at the rout of Jena, for example, were divided in three, partially to accommodate Prince Hohoenloe, who considered it beneath his dignity to serve under the commander in chief, a duke. The duke in question then deferred to the king, whose unanticipated arrival on the battlefield threw court etiquette into turmoil. The king, militarily inexperienced, relied on the duke but muddied the waters by interjecting advice of grotesquely amateurish character that some officers considered themselves dutybound to accept, however disastrous to the outcome.

lated Austria's willingness to continue war with France. At Jena he
pretty much annihilated the entire Prussian army.

It was a battle Prussia need not have fought. Obsessed and distracted with the feeding frenzy on Poland's former domains, Prussia
had come too late to the coalition opposing Napoleon along the Rhine.
Diplomatically outwitted by the scheming emperor, blundering from
one inauspicious policy decision to another, Prussia suddenly found
itself where no country wishes to be, alone and in a bind. A dithering
king and a strong-minded queen—never a happy combination—both
surrounded by bellicose though feuding soldiers, resolved to fight.
Napoleon scorned their whimsy. "If the King and Queen want to see a
battle, they will have this gruesome delight," he wrote Josephine in
Paris. "I feel splendid." On October 14 he took 27,000 men, dead or as
captives, colors beyond counting, and some 200 artillery pieces. Prussian discipline, perfect in any advance, dissolved when defeat became
apparent, precipitating one of the most ignominious routs ever known
to German history. The Hohenzollerns fled to Königsberg as Napoleon
sat at the queen's desk in Berlin and read her mail.*

German writers generally view the Napoleonic catastrophe as the
inevitable trial by fire that always precedes purification, a pattern of
racial behavior, to put it another way, that refuses to accept any defeat
as final or irrevocable. The prestige and glory that Frederick the Great
had bequeathed to Prussia was noble beyond all expression, but that
formidable commander's reliance on his aristocracy as the backbone
of army command was now perceived by many as inadequate for the
times confronting them, a Napoleonic era that valued competence
over bloodline. Many generals in the French army had been butchers,
grocers, even peasants in their prerevolutionary lives, and no matter
how foppish they might appear in plumes and cockades, there was no
denying their élan and skill.

Certainly the Prussian humiliation of 1806 was most keenly felt
among the professional military, many of plebeian or minor gentry
status themselves, who had seen their reputation gone asunder, their

---

*The emperor was piqued that at Jena he had not defeated the main body of the Prus-
sian army as he originally thought, only one of its wings. At the village of Auerstädt,
some dozen miles away, Davout routed a force three times larger than his own and secured the greater victory. "Glory was what he chiefly lived on," wrote one of
Napoleon's generals later, and "it should excite no surprise that in his triumphal bulletin of the following day, he chose to merge Auerstädt with his own Jena."

honor sullied, and their competence questioned, often through actions initiated by noble though maladroit commanders. In the distractions of defeat, to say nothing of its carnage, the spirit of reform perked its way through the ranks of disgruntled officers. These were often lonely men, despised by many as parvenus, discounted by most, ignored by the royal court itself, who persevered mostly out of devotion to their profession and to their fellow "conspirators." At first they made up a very small percentage of the Prussian officer corps, but ideas they espoused eventually molded a German army the world would again come to fear just a century later.

The prophet was Gerhard Johann Scharnhorst, a Hanoverian by birth, whose family and relations were farmers, millers, and fishmongers. His military education, not surprisingly, was at first that of artillery. He did not, from contemporary accounts, cut a very dashing figure, and his work seemed to many of a somewhat literary and thus unheroic bent. As was usual for the times, he sought and received employment in several of the various armies that were busily fighting France, generally hiring on where the pay was highest. Considering the age and his profession, neither conducive to scholarly pursuit, Scharnhorst can only be regarded as an intellectual man. He actually wrote for a living, founding a military journal and jotting off essays of observation and critique on the military issues of his day. In 1801 he joined the Prussian service, was present at the disaster of Jena-Auerstädt, and amid the disorder of retreat, "filled with disgust at the sight of suddenly dispirited generals," he attached himself to the rear guard of Marshal Gebhard Blücher, later the hero of Waterloo.

Blücher has been charitably described as a man "of ardent and vivid temperament," which naturally means he was an uneducated, boorish individual given to excessive behavior both on and off the battlefield. No one ever questioned his bravery—at age seventy-three he could still find himself in the thick of things, being trampled near to death by a squadron of French cuirassiers in Belgium—but few ever thought to overwhelm the marshal with praise for his intelligence.

In the squalid retreat before the French in 1806, however, only Blücher distinguished himself, and over the monthlong rear guard action he found himself relying on Scharnhorst, who seemed always to be at his elbow. In this strange friendship can be seen the origins of the German general staff.

Frederick the Great never had the need for a right-hand man. He viewed the field and gave his orders, and officers were in attendance for the sole purpose of carrying them out. By the nineteenth century, however, battlefields were too immense, forces too big, and foes too numerous for any single individual to handle. Great commanders took to leaning on their generals for advice. Engineering, logistics, supply, artillery—these areas of specialization (and others) were breeding expert officers in single fields of the service who knew more in their departments than any commander in chief could ever hope to master on his own. Blücher was a man of action, but Scharnhorst, master of theory, could direct, advise, and intellectualize the landscape, point out the little niceties of tactics or grander strategy that a bull such as Blücher might miss. Blücher himself recognized this dependence and gratefully accepted it, but a relationship of this sort can be tricky. Who would garner the praise for victory or the shame of defeat, the man whose idea it was or the man who gave the order?

In Scharnhorst we find the exemplar of what was soon to be the Prussian ideal: anonymity. In modern times this trait was deemed sinister. After both world wars the desire was acute to criminalize the often nameless officer corps who toiled in obscurity, marking maps, adjusting timetables, arranging depots for ammunition and fuel, scheduling troop movements, and fomenting strategy. At Nuremberg in 1946, the entire apparatus of the general staff was actually indicted for war crimes. But after 1806 the selfless character of a staff officer was the highest virtue.* Scharnhorst could have held supreme command of Prussia's forces in the 1813 coalition against Napoleon but chose Blücher instead, whom he served as chief of staff.

Over time a general staff independent of field commanders would evolve, giving orders that generals in the field were expected to obey. In the complicated theaters of operations in World War II, for example, when German armies were engaged on several fronts hundreds of miles from home, a central enterprise issuing directives and supplies was indispensable. By then, of course, the staff had in its turn become a haven for the elite. Their disgust at being led by a rank amateur such as Hitler, the former corporal, leaves little to the imagination.

Blücher and Scharnhorst surrendered their tattered remnants of force before Lübeck in November 1806. By then Napoleon had proceeded with the Grande Armée to Warsaw, relieving Prussia of its Pol-

*This dictum was most famously expressed by Alfred von Schlieffen. "General Staff officers have no names," he said. Nietzsche wrote admiringly that the Prussian officer corps was "the work of art where it appears without an artist."

ish spoils and raising the hopes of fervid nationalists there that the country might be reconstituted once again. Napoleon hinted at such a restoration but called for recruits as a show of personal commitment. No nationality would support the emperor with more zeal than the Poles, once again committing themselves to a losing cause.*

Scharnhorst was eventually exchanged for one of Napoleon's captured generals, Claude Victor, a former drummer boy in the revolutionary army. For all intents and purposes, Prussia was now out of the war. Only Russians remained in the field, and toward them major elements of French forces headed, leaving Warsaw with the emperor on December 23, aiming straight for the heart of East Prussia.

No march had as yet discouraged the ordinary foot soldier of France as this one did. Poland was a country without roads or even cart tracks, the soil a watery mire as frost and alternating thaws turned the army's course to mud. It has been said by observers that their advance resembled a giant caterpillar, the main body of men a long black streak on the plains, flanked on either side by huge clouds of dust and debris as outriders scavenged the countryside for supplies and fodder. Napoleon had expected more of a breadbasket from the Polish countryside, not the empty, cavernous steppe that it truly was. The troops starved, making millionaires of enterprising Jews who rode alongside selling sundries and food to the hungry men until they, too, their wagons empty, turned around and headed back to Warsaw. Soldiers learned two phrases in Polish: "Any bread?" and "Any water?" Fights broke out over the few rations still available; order broke down. As Napoleon himself estimated, by the 28th of December over 40 percent of his men were off on their own, scrounging for food. Meanwhile, it started turning cold.

For once, it was Napoleon who was caught off guard. Failing to engage the Russian army under the sixty-five-year-old Count Levin von Bennigsen in decisive battle, he dispersed his troops from the Baltic to Warsaw for winter quartering. The countryside suffered grievously as soldiers from both armies foraged continuously. But as Napoleon plotted his geopolitical future, Bennigsen moved, hoping to isolate Marshal Michel Ney, whose position was too exposed in the town of Soldau. This bold maneuver brought out the best in Napoleon's character, as he quickly formulated a riposte designed to encircle the Russians

---

*Of the 82,000 Poles who made up V Corps of Napoleon's Grand Armée that invaded Russia in 1812, only 2,300 returned alive.

and destroy them, and had not a courier been captured with a dispatch detailing the emperor's plans, Bennigsen might never have realized the trap about to engulf him. Withdrawing from the noose, he retreated toward Eylau.

No Frenchman, need it be said, relished the notion of marching to and fro through the wasted, frozen landscape of East Prussia, hungry as he was and hating the frigid winds that tore through his greatcoat. To the professional officer, however, it was the game that counted, the hunt for prey, the noble "art" of war undertaken no matter the weather or season of the year. Baron Antoine-Henri Jomini, a Swiss professional under salary to the French, whose theoretical works on military practice would equal in prominence those of von Clausewitz, saw Napoleon's qualities as a field commander in four general areas: his flexibility, his use of surprise, his offensive spirit, and most important, his concentration of force. The sport with Bennigsen involved all these elements, and Jomini, who fought at Eylau, reveled in it. During the height of this gruesome battle, Jomini could detach himself from the bloody business at hand and conceptualize himself as the enemy. "If I were the Russian commander for but two hours!" he was heard to say. Never were men such as he so exhilarated. Von Clausewitz equated battle with his wedding night.

The one constant of Napoleonic purpose was to bring one's enemy to bay for the great climactic battle. Time after time throughout his career, Napoleon would extend one of his divisions—self-sustaining, with cavalry, light infantry, and cannon—far to the front to nip at the heels of his opponent, "to stick the sword in his back," as an old French maxim had it, hoping to lure one's foe into a stand and a fight. The trick was then to follow up with the main force with all due speed, if possible in two wings, to envelope the enemy, perhaps encircle him, but in any event to engage him. At Eylau Bennigsen decided to hold his ground.

In fourteen years of active military experience, Napoleon had yet to suffer a major reverse, incredible as that may be to realize. But at Eylau he did. On the bitterly cold day of February 8, 1807, in the midst of blinding snow squalls and piercing winds, a scene of unparalleled butchery unfolded. The old French veteran Pierre Augereau, his head wound tight with a scarf, led his infantry to the attack. Each soldier barely able to see the man next to him, the entire immense column lost its direction, blundering en masse across the very head of the enemy. Russian grapeshot and musketry shredded the previously invincible Grande Armée with continuous broadsides. Augereau fell to the

Napoleon at Eylau *(detail from a painting by Antoine Gros, 1808)*

ground, as did 11,000 of his men, opening a tremendous hole in Napoleon's line. As the Russians prepared to move forward, however, the emperor launched a saving stroke unheard of in the annals of warfare, sending his entire cavalry strength of over 10,000 men into the breach. Lead by Marshal Joachim Murat, "that spoilt child of glory," resplendent in a wild outfit of satin and jewels, waving a cane with gold top, this wall of horseflesh battered the first Russian line, plowed through the second, and pierced the third. It then wheeled, sabers slashing, and plunged through the sea of bodies back again to its own lines. In this, the largest cavalry charge ever seen by any contemporary, losses by the French were grievous, but a bold stroke of immense force had saved the day. Scharnhorst, commanding his few Prussians on a wing, prevented a French victory by attacking an advancing Ney in the flank, and by the end of the day the two armies lay in bloody stalemate—frozen, exhausted, dying.

Who had won? Napoleon didn't know. "What news? What news?" he cried to couriers reporting to his bivouac. That evening he entered the charnel house of his medical corps and ordered the doctors out. The amputation block was wiped down, maps spread across it, and candles brought closer. Generals, colonels, aides, messengers, the emperor himself, stumbling over severed arms and legs scattered on the ground, studied their options. "The Russians have done us great harm," the emperor was heard to mutter, but in the middle of the night word came in that Bennigsen had withdrawn. To Napoleon, whoever stands on the field, "armored in constancy," as he put it, was indubitably the victor. The next day he issued a customarily bombastic proclamation, to be galloped all the way to Paris, proclaiming a triumph he himself was never certain belonged to him.

The scene of that following morning appalled all who witnessed it. One general declared, "I have never seen so many dead collected in such a small place. Whole divisions, Russian and French, had been hacked to pieces where they stood, and for more than a quarter of a league there was nothing to be seen but heaps of dead bodies. An enormous number of horses had been killed as well, which enhanced the bloody effect of this picture." Marshal Ney, never a man to quail at the sight of mayhem, exclaimed, "What a shambles—and no result!"

For Napoleon, this first considerable setback had no immediate effect. He possessed that remarkable ability common to all the great commanders of putting the past behind, often as quickly as it took him to gallop off the battlefield, leaving the wreckage for others to clean up. "What will Paris say?" was often the initial consideration to enter his practical mind, followed up by putting into motion whatever was required to gloss any untoward happening. Soldiers were forbidden to grieve. As the emperor rode past Eylau, he saw black ribbons wrapped around a regimental pike, which caused him "some resentment."

"I never wish to see my standards in mourning," he yelled. "We have lost a good many of our friends and brave comrades. But they died on the field of honor. Their fate is enviable." This was greeted by cries of, "Long live peace!" and "Bread!"

⁂

For his solace, Napoleon took up quarters in Finckenstein, its Prussian overlords having fled their manor house for Königsberg, along with all the other Junkers of the neighborhood. It is said the emperor was relieved to find more or less sumptuous apartments in this God-forsaken province—"Finally," he exclaimed, "a chateau!" Here for six weeks he found additional comfort in the arms of an eighteen-year-old Polish countess who had caught his eye at a ball in Warsaw. To give him credit, Napoleon appears to have deeply loved this winsome creature, unlike most of the women that were thrown his way by members of

*Napoleon's headquarters, Finckenstein*

his procuring household. Napoleon's valet recounted a Berlin tryst where a teenage girl had so drenched herself in perfume that the emperor had a fit of nausea. The only words she reportedly said in the course of lovemaking were, "Das ist miserable" and "Das ist gut."

Marie, Countess Walewska, was a different sort. Though married to an aged nobleman (evidently for cash, her family being impoverished), she was virginal in appearance and coy when besieged with letters and flowers by the infatuated Napoleon. "Kings do not sigh long in vain," however, an intimate of the household wrote afterward; "they cast too heavy a wait in the balances of discretion." The affair was passionate on both sides, and Marie was to appear, fitfully, throughout the emperor's life, at times for only a night or two, at others for a stretch of weeks or months. When least expected, she could appear in coach at his doorstep, often carrying the infant son that Napoleon openly acknowledged as his own.* Out of the imperial treasury 10,0000 francs a

---

*Alexandre Walewski, the issue of this liaison, had an active youth evading conscription to the Russian army. He later entered the French diplomatic service, and his career, unspectacular to that date, bloomed with the rise to power of Napoleon III in 1852. Marie eventually remarried, this time to a French nobleman, the news of which Napoleon heard on Elba. "She is rich," he said. She died in childbirth, 1817.

month were transferred to the countess, who, according to Napoleon, was thrifty and saved most of it, a fortunate circumstance when the money stopped after Waterloo. During the frigid months that followed Eylau, in the opulent drawing rooms of Finckenstein, Napoleon ran his empire's business, issuing commands, receiving ambassadors— some of the outlandish variety, from Persia and Turkey—and plotting his future campaigns. Marie occupied the room adjacent to his. She was rarely seen out of doors.*

In June, bursting east from the Prussian heartland, he resumed the pursuit of Bennigsen and lured his older opponent into battle at Friedland, another small town just a few miles from Eylau. Napoleon's advance division, under Jean Lannes, had tempted Bennigsen by its inferior numbers. The Russian general turned at Friedland, his back to town and river (a fatal error), intending to devour the leading French who had followed too closely. But the art of skillful maneuver had yet to be mastered by the laboring Russians. It was well past 2 P.M. before Bennigsen could arrange his lines and batteries, by which time Napoleon had arrived in full force, sending enveloping wings to cut off avenues of retreat. Bennigsen must have gulped when he realized what had happened, faced as he was with superior strength and hemmed in by a cramped little village tucked in a river's bend.

Successful attacks by the emperor pushed both Russian wings back onto their constricted center. Friedland erupted in flames; bridges crumbled; Russians were slaughtered as they waded or attempted to swim toward safety. French batteries that day were the real killers, firing grape and canister into mobs of panicked soldiery, 10,000 of whom were dead by evening. Riding through Friedland after the battle, a Frenchman noted his horse's four legs bathed in blood from wading through the heap of corpses.

This overwhelming victory brought Tsar Alexander I to the conference table immediately, a political denouement without which Napoleon never considered his battles complete. Their famous meeting, on a raft moored in the center of the Memel (the Niemen), isolated Great Britain as the only opponent left whom Napoleon had not swept aside, and for that the English Channel seemed mostly due the

---

*Finckenstein was used as a stage set in 1934 when Metro-Goldwyn-Mayer filmed *Conquest,* starring Charles Boyer as Napoleon and Greta Garbo as Marie. The picture was a box office disaster and generally regarded as the beginning of the end for Garbo's career as a leading lady.

credit. Prussia lost half its territory and essentially took on the status of a client state to the French, liable in any future campaigns to levies of money and troops. It was left little self-esteem in the bargain, its king, in the words of the emperor, no more than "a blockhead."

As Goethe remarked after meeting the great conqueror, "Napoleon knew men well. He knew how to make use of their weakness." He rewarded his vainglorious marshals with treasure, spoils, estates, marriages, decorations, and best of all, titles, many signifying their role in the greatest victories. Thus Louis-Nicholas Davout was made duke of Auerstädt; Ney, duke of Elchingen; Augereau, duke of Castiglione; and Lannes, duke of Montebello. But Friedland Napoleon gave to no one. It was one of the four battles he reserved for himself, unwilling to share its glory with anyone.*

⚛

On my final day in Kaliningrad, I meet a Luftwaffe veteran, here to revisit his wartime base, wandering about the cathedral in a reflective mood. "In Dresden, the Frauenkirche—it had been destroyed by bombs during the war, in worse shape than even this—will be completely rebuilt in ten to fifteen years. But putting our cathedral back up here would take a century. Just like medieval times!"

The more revealing resuscitation, however, is that of Russian Orthodoxy. Touring the seacoast on Easter Thursday, I encounter a scene that would have disgusted some of the old Junker families who once owned these lands. Leaving a refurbished German church from the nineteenth century, a heavily robed Orthodox priest leads a procession consisting of eight seminarians, two deacons, thirty-five women, and three men around a village. Icons are held high; hymns loudly sung; incense curls through the scraggly pine woods. Russian bystanders on the sidewalk or strolling through the park appear stunned, as though viewing a scrapbook from the far distant past or perhaps a wish come true. Several cross themselves, hesitantly; some join the service; and most seem genuinely moved by the sonorous chants, particularly the heroic basso profundo bellowed forth by one heavily bearded bull in the choir. "Christ has risen!" yells the priest, splashing the face of his deacon with holy water so many times that vestment and face are soon dripping wet.

---

*Marengo, Austerlitz, and Jena were the others.

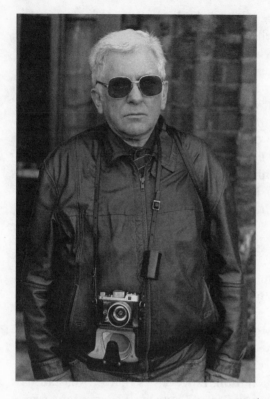

*Luftwaffe veteran at cathedral*

After the service I inquire as to the spiritual progress of the mission here. "We are starting from the very beginning," the priest tells me. "The Russian people, they have no memory of God's word whatsoever. There is a reflex in their minds and bodies left over from several centuries of devotion—they know how to cross themselves, they know to take their hats off in church—but they have no idea what any of it means. It may seem too dramatic to say this, but holy Russia is now a field for missionaries. We have lived for a hundred years through a Dark Ages, and the light must be brought here anew."

In the meantime, some purveyors of "the light" wear a different sort of uniform. In a throwback to the more autocratic days of yore (in fact, to just a year or so ago), a semimilitary force has recently been organized to combat the spectacular rise in crime that plagues Kaliningrad. An evening driving about at high speeds with a three-man patrol would not remind any American of life in his or her down-home ghetto. At least there a semblance of civilian rights can still be recog-

*Orthodox priest and deacon*

nized, but in Kaliningrad the urge to restore order—or in the words of the young officer commanding this rambunctious jeepload of militia, to keep even—recognizes none of the little niceties of justice to which we pay lip service with our Miranda rights. Public drunks, streetwalkers, anyone seen with drugs, rowdy street brawlers, and purse snatchers all get the same rough treatment. Bashed around with clubs, firearms waved in their faces, cuffed and thrown roughly into paddy wagons, these miscreants are hauled off to jail by the dozens every night. Several arrests that I witness are bloody affairs indeed, though strangely good-humored. After the action, officers and "detainees" often share a laugh.

⟡

On my return trip to Poland, the Kaliningrad Express is again sparsely peopled, about a hundred passengers. At the border everyone is cleared out onto the platform with luggage—everyone but me. I watch from the window as sullen men and women file into the same tiny shack that I had the pleasure of visiting just ten days before. Snippets of argument, cajoling, even crying can occasionally be heard. I see cartons of cigarettes, bottles of homemade vodka, and contraband I

*Arrested*

cannot identify come flying out a rear window onto a luggage cart. Some half dozen people are not allowed back on board. As we inch across into Poland, the mood suddenly becomes jovial. Flasks come out. Offers of a smoke go back and forth. Women flounce onto the floor, oblivious of the dirt and muck that sullies their overcoats, stuffing what liquor they still have underneath the springs of their seats. Next up, those angry Poles. By the time we finally reach Braniewo, my papers have been checked five times.

# Part Three

# BLOOD AND IRON
## Bismarck and Wilhelm

## ⚜ Select Chronology ⚜

| | |
|---|---|
| 1815–1848 | The Metternich system: Conservative rule in central Europe and German states. |
| 1830–1832, 1848 | Revolutionary disturbances in Germany and elsewhere. |
| 1848, March 15 | "March Days." King momentarily a hostage to the mob in Berlin. From 1848 on, numerous antagonisms between liberal and conservative movements, expressed in struggles between king and parliament. |
| 1862 | Otto von Bismarck appointed minister-president of Prussia, later named chancellor. |
| 1864 | Successful war with Denmark for the Schleswig-Holstein provinces. |
| 1866, July 3 | Climactic Battle of Königgratz obliterates Austrian claims to hegemony in north German affairs. |
| 1870, July 19 | France declares war on Germany. |
| September 1 | Prussian victory at Sedan; Napoleon III captured. |
| 1871, January 18 | German empire declared at Hall of Mirrors, Versailles: Germany united, William I of Prussia proclaimed emperor. Franco-Prussian War ends in complete victory for Prussia. |
| 1888 | Wilhelm II assumes the throne. |
| 1890 | Bismarck resigns under pressure from Wilhelm. |

### World War I

| Western Theater | | Eastern Theater | |
|---|---|---|---|
| 1914, | | | |
| August 4 | Germans invade Belgium, initiate Schlieffen Plan. | | |
| August 5–6 | Liège invested. | | |
| August 20 | Brussels occupied. | August 19–20 | Rennenkampf's initial "sortie in force" successful at Gumbinnen. German commander von |

| | | | Prittwitz contemplates retreat. |
|---|---|---|---|
| August 23 | Battle for Mons | August 23 | Von Prittwitz relieved. Von Hindenburg and Ludendorff arrive at Marienburg to assume command. |
| August 25 | Troops siphoned from right wing, entrained for eastern front. | | |
| | | August 26–30 | Tannenberg |
| August 30 | Extreme right wing forgoes western sweep around Paris, turns east, exposing flank. | | |
| September | Battle of the Marne, Schlieffen plan fails. | September 6–15 | Russians defeated at Battle of Masurian Lakes. |
| | | September 18 | Von Hindenburg made commander in chief of German armies east. |

⸎

| | |
|---|---|
| 1916, August 29 | Von Hindenburg named chief of the general staff. He and Ludendorff transfer to the command of western front. |
| 1918, March 21– August 7 | Last offensive attacks, designed by Ludendorff, of German forces in the west. |
| October 27 | Ludendorff resigns. |
| November 10 | Wilhelm abdicates, flees to the Netherlands. |

# 9

# Cadinen
## 1888
# Rush for Glory

*"You have a little cold."*
*"No, it is a big cold. Everything about me
must be big."*
**—Wilhelm II, 1906**

COPERNICUS CALLED FRAUENBURG on the Frisches Haff, along
the Baltic, "the remotest place on earth," and so it seems driving out
of town into rural landscape, cultivated, to be sure, but strangely devoid of life. Perhaps I read too much into all of this, but Ostpreussen
seems to the eye a contradictory, ironical sort of place. Catholics worship in Protestant churches; Poles own the soil of Prussian Junkers;
the faithful Copernicus sends his apostate manuscript to the heretics
for publication; scrub farmers piece together fragments of old German
china tilled up from summer gardens. "I have their estate; soon I'll
have their place settings, too," one said to me.

A few miles down the road is Cadinen, Kaiser Wilhelm II's former
stud farm, recently refurbished by a luxury hotel chain and appropriately glossy. This afternoon, quite clearly, the boss is away, since the
front desk has been commandeered by a jovial, bare-chested muscle-
man from out back in the stables. He is seated with feet on the guest
register, two receptionists on either side feeling up his biceps. They
greet me nonchalantly as though nothing untoward or undignified is

*Prewar military maneuvers: The kaiser instructs his generals*

going on and happily toss over the keys to Wilhelm's private chapel. Nothing but laughter and merriment follow me out the door.

Because of his stunted left arm, the young Wilhelm often had trouble handling horses, but with admirable Prussian stubbornness he always remounted after being tossed and became an adequate rider. At his writing desk, in fact, he spurned the customary chair, preferring to work on a specially mounted saddle, which must have been a curious sight indeed.

In *Thoughts and Adventures*, one of his interwar books churned out to keep creditors at bay, Winston Churchill, who thought the kaiser "an extraordinary man," described Wilhelm at the field maneuvers of 1906. Martinet that he was, the kaiser took command of what Churchill called "the Grand Finale," leading a charge of thirty cavalry squadrons uphill into the teeth of several "venomous-looking little cannon," a spectacle as ostentatious as it was absurd. Churchill, who "galloped along in the greatest glee," witnessed the happy outcome as umpires declared Wilhelm victor of the field, guided in their verdicts, no doubt, by the comic opera of 1890, when the kaiser was judged "deceased" after an equally impulsive mock melee with his horse guard. It has often been said (though denied) that von Hindenburg had been

*The kaiser's chapel*

forced into retirement that disastrous afternoon for allowing the kaiser full rein to this delusion.

There are stalls here at Cadinen for well over one hundred horses, and German businesspeople and nouveau riche entrepreneurs have acres of pasture and wood through which to roam. Those of more aristocratic lineage, I am told, avoid the place. They have estates of their own. And besides, who wants to be haunted by dead Hohenzollerns? Certainly the kaiser would have hated this place were he to be here now. His chapel still retains the faded outlines of fresco and scroll, and his pews, though scratched, are original to the little building. The flowers, however, are plastic, the vestments of a cheap and glimmering polyester, and the beaming visage of John Paul II would not be an image to soothe the royal temperament. "Well has it been said," wrote Churchill, "'Thought which cools the minds of other people, inflames the German.'"

⚞

As a prelude to Wilhelm's assumption of genuine (as opposed to purely ceremonial) political power, an event achieved when he dismissed the aged Bismarck in 1890, we have the long and tumultuous saga of the nineteenth century, a span of some seventy-five years between Waterloo and the unfettered kaiser. Without hesitation most conservative Germans would label these decades as the high point of their nation's existence: a period of liberation, reform, consolidation, industrial growth, and eventually the unification of Germany under Prussian auspices, the so-called Second Reich. The inherent contradiction in bandying about the word "Prussian" in any of these areas, however, is that Prussia itself, the nucleus of the old Teutonic March, was in fact peripheral in many ways to this stupendous national growth.

Essentially agrarian, cash poor, and needy, Prussia certainly contributed manpower to stock its famously unwavering army, no insignificant element to Germany's gradual emergence as a major player on the European scene but an unspectacular one just the same. The upper reaches of Prussia's officer corps briefly flirted with the principles of liberalism following Napoleon's defeat. But after 1819 the landed gentry and Junker classes, who monopolized the upper ranks of the armed forces, generally followed the policy of reaction and suppression of Austrian foreign minister Klemens von Metternich. Brief revolutionary scares in the early 1830s and 1848, most originating (as usual) from France, produced dreadful jolts throughout the country. The army, however, never hesitated in its support for Hohenzollern order above all else, be it "constitution" or "Germany," even as individual monarchs wavered during crisis, at times contemplating concessions to the mob or, after 1848, the newly formed parliament. The people and the legislature were synonymous evils in the opinion of Prussian generals. Field Marshal Friedrich von Wrangel in 1848 had no qualms about browbeating his sovereign when the latter proved fainthearted in dealing with contentious liberals. The king, he stated, would be court-martialed if he didn't do his duty.

The Prussian officer saw little need for compromise. Generally speaking, he had nothing in life worth owning. The agricultural crisis following Waterloo in 1815 had devastated the smaller Junker landowners of East Prussia in much the same fashion as it had bankrupted the minor gentry in obscure, far-flung corners of England and Ireland, but with one crucial difference: Junker poverty became, by necessity and even temperament, a source of pride, however bitterly attained. It was a matter of faith and honor that one's only possession was a uniform. Renunciation of worldly goods and service to the king became life's solitary justification. The notion of estate was measured by the dimensions of a barracks; one's family became fellow cadets at the military academy, then one's brother officers. German military codes of behavior, handed down from the Teutonic Knights themselves, stressed sacrifice and mission, neither of which is necessarily conducive to the accumulation of treasure or comfort. Exaggerated conceptions of honor and duty were usually the result, which tended to constrict the ordinary officer's breadth of vision, producing the narrow-minded, priggish stereotype of the Prussian officer that German liberals and later a worldwide population came to detest.

Nowhere was this more evident than in the socially backward and often semifeudal reaches of the East Prussian countryside, untouched by the workings of even its regional metropolis at Königsberg. This was the outback. Thus the memoirs of Field Marshal Colmar von der Goltz beatifically describe the Junker estate on which he was born in 1843, the thatched cottages of its peasantry barely differentiated from that of the paltry manor house in which his widowed mother strove so laboriously to keep family and farm together (she failed). Von Hindenburg himself—born on the Junker soil of his ancestors, a von Hindenburg among those killed at Grünwald in 1410—saw his family living hand to mouth in apartment buildings, a fate he stoically accepted. This was not an aristocracy bred to Greek and Roman classics or even the homegrown Kant, for that matter. Poverty and the threat of bankruptcy or forced sale kept these haughty minor landlords hard at work to ward off the wolf. Crops were sown and gathered, their peasant tenantry exploited wherever possible, and technological advances of the growing Germany were daily deprecated as threats to a deeply conservative way of life. Additionally, all manifestations of Poland—its religion, culture, and most particularly its language—were oppressed at every opportunity.

Bismarck's Second Reich directly threatened this constituency. Although a Junker as reactionary as the next, Bismarck had a larger desire that transcended the petty provincialism of his class—his own glorification. He saw the achievement of his personal destiny in direct correlation to a step-by-step plan to unify the northern German states into one nation dominated by Prussia. And by "Prussia" he did not mean the swampy hinterlands of Memel or the East Prussian steppes but its army and its king.

Bismarck was a classic guns-and-butter politician, a master of barter and intrigue both in his foreign and domestic policies. He had a knack for going too far when conventional wisdom dictated restraint and for pulling back when others, appealing to his well-known greed, cried to advance (noting perhaps his prodigious and appalling appetite—some of Bismarck's gastronomic intakes produce indigestion just in the retelling).

A fervent militarist and devotee of the crown, at least in the abstract, he distrusted most officers and considered the Hohenzollerns little better than dolts. He campaigned against socialists and liberals all his life, while simultaneously instituting progressive and—there is no other word for it—revolutionary schemes in education, health services, and insurance programs designed to better the lot of a hardworking proletariat. A juggler of impossible alliances, plots, and friendships, he ended up enshrined in German mythology but essentially unloved by all who knew him. To the Junkers of East Prussia, he was an out-and-out traitor.

In the course of but seven years, 1864–1871, Bismarck fought and won three wars. The first, with Austria as an ally, put Denmark in its place and secured the provinces of Schleswig and Holstein. The second, and most appalling to traditionalists, reduced Hapsburg Austria to a quaking shell at the Battle of Königgratz, after which the king of Prussia and his generals demanded a triumphal march into Vienna, which Bismarck denied them. This alone is proof of the man's undeniable authority, even majesty: to deflect a triumphant army's insatiable bent for flouting its victory in the enemy's capital is well nigh an impossibility. The third humbled France and Napoleon III. The latter individual, in the process of dying and less than enthusiastic for battle, was of no particular prize as an opponent, but his nation was another matter indeed—the world's most famous army, ineptly led, to be sure, but handled in straightforward fashion by the methodical Germans. This conflict resulted in the formal creation of the German empire at Versailles Palace on January 18, 1871, its Hall of Mirrors then full of generals in cuirasses and pointed helmets, their swords drawn and yelling Hunnish war cries to the new Emperor William I. Twenty-six independent German states and cities were now a single Germany under a single Prussian monarch.

William I no longer presided over a backward nation. All available statistics—regarding coal and steel production, armaments manufacture, construction of railroad lines, advancements in the chemical and electrical industries, education and literacy—demonstrate an unbelievable surge in productivity, much of which passed East Prussia by. The province had no coal as the Saar and Ruhr and Silesian fields spewed forth in plenty. It had no manufacturing firms the likes of

Siemens or AEG or Bayer and Hoechst. It had but the single university at Königsberg, and Wagner's interest in old German knighthood centered on the mythic Rhine, not the brambles of Lithuania. Prussia manned the great general staff, however, and there the ethos of the east flowered in the long line of dutiful, faceless officers, myopically poring over maps and planning each year for whatever inevitable war there was to come.

The mindset of the general staff was, of course, constant preparation. From meager beginnings in Scharnhorst's day, the staff by 1867 under the mythic Helmuth von Moltke had in effect taken command of the army, and had a man of forceful character such as Bismarck not been in control of diplomatic policy, it would have taken over the entire government as well, no doubt with disastrous result. As it was, the army consumed 25 percent of all incoming revenues, and with universal conscription and the Landwehr (or reserve army) touching with some obligation or another most every German male, its reach grew pervasive. Inescapably, the ethos of the army wound its way into the very fabric of everyday life to an extent entirely unwarranted given East Prussia's thin population and its often retrograde point of view.

The army was to some degree in a state of flux itself. The general staff was larger than ever before and no longer the special preserve of aristocrats. In 1871 the staff comprised 135 officers, a full third of whom were commoners. This reflected both the growing size of German armed forces and the pressing need for specialists in areas not hitherto associated with glory and renown, railroads being a fine example. Still, the influx of plebeians did not democratize headquarters on the Königsplatz in Berlin. Quite to the contrary, those who joined the elite sought to preserve and nourish its élan.

Controversies generally revolved around dealing with the parliamentary Reichstag over army budgets, one of the few areas of leverage that civilian legislators could find to influence military policy. Bismarck, von Moltke, and other conservatives were often infuriated by the nuisance of it all and periodically gave way to their passion by contemplating coups d'état and the scattering of their debating foes with force, but they usually won their way without extreme measures. More serious theoretical disagreements within the command apparatus were waged over the changing nature of warfare and, more particularly, identifying an opponent for the next war. There were certainly a myriad of options to consider. Germany's position in the center of Europe's landmass, with few defensible borders, made it extraordinarily vulnerable in the army's view. It was surrounded by a range of foes, all with sinister motives for attack, ranging from revenge (France) to racial animosity (the Slavic, Orthodox tsar). In general, from 1879 on plans were annually drawn up and reviewed that contemplated fighting on two fronts at once, no matter the state of relations east or west. According to one German historian, this resulted in a certain "morbidity" of view that was if anything quintessentially Prussian: the burden of fateful inevitability. The great Alfred von Schlieffen was in the habit of devising a military conundrum on Christmas Eve for his staff of protégés at general headquarters. He expected to receive its solution the next day. Singlemindedness was the vice, or virtue, of the general staff.

⁂

Klaus von Holleben, whose mother's family originally came from the Memel, guides me about his house. Family photographs invariably show ancestors in uniform, some on horseback, others in formal pose. "War to these men was their professional life, it was their career," he says. It is to me a fascinating collection, used as I am to my own parent's home, where snapshots of my great-grandfather in regalia from the Grand Army of the Republic, my father in naval uniform, my uncle from General George Patton's Third Army Group, along with various other relations in the service adorn the wall. Instead of Bronze Stars and Purple Hearts, I'm surrounded here by Iron Crosses.

"My family is one of military officers, civil servants, and diplomats for the most part. Since the Middle Ages we have always been officers, and as a matter of fact through marriage we are remotely related to von Clausewitz. Before World War I that was an exciting combination, I can tell you, but for today it has little meaning." We pause before a full-length portrait of a martial ancestor. "This is the sort of thing you had painted before you went off to war, in case you didn't come back. Quite mediocre." More self-deprecatory remarks follow. "My great-great-grandfather, and this will interest you, introduced underwear to the Prussian army." This figure turns out to be Count Albrecht Theodor Emil von Roon, the self-styled "king's sergeant" and war minister, whose duties and achievements went far beyond the realm of sanitary improvement.

Von Holleben is my age, born in 1945, and reflects the "little Germany" that seeks an almost anonymous immersion into the greater Europe of today. He is thoroughly conscious of other peoples' often

*Klaus von Holleben
with ancestor*

negative feelings about the determination and drive for which his fellow Germans are so well known. "We have a severe problem in this
country with history, with coming to grips with the past. But I honestly believe that the rest of Europe need not worry anymore about
'Germany' and 'German destiny.' You Americans should be proud of
the democratic system that you gave us after the war. These checks
and balances—the sort we'd never had before—will prevent war in the
future, and our educational system fully explains to all our young people the terrible errors of our historical behavior. They know all about
Hitler and Nazis, and I can say clearly that the loyalties we always
gave to officialdom—to the kaiser, for instance, then to Hitler—that's
all done. We are far beyond that."

Later we drive through wasteland in the former GDR and talk about
Prussia. "My family owned quite a stretch of forest over here before
the war. You could see it from the West. My father could never bring
himself to come to the border and look at it; that was a common reac-

tion [for] people of his generation. Frankly, even today I myself have a hard time dealing with its loss, and I wasn't even alive then. But most young people in Germany now, they lack this emotional hitch. I think I read that 75 percent of Germans today were born after 1945. The notion of Prussia has no meaning. As for the kaiser, many of them would pretend they had never heard of him."

※

One hundred years ago there were few people anywhere in Europe who had not heard the trumpet blasts of Kaiser Wilhelm II, a saber rattler of infernal energy whose varied pronouncements both amused and terrified newspaper readers everywhere, who were often unable to distinguish between high comedy and impending disaster.

Wilhelm had been introduced to the German body politic in a typically Prussian fashion. The crusty Field Marshal Wrangel had taken the newborn heir to the throne from his cradle to wave aloft before a Berlin crowd awaiting news outside the palace of this royal birth. Finding French doors blocking his entry to a balcony, Wrangel plunged his fist through the glass panels and pushed his way through. "Children, here's a fine recruit!" he bellowed to the mob.

But nature, as his aunt was to say, "did not fit Wilhelm for the soldier's life," his constitution being frail and his psyche undermined by the physical deformity of his left arm. In rather classic fashion he made up for these deficiencies by a bluster and a swagger that few of his more cultivated contemporaries could stand. Vain, pampered, excitable, and neurotic, Wilhelm merely confirmed Bismarck's low esteem of the Hohenzollern bloodline, the Iron Chancellor hoping (in vain, as it turned out) that Wilhelm's wife, "the Holstein cow," would help regenerate the family gene pool. It seems even his own parents disliked him. Wilhelm's father thought the crown prince "selfish and domineering"; his mother hoped "to put a padlock on his mouth." Inattentive to detail, easily bored and rather loutish, he insisted nonetheless that he be in charge of all the empire's governmental intricacies. One moment he might be plunging ahead for naval rearmament, the next threatening some neighbor with military annihilation. One morning he could be the sworn enemy of Russian pretensions, by afternoon a teary-eyed friend to the tsar for evermore. Few figures in modern European history have been so universally cast aside in capitulative judgments than this man. Bismarck's son mocked him with the sobriquet "Wilhelm the Great."

In 1890, impatient of restraint and certainly uncomprehending of Bismarck's more subtle appreciation of affairs (which after his initial flurry of battles had produced a span of twenty-two boring years unmarked by war or serious discord), Wilhelm dismissed his chancellor, a move that Hitler, for one, could not believe and compared with Nero's giving balls while Rome burned. The Führer ascribed such stupidity to strains of Jewish blood that somehow had infected the Hohenzollerns some generations before. The current Hohenzollern heir disagrees, however, saying in 1979 that "Bismarck was aspiring to establish a kind of shogunate and hoped to treat our family in the same way that Japanese shoguns treated the Japanese emperors in Kyoto. My grandfather had no other choice but to dismiss him." Be that as it may, Wilhelm's then solitary and unchecked plunge into global affairs set Germany on a tempestuous course that inevitably led to war, the likes of which the kaiser could neither comprehend nor stomach. He was the quintessential cardboard warrior.

❧

The prelude and outbreak of the Great War in 1914 is a historian's delight, a time and place in the affairs of Europe when honor was a concept still understood, respected, and obeyed. There were no villains on the stage, no one to compare with a Hitler or a Stalin, and there were no treacheries or undiagnosed pathologies to disfigure the rather straightforward diplomatic record. The web of alliances, the decorum of formal notes and ultimatums, and the almost leisured inevitability of conflict make for an ordered, chronological tale with an absolute abundance of official documentation. Entire volumes of prewar governmental correspondence between the powers is about as clear a trail as any detective could ever wish for. They illustrate the capacity of human beings for immense stupidity and pretension, but for the most part the aura of evil is hardly to be seen. There is something almost sanitized about the whole process, an innocence that four years of resulting combat, the destructive nature of which no human had ever witnessed, would bury forever. Great mechanisms slowly clicked into gear; mobilizations once started refused any effort at delay; war plans that would tolerate no deviation in timetables and forces dragged into combat nations that had no desire for it.

The kaiser, to take but one example, behaved in the few weeks before the outbreak of hostilities in his usual erratic fashion, warlike bravado alternating by the hour with a frenzied "search for peace." In the end, he who so fanned the excitement for war found it impossible to influence the final, creaking move toward bloodshed. This makes for a clear and very sorry picture.

For Germany, the war plans and objectives of nearly forty years went ahead almost monolithically. The two-front war—as unimaginable to most civilian observers in 1914 as it was in 1941—was nevertheless a mindset for the restless general staff. Each version may have differed in its detail (for instance, where to strike first, the east or the west), but the notion of fighting on all sides had become de rigueur. In its latest manifestation, the famous von Schlieffen plan, the strategy was to hit France with the initial blow, then turn on the slower Russians. The key was to envelop the French army with a rapid, numerically overwhelming surge of a right wing through neutral Belgium in order to trap the enemy against its eastern frontier in one vast, climactic "battle of annihilation." The notion of fixed and rigid lines leading to stagnant, draining, prolonged engagement was every German's nightmare, for lurking over the horizon in the East was the lumbering colossus of Russia, what Churchill at the time called "that mighty steamroller." Victory delayed in France meant a fearful day of reckoning on the banks of the Niemen or, even worse, the Vistula and Oder, but no other strategy seemed available. The German army could not simultaneously fight its two major enemies with enough force to beat either. But in 1914, as the first month of war began, such was the catastrophe facing the High Command.

German troops entered Belgium on Tuesday, August 4, and ruthlessly commenced the application of von Schlieffen's so far theoretical plan. Seven of the eight German armies began the immense flanking drive for which every disposition, objective, and schedule had been meticulously planned in advance. Delays at the great Belgian fortresses at Liège were irritating but not unduly disruptive to the all-important timetable, and the German wing crossed into France more or less as envisioned. Casualties on both sides were unexpectedly high, particularly for the French, who as yet had misunderstood the enemy's intentions and frittered away their strength through the misguided élan of *offensive à outrance,* or "offense at any price." The horrific five days of August 20 to 24, when the northeast frontier of France found itself engulfed in battle and pierced everywhere by German troops, were among the darkest in French military annals.

At German headquarters the chief of staff, Helmuth von Moltke (known as "von Moltke the Younger" to distinguish him from his famous uncle, "the Elder"), found his nervous system equally tormented. The great envelopment of France was proceeding just as von Schlieffen had predicted. The question was, could the German army sustain its momentum, maintain its strength, and essentially continue to dictate the character of battle as a gun-and-chase affair—the very mobility von Schlieffen's ghost demanded? But with all eyes riveted on France, von Moltke heard news that shriveled his spirits. Contrary to all expectations, the Russians had launched not one but two field armies toward the core of East Prussia, forces that totaled well over half a million men and something like 600 pieces of artillery. The sacred soil of Germany, the emotional heartland of its martial spirit, was being trampled by barbarians just as Paris lay within reach of German arms. What good a triumphal march down the Champs-Elysées if Cossacks put Berlin to the torch? Such was the inevitable result should the sole German army in the East, the Eighth, numbering only 210,000 men, be brushed aside, and that seemed unavoidable.

Von Moltke could hardly stand the strain. A man of great abilities but incapable, as he had warned the kaiser, of generating the sangfroid that every great commander must sustain during crisis, he saw himself staring down the abyss of utter ruin. His knees may have shaken even more when he spoke by telephone on August 20 with Max von Prittwitz, commander of the Eighth and a favorite of the kaiser. Von Prittwitz, known as "Fatty" to his fellow officers, reported that his forces had been sufficiently bloodied by one of the Russian pincers and threatened in the rear by the other, that a withdrawal beyond the Vistula was now necessary. East Prussia was to be abandoned.

## ⚜ 10 ⚜
# Tannenberg
## 1914
# The Siamese Twins

> World history knows three great battles of annihilation: Cannae, Sedan, and Tannenberg.
>
> —**Adolf Hitler**

THERE ARE NO SIGNS to direct a traveler to the site of Paul von Hindenburg's first grave, the great mausoleum of Tannenberg, which the Wehrmacht blew up in the winter of 1945 as they retreated west. According to people I've met and talked with who were born and reared in East Prussia and who have had the courage or just the curiosity to return to their old province for a visit, there isn't even a pile of bricks or rubble masonry at the former gravesite. What the Germans started to destroy the Russians and then the Poles finished, leveling the place and leaving it for future generations of archaeologists, who might be interested in the odd button or medal, to poke around in several centuries from now.

In 1934, however, this monument was Germany's equivalent to the enormous memorial that the French constructed at Verdun. From postcards that I've seen of the place, it was a huge ersatz castle with towers and outer walls all put up in the customary Teutonic brick, within which Hindenburg lay buried amid flags carried into combat by the famous regiments that fought here in the summer's heat of 1914. A complicated diorama with blinking lights showed the movements of armies and divisions, guides led groups of schoolchildren from one martial exhibit to another, and a hostel catered to Boy Scouts and

*Battle standards, Tannenberg*

youth corps who dutifully marched about the countryside reliving the fight. Nowadays the battle this heap of stones commemorated shares the same fate. Not too many people have ever heard of it, despite the fame of Aleksandr Solzhenitsyn, whose novel *August 1914* is a brilliant recapitulation of those frightening days. Tannenberg, though it affected nearly the entire province of Ostpreussen, represents just one too many battles that Germans have fought, no matter its repute as one of the most convincing victories ever achieved by any army in this century.

"The best thing for you, I think," an old German gentleman said to me, "is to ask at the restaurant called Mazursky for directions. If they can't tell, you never mind, for it stood on the little hill just behind the place. Look carefully, you'll see evidence that something was there."

The Restaurant Mazursky, as things turn out, is a dilapidated shack that seems not to have been in business since the battle itself. I leave the car behind in its overgrown lot to wander a bit through some woods, and sure enough, I see in the undergrowth carefully fitted cut stone ramps that may have been walking paths or retaining walls leading into the mausoleum. The mound I explore is roughly circular, like an Irish rath, and thus generally consistent with the pictures shown me.

Around its outer edges are three or four graves, all marked with sim-ple wooden crosses that carry only the inscription "A German Sol-dier." I am told later these remains were plowed up in neighboring fields, then identified as Germans from scraps of clothing or boot heels that were judged as certifiably military, though no one could positively state from which world war they may have originated. Ger-man donations paid for the burial and crosses. "It was probably just a piece of luck they ended up in graves," a German veteran said to me later when I related my tour. "If it was just the Poles, they'd have dragged the bones over to some drainage ditch and thrown them away or just put the tractor in reverse and turned them over into the ground again, where they came from in the first place. But Germans are now visiting the East in very great numbers, and many are investing there, and I would wager that they heard talk or rumors about these dead sol-diers, investigated further, and took command of the situation to arrange for the proper burial of our people. We are a race that appreci-ates and honors the sacrifice of our forebears."

Several workmen are burning garbage in a giant pit that may have been—who knows?—Hindenburg's crypt, and further on I come across a miserable-looking institution of some sort, whose elderly inhabi-tants shoo me away in some anger. "Nie fotographia! Nie fo-tographia!" they yell. I read in my guidebook that the masonry from Tannenberg was used by the Russians to build their own war monu-ment in nearby Allenstein. I go to take a look, but at the tourist office Poles inform me that they in turn bulldozed the Russian memorial. Out of curiosity, I ask where the rubble went. Thinking optimistically that here's yet another wealthy German wishing to build a chalet or summer house in the vicinity, they direct me to a local contractor.

Later that afternoon, I drive about the environs with maps in hand and a chronology of the battle I assembled before my departure. Cer-tainly in this respect the relief maps and the trail of dots moving hither and yon about the countryside at the old Tannenberg memorial would have come in handy, for the battle they outlined was no single engagement decided on a front of just a few miles over the course of an afternoon. Tannenberg represented instead a vastly complicated se-quence of fighting: Because of the broken terrain, with lake and forest thrown scattershot among the combatant armies, each piece of the battle often seemed disconnected from others taking place 30, 40, 50, even 60 miles further away. This was in many ways a modern battle in the sense that it involved nearly all of East Prussia. It presented a tableau that could daunt soldiers of the old school but excited those of a more youthful disposition.

-⧈⧈-

The newness of war—many generals had last heard the sound of serious gunfire some forty-four years before, in 1870—may partially explain the timidity and upset that officers such as Max von Prittwitz displayed when adverse tidings reached their headquarters. Von Prittwitz, sixty-six years of age, had certainly panicked on that August 20 when he heard that General Pavel Rennenkampf's First Army had advanced to the Insterburg Gap, a 43-mile stretch of level country between the fortress city of Königsberg and the obstructive maze of Masuria's forests and lakes, dealing two serious blows to German forces in the process. Simultaneously the staff of XX Corps, acting as a screen on the southern side of Masuria, signaled the approach of Russian general Aleksandr Samsonov's Second Army from Warsaw, advance units of which were now pouring over the border and threatening the town of Neidenburg. Von Prittwitz should have known better but signaled his intention to retreat, thus marking the end of his career.

German officers had been trained to withstand adversity. It was their duty when confronted with a deteriorating front to consider alternatives and countermeasures that would stem the decline and reverse the fortunes of battle. The aid to this process had supposedly been the decades' worth of war games and simulations that every staff officer had participated in, along with the annual "ride" of the high command, whence the terrain for every and all conceivable action was personally reconnoitered on horseback and debated ad nauseam in what-if scenarios. Von Prittwitz momentarily forgot himself, whereas members of his staff did not.

Colonel Max von Hoffmann, a cynical man whose diary is one of the few eyewitness accounts of the great battle that has any verve or nuanced assessment, saw opportunity in the tactical situation, not ruin. Appalled at the notion of retreat, he pulled calipers from his pocket and demonstrated that Samsonov was actually closer to the Vistula than the Eighth Army and could beat them to the river if it came to a race. The key was to turn once again to the von Schlieffen gospel. Draw off strength from before one of the Russian armies and attack the other with all your might, then turn and strike the survivor down. The essential requirement for such a scheme was in place: the

Prussian railway grid. Since 1862, annual war games had relied heavily on the transport and maneuver of troops by rail, and indeed Hoffmann was an expert in their deployment. He proposed denuding the forces ranged against Rennenkampf and shifting them southwest to deal with Samsonov, relying on the commonly held conviction that the Russians were incapable of exploiting their earlier successes with any speed or vigor. This, in keeping with von Schlieffen's maxims, constituted a gamble, but Hoffmann felt sure of success. After Samsonov was defeated, the Prussians could concentrate another blow against Rennenkampf. "Enough of war on two fronts," von Schlieffen had said in 1899; "one front is ample." Von Prittwitz was brought around to Hoffmann's view and issued the necessary instructions. He was then relieved of his command by von Moltke.

The savior of East Prussia arrived in a special train from the western front on August 23. Headquarters staff at Marienburg gave him a chilly reception, their honor doubly offended when they realized that new commands intended to rectify the position were in fact no different from Hoffmann's. The newcomer was indifferent to their notions of self-esteem, however. Erich Ludendorff was not a sentimentalist. He had come to take charge, to issue orders, to win a crucial victory. In his train came the nominal commander in chief, Paul von Hindenburg, a man neither Hoffmann nor anyone else "had ever seen before."

The partnership between von Hindenburg and Ludendorff is undoubtedly the most revered in the tradition of Prussian arms, on certain par with its illustrious predecessor from the Napoleonic era, that of Blücher and Scharnhorst. Whereas the latter arrangement was more or less between equals, however (though their strengths as either tactician or actual commander differed in degree), that of Ludendorff and von Hindenburg was very much weighted in the younger man's favor.

Ludendorff was forty-nine at the time, a general staff officer of Prussian, though nonaristocratic, background whose abrasive personality and dogged adherence to principle had actually earned him disfavor and demotion before the war. A fervent disciple of von Schlieffen and his plan, many of whose intricacies he had himself put into the detailed minutes of the battle orders, Ludendorff was the lucky recipient of gratuitous opportunity before the gates of Liège in the first days of August. Encountering a leaderless brigade mired in confusion, Ludendorff immediately took command and fulfilled its orders to force an entry into the ring of Belgian forts surrounding the city, orders he knew by heart. This achievement won him instant fame.

Von Moltke, in urgent need of merciless housecleaning for the Eighth Army, detached Ludendorff from what everyone thought was the brink of a glorious victory on the western front with renown for all and ordered him to "prevent the worst from happening" in Prussia. Within fifteen minutes of receiving this message from von Moltke, Ludendorff was packed and on his way, first to an audience with the kaiser and from there by train to the East.

What went through Ludendorff's mind as he sat in his private coach is unknown. Ludendorff's memoirs are spare in color, being, like their author, direct, plain, to the point. He was not a complicated or reflective man. His entire attitude toward life was aptly summarized in his remark that "all I stand for is authority and order." His path, as he also frequently observed, was nothing if not "straight." A pathological worker, Ludendorff proved the master of detail, the epitome of drive, the cliché of a merciless, single-minded Prussian officer to whom the pursuit of personal reward was mere afterthought in comparison to the greater glory of kaiser and Germany. No comparable figure in any army, any war, or any epoch so wholeheartedly sunk himself with such unrelenting concentration into his work as did Ludendorff. In the end he emerged from the four years of war in a kind of shell shock, utterly devoured, a wreck of nerves, the victim of what von Hindenburg himself called his "ruthless energy." It is probably with some confidence, then, that we can assume what Ludendorff was thinking on that train. He was thinking, in a clinical sort of way, just how to annihilate as many Russians as possible.

One necessity of army protocol remained, however, before he assumed his new duties. At 4 A.M. on the morning of August 23, Ludendorff's command express consisting of three cars stopped at the Hanover station. Standing on the platform, dressed in the outmoded blues of a Prussian general and unable to clasp his formal collar on account of a bulging neckline, was von Hindenburg with his wife. Eleven hours before he had been just another retired officer, a man whose climb through the ranks had been steady if unspectacular, whose decorations, in the none-too-charitable assessment of a contemporary observer, had been the "minimum consistent with his rank." When war began, he had written letters to old friends still in the army, obsequious pleas not to be forgotten, but he had abandoned hopes of any further employ. His routine seldom varied, his meals never so. Ten hours of sleep every night; mornings in his apartment; a short daily walk; afternoons at the Linden cafe drinking beer "with

the gravity of a hippopotamus." No one was more shocked by his recall than he, but his reply to the summons was resolute—"I am
ready."

How von Hindenburg received command of the Eighth Army was
chance and little else, a decision that caused no one at headquarters
undue amounts of time or hand-wringing. It is doubtful von Moltke
gave it a thought. Ludendorff was the key element, the man entrusted
with responsibility and worry, the "robot Napoleon" (in Liddell Hart's
phrase) who was to seize control of the Prussian situation and redeem
it. What the brash and impolitic Ludendorff required was a figurehead
of some respectability to give authority to whatever orders Ludendorff
deemed necessary. Von Hindenburg was merely a name on the list, a
figure of age, lineage, and the required deportment. As the train left
Hanover station, Ludendorff briefed von Hindenburg on the general
situation, outlined the remedy, and went to bed. Von Hindenburg's
value was not at first sufficiently appreciated.

Proceeding east, the train stopped in Berlin to pick up another passenger, Ludendorff's wife, who accompanied her husband for several
hours before being dropped off at a later station before the battlefield.
She found Hindenburg a sweet old gentleman, "calm and almost
cheerful," in contrast to Ludendorff, who was absorbed and immersed
in his own thoughts, not a very personable companion in the private
dining car. "There was a time when he could be cheerful," she wrote
in her memoirs later. "His features did not always wear that look of
unbending obstinacy, the expression of a man whose feelings had
turned to ice." Looking out the window, she noted endless lines of
military troop trains and motorized convoys, all heading to the front,
all "decked with flowers."

Arriving in Marienburg on the twenty-third, the two generals found
that Colonel Hoffmann's dispositions were already set in motion,
with neatly scheduled trains hauling all the scattered elements of the
Eighth Army save two corps southward to face Samsonov and his
Russian forces heading up from Warsaw. In just forty hours, for example, General Hermann von François's I Corps, later to play a key role
in the coming battle, would be dropped quite precisely on the right
wing of Ludendorff's force. Some troops marched only 3 miles from
their depots to the front line.

In contrast, Russian soldiers of the Second Army were shambling
forward with only the vaguest notion of where they were or where
they were going. What they did know was hunger and fatigue. The

Russian mobilization had been haphazard and chaotic, Tsar Nicholas and his uncle, the commander in chief, Grand Duke Nicholas Nicolaievich, being anxious to fulfill their pledge to France and Great Britain that Russia would take the field immediately to create a second front. As a result, Samsonov's forces in particular were in disarray on their march to the Prussian border. The weather was hot, the Polish roads sandy and difficult going, the bread ovens far behind, and their orders contradictory and often inappropriate to immediate circumstances. Once on or near the battlefield, units were sometimes marched all day in one direction and, come evening, commanded to turn around and tramp back just the way they had come. Officers were irresolute or unaware of a general tactical plan other than the vague notion that they should advance. It was their universal expectation that they would soon encounter and mop up the desiccated elements of the Prussian field army that Rennenkampf had so proudly announced he had routed some days before. They were to a man ignorant of the German forces being arrayed against them.

The British equivalent to Hoffmann's diary is that of Major Alfred Knox, the military attaché assigned to the Russian high command. Knox was a breezy fellow, a typical British officer of the period: addicted to the hunt, full of admiration for "good chaps" hither and yon, a lover of wine and port, an eager photographer who snapped away at peasants and princes alike, a kind of rumpled figure, his pockets bulging with scraps of paper and notes to himself. He also had an eye for terrain. In 1911 he had bicycled from Warsaw all the way to Königsberg, a "staff ride" of sorts, and understood that although Prussia was not strategically important in and of itself, the province certainly represented a "delicate spot" in the German psychological armor. He was delighted with the Russian plan to take it.

Knox was a professional traveler and managed in his usual insouciant fashion to secure a berth on the last prewar train from Berlin to Moscow. Russians on board reserved comment until they had crossed the border between the two countries, whereupon the conversations became animated about "those pigs of Germans." Knox eventually made his way to the grand duke's railroad command car somewhere in Poland, commenting with approval on its cuisine ("We lunch at 12:30—three courses—and dine at 7:30: soup, joint, and sweet, a glass of vodka, claret or Madeira, and a glass of cognac with our coffee"). Nicholas granted Knox's request to join General Samsonov at the front, more than delighted, perhaps, to rid himself of the determinedly cheerful Englishman. Knox noted the ragged villages through which he passed, "dirty and dusty, the streets swarming with Jews," and jotted down the prophetic remark of a despondent Russian recruit—"They say it is a wide road that leads to war and only a narrow path that leads home again."

The attaché reached Samsonov on the twenty-fourth, headquarters still being in Russian Poland. The general struck Knox as a fine fellow "of a simple, kindly nature" yet possibly over his head in this command. Knox nonchalantly observed that neither Samsonov nor Rennenkampf had ever commanded forces any larger than a division, the implication being that their understanding was necessarily no broader than what they saw with their own eyes in front of them.

The vision at German headquarters was decidedly more expansive, though it is now impossible to say in whose mind the idea of maneuvering a full-scale envelopment of the enemy had originated. Quite possibly it was a collective notion, a process absolutely in keeping with the general staff tradition of orchestral management, wherein disparate elements or talents blend toward the same solution, although occasional soloists might take the lead. Uniting them all, as students of von Schlieffen, was the notion of a monstrous Cannae, a replication of the famous battle of the Second Punic War where Hannibal destroyed a far larger Roman force. Von Schlieffen had spent his retirement years completely absorbed with this one quite brief struggle, seeking lessons that could be translated from 216 B.C. to the arena of a modern battlefield hundreds of miles large and encompassing numbers of combatants that Hannibal, for one, could never have imagined. The guiding principles were clear and transferable, according to the old general. Give way in the center but do not break, then send stronger forces around the flank of your enemy and, in effect, overwhelm with superior force at a point of weakness. A double envelopment, if possible, would bring even greater profit; that is, send out two flanking forces that could meet in the enemy's rear, thereby surrounding your opponent. Ludendorff, Hoffmann, François, and Hindenburg all saw that exact possibility here in southern Prussia, though as Solzhenitsyn remarked, "the task of convincing history that *he* had thought it first still lay ahead."

The disquieting element to their plan, however, was Rennenkampf. If the Russian First Army sensed the enemy had decamped from its front, the road into East Prussia lay clear and open. A resolute commander could burst through to support Samsonov by taking the Germans from the rear. With superior manpower it lay well within the Russians' ability to crush the Eighth Army, and nothing would then lie between a rampaging horde of Slavs and the capital city of Berlin. On the evening of the twenty-fourth, during dinner, Ludendorff quailed at this possibility and questioned the disposition of his battle plan, some of which already was in motion. Hoffmann, a heavy drinker who never had qualms about anything, was aghast at these remarks. Was yet another general officer about to lose his nerve? It was here that von Hindenburg won the Battle of Tannenberg.

No one witnessed the conversation between Ludendorff and Hindenburg that took place outside the officers' mess that evening, neither man giving details in his respective memoirs, but its broadest tenor is clear. Von Hindenburg, the old bear, in a few minutes of honest, quiet, deliberative counsel, calmed the excitable Ludendorff with a show of stoicism and fortitude, a "trust in yourself and the Almighty" kind of performance: Ludendorff had done his best, the execution of his orders was under way, so let the matter take its course. Hindenburg would take the responsibility in case of failure. The next day, intercepted wireless messages sent in the clear between the Russian commands ("quite incomprehensible thoughtlessness," according to Hoffmann) showed that the gamble could work, as Rennenkampf was advancing too slowly to influence the outcome of battle in the south. Ludendorff immediately ordered the second enveloping wing, hitherto in a holding pattern in front of Rennenkampf, to head by forced march immediately to the new battlefield. Samsonov's doom was now seriously in motion.

In broadest terms, the German plan was to entice Samsonov forward into what Solzhenitsyn would later term "the wolf pit." At the very moment that the Russian general was trading toasts with Major Knox, the center of his army was already engaged with the German center, XX Corps, near the village of Orlau on a front about 10 miles long. It is interesting to note that XX Corps contained units of the Landwehr, or reservists, older men not previously considered first-line troops. But XX Corps was an East Prussian regiment. These soldiers were truly fighting to save home and hearth, and thus they unwaveringly accepted the sacrificial nature of their task, for XX Corps was to be the "anvil" the Russian army would repeatedly be lured into striking. It might bend, but it must not break. In a series of sharp contests, the XX absorbed a rain of blows and frequently came close to collapse, yet it managed over the course of the battle to realign its formations in such a way that Samsonov, still far to the rear, remained assured that the Germans were fleeing in some disorder.

In fact, with each localized victory and marginal advance, the Russian center was sliding further toward destruction. On the twenty-fifth, Ludendorff's noose began to tighten, aided immeasurably by the steady stream of intercepted Russian messages that indicated little change in the enemy's intent. Hindenburg was sufficiently confident that he retired to bed at an early hour. "We can sleep soundly tonight," he said to Ludendorff, a man to whom rest was anathema.

Over the next three days, a Cannae the likes of which the deceased von Schlieffen had designed for the western front played itself out in the East. Though Ludendorff faltered on one or two occasions, the resourcefulness (and often insubordination) of his generals, in particular the aggressive von François, put all the finishing touches on what became an utter rout. Although the Russian center performed heroically, its right and left wings were summarily shattered and reduced to ineffectiveness, separated corps acting independently of each other in the absence of both communications equipment and any knowledgeable direction from Samsonov, who initially had no idea as to the seriousness of his position. Knox recorded in his diary that "things have developed rapidly," but it was not until the twenty-seventh that he observed the onset of "nerves." By then the Russian right had already dissolved, with the left about to, their commanders disgraced and fleeing helter-skelter for the border. Samsonov, completely out of touch, had only just entered Germany. Already he was receiving messages from headquarters that his lack of forward progress had been deemed "cowardly," but on the very next day he suddenly realized that the battle was as good as over.

Knox caught up with Samsonov in fields north of Neidenburg. He found him "sitting on the ground poring over maps and surrounded with his staff. I stood aside. Suddenly he stood up and ordered eight of the Cossacks who were with us to dismount and give up their animals. I prepared to go off too, but he beckoned to me and took me aside. He said that he considered it his duty to tell me that the position was very critical. His place and duty was with the army, but he advised me to return while there was still time." Samsonov then broke off all contact with his superiors and rode northward into the hopeless battle and oblivion.

Tonight I am driving the lonely road from Neidenburg to Willenberg, enjoying a panorama little changed from those days in 1914. The usual avenue of ancient trees lined up on either side of the road heads due east. Farm fields spread in parallel strips 200–300 yards off to either side, boxed in by stands of pine through which dirt tracks crisscross. In this morass of wood, fragments of the Russian Second Army thrashed about seeking escape. Units that still had officers generally followed compass readings south, while stragglers or bands of common soldiers fled wherever the sounds of gunfire seemed least appalling. The general retreat was therefore aimed for this road.

The two corps detached from Rennenkampf's front had done their work, wrecking the Russian right flank and closing in from the northeast. Von François, after dispensing with the Russian left and in direct disobedience to Ludendorff, who had ordered him to stop, plunged eastward toward Willenberg to close off the cordon. Ludendorff realized his mistake and later sanctioned this move. Von François emphasized speed to his men, many of whom traveled on bicycles. At intervals along the narrow road, detachments peeled off to take up firing positions toward the forest. On the twenty-ninth, the Russians began to emerge.

This was a glorious finale for German arms but little more than slaughter for the dispirited Russians, who found themselves cut down in the killing zone between forest and road. From my vantage near Muschaken, where I camp for the evening, my sight line is totally unrestricted. Groups attempting a breakout fell back on fresh stragglers trying themselves to push forward, resulting in dreadful mayhem throughout the tangled undergrowth. The final, semiorganized attempt to escape encirclement occurred exactly here. German soldiers saw an Orthodox priest come out of the woods holding a crucifix. Behind him several hundred starving Russians, many of whom had not eaten so much as a crust of bread in the last five days, charged with bayonet. Not a single one made it through the German line. Von Hindenburg referred to this final operation as "the harvest."

Knox heard about Samsonov's fate several days later. The befuddled general had gone to the center to take personal command, but there was by then little he could do. Despair and fatherly concern for his poor recruits, the men of the army, racked his soul. "How can I face the tsar?" he was overheard saying. When Knox reached Russian Poland on September 1, he asked an officer to direct him to Samsonov. "He shook his head, and as I pressed for a reply, he drew his hand significantly across his throat." Samsonov, on foot with his staff, lost in the great wilderness of the forest, had shot himself in the head. "This is a disaster," Knox wrote down in his diary. "The Russians are just great big-hearted children who had thought out nothing and had stumbled half-asleep into a wasp's nest." The Germans, by contrast, thought of everything. As night fell, searchlights were brought up and splayed across the landscape. They didn't want anyone to escape.

No more authoritative military victory could have been achieved, and even von Hindenburg and Ludendorff were overwhelmed at its immensity. To have accomplished the utter ruination of such enormous forces on a fluid battlefield in modern times may have been theoretically feasible, but it was an outcome hardly anticipated. Yet the Germans had prisoners and spoils to prove it, over 125,000 captives and untold thousands dead and rotting in fields and wood. It took weeks for the methodical victors to scour the forests for all the booty left behind, and the final tally amounted to some 500 artillery pieces.

In Allenstein von Hindenburg and Ludendorff went to church. When the Russians first entered the town just a few days earlier, they had in their naiveté thought they had captured Berlin. Most of those men were now dead. Von Hindenburg found himself overwhelmed with emotion. In the shadow of the red brick castle built by his revered Teutonic Knights, he piously gave thanks for the victory. Ludendorff knelt beside him and went through the motions of prayer, but his thoughts were elsewhere. Already formulating in his mind were plans of action against Rennenkampf.

⊱⊰

One could reasonably expect in driving about the countryside to find some indication that a battle so famous in the annals of war had taken place here, but such is not the case. The great mausoleum is gone, of course, and so, too, is nearly every other trace of battle. Unlike a Gettysburg or a Verdun, the landscape is devoid of memorial or remembrance. Taking a chance in the village of Willenberg, I approach a group of Polish officers standing by the roadside in charge of a convoy with twelve enormous tanks that are being trucked to who knows where. They strike extremely noble poses in their handsome uniforms and distinctive caps, known in Polish as *rogatywka*. Two of these gentlemen speak some French, and I ask if the grave of General Samsonov has ever been formally located in the wilderness or marked by any sort of commemorative stone. They have no idea who Samsonov was and in fact are ignorant of the battle itself. "There were so many fightings here, so many campaigns," one said, "but they have nothing to say to us. Even these tanks are obsolete, very good for controlling crowds in a city street, but in nuclear war of no value whatsoever." As I go back to my car, each of the officers gives me a very smart salute.

Despite the enormity of its success, the Battle of Tannenberg, as it came to be called (in revenge for the drubbing German knights had received 500 years previously on these very grounds), resulted in no lasting influence over the course of the war and in one respect may have negatively affected German fortunes. Von Moltke, impressed by the kaiser's fury that Prussian soil had been violated and responding to reports of civilians' fleeing en masse from the province in terror, diverted two entire corps and a cavalry division from the von Schlieffen right flank then wheeling into France and entrained them to reinforce Ludendorff in Prussia. These troops failed to reach the battlefield in time and thus assisted neither front. Military historians have long debated whether the French recovery at the Marne (September 5–12), which in effect destroyed the German effort for a short, knockout war, could ever have succeeded had these troops remained in line. A French officer called this error "our salvation."

Tannenberg did, however, save Prussia, and Ludendorff's immediate follow-up against the enemy's First Army proved another humiliation for Russian arms, its commander, Rennenkampf, so unnerved that he jumped into a staff car and ran away from the field of battle. Foreign attachés at Nicholas Nicolaievich's railroad command car behind the lines commiserated on these dreadful losses—"Nous sommes heureux de faire de tels sacrifices pour nos alliées"* was his famous reply, wherein lie the seeds of the Bolshevik revolution.

Ludendorff and von Hindenburg continued to inflict enormous suffering on the various Russian armies that opposed them over the next two years. Gigantic battles raged throughout East Prussia and then further afield in Galicia and Poland, campaigns about which most Western readers know very little, their attention more focused on the Somme, Ypres, Passchendaele, and Verdun. But to Germans, the dual focus is a genetic trait, warfare in the East a logical extension of too much history, too much racial animosity. "Will any German now, as then, suffer the Lett, and more especially the Pole, to take advantage

---

*"We are happy to have made these sacrifices for our allies."

and do us violence?" wrote Ludendorff. "Are centuries of German culture to be lost?"

And yet German victories could not eliminate Russia from the war, no more so than the single Battle of Tannenberg, though a dreadful battering, could prevent the tsar from fielding another new assemblage of ill-equipped and ill-trained peasant armies, and another and another after that if necessary. Ludendorff's great sweeps, envelopments, pincers, and Napoleonic movements repeatedly staggered the Russians and shamed them, but no defeat or even series of defeats brought cries for surrender. A partial explanation lay with Austria's performance as Germany's ally, Ludendorff himself ruing the day that ever brought him dependent on such "a corpse." And of course Germany's resources were wearing thin, the eastern front at one time stretching from the Baltic city of Riga in Courland all the way south to the Black Sea, though still secondary in terms of men and material to the cauldrons of trench war that raged from the North Sea to Switzerland.

In August 1916, with stalemate everywhere, the eastern commanders were brought west, thereby initiating Ludendorff's reign as virtual dictator of Germany. It had been the hope of the general staff that this by now almost legendary team could somehow transfuse their penchant for mobility into the stagnant morass of stationary warfare in which the western front was mired. This "ironmongery," as one German officer put it, was an affront to what many men considered the "art" of war. Mobility, however, required a breakthrough, and by that time the front was a churned-up sea of mud and fortified lines, a ground fought over so many times that it lacked any feature at all. Ludendorff's tremendous attacks burst through at one point or another, but logistical nightmares of bringing up artillery through shattered terrain often meant that advancing infantry outran its cover, thus opening itself to snuffing countermeasures. None of Ludendorff's offenses achieved the desired Tannenbergian result. No allied armies were enveloped from the rear; no blow however strong brought enemy proposals for an armistice.

By 1918 even the German will for victory had flattened, calls for "the old élan and spirit of 1914" falling on many a deaf ear, something Ludendorff could not understand and blamed on German society behind the lines—it had gone soft and was contaminating the spirit of the common soldier. Ludendorff lost touch with the actual rigors of the front, failing to grasp the weariness that squalor and modern war could produce. As a Prussian, he had no sympathy for weakness and thus continued to plan sledgehammer frontal assaults on prepared positions, a conception von Schlieffen—by then barely relevant—would have deemed madness. At Tannenberg Ludendorff had 500 guns at his disposal. His last great offensive four years later, Operation Michael, employed 6,000. Whatever strategic subtlety Ludendorff had once possessed was gone forever. He became, in the words of the novelist Arnold Zweig, "unapproachable, enclosed in his own atmosphere like a planet in icy space."*

Hindenburg, as was his wont, supported Ludendorff throughout these trying years, though his later characterization of their relationship as that of a harmonious marriage is utterly false. The aging field marshal (his new and exalted rank) had not yet descended into senility, and he was conscious in his slow and ponderous way that Ludendorff held the actual reins of power and exercised them relentlessly without regard for Hindenburg's feelings or opinions. Hindenburg found the situation quite appropriate if often awkward. It made sense for young men with young ideas to take control, and with his antique notions of honorable behavior he felt comfortable in providing the legitimacy of his position as commander in chief to cover their designs. But Ludendorff's brusque disregard for the field marshal was discourteous to say the least, and as 1918 and the final crises of the war engulfed the high command, an estrangement developed between the two. Ludendorff, under crushing strain, grew less tactful in conference, could not resist rolling his eyes or snapping at von Hindenburg when the old man offered some particularly quaint strategic observation, and brooded quite uncharacteristically over slights to his own past achievements that Hindenburg's burgeoning popularity had blurred. Who had won Tannenberg? Certainly not von Hindenburg! As Hoffmann was to say when leading fellow officers on tours of the old site, "Here is where Hindenburg slept before the battle, here is where he slept after the battle, and here is where he slept during the battle."† Ludendorff took to mentioning the dreaded "I" when referring to those glorious few days that seemed an eternity ago— "when I won the battle." Many officers commented disparagingly on Ludendorff's lack of breeding.

---

*Churchill remarked in one of his postwar books regarding Operation Michael, "The reader will now observe how low the art of war had sunk."

†Hoffmann was promoted to major general, became the de facto commander in chief of the eastern front, and negotiated the infamous Treaty of Brest-Litovsk with the Bolsheviks from December 3, 1917, until its acrimonious conclusion on March 3 of the next year. He is memorably portrayed in the novel *The Crowning of a King* by the German author Arnold Zweig as a man possessed of an "inner poise, a sound, firm back-

Certainly the kaiser could stand him no longer. Wilhelm's mental fluctuations had hardly ceased during the course of war; indeed, his mind remained in its usual high state of volatility. As Ludendorff humiliated the kaiser by appropriating his powers as supreme warlord, the kaiser was reduced to the status of a mere tourist, a "crowned observer" in Walter Goerlitz's helpful phrase, whose only job was to tour the trenches giving pep talks. Ludendorff had seen no choice in the matter. The dire threats facing Germany forced a man with Ludendorff's convictions to take the drastic steps required, the notion of "total war"—a title Ludendorff would in 1935 give his book of military theory—being all that prevented Germany from collapse. Political infighting, parliamentary squabbles, civilian lassitude, and socialist intrigue—these distractions could be curbed only by draconian measures, and the kaiser, in Ludendorff's correct opinion, was too much the dilettante to handle such a responsibility. Using the threat of resignation as a lever, Ludendorff brushed Wilhelm aside, who bitterly resented his grasping subordinate, calling him the "sergeant major." Hindenburg, the other "Siamese twin," was of no help to his monarch, standing aside during conference, deferring to Ludendorff in his grave and silent fashion. Wilhelm suspected this pose of aloofness merely disguised Hindenburg's stupidity. The old man was lost in the past.

In many ways this was quite the truth. Hindenburg, a true Prussian, wept at the kaiser's abdication on November 9 but would not save him. Ludendorff, in the wreckage of defeat, had been cast aside just a few days before. "Politics demanded a victim, the victim was forthcoming," the marshal recorded in his memoirs, and as Berlin dissolved in revolutionary confusion, the kaiser was sacrificed as well, von Hindenburg choosing to save the army instead. For a man of Hindenburg's sensibilities, only the army could never be abandoned.

Wilhelm thrashed about at his headquarters in the Belgian town of Spa, too far from the front and decidedly too far from Berlin. Should he gather up the army and march on his capital, scattering the demagogic mob that sought to dethrone him? Or should he motor to the front, to his son's regiment perhaps, and just remain there with them to await

---

bone," whose "nerves were imbedded in fat like sardines in oil." He died in 1927 "of overwork and old brandy."

The works of Zweig, largely unread today, are the equivalent in eastern terms of Erich Maria Remarque's *All Quiet on the Western Front*. Because Zweig was a Jew (he was friends with and dedicated *Crowning* to Sigmund Freud), his books were burned by the Nazis and he fled Germany for Palestine. He died in East Germany, 1968.

*Kaiser Wilhelm with
von Hindenburg and
Ludendorff*

developments? Neither was possible, said the marshal. He could not vouch for the army's loyalty, meaning that he feared to put his men to the test. If the army marched on Berlin to restore the kaiser's position, he feared the catastrophe of Tsar Nicholas: troops fighting troops, civil war, ultimate ruination. Hindenburg saw his duty in ancient terms; he loved the uniform beyond all. Germany could lose the war, could lose its kaiser, but it could not lose its army. When Prussian units marched back to their homelands, they would return intact, in order, under proper command, and essentially unbeaten. The victors might shackle them with restrictions, cut their numbers, and humiliate the colors in any thousand ways, but the army would survive and regroup for another day, another era. Hindenburg, in fact, was not stupid.

The kaiser, a "byzantine figure" to the end, could rail and vacillate, strike his theatrical pose and cry bitter tears of anger, all of which moved the old marshal to inarticulate grief, so much so that a subordinate had to say the treasonable words that von Hindenburg could not. "Military oaths? Warlords? Those are only words; those are, when all is said and done, mere ideas." Less than twenty-four hours later, the abandoned kaiser was on his way to exile in the Netherlands.

# ⊰ 11 ⊱

# Gross Pötzdorf
## 1930
# Weimar Interlude

*Hitler came from no man's land. Only one who was fundamentally alien could fascinate and subjugate Germany as this man managed to do.*

**—Golo Mann**

IN THE FEDERAL REPUBLIC OF GERMANY, I am sitting in the living room of a pristine little row house in a new town somewhere in the countryside. We have just finished lunch in the small dining salon that takes up a corner of this room, all the windows overlooking a small and immaculately manicured garden. A scrapbook is being passed around, scenes from the 1930s at the old family estate of Gross Pötzdorf in East Prussia, also a family ledger or diary. The Germans are a meticulous people when it comes to remembering the past.

Bernd Volprecht, his wife, a neighbor, and son-in-law reminisce about the old days. "My family got this property in 1830," Volprecht says, "when it became possible for someone not a noble to purchase land. It totaled 700 hectares, or about 2,800 acres, and it was located on the western border of Ostpreussen. Thus when we traveled to Berlin we had to cross the Polish Corridor. By train it took about three hours to cover the 120 miles. The Poles, they sealed the passenger cars and pulled down all the blinds so you couldn't see out. Hindenburg remarked on this as an insult in his memoirs.

*Weather vane, with
Russian bullet holes*

"We had thirty-two families living on the farm, and I believe it averaged out to something like two workers per family. We had a foreman. He managed the ten teams of horses that we had; I think it was four horses per plow. There were forty heavy work horses in our barns, along with several riding or military horses for hunting and pleasure. We also had a tractor. I still have the weather vane from one of our buildings, a cow. I got it back a few years ago. You can see the Russian bullet holes.

"Life on the estate was completely different to anything like today; the style was so different. You were completely independent on the property you lived on; you produced everything you needed. The soil was light, so we grew potatoes. The potatoes, of course, we ate, but we also distilled, getting 96 percent alcohol for lighting, pure wood alcohol really. When the Russians came through in 1945, they drank all this stuff on all the farms they plundered, which is one reason so many were burnt. After the distilling process, you had a mash left over, and we fed that to the cattle. Everything was consumed. We used the farm product and the end product, no waste. My father made one concession to modernity in 1936: He brought electricity to the farm.

"The person who owned such a property had an obligation to entertain family during the summers. We had an extreme Continental climate at Gross Pötzdorf—cold winters, wet springs, hot summers—so
relations always came for long stays when the weather got too awful
in summer. There was in a sense nothing for entertainment: no cinemas or movies—the nearest theater was 50 kilometers away—and of
course no television. There was hunting, riding, bridge parties in the
evening, but I think the real pastime was just having the guests
about."

"It's funny about the thirties," his son-in-law interjects. "My extended family entertained all summer as well, but the climate of the
times could often intrude. The sister of my grandmother married a
German Jew. He was an outstanding banker, very well known, a member of the German Imperial Bank, which was the equivalent of the
Federal Reserve Bank in your country. He was never in the house of
his wife's sister. The wife occasionally visited her sister's estate, but
he chose not to come for the summer as everyone else did. This was
something she probably realized would happen when she got married
to him. She just accepted it." Everyone nods their heads.

"Your life, well, it was predictable," continues Volprecht. "It's
youth; it's school time; it's right into the military to do your term of
service. We went first to primary school nearby, then you had a private
teacher. When you got older, off to boarding school."

His wife, who grew up on a neighboring estate, agrees. "I went to a
nunnery in Stettin called the Holy Grave. Baltic families sent their
children there if they were 'young girls with a future.' This, of course,
all ended with the war and the Great Trek." All nod again in agreement.

"The uniform, it was very important to us, and everyone had one,"
says Volprecht. "Prussia created loyalty by giving us benefits and giving us a position in which to serve the country. Army status was very
real. No matter how long or how short your actual duty, you had the
right to wear your uniform for the rest of your life. Affinity to the unit
was something you carried forever." Everyone here is an expert on the
etiquette and particularity of regimental adornment. As photos are examined, the minutia of various insignias are debated. "That is my
white tie uniform."

"No," says his wife, "it doesn't have the proper braid. *That's* his
white tie uniform."

"I believe you to be mistaken."

"Nein, nein."

The older gentleman sitting with us points out a postcard in the album. "The Führer," he says. "There he is." We stare at the photo of Hitler presiding over von Hindenburg's funeral at the Tannenberg mausoleum in 1934, the site of which is only a few miles east of Gross Pötzdorf. "I remember that day very well; it made a deep impression. I was fourteen, and naturally to us Hindenburg was such a personality because he had saved our province at that battle in World War I. My father was inside the memorial because he was the leader of our village Warriors' Association of Tannenberg. He had been an uhlan. But he did not like Hitler. He was essentially a monarchist. That ceremony, though, it was immense. The uniforms, the marching, the music! We waited hours to watch everyone go by. Hitler stopped on our street for three minutes to shake hands."

We look at more pictures of Volprecht and his wife in 1945 and 1946, resettling in the West. "These were hard years, but we were young. I think we knew we would never regain the life we had in East Prussia."

"My father could not go to the border between East and West Germany after the war," the son-in-law says. "We had property just over the line, and he could not bear to go and look at it over the wire."

Volprecht understands. "For people of my generation, it is hard. I returned to Gross Pötzdorf in 1973 for the first time. That was difficult. We remember a very free time in our youth, but we must accept the political development as it has been since the war. To see the old home the very first time . . . I had to work to avoid sentimentality. I wanted my children not to see me upset. They must develop their own outlook uncontaminated by their father's sadness.

"The old house, four or five Polish families live in it now. A pharmacist, I think, some other people, and the director of the local co-op. I am a professional agriculturalist, and when I went over, this man, who was very friendly, kept asking me questions: 'Where are the drainage pipes? Point out for me the old field system. How was the property run before the war?' He knew I had irrigation know-how and knew they weren't getting the most from Gross Pötzdorf. If they had modern equipment there, it would be once again a very fine farm.

"I go back each year. The attempt now is to build up a good relationship with the Poles despite the past. My school friend has bought with Polish counterparts an estate in East Prussia. He finances it. Poles work it. The aim is to set up a vacation camp." We examine some of

*Bernd Volprecht with trophies from his former estate, shot since 1989*

Volprecht's hunting trophies on the wall. "These are from Gross Pötzdorf. I shot them all around my old estate." I comment on how strange
this must have been for him. He says a word in German that I do not
understand, and his son-in-law translates for me—"bittersweet."

Later that month I stop in at what I take to be a grocery store at a
village crossroads to inquire as to the whereabouts of Gross Pötzdorf. I
realize I'm not in a grocery at all after tripping over the outstretched
body of a man in the dark foyer, an occasion for merriment from all
the other drinkers lined up at this aptly named establishment, "Non
Stop Bar." The intoxication level here is so pronounced that I give up
my geographical inquiries and have a beer. These are the first friendly
Poles that I have met, though their speech is slurred and their odor
redolent of stale brew. Against my better judgment, I buy them all a
round. Since no one here owns a car, I figure I'm not endangering any
innocent bystanders. A boy coming in to find his father or brother
knows where Gross Pötzdorf is, just a few miles down a dirt road leading out of town.

The long and twisting formal avenue is lined with beautiful trees,
and fields off to either side are rolling, pungent, neatly hoed. The old
manor house, sitting on a slight rise, looks to be in fairly decent shape,

*Gross Pötzdorf*

though clearly the decorative arts of landscaping and house painting leave much to be desired from a Western point of view. The outbuildings and farmhand cottages are equally threadbare, as are the variously dressed children who soon surround me in cheerful awe. Old women head for the barns with small tin canisters. It must be time for free milk or cream. There is something timeless about this scene. I go up to the main house for some photographs to send back to the Volprechts. A young man comes out in a fury. "Who would want to photograph *this*," he seems to be saying. "Go on, go on, leave!" He must think I'm a German, come here to throw him out of his rooms.

⚜

Certainly the Weimar period witnessed a Junker ascendancy class at the end of its tether in Prussia. Artificially supported for over fifty years by tariff protections, direct subsidies from the state, and a plentitude of indentured peasant labor, its estates nonetheless lay encumbered in debt and sunk into feudal decline. Junkers had resisted every innovation, whether social or mechanical, preferring to live in a warp of nostalgia for the ironfisted past. Their idea of progress was an hourglass that never drained, the maintenance of a status quo that relied on serfdom and freedom of action little different from what the Teutonic Knights had enjoyed centuries before. Time and circumstance, however, had caught them by the neck. The serfs had been freed, and industrialization to the west had lured their labor force from the land. A greater calamity was the new status of Danzig, lost to the German empire after its surrender in the Great War, now a "free city" administered by the League of Nations and surrounded by a Polish Corridor that, in the words of contemporary observers, had "amputated" East Prussia from the homeland. To bring their produce to market involved the payment of Polish duties and taxes and often the use of Polish railroads. Access to the home market and indeed the European market was impeded. Poland, a country that had not existed for a century, whose people constituted the day laborers whom Junkers were used to ordering about, had been elevated to the position of determining the economic fate of Junker landowners. It was a reversal of fortune too bitter to contemplate. Friedrich Engels fifty years before had called the Junkers "callous, narrow-minded, conceited." During Weimar, as their economic horizons contracted, they turned bitter as well. "We have never been good losers," is the way one of these gentlemen put it to me. "We tend to be very great brooders."

Much has been written on the Weimar period in German history, the curiously flawed interim democracy that died in 1933, "part murder, part wasting sickness, part suicide" in Peter Gay's trenchant postmortem. Looking at it today, the inevitability of Hitler's emergence from obscurity and indeed his ascension to power seem almost taken for granted in both popular perception and many textbooks, though this represents a revisionist view at best, an attitude that William Shirer's enormous best-seller of 1960, *The Rise and Fall of the Third Reich,* did much to inspire. In Shirer's recitation, Prussia and Hitler marched hand in hand into the furnace. Without Prussia and its militaristic traditions, no Hitler would have been possible. Ergo, the evils of the Third Reich, not only its expansionist warmongering but its racial crimes as well, are all logged to Prussia's generalized debit. According to Shirer, the Nuremberg trials condemned to death, figuratively and literally, not only nazism but "Prussianism" as well. This widely misses the mark, as many furious historians and academics, many of them German, noted when they brushed aside the Shirer opus as a piece of simplistic "journalism."

The matter of von Hindenburg was a crucial case in point. Though elected in 1925 as the president of a republic that he himself detested, he was in no mood for an Adolf Hitler. "I'll make him a postmaster," he had once remarked, "and he can lick the stamps with my head on them." But Hindenburg grew senile over his terms in office, spending more time than ever in seclusion at Neudeck, his East Prussian estate, there to be manipulated by his greedy son, Oskar, who grew increasingly receptive to the pay and shadowy blackmail of Nazis. The final sketches of Hindenburg are sad ones. "They say the old man signs anything now," a diplomat related. "The other day Meissner left his sandwich bag on the table and when he came back, the President had signed it."

Ludendorff represented another unhappy story, part of the confused welter of dreams, ambitions, and politics that tend in retrospect to mingle Prussian aims with Nazi aims, though the two were in many fundamental ways irreconcilable. Ludendorff had suffered a dazzling downfall, one moment the most powerful man in Germany, the next a near fugitive who fled the revolutionary mob in Berlin disguised in a false beard and sunglasses. Alone on a country estate in Sweden, Ludendorff's sanity weighed in the balance, "the solitude in a strange land particularly hard to bear," according to his wife, who attempted to share his exile but could not. "I am at war with myself and the whole world," he later wrote her. "It isn't easy to pull myself together again." Returning impetuously to Germany, he erratically involved himself in what Count Harry Kessler, the Weimar ambassador to Poland, called "the Kapp farce," a "preposterous coup" of "tragicomic" proportions. Three years later he participated more wholeheartedly in Hitler's beer hall putsch. On that less than memorable occasion he had marched straight ahead into the gunfire of a police unit ordered to break up the Nazi march, who parted like the Red Sea to allow him past. Hitler, in contrast, ran away.

For Ludendorff, of course, the insignificant Adolf Hitler was a mere errand boy, the means to an end. He viewed him as a provider of manpower that would again position the general as a power behind the throne, power he would use to prevent a fate for Germany that he saw in apocalyptic terms. In his wild dementia, he could not appreciate the reality of who was using whom.

In the eyes of contemporaries, of course, Ludendorff had become a "political imbecile" (as one aristocratic observer put it), the fool who had allowed a gang of uncouth street rowdies to appropriate his good name to a more or less proletariat movement. Prussian officers excoriated the Weimar regime as much as Hitler did and had proven themselves more than willing to dream up and originate right-wing coups, but they had little interest in funneling authority to anyone the likes of an Adolf Hitler. A monarchist candidate or, more likely, a military dictator was much more their preference. (The exiled kaiser, for example, was quite excited at news of the Kapp putsch, according to his attaché. "'Tonight we shall have champagne!' he said, grasping my hand in excitement and joy.")* Hitler caught these people as much by surprise as he did the rest of Germany. He was a man of the masses, a sin of association that Junkers seldom committed.†

When the mausoleum of Tannenberg was officially opened in 1927, Hindenburg, twenty-seven generals, countless officers, and a host of sergeants, corporals, and privates who had all fought and survived those frantic days of thirteen years before gathered at the battlefield. Ludendorff stood alone, shunning his former associates as they in turn shunned him. When the ceremonies finished, he marched alone back to his car. His final years were spent in a bizarre, pseudo-Wagnerian haze—a *Twilight of the Gods* scenario—writing books and articles on Teutonic mythology and superheroes. His Tannenberg League, an organization that once numbered 30,000 members, was outlawed by the Nazis in 1933 when they had no further use for it. By then the occult of torchlight parades, Nietzschean oratory, and Hunnish pomp had become a state monopoly.

⚌⚌

On Junker estates in Prussia, and for that matter on aristocratic estates everywhere in Germany, the rise of Hitler was a profound surprise that few could comprehend. Most thought of Hitler as a temporary solution to the country's problems, a convenient barricade behind which a power with more suitable pedigree might develop and then appear to combat Germany's traditional enemies of disorder and so-

---

*The kaiser maintained a quasi court at his estate in the Netherlands, where the particularities of etiquette and form were fully maintained. The British writer John Wheeler-Bennett was less than impressed with Wilhelm's entourage. "Though the bluest of East Elbian blood flowed in their veins, they had the manners of wart-hogs and the political intelligence of low-class morons."

†Wilhelm disdained Hitler and the Nazis. The Third Reich was "a mustard republic," in his opinion: "brown and sharp."

cialism. The Junkers, like industrialists, clergy, and generals in the
Wehrmacht, underestimated the upstart and thought in the end that
they could control him if it came to that. The power of his dema-
goguery eluded them.

"The people of my family's social strata never understood Hitler's
appeal," one member of the aristocracy, Count Otto Friedrich Wilhelm Grote, said to me. "They were willing, emotionally, to accept
the 'stab-in-the-back' theory, despite their intelligence and education.
To this day this legend, this myth really, that Hitler exploited to the
fullest—you talk to rational Germans and they will repeat it: 'We were
fooled at Versailles! We could still have won the war!'"

"How is it possible they could have felt that?" I asked.

"Because the French army was finished. There were mutinies in
something like 70 percent of their regiments. And the casualties that
Britain took on the Somme were unbelievable, to this day it suffers
from it. They had beaten the Russians on the other side, so who was
left? Many Germans felt they had won the war. The mistake of the Allies was to let that armistice happen. And not only to offer the
armistice, but Wilson, with his Sixteen Points, made it palatable for
Germans to stop fighting. I mean, the Germans were finished, too, but
the German *people* as such would not believe that. They would only
have believed it if the Allies had invaded their country, occupied it,
and marched into Berlin. Hitler and the other nationalists never let up
on this theme, and it was fatal to the Weimar Republic, born as it was
in a sham defeat, or so the people thought.

"Add to that Hitler himself, his effect on ordinary people. I mean, to
this day I still can't believe it, and I'll give you my own personal experience. I don't know when this was, in the 1930s, I suppose, and the
German army was having maneuvers in our province, soldiers all over
the place. Somewhere along the line, Hitler came through our neighborhood. I was in my rubber boots, mucking about in the barn, the
cows and the pigs and so on, and at 9 in the morning there was no one
there. I couldn't believe it. You know, there were milk pails half full,
the cows just standing there munching away, but no one there to tell
me what was going on. Finally I ran into somebody; he was running up
to the main road there, and I said, 'What's going on? Where is everybody?' And he said, 'The Führer is coming!' So I went up there, too,
and found all the women standing on the left and all the men on the
right. After two hours of waiting—and it was a gray, cold day—in
comes these armored cars and whatnot driving through. And then he

comes by in his black limousine, up front in his usual posture, going very slowly, he was not even as far away from me as you are. And you know, I looked around me and all the women had tears coming out of their eyes. They were all crying, completely overwhelmed. Then I crossed the road to the men's side and the men couldn't even look at me straight; they had water in their eyes, too.

"It was the same thing when I first heard him on the radio. There were a bunch of women—they were governesses, nurses, cleaning ladies—and we had this radio, also a rarity, in the children's room, and I was walking by when I heard this crazy voice yelling and screaming, and music, too, and one of the girls says excitedly, 'Come in here! Here's the way Germany is going to be run; here's what's really happening in Germany; this is it!' and I listened. I didn't understand what it was at the time. I was only seven or eight. I was completely confused by this, but here, a second time of my exposure, these women all were so emotionally moved that they were crying. I ask you, what was it? I mean certainly, it wasn't normal."

"Well, what do you think?" I ask. "In *Triumph of the Will* the speeches strike me as banal, crude, gangsterish, emotional, and ranting, an appeal to the gutter really. Is this what attracts ordinary, common people?"

"Obviously not. Educated people could get swept up by it, too. It was the delivery, the way he said these things, the enormous emotional content. He clearly triggered things that were in the German psyche, that were explosive and that moved people. I often have thought that he conveyed an enormous sense of suffering; he translated to others that he was in pain. In a religious sense, I would equate it to the suffering of Jesus Christ on the cross—that's the kind of intensity he brought across. People saw it; they perceived almost by instinct that this man was suffering along with them in some inexplicable way and that he was going to do something about it. The genius to it, of course, was that Hitler wasn't faking. I think in the beginning, at least, he meant everything he said. Otherwise he could not have succeeded."

A Prussian officer from World War II agreed. "My father was an educated man. He had never cared for Hitler, he was completely against him. He said in the very beginning, 'When he gets the power, that means war.' But I was young, and in those mass meetings you really started to get goose pimples all over your back. He had suggestive mass psychosis. You were moved, and it usually took a few hours to get yourself back again. He was a very, very able speaker to move the masses as he did."

"Did he strike you as an educated man up there or as a rabble-rouser?" I asked.

"To be honest, I never had this feeling that he was a rabble-rouser. I had the feeling he knew what he was talking about. He spoke freely; he never read anything from notes. He spoke from the heart. He meant it. You cannot move German people for so long if you are just a fake or a hypocrite. I believed he believed in what he was trying to do."*

---

*The English historian Hugh Trevor-Roper remarked in a 1995 article that Hitler "certainly had an extraordinary power. When he wanted to mesmerize, he did have this effect. It didn't work on everyone. It didn't work on—to put it crudely—aristocrats or on people who were sensitive to the vulgarity of his behavior."

# Part Four

# EXTINCTION
## The Second World War

# Select Chronology

| | |
|---|---|
| 1919–1933 | Weimar Republic. |
| 1920, November 9 | Danzig proclaimed a free city. |
| 1923, November 8–11 | The beer hall putsch. Hitler and Ludendorff arrested. |
| 1925 | Hindenburg elected president of the republic. |
| 1932 | Hindenburg reelected to second term. Outpolls Hitler by 6 million votes. |
| 1933, January 30 | Hindenburg reluctantly names Hitler as chancellor. |
| February 7 | Reichstag fire. |
| March 21 | New Reichstag convened at Potsdam garrison church. |
| 1934, August 2 | President Hindenburg dies at Neudeck. |
| August 19 | Plebiscite approves Hitler's assumption of presidency. |
| 1938, February 4 | Von Blomberg and von Fritsch removed from roles as minister of war and commander in chief of army, respectively. |
| March 12–13 | Germany annexes Austria. |
| 1939, March 21 | Germany annexes Memel. |
| September 1 | Germany invades Poland. |
| September 17 | Russia invades Poland. |
| 1941, June 22 | Germany invades Russia. |
| June 29 | Germans occupy Vilnius in Lithuania. |
| July 1 | Germans occupy Riga in Latvia. |
| September 19 | Germans occupy Kiev. |
| November 1 | Germans enter Crimea. |
| December 5 | German army observes outskirts of Moscow. |
| December 6 | Soviet counterattacks stall invasion. |
| 1942, January 20 | Extensive Russian resistance. |
| Summer | Germans continue offensive. |
| September 14 | Germans reach Stalingrad. |
| September 21 | Russians counterattack. |

| | |
|---|---|
| 1943, January | German siege of Leningrad is broken. |
| February 2 | German Sixth Army destroyed at Stalingrad. |
| Summer | Russians carry the fight. |
| 1944, June 7 | D day in France. |
| July 20 | Assassination attempt on Hitler, Wolfsschanze. Stauffenberg executed in Berlin. |
| November 20 | Hitler leaves Wolfsschanze. |
| 1945, January 13–14 | Two-pronged Soviet attack into East Prussia, one pincer directed toward Königsberg, the other to Marienburg-Danzig. |
| January 16 | Hitler returns to Berlin bunker. |
| January 17 | Warsaw falls. |
| January 26 | Elbing, Thorn, and Marienburg in Soviet control, Russian forces having advanced 125 miles in twelve days. Königsberg cut off; civilian exodus over frozen Frisches Haff well under way. |
| January 27 | Memel falls. |
| February 10 | Soviets push into Pomerania, isolate Danzig. |
| March 26 | Final assault on Danzig begins. |
| March 30 | Danzig surrenders. |
| April 6 | Final storming of Königsberg begins. |
| April 10 | City capitulates. |
| April 13 | Vienna taken. |
| April 30 | Hitler's suicide. |
| May 2 | Berlin captured. Armistice six days later as Russians near the Elbe. |

# ⇥ 12 ⇤
# Suwalki
## 1939
# War

*For me, Poland is a cemetery.*
—**Aronek Kierszkowski**

TO REACH THE BORDER TOWN of Suwalki from the heart of old
Prussia, one passes through the former no-man's-land of Masuria, once
an impenetrable track of forests, lakes, and undergrowth, a natural
barrier separating the welter of peoples whose distant borders all
merged in this morass.

It is attractive country, undeveloped and sparsely populated, prized
nowadays as one of the few environmentally sound regions left in
Poland, "the green lungs" of its virgin stands of timber boasting an in-
finitesimal pollution average as compared to that of industrial Silesia.
In summer the lakes are thronged with tourists, many of them German, lured as much by the unbelievably low prices as they are by pristine surroundings. This bonanza, in a region unused to attention in
any area other than war, has produced the usual run of exaggerations,
various waterside towns claiming to be "Poland's Venice" or boasting
more than their fair share of folk traditions or ancient crafts. Poland's
biggest country-and-western festival is held here each July, an opportunity for aging, second-rank musicians from Tennessee to pocket a
few easy dollars. The phenomenal popularity of American pop culture
here in the former Eastern bloc, though much commented upon, must
be seen to be appreciated.

I have never cared for woods. They are to me too Gothic, claustro-phobic, and dank, but they give good cover for clandestine campers, even though my brightly painted rental car does not exactly melt into the landscape. This morning, upon rising, I find three mute woodsmen transfixed at the sight of this wholly unexpected apparition parked in the middle of their place of business. I arise, offer a few breakfast salu-tations, roll up my sleeping bag. Not a word or gesture from any of them. They do move to the side of the road as I depart, sparing me the need to honk or run them over.

The road to Suwalki emerges from the cover of forest and foliage to a broad plateau of level fields all cleared of cover. It is extraordinary that the ambience of the area changes so dramatically in step. We are no longer in the ordered symmetry of Prussia but have entered a Slavic realm.

Suwalszczyna Province, though incorporated within German fron-tiers at various stages in its history, is in feel and texture a countryside entirely alien to that of its Teutonic neighbor: no more brick barns or the footprint of great landed estates, no more tree-lined avenues that resemble soldiers at attention. The villages here are wooden and ram-shackle; the churches sided in wood; the fences all slat and board. There is a dusty element to every approach to town or hamlet, many of the roads dirt, gouged with ruts and potholes. One drives about here with the notion that if it rained too hard everything would turn to mud. Although not the steppes of Central Asia, that great expanse of empty plain seems to hover just over the horizon.

Suwalszczyna is hemmed in from south and east by forests, one enormous swath of which is a national park. The Germans called this region Südauen, or the "southern fields." To the Poles it was Kraj Za-puszczanski, "the territory behind the virgin forest." The Lithuanians, in remembrance perhaps of the Teutonic Knights who forayed from this wilderness in vicious raids and slaving expeditions, named it Sussi Vilki, the "land of the vicious wolves." All three of these peoples—Germanic, Slav, and Balt—vied for control of the region, not so much for the wealth or mineral resources that might have been there to ex-ploit (few if any) but more for the pride of excluding others from having it themselves. It was a convenient "outermost frontier," a place where probes were directed and met, a desolate wasteland from which mes-sages of warning and alarm were sent back to more settled homelands.

The greatest shadow was of course cast by Russia. When Russian forces lumbered west, they generally churned through Suwalszczyna.

Conversely, when enemies took the road for Moscow, they used the same route east. Napoleon did in 1812, and Hitler, foolishly, would again in 1941.

The town of Suwalki was a coach stop. In the 1800s the great highway from Warsaw to St. Petersburg passed through town, generating traffic and sustaining a hotel and provision trade. The railroad followed. Nobles from Russia traveling west and south often stopped here for the night, entertained in the governor's mansion before reembarking on their travels of enlightenment to the glories of Vienna and Paris. A few municipal buildings of some original splendor, considering that Suwalki was a backwater town, were constructed on the single major street. Some of these still survive and reflect a decidedly Russian influence, mingling in curious ways both elegance and squalor. In order to develop Suwalki as a more viable commercial metropolis, Catholic monks in 1715 set aside a section of town for Jews. By 1827 there were 1,200 Jews residing in their quarter. Thirty years later the figure had risen to 6,500, and by the turn of the century, over 13,000. I drove into the place looking for Naum Adelson, the last Jew of Suwalki.

Aronek Kierszkowski, a Polish concentration camp survivor, had warned me over the telephone, "Whatever you do, do not associate with him. Do not ask for Adelson by name. Ask to see the Catholic church first, or even the German church—make sure people know you're gentile. Then go see him. Otherwise you could find yourself in difficulty if they think you're a Jew. They won't answer any of your questions."

By "they" Kierszkowski meant Poles in general, and his wariness, though seemingly paranoid, is well grounded in both his own gruesome experiences and the broad historical record of Polish anti-Semitism that cannot be denied. The controversy over the fiftieth anniversary of the liberation of Auschwitz in 1995, involving every Pole from Lech Walesa to the pope himself, presented to a global television audience the most pallid minuet of studied utterance ever performed by public personae, whereby every word written or delivered was deliberately designed to obscure in large part the truly held opinions of those whose duty it was to go through the motions of comment or ceremony. Never in the history of Poland have so many people bitten their tongues to keep from lashing out, gyrating instead through a mishmash of diplomatic body language designed to offend no one but that ended up, inevitably, offending everyone. "The Poles are not very smart," said Kierszkowski. "They know the reputation they have around the world; they must know what the world thinks of them from the point of view of their behavior toward the Jews during and after the war. So here they have an opportunity with the Auschwitz ceremonies to put a good face on things, and they end up smearing black on white. Even Walesa, it took a tremendous amount of soul searching and outside pressure for him to finally come around and speak the truth, that the majority of people who died at Auschwitz were Jews. Such a simple fact, but this was the major issue of contention in Poland! They are so dumb."*

Aronek Kierszkowski speaks his mind. Having seen everything in his life swept away in the colossal wreckage of Polish Jewry, his attitude is typically, "What else have I got to lose? Nothing!" This, of course, is hardly true.

I found Kierszkowski, after phone calls and references from a friend of his whom he met at a displaced persons camp after the war, in a luxurious suburban home in Delaware, not far from the university where he pursues a distinguished academic career in engineering (he is the author of over a hundred learned papers and was recently elected a fellow of the American Society of Mechanical Engineers). The walls of his home are covered with original art. A splendid Milton Avery overlooks the elegant dining room. "This is a gift from Germany," he tells me with a sardonic laugh. "I got $12,000 in reparations money from the Federal Republic, so I said, what the hell, and I bought this." We review the palatial lawn and garden, with immense oak trees over 80 feet high shading a formal landscape of statuary and sculpture. This is a long way from Suwalki.

"If it hadn't been for the war, I may never have come to the United States," he says, "but I doubt I would have stayed in Suwalki. I had an interest in mechanical things, and my parents would probably have sent me to the university in Königsberg or Berlin, and I may well have ended up as an engineer, just as now. But who knows?

"My family was traditionally Jewish, though not fanatically religious by any means. My father didn't have a beard or regularly wear a head cover of any sort, but we maintained a kosher home and just carried on the tradition. At home my mom and dad spoke to each other in

---

*The Polish mayor of Olsztyn (formerly Allenstein) was quoted in 1994 as saying, "There is no sense in being offended with one's history."

*Aronek Kierszkowski with Avery's* Reclining Woman

Yiddish, but with the children they spoke Polish. My brothers and I spoke Polish very well and one of them, Dudek, the oldest, went to the local *Gymnasium*.

"My dad and his brother ran a fur business, import and export. He traveled to London and Paris each year, and to the Leipzig fair in Germany. By Polish standards he was a multimillionaire, the wealthiest person in Suwalki, people claim. Only two weeks before the war broke out, my dad was in London on a business trip, and from his transactions there he had $75,000 left in England. Sure, this was in sterling and it was devalued a few times, but several years after the war I got about $15,000 out of it. That was all that was left; everything else disappeared. I spent it on my university studies.

"In Suwalki we had several properties. We lived on Kościuszki Street, the major road in town. You went through a gate into the courtyard, and we lived on the second floor in twelve rooms. My father put in flowing water in 1936. Ours was one of the few places in Suwalki that had it, although there was a big outhouse in the back for the whole complex.

"As far as I recall, my mom, who attended *Gymnasium*, had a high regard for German education. Germans were the *Kulturvolk*, the cultured people of Central and Eastern Europe. In 1932, when I was four and my older brother, Dudek, was six, she wanted to get a German governess from East Prussia, which was only 15 or so miles away. She felt the older boys should be exposed to German discipline and culture. But then Hitler came to power, and the Poles, especially border Poles, thought anyone who was German had to be a spy, so my mother decided to get a *Gymnasium* graduate instead, a Polish girl who lived with us in our house. In retrospect, I wish we had gotten a German governess because we were quite a nice bunch of kids and she would have liked us. Then she might have been able to warn us and maybe even try to convince my father that nothing good was coming out of Nazi Germany. But we were completely isolated, completely surrounded by forests. Suwalki was the kind of place where people looked inward, not out.

"We had no social contacts with the Poles or Germans who lived all around us, whether in town or the countryside. That's the way the rabbis wanted it. They preferred to have the Jews isolated, because then they could control them religiously. I remember a German butcher in town, his name was Kizel—he had a beautiful horse and a colt, as I recall—and on the way to school I used to look at what was in his display windows, like roasted pig legs, bloodwurst, and all those sausages, and I was told, 'When you pass by this store, you should look away. This is all nonkosher food.' What kind of nonsense! Some of our rabbis were just like the mullahs in Iran. They were still in the Dark Ages.

"When I grew up, Suwalki was like the rest of Poland, a very anti-Semitic place. As a matter of fact, in 1936, the year of extensive anti-Jewish rioting, I remember I was at school and somebody came from my dad's business saying he was going to take me home because there were some people breaking windows and attacking Jews on the streets. This was a year after Marshal Pilsudski died, the semidictator who did not subscribe to these ideas. But after him the government turned fascist and anti-Semite.

"To give you an example of what was going on, in 1937 or '38, the Poles came out with a new decree that all stores, since they always had the owner's last name on it, would now have to display their first name on it, too. This doesn't seem like a big deal, but in fact it was sinister because while many Jews had Polish last names, like we did, they very often had biblical first names. In America this would not mean anything, because David, you know, every tenth name is David.

But in Poland if your first name was David, you were a Jew. Likewise with Abraham or Isaac. In England Isaac Newton was a very famous scholar and non-Jewish, but in Poland whoever had the name Isaac was automatically considered to be Jewish. So instead of getting ready to fight Nazi Germany and possibly Communist Russia, the Polish government was preoccupied with identifying which stores belonged to Jews so the population could boycott them. The National Democrats had a slogan, 'Don't buy from Jews.' Sounds like Nazi Germany, doesn't it? And I remember that you could sometimes hear Poles say to Jews, 'Oh, you wait, just wait. When the Germans come, we'll teach you a lesson!' This is the spirit of independent Poland before World War II, looking inward to solve its Jewish problem, looking outward to France and England to fight Germany for Poland."

I asked Kierszkowski why, in his opinion, the Poles so hated the Jews. Most commentators tend to point out the historic role of Jews as moneylenders, estate agents, rent gatherers, and so on, all occupations that, especially in hard times, might excite the animosities of an impoverished peasantry. He did not think so. "It's mainly religion and the teachings of the Church. Jews quite simply were blamed for killing Christ, and they were persecuted as a result. You have to remember that Christianity came to Poland and its eastern neighbors quite late, around the year 1000 A.D., and the brand of Christianity they got was quite severely anti-Semitic, unlike the variety that other Western countries had received earlier in history.* You also have to keep in mind that many eastern peoples were rather primitive. When the Polish king Casimir the Great called in Jews, Italians, Germans, whoever, to help modernize Poland in the fourteenth century, to make it into a modern state, these minorities came in under the king's protection. The Jews started their own towns, the so-called shtetls, without any Christians whatsoever, and they were looked after by the aristocrats and the kings, who needed them.

"Our problems started in the 1500s, when priests and Jesuits intensified their attacks on Jews. In the next century the situation deteriorated further when Ukrainian peasants rebelled against the Poles, attacking nobles and Jews alike. After that you had the partitions and

---

*The Swiss theologian Hans Küng has said in reference to Germany, "Nazi anti-Semitism would have been impossible without two thousand years of Christian anti-Judaism. It was not racial. It was religious."

then Napoleon, and suddenly there were no kings to serve as Jewish protectors.

"But Polish nationalism had to find a home somewhere, and that turned out to be the Catholic Church, which was very anti-Semitic. Most Poles, in addition to their frustration about their occupied homeland, were also fed this hatred of Jews from the Polish pulpit, which has really lasted until this very day. You were Polish if you were Catholic and vice versa. The odd men out were 'Poles' who did not speak Polish. Poles were not created anti-Semites. Over time they were just born that way."

When war broke out in September 1939, the Kierszkowski family, like Poland as a whole, was broken into pieces. Aronek, his younger brother Maksik, and their governess were at a riverside resort near the town of Grodno on the River Niemen. He remembers the utterly chaotic scene of Polish regiments rounding up horses and wagons from the peasants. These would later be shot to pieces by Nazi warplanes. Suwalki was occupied twice: first by Russians, then by Germans in their amicable and devious (especially on Stalin's part) division of Poland. In these desperate days of that first week in September, the elder Kierszkowski then made a fateful decision. "My mother told the governess over the telephone, which still worked, that she should take us to Mom's family in Sokólka, near Bialystok, where she came from, and she would meet us there, which she did. My older brother, Dudek, and two of our employees, the Krawczynski brothers, accompanied three horse-drawn wagons full of fur to Sokólka to join us. But my dad, well, he made a huge mistake. From our big warehouse in Suwalki, he took the most expensive furs and packed them up in three large trucks, and along with my uncle, they drove to Warsaw."

"You mean right into the mouth of the dragon?"

"Exactly. In retrospect, he should have gone to Wilno, because Wilno was near the Lithuanian border. It was further from the Germans; it was not a war zone at the time; it was safer. I don't know. What was he going to Warsaw for? Did he think, as some people did, that the Poles would beat the Germans? Did he think that Warsaw would never fall? I just don't know, but it was disaster. He apparently was lulled by the fact that right up to 1939 he had been doing business with Germany, and that he used to go there every year. And historically the Poles, and particularly Jews, preferred German armies to those of the Russians, which consisted not only of Russians but Ukrainians, Cossacks, all manner of eastern nationalities. During the

First World War no one wanted Russians to take their town; they were a horror, burning villages and all. People wanted to be occupied by Germans; they were the civilized ones. My father never trusted Communist Russia. Before the war he had gone there twice as part of Polish trade delegations, and he disliked them immensely. So I guess he wanted to be as far away from them as possible.

"Well, that was the last time I saw my father, when he brought us to the Suwalki railroad station in that July of 1939, when we left home for our summer vacation. He wrote to us on occasion. There were no phone connections after the war began, or regular postal service, but if you knew someone who knew a locomotive driver on the Warsaw-Wilno route, he would take a letter and bring one back. This encouraged my mom to wait, to wait for my dad. Some of our friends, if you can believe it, made their way to Japan through a friendly consul in Lithuania: across Siberia by train, then to Japan, then by ship to the United States. We had the money; we could have done that, too. But we waited too long.*

"After the end of the war, I found out that my father had been killed. I wasn't surprised. He hadn't shown up anyplace—Suwalki, a displaced persons camp, anywhere. I sensed he was dead. In 1964 I met somebody in Munich who had been in the same camp as my dad, and he told me that my father had been shot in an 'action' at Trawniki, near Warsaw, a place where concentration camp guards, many of them Ukrainian, were trained. Looking back, he did everything wrong. My uncle, for example, smuggled himself out of Warsaw and came to Wilno, but my father, who could have done the same thing, did not. After storing his fur, he supposedly went to the Germans in Warsaw and told them he wanted to go back to Suwalki. He didn't understand the situation. It's amazing."

Suwalki, meanwhile, was made *Judenfrei*, or "Jew free," soon after its occupation by German troops. Many Jews fled through woods across the Lithuanian border, guided by peasants—or betrayed by them—for preposterous sums of money. "In Sokólka we gathered up

---

*For three weeks in August 1940, the Japanese consul general in Kovno, Lithuania, wrote over 2,000 transit visas for Polish and Lithuanian Jews. Sempo Sugihara, who died in 1986, proceeded on his own initiative issuing papers and travel documents that enabled refugees to cross Russia by train for embarkation to Japan and from there to the United States or Palestine, supposedly via the Dutch island of Curaçao, one of the few ports of entry in the world where landing permits were not required.

*"My parents and our employees at the fur company. I'm in the middle between Mom and Dad, and that's Dudek on the right, with the Gymnasium insignia on his jacket. The Krawczynski brothers shot in Lithuania are in the second row. Besides myself, only one other person in this photograph survived the war. He lives in Brooklyn now."*

our furs," recounted Kierszkowski, and "took the train to Wilno, which the Lithuanians renamed Vilnius, while the border was still open. We thought we were safe." But in 1940 Stalin seized Lithuania. Many Jews, including relatives of the Kierszkowskis, were deported to Siberia. "At least some of them survived," he says. In June 1941, however, the fate of those left behind was sealed. Germany invaded the Soviet Union, and within three days German troops had occupied Wilno. "I remember the Lithuanians greeted them with flowers." It didn't take long for the death machine to start up.

"Immediately there were official pronouncements, usually degrading, coming out each day. Armbands, yellow badges, don't walk on the sidewalks, that kind of thing. Then roundups when Lithuanian police and civilians—not Germans, but enthusiastic Lithuanians, many of whom were admitted to the States after the war—would come down to Jewish apartments and take away every man they could find. Two of our fellows, the Krawczynski brothers, and a friend of theirs named Palnicki were caught by Lithuanian auxiliaries, who were so anxious to help the Nazis get rid of Jews.* They had started to search apartments, and they got the Krawczynskis in our rooms, and Palnicki, who was hiding in the backyard. These people were marched to Paneriai, oh, about 5 or 10 kilometers outside the city, and murdered there. This is how they began to thin out the Jewish population. In the following months, Paneriai became a notorious killing place for the Jews of Wilno. Finally the word came around to those of us who were left, we all had to leave our apartments. We were all going to the old Jewish ghetto.

"A neighbor upstairs from where we were staying knew what was going on, a woman with two children. Her husband was an officer in the Polish army, presumably a prisoner somewhere, and my mom kept helping her, gave her food, sometimes some clothes. When we were ordered to move, she came to my mother and said, 'Ohhh, the ghetto is being formed. You cannot take too many things, so whatever you have to leave behind I'll keep for you.' So my mom gave her a fur coat and a few other things. But in the ghetto, when things got really desperate, my mom smuggled herself out one night, at the risk of her life, and went to the Polish woman and said she'd have to take some of the things back to sell for food. And do you know what the reply was? She told my mother that if she didn't run away quickly she'd call a friend of hers, a German soldier. This is the wife of a Polish officer!

"Another event I will never forget took place about a week after the Germans occupied Wilno. Near us there was a bakery owned by a Jewish family, and about a week after the German occupation heavy smoke was coming out from this building as I walked by. It had been set on fire. In front of me was this short Lithuanian woman, and she started yelling 'Zydas! Zydas!' ['Jews! Jews!']. I never heard a person express so much hate in just a few words. She deserved to be fixed right on the spot, this bitch. I mean, I went through the Holocaust and saw so many atrocities, but the hatred of this Lithuanian woman. . . . What could the baker have done to her, for God's sake? I was really shocked. It showed me what kind of neighbors we had.

"Ghettoization has always been a problem for Jews. When there's danger, Jews tend to congregate. Then of course you're a target concen-

---

*About 220,000 Jews, or 4 percent of Lithuania's Jewish population, did not survive the war.

trated in one spot. We all went to the ghetto, as we were ordered. Many mothers, not mine particularly, but most, said, 'Let's stay together. Let's keep the family together.' No, wrong! Get out, don't concentrate! But to escape the ghetto we had another problem: our accent. By living in ghettos for generations, some Jews who spoke Polish pronounced certain words with a Jewish accent. Instead of going to a Polish *Gymnasium*, many went to a Jewish school because community leaders wanted to keep Jews together. Thus if your parents and grandparents spoke Yiddish, so did you. This was disastrous for us. Some Jews spoke Polish very well and they could go outside the ghetto and not be known as Jews. A number of these people survived. But there were many that spoke certain Polish words or phrases with a heavy Jewish accent, and they were recognized just like that even if they didn't look Jewish. I remember in the camps I had friends who were so blond and blue-eyed they could have been Germans or Swedes or something like that. But their accent betrayed them for the Jews they were.

"These were problems our leaders could not cope with. For centuries, everyone relied on rabbis for advice, but they couldn't help here. They knew how to interpret the Torah, but they didn't understand what was going on beyond their world. Added to that was the fact that because of their isolation, Jews had very few Christian friends, people who could hide their identities and help them survive. Those Christians who did help should be declared saints, in my opinion. They were true human beings, but unfortunately there were very few of them in Eastern Europe."

With thousands of refugees packed into the medieval Jewish quarter of Wilno, life took on a prison quality as Lithuanian police boarded up windows that faced outside, barricaded all the streets leading in and out of the ghetto, and restricted the Jews from freely moving about. For the first time, the Kierszkowskis started to go hungry. "A week or two after we were packed into the ghetto, an order came that all men were to go to work outside. We used to go in columns, my older brother, Dudek, and I included, out the main gate and back the same way at night. When coming back, the Lithuanians often used to search us, looking for food and provisions, and whoever had anything they would beat them up. Whenever that happened, people in line would drop whatever they had. One day we had something, some food we bought from a Pole, so we dropped this when a search began at the gate. After it was over, of course, we didn't have anything for dinner.

So later we went back to the gate. It was kind of empty, no guards or anything, and there were all kinds of things lying there. And Dudek, who really was fearless, found a piece of meat—I still remember the scene—a pound or so, and I found something, too, and we ran back into the ghetto and had dinner. This was my first nonkosher dinner, and as a matter of fact since then I have been eating nonkosher food. It's a minor thing in terms of events that later took place in my life, but it shows how the old traditions were just breaking down.

"The only good thing to come out of all this, my mom started to lose some pounds. She used to joke, 'All my life I tried to lose weight; now it's not a problem.'"

In 1943 the Germans decided to liquidate the ghetto of Wilno. "There was a major action that summer. All men of working age were to be separated from the women and children and sent to labor camps. We had heard they were rounding up the older boys and what men were left, so we hid in cellars. They started throwing grenades into the basements, though, so people thought, 'Better get out or we're going to be killed altogether.' They lined us up in columns, all the men and boys, my two brothers and me included, and they marched us out towards the ghetto gate. I will always remember the scene when we passed my mother in front of our apartment, and she held our youngest brother, Isaczek, who was five, in her arms. We didn't say a word to each other as we passed by and were led away. That's the last time I saw them.

"So the three of us came to Rudnicka Street, where the main ghetto gate was. A young German soldier helping the SS and the Lithuanian police to gather up the people looked at my younger brother and said, "Schade, schade," which means "a pity, a pity," and he sent him back to find his mother. And that's the last time I saw him. That German soldier didn't realize that by sending Maksik back, he had condemned him to Auschwitz.

"I found out about my mom and my two younger brothers after the war. When they liquidated the entire ghetto a few months later, they brought the women and children in freight cars to Estonia, and they told the women, 'Whoever wants to leave the kids can go out to the labor camps.' Well, my mom and her sister-in-law, they weren't going to leave their children. In 1946 I met a man from my hometown of Suwalki, and he told me that he saw my mom at Auschwitz in a transport of women and children. My mom was good-looking, and even in this condition she stood out in a crowd. He said, 'She was with two kids, two young kids, is this right?' And I said yes, this would be my two younger brothers; one was five and one was about twelve. So they were all gassed in Auschwitz, which was not a concentration camp as much as a death factory. At least they didn't suffer for months and months. You arrived and just got killed."

※

In Suwalki I find myself driving around to get my bearings, looking for the Kierszkowski house that Aronek told me is still standing on Kosciuszki Street. The numbering has all been changed since the war, however, and my flash cards in Polish asking for information are blankly received. I now have a handle on how beggars feel when they approach people for change. I head for the local hotel—owned a century ago by a Jew who advertised in three languages that his kosher food was the finest—to look for a translator.

A very personable man in his early thirties comes by in about an hour. He is from Warsaw and works for the regional development agency, trying to induce companies from the capital or, more hopefully, from the West, to settle their manufacturing operations here. He hands me perhaps the glossiest and most professional-looking brochure on the attractions of Suwalki that I have ever seen anywhere. It glistens with promise. "We had no choice," he explained. "This place is Poland's Siberia."

We begin by looking for Ciecierski's Cafe and Maszewski's Restaurant, near which, as Aronek had explained to me, his old home stands. In the prewar years, Kosciuszki Street had been lined with shops, many owned by Jews, but most of these are long gone now, their space broken up into single-room apartments. No one has ever heard of Ciecierski's Cafe, but after a half hour or so we narrow down our possibilities to a single address that seems to fit Aronek's description. Standing in the shabby courtyard of a run-down building, we start to ring doorbells and knock on doors. Most people refuse to answer or yell for us to go away. My guide shrugs his shoulders. "People here are suspicious by nature."

Back outside a scene from some old Thin Man movie unravels. A legless and conspiratorial war veteran seated in a jerry-built wheelchair of some unknown and ancient provenance propels himself over the cobblestones with a hand winch contraption of some sort. He has heard of the Kierszkowskis. "Oh, yes, this was their home. I remember them well. One of the Kierszkowskis, he funded the Jewish soccer

*Current tenant*

club. They were called the Maccabees. They used to play the army team and anyone else who'd take the field with them. He was a nervous sort; he'd pace the sidelines back and forth. They're gone long ago, though, long ago." We chitchat. I have several packages of stale American cigarettes, uncovered when I cleared out my father's dresser after he had died. I ask my translator to ask our informant if he'd like some. "He certainly would," came the reply, "and so would I." I hand out the packs.

We go back inside and finally get someone to answer our knocking, a single mother living in two rooms, one of which, I later learn, had been Kierszkowski senior's study. A makeshift toilet has been installed in the corner, separated from the kitchen stove by a hanging blanket. This woman knows nothing of the Kierszkowski family. "I have troubles enough to worry about." I hand out a few more cigarettes.

We set out to find Naum Adelson. My guide is cosmopolitan enough not to care whether Adelson is a Jew or not. We find the old man in a derelict, crumbling masonry building that reeks of boiled chicken. He is delighted to have a visitor.

"I never knew Aronek. He was just a young boy. But I knew his father and his uncle; they were very successful men, very good at business. They owned several buildings in Suwalki. I recall one of them near here that Aronek's grandmother lived in. It was a wooden house with a courtyard; it had a beautiful pear tree in the middle. Aronek was probably brought up eating that fruit. When Germans cleared out the Jews, the Poles swarmed all over the building. They took it apart piece by piece, looking for gold, if you can believe it. All that was left was a bare piece of ground and the pear tree.

"There used to be 15,000 Jews here. Now look at me: I'm the last one left." We discover that both of us speak French, so I no longer have need for a translator. As I settle up outside on the street, my young Polish acquaintance tells me, "He's not the last Jew of Suwalki."

"No?"

"Not at all. There are at least four or five others."

Adelson's mission in life, reluctantly assumed, as I discover, is the old Jewish cemetery. I drive him out to it, a great empty green field. "There used to be over 20,000 tombs here," he says, "all vandalized and destroyed by the Poles, with a little help from the Germans. After the war, farmers let their horses and pigs graze here. You'd find bones and all sorts of matter lying about that animals had routed up. Then the Christians needed more space for their graveyard, and the sports facility over there wanted more room, too, and they were just going to take the land. That's when some Jews originally from here, they're Americans now, came over. They were outraged and started to harass the local authorities, who of course had no use for them. The Jews raised some money and decided to rebuild the outer wall and put up a gate. There were a few gravestones left—the German commandant had taken some to line an ornamental pool—and they wanted to get them back and remount them in a special wall. Since none of them live here, they gave me the job of overseeing the whole thing. What a nightmare. The authorities!" He waves his hands in the air. "I can take the Germans, but the Poles? Ah, *les Polonais*, some are good, some are bad." We continue to wander over the great desolate field.

"I look at this and I can't understand it."

"*You* don't understand it?" he replies. "How do you think I feel? Twenty-two members of my family, lost forever."

❧

"After the war, and this defies belief," Aronek Kierszkowski says to me, "they had a pogrom* in the Polish town of Kielce, killing Jews. I know a girl, Paulina, she was studying dentistry in Munich. Her parents had both been dentists, too. They had all survived on Aryan papers. One of the partisan groups, the Armia Krajowa [the AK], who had taken their orders from London during the war, they were real anti-Semites. They would hunt for escaped Jews in the forest and kill them, often in collaboration with the Germans, who they were supposedly fighting. So they came into her house and they murdered her parents while she hid under the bed. This is how she survived. My cousin Lisa, who had been sent to Siberia but after the war returned to Poland, told me a similar story. The AK were stopping trains, pulling Jews out who had returned home from concentration camps or Siberia, and shooting them. Incomprehensible! She was on the train from Warsaw—oh, this must have been '46, a year after the war was over—and met a Polish school friend from before the war; they had gone to *Gymnasium* together. The train was stopped; the AK were searching for Jews. They caught one Jewish fellow and executed him right on the spot. They came to the compartment where my cousin was and the student pushed her under the bench and said, 'There's no one here.' Now *there* was a good kid!

"You know, I look at most Poles, I look at them as traitors. They betrayed us, and we were as good Poles as they were. I despise them more than the Germans. Most of them are inherently bad.

"After the war, I returned to Poland from Germany. I wanted to go to my hometown of Suwalki. In Bialystok I met my former gym teacher, who went to Suwalki once in a while, and he told me that I can go with him, but I have to leave my papers behind, papers that indicate that I am Jewish. He told me, 'Your name is Polish, but in Suwalki everyone there knows who the Kierszkowskis are, that they're Jews. Adopt another Polish name,' he told me, 'because if they catch you, they will kill you.' Can you imagine! After I returned from the camps in Germany, I had to hide my identity because the Poles would kill me!

---

*"Pogrom" is from the Russian and means "devastation."

"So when I went home to Suwalki, I looked up our old maid. She had worked for us for fifteen years, and before the war my parents had married her off to a plumber who serviced our buildings. They bought her a commercial laundry wringer as a wedding present, as I recall. So when I came after the war, she said, oh, the gold objects, the watches and so on that my mom left with her, she didn't know what had happened to them. Her husband must have buried it all someplace—who knows where? When my mother left for Sokólka, she was probably the first one in the door looking for things. So I said, 'Listen, just give me the family photos. That's all I want.'

"But you know, out on the street, a Polish woman I never knew came over to me and said that at the beginning of the war, when my family left, she had picked up something from our place, a table or something, and she would like to offer it back to me. That was real. I was touched. I had nothing, but I told her to keep it.

"After getting out of Siberia, my uncle went back to Suwalki. I wrote him from Germany. I said something like this: 'The Poles let us Jews go to the slaughterhouse. Leave Poland—get on a train, go to Vienna. I'll meet you there. You can start all over again in the West.' But no, he wouldn't. He had a heart attack standing in a line in Suwalki with some Poles. He asked for water. They wouldn't give him any. These Poles, they're a bunch of bastards. I disagree with Nazi ideology, needless to say, but one point they were saying may have a certain validity. The people from Poland, the Ukraine, Lithuania—the Nazis called them *Untermenschen,* or subhuman. Many of them are. Sure, there were some saints who risked their lives to save the Jews, but they were extremely rare. Among the rest were many collaborators who denounced the Jews to the police. Pope John Paul II, I give him credit; he's a Pole, but he's a good man and honest. He was in Poland before, during, and after the war; he knows exactly what happened. He has apparently made up his mind that he has to solve this question of Catholic anti-Semitism, and I wish him every success."

❧

Naum Adelson walks me out to my car, parked in his yard. He had insisted that I drive it in for fear someone would steal it. He asks me if I have seen the movie *Schindler's List,* with its graphic depiction of life in a concentration camp. "I don't think I could bear to," I reply. He nods. When it comes to Poland, he says, he plans to see it, no matter

*Naum Adelson, the last Jew of Suwalki*

how painful. He gives me a kiss on both my cheeks. "Drive straight through," he says. "Don't stop for anyone. Watch out for bandits. They're all over Poland these days."*

---

*Suwalki was also the birthplace of Avraham Stern in 1907, whose mother, the local midwife, delivered all the Kierszkowski children. Stern founded the terrorist group Lehi in Palestine at the start of World War II. Following the example of Irish revolutionaries from 1916, he saw Britain's mortal struggle with Hitler as an opportunity to strike for a Jewish homeland. He not only initiated contacts with German diplomats to coordinate a military strategy against British forces in the Middle East but demonstrated his commitment to force by ordering assassinations of high-level figures in what he called the "occupying" administration of the crown.

In Jewish underground circles, Stern's radicalism was not appreciated. Arguing with him, as a contemporary recalled, "was like talking to a wall." To his followers, however, men like former prime minister Yitzhak Shamir, Stern was a godlike figure, "the world's first truly free Jew."

Because there was a reward on his head as leader of the Stern Gang, Avraham's whereabouts in Tel Aviv were leaked to the military, who stormed his hideout on February 12, 1942. During the ensuing scuffle, Stern was shot three times, rolled up in a blanket, and kicked down a stairway. He died within the hour in police custody, thirty-four years of age. In an autopsy photo taken of his body, graphically showing a bullet hole through his heart, Stern's open eyes seem riveted to the camera lens, a zealot to the end.

# ⊰ 13 ⊱
# The River Memel
## 1941
# Into Russia

*Hitler wanted to be another Napoleon, who had only*
*tolerated men under him who would obediently carry*
*out his will. Unfortunately he had neither Napoleon's*
*military training nor his military genius.*

**—Field Marshal Erich von Manstein**

I HAVE A NEW DRIVER TODAY here in Kaliningrad whose English is
nonexistent. We wade through the usual horde of clamoring street
kids selling postcards of old Königsberg to German tourists and head
northeast for the Memel in his creaking, beat-up old car. About thirty
minutes along we have a flat, replaced by a tire as bald as a baby's rear
end. Fifteen minutes or so later it, too, blows, and from the plaintive
look on my associate's face I can tell we're in for a long day, facilities,
as they say, being in short supply out here in the countryside. I am left
alone with the vehicle and this assortment of shredded tires as my
man walks off for help, and this does me little good when a military
police patrol comes by and inevitably asks for papers. I sit in their vehicle for over two hours waiting for the driver's return at about noon,
and his discomfort as they plow through a wad of dirty and tattered
identifications, permits, registrations, and God knows what else
pretty much dooms our excursion. I am returned to Kaliningrad by
these conscientious supporters of law and order.

*Postcards of old
Königsberg*

The Memel I had wanted to visit for several reasons: Napoleon's conference site with Tsar Alexander at Tilsit; his bridgehead over this river in 1812 near Kovno for the drive on Moscow; its status as the true northern border of Prussia. Most particularly, though, I wanted to see the jumping-off point for Erich von Manstein's First Tank Division in 1941, Hitler's fateful imitation of Napoleon's that led, some have judged inevitably, to the same catastrophic conclusion. I rely here on the recollections of a panzer veteran.

It seems incongruous to speak of war and all the mayhem associated with such a subject while looking from a veranda onto a lawn strewn with rhododendrons and other flowering shrubs. The gentleman sitting across from me is a professional landscape gardener, now retired, whose proficiency with plant material no doubt rivals in skill and dedication what he brought to bear as a leader of men and tanks some fifty years ago. We speak of his East Prussian origins and family, the military background of various brothers and other blood relations who fought in World War I and the Freikorps units after 1918, and the devotion of a Junker to his land.

He tells me with pride that Wilhelm II was his godfather. The kaiser, father of six sons, took the position of sponsor for the sixth or seventh son born to any Prussian family, an officer generally representing Wilhelm at the christening. The panzer veteran was, in his turn, named after the crown prince. "You can imagine, this was a very special thing for my family.

"I was sent to the academy in Potsdam after I had grown up, the West Point of old Prussia, where I had many, many doubts that I would make it, the training was so hard. They always make you feel you never measure up. But when you had this behind you, you really felt you had a kind of pride. And frankly, I found out I was good at it and that I liked it. I saw [the tank commander Heinz] Guderian many times; he was my division commander in Poland, a charismatic man, a born leader. Well, after my hard training at Potsdam, I began to feel I was a born leader, too.

"I was in the Polish campaign and the French invasion, then into Russia. By this time I was different than civilians, which will be hard for you to understand. To be a soldier, to be always successful in a military campaign, that can mean a lot to a young man. It's hard to believe, really.

"I will never forget the first dead soldiers I saw, but you had to get used to it and go on. I had one case in Russia, a young lieutenant right next to me. We were forward observers, and he got a 2-centimeter grenade right in his head, his whole head popped off, and I got it all over me. But I had to get used to it. I had a company commander; after he stepped on a mine I took over the men. It tore one of his legs apart and the other was terribly injured. I gave him first aid and he said to me calmly, 'Now it's up to you to help out for a while, but I will be back soon.' It was all matter-of-fact."

"What was your frame of mind invading Russia? Guderian says in his memoirs that he gulped when he heard the order."

"I didn't feel daunted. We felt we were invincible. We had won in Poland and France; we were practically before Leningrad in days, not weeks, and nobody could stop us from Moscow. I thought the war would be over in half a year, and it seemed like we were right. I still can see thousands and thousands of Russian soldiers, our prisoners hemmed in on hillsides. And in a way, people my age saw the war as

*Panzer veteran*

inevitable. I had always been interested in history, and I remembered what I had learned from my instructors and my books, what was going on in the tsar's times and everything. There was always this pressure from the east towards the west, and now with Hitler in power, he knew what the Bolsheviks had openly said—we will take the Western nations, and the worst of them all is Germany. The Russians had this kind of fear of Prussia. In our classes we were instructed, and we believed, that it was only a matter of time before they come and get us, and it was therefore advisable to hit them first, hit them hard.

"I was trained as an artillery specialist in the panzers, and I was frequently a forward observer directing the fire of our tanks and guns. Our innovation was to use heavy mobile forces to plunge ahead, later to be supported by infantry which could often be very slow following us up. Sometimes we combined our heavy weapons from various divisions and put them into larger, corps-sized units, often under the command of an artillery general, and emphasized speed and very concentrated fire.

"Our First Tank Division was stationed in Brandenburg. I was then a first lieutenant, and we were under the command of von Manstein. I saw him several times, at meetings and such, but never met him personally. Most Prussian generals, they were very reserved.

"There were some 2 million men ready to jump off into Russia from the eastern front. I remember that because in Königsberg, which was unbelievably full of soldiers, I just happened to stumble into my brother at a cafe. Can you imagine?

"We invaded in June of 1941. This was not ideal terrain for us, plenty of swampland. We would have been a lot faster into Leningrad if the conditions had not been so primitive. We had to cut down trees and branches to cover the mud to get through all this. Spring and early summer were often worse than winter. When the ground froze you could at least move on it."

I asked him about the caliber of his Russian opponents. "It changed all the time," he replied, "especially in the early days of this campaign. At the Riga River, all of a sudden they sent in against us elite divisions with T-34s, this famous Russian tank. We thought, my God, how would we be able to get through their armor; our shells would just bounce off them into the air. We had to use our infantry, the panzer grenadiers who rode with us on the tanks. We would stop, the infantry would jump off the back and dig trenches, and then we'd go into reverse and the Russian tanks would come forward. When they would cross the trenches, our grenadiers would get up and put magnetic mines on their armor, and these would disable the tank. Those first few days were critical, and the grenadiers saved us. Eventually we increased our cannon size so we could handle these tanks, because they were hitting us, and thank God their fuses were bad. Their shells had a time delay. They should have been ready to explode once they pierced into our tanks, and exploded on the inside; then naturally they would destroy everything, the tank crew and all. But instead they just shot right through. I had a few holes in my tank; we used to joke about it.

"You know, it's very interesting: Those Russian tanks, even the T-34s, were very crude machines. We got to see them because our mechanical people often salvaged disabled material and our troops used them later on. They were very simple machines. If a transmission broke down, the Russians could replace it with a truck transmission—many of their important parts were virtually interchangeable with civilian parts. They were easy to fix, in other words. Our tanks were technologically superior in every way, but because they were so complicated, they were hard to repair.

"Some of those Russian troops in front of Leningrad, they were marvelous. They would never give up. They would dig themselves in, these round, deep holes, and let the fast-moving, shock-killing troops pass them by. Then our infantry following up, occupying the land, they would have to deal with them. And our men used to complain about it; the Russians would never stop shooting. They were tough. I think they fought that way out of fear. They had been told by the commissars, 'The Germans are the worst devils. They never take prisoners of war. If you surrender, you will die. And if you take one step backwards, we will kill you.' So many of them may have felt they had no choice but to fight to the end.

"Despite all you read, I never saw anyone kill a Russian prisoner of war, never! The Russians, because they were always on the run, they could never take prisoners with them, and they killed whoever they could get, but I never saw anything of that on our side.

"When Leningrad looked as though it would fall, we were pulled out for the drive on Moscow. We came into our own then; the land was ideal for tanks. Very often we were pulled out from our division and combined with other tanks and armored divisions, and you belong now to a very powerful *Heerestruppen*. Believe me, we were the best of the best. We got special treatment in armaments and supplies, and very often we were the ones who broke through.

"As spearhead divisions, we were always surrounded. We had enemies in the front, on our left, on our right, often at the back. Ground troops couldn't keep up with us. Very often they were too exhausted, and that could be very dangerous. That's why they often resupplied us from the air. We could move as few as 5 or 6 kilometers in a day, but we could also drive 60, 70, 80 in a day, then turn around and roll up from the back a whole front. This was the way to wage war! Taking hundreds and thousands of prisoners, saving lives if you will. Good officers can save lives, and we had the best officers in the world. If you get bad officers, you are really in trouble. Guderian said this to us many times. We are not a killing machine, he said. We break through and end wars quickly. By waging quick warfare, the generals believed fewer lives would be lost. This is what they meant by "blitzkrieg." Look at the trench fighting of World War I. Thousands of people shooting at each other for years, terrible casualties. We were quick. Of course you, as an American, you would say, What happened to all those prisoners? I will admit that the thought has often crossed my mind, too. You can believe what you want, but I never saw any unnecessary brutality. We captured those men; we never mistreated them. What happened afterwards to them, I do not know. I never sat behind a desk. I was on the front line risking my life every day."*

"What happened to the German army in Russia?" I asked. "After such success, on a scale never before known in warfare, how did you come to lose in the end?"

"Not through bad luck, I can tell you. It was our fault completely. It started—I know the time very well—when we were so successful towards Moscow. It is unbelievable to me, but when I visited Russia a year ago I was able to see again the places I was as a young officer, Leningrad and so forth. And before Moscow, there's an area where they built this big university. It's a high section you can overlook, and from there I took 'skyline sketches' of Moscow as a young officer; and there I was, some fifty years later, standing on the same spot. I closed my eyes and opened them again. It hadn't changed all that much. So we were there, just like Napoleon.

"What happened? I don't know. Being involved in continuous combat all the time, you didn't recognize what was going on in higher places, but clearly they couldn't make up their minds what to do. I know these things like you do, from books, and it is clear that Hitler interfered and spoiled the good planning of our officers. What I do know is that all of a sudden we had nothing to throw against the enemy anymore. They had turned all the supplies to the south and gave up on us. And we were so close. Then to tell us, 'Retreat!' This was bitter, and I never forget it! When you go forward, you can take a lot, but when you go backward, it really gets to you. That was the first time we had a retreat. We did not learn about this in our academy. 'Retreat,' 'surrender,' these are words they never mentioned there.

"The worst of it was, they gave us nothing, left us completely without supplies: no winter clothes, no food, no ammunition, no gasoline. We had to fight our way back like infantry. We left so much of our equipment behind. Many of us had only rifles, and we were fighting against very well equipped, really tough Siberian troops. So many of our men lost arms and legs. It was a rotten shame.

"The exhaustion level, it was unbelievable, and the weather conditions, I have to tell you I never experienced this ever. The tanks we

*Estimates vary widely on the number of Russian soldiers captured in combat by the Wehrmacht, anywhere between 4 and almost 6 million being the parameters. One German historian has written "that four out of five Russian POWs died by starvation, maltreatment or execution."

Snapshots from the scrapbook of a panzer veteran

*"This is what it was like being a forward observer. This was during maneuvers in East Prussia."*

*"That's me, a short way from Stalingrad. My vehicle here, all stuck. We had to get out and push."*

*"After I was wounded at Stalingrad, I was stationed at the academy in Potsdam. I had a class of reserve officers. Even though I was younger than they were, they respected me. It didn't take them long to find out this guy's from Stalingrad."*

*"On our way to Stalingrad. This was perfect ground for tanks. That's me getting into my wagon."*

*"This was my class at Potsdam, reserve officers. That is me, the officer with the sword. You can see some of them had some experience already; they had decorations. But reserve officers, they were cannon fodder. In my experience, each and every time we put reserves to the front, in no time they were dead. With luck, maybe 10 percent survived the war . . . a rotten, rotten shame."*

still had, you couldn't start them in the winter without making a bonfire underneath to get the oil moving. When you touched something metal, your skin came off. Sometimes we tried to push vehicles, and if a man had holes in his gloves, it ripped his skin off. And our wounded? We had to leave them behind. In a month or so we established a winter line. Once again I was reminded of Napoleon.

"What broke the rest of our strong belief that we were on the winning side was Stalingrad. That was really . . . I will never forget Stalingrad."

# ⇥ 14 ⇤
# Stutthof
## 1943
# Final Solutions

*Here you have Western civilization, our achievements these past 2,000 years—what we refer to in the old German slogan as "the Christian love of your neighbor." This place just shows you where we ended up with all these slogans.*

—**Aronek Kierszkowski**

THE LITTLE VILLAGE OF STUTTHOF lies just a half hour's drive down the road from Danzig, its commercial viability ensured by the long and narrow strand of pristine beach that plunges eastward into the Baltic beyond its last row of ice cream shacks and guest houses. This place is a bottleneck in summer, as busloads of vacationers from all over the former Communist bloc—and now Germans from the West—line up to enjoy the pleasures that Frisches Nehrung (in Polish, Mierzeja Wiślana) can offer, a relatively unpolluted stretch of seaside amenities some 30 miles long, studded with stands of pine for nature walking and bird sanctuaries. When winter winds blow in January and February, however, the "Zimmer Frei" ("Vacancy") signs can be ripped right off their shingles. The population shrinks to nothing.

I never saw any signs directing tourists or visitors to the Stutthof concentration camp. I knew I was close only when graffiti began appearing: swastikas painted on traffic signs and the like. I do not hold this desire for anonymity against the Poles in particular, nor those from the local chamber of commerce who might wish to emphasize some of the region's more pleasing attractions. Touring Stutthof, after all, is a good way to lose your appetite for some of the fine kielbasa and equally good beer that is served up in local restaurants. Why discourage business unnecessarily? Even so, over a million visitors a year tour the place, and most of them are Poles.

I had never heard of Stutthof, nor, do I imagine, have most others from Western Europe or America. William Shirer's encyclopedic tome on the Third Reich dutifully orients us to the gruesome work performed by SS murderers at Auschwitz, Dachau, Buchenwald, Belsen, Treblinka, and the many, many other death camps, but Stutthof is mentioned not once. I asked twenty-five friends in the States if the name rang a bell, and for all twenty-five it turned up a blank. But every Pole, Jew or gentile, knows Stutthof.

The camp is on the very edge of town. In 1940 the only people living here were fishermen and farmers. Heinrich Himmler ordered beach facilities constructed "for recreational purposes," a place where SS guards could relax from the rigors of a day's bloodletting. It was constructed upwind of the camp, so that smoke and ash from the crematorium, an odor that one survivor equated with roast pork, would not offend.

As I'm here well before the season would ordinarily begin, mine is the only vehicle in the rather modest car park. The gate to Stutthof is open, not an employee or caretaker in sight—a rather eerie sensation, to put it mildly. A sign in several languages reads, in its English translation, that "not allowed are children up to 17, unsober persons, seaside wear persons." Passing the commandant's villa, one enters by a guard tower and through barbed wire into the compound.

Stutthof has the distinction of being the first labor camp established outside of Germany once hostilities began. War commenced on September 1, 1939; Stutthof received its first prisoners a day later. Günter Grass in The Tin Drum asserts that all thirty defenders of the Polish post office in Danzig (including his character the unfortunate Jan Bronski) were put against the wall and shot for "irregular military activity." Be that as it may, the initial batch of those incarcerated at Stutthof were Danzig postal employees, followed by railroad workers, soldiers from the Westerplatte garrison, intellectuals, writers, artists from the city proper (mostly turned in by local Germans), and over 200 Polish priests. Their first job was to create a prison.

Stutthof was cleared almost by hand. Trees were felled by ax to be sure, but the SS saw no need for horses or tractors. Work gangs hauled the trees away, removed the stumpage by manual labor, and leveled the fields with their own sweat and muscle. Those who couldn't handle the job were summarily shot. Food was inadequate, hygiene nonexistent, clothing threadbare as the first winter joined this dismal scene. Cheap barracks thrown up by inmates were drafty and ill heated. A greenhouse for ornamental flowers, however, was carefully monitored for temperature control, Stutthof becoming well known throughout the SS system for its horticultural achievements. A rabbit farm, of all things, was also highly praised.

Stutthof's character radically altered in 1942 when its status as a work camp was upgraded to that of concentration camp. No longer was it a provincial detention center for "antisocial persons" of Polish descent numbering some 3,000 people; now it was blueprinted for 25,000 prisoners, and these began streaming in—Russian POWs, Polish Jews, Hungarian women, the usual assortment of social riffraff, Gypsies, and unfortunates from some thirteen European countries. In all it is estimated that 115,000 people were trucked or trained into Stutthof. Of these, 65,000 never made it out.

The crematorium, it seems, could not handle the load. Mass graves are scattered about the old Prussian countryside, periodically disturbed by inadvertent farmers during springtime plowing. Even bathers on vacation have at times uncovered bones in the sunbleached dunes, their beach umbrellas jammed through corroded skulls.

Stutthof was the tip of an organizational pyramid, its web of satellite camps numbering over a hundred. Many of these were located next to industrial or manufacturing concerns that required manpower, some of it skilled. Labor was by no means freely supplied, businessmen paying on numerous occasions an equivalency in wages into SS bank accounts. Submarine and Luftwaffe parts, bricks, wood products, roads, plantings, and harvests were made, delivered, or gathered by emaciated and easily replaced units of prisoners. No one in the countryside could claim they didn't know that Stutthof camp existed. Work squads marched through the countryside every day, back and forth to job sites.

Some barracks still remain here. Most were torn down and used by prisoners—skilled as they were in stretching what resources they had to the fullest—as firewood after their deliverance in 1945. Whereas their Soviet liberators, when in need of warmth, often ignited an entire cottage, then huddled by the tens of dozens around the blaze, survivors at Stutthof neatly stacked their planks in little piles and consumed them very carefully in campfires. These barracks are now marked by rectangular blocks of concrete, their identification numbers molded within.

In several adjoining wooden shacks, a small museum has been installed, depicting the fall of Poland, the creation of Stutthof, and the efforts of resistance groups to free their country. Included are exhibits devoted to Catholic martyrs who died both here and at other camps. Only a few panels specifically highlight the plight of Polish Jewry. Although Stutthof was originally a camp designed for all the captive nationalities no matter their status or religion, it is also undeniable that in the summer of 1944 the balance tipped. In only four months that year, Stutthof swallowed up 37,000 prisoners, and over 70 percent of these newcomers were Jews. The final two years of the camp's existence were primarily of a Jewish coloration. The death marches, the executions down by the Frisches Haff, and the train traffic to and from Auschwitz involved the Jews to near exclusion.

This museum as a result becomes yet another focal point in the recriminatory Jew-Pole relations, symbolized in many ways by the convent controversy at Auschwitz and, by extension, the fiftieth anniversary of that camp's liberation that was held in February 1995. A survivor put it to me this way: "What I went through as a young girl during those times, it has scarred me forever. My family gone, the things I saw—this is my whole life. It defines everything, no matter that I pulled myself together afterwards and could put it behind me if I chose to. I am a Jew, not a Pole—and the camps, they killed Jews, not Poles."

This relentless dogmatism amazes many Poles. What in heaven's name, they cry in exasperation, can anyone have against Carmelite nuns praying for the souls of those martyred at Auschwitz, no matter the religion of those who died or those who remember? Auschwitz and all the camps stand for man's inhumanity, an object lesson from which every country and every individual should learn, especially today in a world riven with minor holocausts. As Jewish groups blistered Lech Walesa and his government's plans for the Auschwitz ceremonies, a Polish official was even quoted as saying, "I don't know whether in this atmosphere created by some Jewish circles and media it will be possible to continue a dialogue. First we are attacked for poor organization, then for the Polonizing of events. It is, in fact, a universalization."

"That's the sort of thing people say who have a bad conscience," another camp survivor told me. "Universalization? I don't want to hear the word. These camps were primarily run to murder Jews. It's really quite simple."

As Pontius Pilate asked, "What is truth?" Can it be found here at Stutthof, given the tempers and traumas of such a subject, a setting wherein our emotions can so easily be swayed or manipulated? Probably not. The safest thing to do would be to retreat or withdraw into some sort of mental reserve when we are in a place like this, but the graphic visions are much too powerful: one shack stacked high to the ceiling with thousands and thousands and thousands of old brown shoes, the leather seemingly slagged by the heat into an immutable solid whole. I note one pair on the top, children's size, and all I can think about are my own two daughters. Nor does the gas chamber give one a moment of reprieve for studied contemplation, especially with the crematorium to its side, where bodies were stacked in between layers of firewood, then doused with gasoline and lit up. A few wreaths, several plaques, and many flags give a sheen of respect and memory to this befouled building, but "sweetening the horror," as one scholar put it, seems to me to make matters worse. A large Soviet-style requiem impresses the visitor, but who can enjoy looking through glass panels at bone and ash? The latrine area makes you want to vomit. "Afterwards, Jews were ordered to jump right into the cesspit," wrote a Polish prisoner. "This was full of urine. The taller Jews got out again since the level reached their chin, but the shorter ones went down." And the soap recipe? Well, why should a British POW lie? "The process of melting down took about 24 hours. The fatty portions of the corpses and particularly those of females were put into a crude enamel tank, heated by a couple of bunsen burners. Some acid was also used in this process. I think it was caustic soda. When boiling had been completed, the mixture was allowed to cool." A German laboratory technician who participated in this experiment claimed that "25 kilograms of soap were produced. The amount of human fat necessary for these processes was 70 to 80 kilograms, collected from some 40 bodies. I used this human soap for my personal needs, for toilet and for laundering. For myself I took 4 kilograms of this soap."

The truth, in perfect impartiality, cannot be found at Stutthof, but opinions? They flood through a person's mind like a dike in Holland giving way to the rush of the wild North Sea.

*"My shoes are probably in there" (Aronek Kierszkowski)*

The "Auschwitz lie"? Anyone who denies the Holocaust should be whipped. Extreme punishment for extreme falsity. Of all the bogus catchwords in this century of political doggerel, from the "stab in the back" to McCarthyism, the "Auschwitz lie" is perhaps the most specious.

Universalization? I side with the Jews. There are holocausts aplenty in our modern world, whether they be called ethnic cleansing or tribal feud, but they derive their example from the single figurehead of monstrosity that Stutthof and all the camps represent. The German philosopher Karl Jaspers said as much, the Holocaust in his opinion being "something that is fundamentally different from all crimes that have existed in the past." Nazi Germany singled out a particular group for extermination and marshaled its considerable force to do so in a sweep of magnitude never before envisioned or carried out. The Jews were its specific target.

Had Stalin murdered greater numbers of people? It seems he did. Did he single out the Jews? No, his purview was more circumferential and paranoid. Did Poles die in concentration camps? Of course they did, in great numbers. Did Russians as well? Indeed so: They, too, were rounded up to some degree and taken away. But did Hitler,

Himmler, Heydrich, Eichmann, and the others seriously believe they could obliterate these Slavic nations from the very earth? These *Untermenschen* could be tortured, humiliated, subjugated, harnessed, enslaved, murdered, and dumped by the wayside when all used up, but despite all his hysterical hypothesizing to the contrary, I doubt whether total annihilation ever entered Hitler's head as a feasibility. The Jews, however, were fewer in number and the objects of a more impassioned malice; they were deemed erasable. This was a job that could be done. Every other ethnic group that SS ingenuity attempted to murder has recovered. Polish Jews, as one of their own has written, will never come back: "The immensity of Jewish losses destroyed the biological basis for continued communal existence . . . in Europe."*

Universalization as an outlook undermines this unique crime. That it might serve to cover long-standing antipathy toward Jews by many Poles both past and present, loath as they are to sanctify their Jewish compatriots, is certainly plausible as an argument and does little credit to this nation. Poles in Warsaw with whom I spoke claim that when and if their nation emerges politically into some form of modern democracy, Westernized in the process both culturally and temperamentally, enormous change in their attitudes will come quickly. "Anti-Semitism is bad for business," one told me. "Everyone knows this." How fast the farthest reaches of the countryside may change is anyone's guess.

It would be, I believe, ungenerous to criticize, by way of example, those fourteen Carmelite nuns who wished to undertake constant vigil at Auschwitz.† There is something comforting about prayer and something quaint or medieval about praying around the clock for the souls of those who perished. The notion of martyrs, of people dying for a sacred cause, is estimable. But as many commentators have noted

---

*Opinion is by no means of one persuasion on this issue, even among Jews. Hannah Arendt criticized "the Jewish perspective" in 1963 when she wrote on the trial of Adolf Eichmann. Nuremberg had emphasized Nazi crimes "against members of various nations," or humanity in general, whereas the proceedings versus Eichmann highlighted "the tragedy of Jewry." Arendt, to enormous criticism, rejected this narrow vision of the Holocaust as presented in Jerusalem, no matter that most concentration camp victims were indeed Jews.

†The Carmelite monastery is dedicated to the memory of Edith Stein, a Catholic convert from Judaism who had joined the order as Teresia Benedicta of the Cross. A philosopher and editor, she is best remembered today for her posthumous book *Final and Eternal Being*. She was arrested in hiding by the SS and gassed at Auschwitz on August 9, 1942. Her canonization as a Catholic saint was proclaimed in 1998.

before me, there is in all of us a desire to find something good in a situation almost by definition hopelessly evil. In the witness literature of the Holocaust, we seek to uncover some message of hope that offers comfort, some sliver of a moral lesson or principle to show us that something redemptive can come out of such terror.

I think the opinion of Jews, or at least the Jews I spoke with, is to let the horror unfold as an unvarnished and fully lit portrayal of villainy: no redemptive features, no lessons, no search for some sort of silver lining, no martyrs. All we have here are murderers and victims—a plan, conceived by a few, carried out by many, to eradicate European Jewry.

Ordinarily I would have taken advantage of this deserted parking lot as a place to sleep. Instead I follow the trail of sun worshipers past and to come and go out into the dunes of Mierzeja Wiślana for a secluded spot.

<hr />

"I came to Stutthof from Tallin in Estonia," Aronek Kierszkowski told me. "It must have been the fall of 1944, and I came alone. My older brother, Dudek, was shot in Estonia before we left there, and for the first time in all this hell, I must have gone into a deep depression. I had no will. That was very dangerous, because you had to go by instinct to survive, you live with the day. But I was in a void, making no decisions for myself. How I got through this period of a few weeks I don't know. As long as Dudek and I had been together, we thought we had a chance, we thought we'd see our family again. Little did we realize they'd all been dead for over a year.

"Dudek and I, after the ghetto at Wilno, worked in a variety of camps in Estonia. The first was a 'good one,' a mine for brown coal, supervised by a German company called Balt Oil. This was a regular SS labor camp. As soon as you got sick, you got killed; as soon as you were unable to work, you got shot all over the place. People died like flies. The work was hard, but they fed those of us who worked in the mines, gave us boots, lamps, and so on, because they needed that coal to produce gasoline for the military. At that time we still had our own clothes but nothing else. It was cold in Estonia.

"When the Russians broke through the first time at Leningrad, things got very much worse. The SS marched us through the snow to a camp called Ereda, a hell if there ever was one, one of the worst camps I ever was in. People talk about gas chambers—gas chambers, you die in about a day. There were people at Ereda that they brought in from all the other camps in Estonia, people that couldn't work anymore, and they just dumped them there in cardboard barracks and didn't feed them. No bunks, no blankets, no furniture, nothing at all, just dumped them in there to die. It was so cold people's hair froze to the concrete floor. I was shocked at this place, and even more so when Dudek came up and said, 'You won't believe this, but I found Uncle Aizenberg and Dodzik' (his son) in one of these barracks. We went down to help him, but my uncle was hardly coherent and, I don't know what the medical condition was, but his skin was turning black. His fourteen-year-old son was holding on to him. What a scene."

"Is there any way that you can describe what your emotions were at seeing such a sight?" I asked him.

"Of course not. I was fifteen at the time. You switch into a survival mode. You couldn't think about the past, and you couldn't think too much about the future. You solved problems as they came up, and these were the problems of survival: getting food or getting work in a place where you could get hold of food. Uncle Aizenberg died. My brother risked his life to get Dodzik to the bathhouse at night to wash him up, give him some food, get the lice off him, so that he might recover and join our barrack, so we could go to work together. But a few days later Dodzik turned black, and he died, too. So that was the past. You couldn't think about it. Day to day, as I said before.

"You had to have luck. You could never tell what might happen. I remember the deputy commandant at Ereda, he was named Scharfeter. He was one of only two SS men there; the rest were Estonian auxiliaries. I remember there were people in the camp who couldn't work anymore, they were called *Musel*-men, a person who put a blanket over his back, a signal that he had given up and was waiting for death. On a Sunday, while we were carrying logs of wood, Scharfeter, who had a stick in his hand, he stopped one of these *Musel*-men. The *Musel*-man, he may have been only thirty-five for all I know, but from far away he looked seventy. And Scharfeter started to hit him with his stick, apparently for nothing. I mean, this was a man waiting to die. He fell, so the SS man ordered him to get up. He got up, and he hit him again. He fell. So he kept this up for about half an hour. At the end the man couldn't get up anymore, so Scharfeter put his stick over his throat, put his boots on either end of the stick, and choked him to death. After 1945 the Western countries wanted to use regular laws to punish people like these?

"In July of 1944, the Germans found themselves in real trouble. During the previous winter we knew they were getting clobbered around Leningrad. We used to see, when we were hauled out to repair railroad tracks, lots of trains going by, Red Cross hospital trains full of soldiers with frozen legs and frozen arms. And as a matter of fact, in the camp latrines people would talk and whisper things like, 'The Russians are coming,' or tell us that some Estonian who might have been a good fellow had told someone, 'Don't worry. The end is coming.' And sure enough, a large portion of the German army soon found itself cut off in Estonia, Latvia, and Lithuania, no way to escape except by sea. They had three ships in Tallin that they planned to use to evacuate some of these troops—this episode was used later in a movie, *The Odessa File*. Well, the SS *Einsatzkommando* unit confiscated the three ships from the German army, and for what? So they could pull out the Jews, fifty to a hundred Estonian camp guards, and maybe twenty-five of themselves? Imagine: They left a German army to fall prisoner to the Russians and took themselves and us out instead. What a patriotic act!

"But since there were too many Jews for the ships to hold, the SS decided to kill off a part of the inmates. They came to our camp and looked for twenty-five strong fellows. This was usually safe, when they asked for strong fellows. Dudek was picked and we were separated. He never came back. He and the others dug ditches in Ereda, where all the 'surplus' Jews were shot. Then he was shot with the other diggers on top of them and the whole mass grave covered over. I heard the details after the war in a displaced persons camp in Germany from a man of this group who had managed to escape during the shootings. This was the start of my depression when I don't remember much that took place in the next several days, a risky time for me because you constantly had to be on your guard, and I wasn't.

"I came out of it on a field in Tallin around August of 1944, waiting to be loaded on one of these ships—I remember it was called the *Mar La Plata*. I was just wandering on the men's side of a fence. Women were on the other side. Suddenly I heard my name called out— 'Aronek! Aronek!'—and you know, it woke me up. The voice sounded like Rose Aizenberg, a cousin of Dodzik who died earlier in Ereda. Rose had lived with her family in one room of our ghetto apartment in Wilno. I looked around, but I never found her. And I did not hear her voice again. This, I can tell you, was a kind of biblical experience, and it saved my life.

"We spent three days steaming on the Baltic and landed near Danzig; then we came by barge to Stutthof. I remember we didn't have a long march from the barges to the camp. I also remember it was cold. They took us into a small area and said that we have to go through *Ent-lausung*, which was delousing, and then we will have to go through a shower. They would be shaving our hair all over. This was a new experience. We still had our civilian clothes, we hadn't been tattooed or shaven, and here they were telling us about showers. We had heard about Auschwitz, and the gas that comes from the shower heads, so we knew this might be the end, but what were we to do? There were walls all around us, soldiers with dogs, SS, Ukrainian guards, all these horrible people. So we concentrated on ordinary things. Some had food; what were they to do with it? They had to give up their clothes, go through a shower, and then get other clothes, the stripes, on the other side—how can you bring anything through when you're naked?

"So I remember we were in this little hall, the gathering place, and I found a half loaf of bread. I said to myself, I'm going to smuggle this through the shower, and if there's life on the other side, then I'm going to take this bread with me. Quick, quick, they hit, and I run, and I kind of held this bread covered with my body. I run in, they shaved off my top hair, they shaved under my arm, and they were shaving between my legs. You had to be careful, because they were using straight-edge razors, and they would make a joke of trying to sharpen their knives on your part like on a barber's strap. I managed to get through that with this half loaf, and I got in the shower with it, too, where it must have gotten wet, but I got through that, too, and out the other side, where they threw us all those striped clothes. Then they led us to a barrack where I was assigned a bunk, my very own bunk. I put the bread under my pillow.

"The next day they called us out, and I thought I'd be coming back, but they put us in a different barrack so I lost the bread. I felt badly about that until very recently. Then I said to myself, Why do you feel bad about it? Some other hungry person got it. Maybe it either helped him survive or at least made a few happy days for him before he was killed. So in a way, now, I feel much better about it. But this event taught me a valuable lesson, that in uncertain times you have to be careful leaving things behind because you may never go back to the place you came from.

"As camps go, Stutthof was pretty clean. We had our own bunks, and food was regularly given out, though meager. It was a real concentration camp in the sense that it concentrated people from all over: criminals, socialists, Jews, even some Spanish soldiers who had volunteered to fight the Soviet Union but then disobeyed German orders when sent to fight the Western Allies. I ended up in a cellblock with Danes who had fought in the Spanish civil war on the socialist side. When the Germans took over Denmark, they rounded these fellows up and put them in Stutthof, but they treated them very well. They were real Nordics, after all, more Nordic than the Germans. We cleaned their washrooms. They used to give us Jews some food. They were real nice people, real human beings.

"There were no mass killings at Stutthof like at Auschwitz, only people dying of starvation and disease or in punishments. There were hangings and beatings. I remember one person ran away and was caught, and we had to stand on roll call while they hanged him. But for large-scale killings, they sent people down to Auschwitz.

"That reminds me of a close call I had at this camp. After our arrival they collected all the teenagers together in one barrack. After a week or so they lined us up and said they are going to send us to a camp where we will meet our parents, younger brothers and sisters, and so on—all lies of course. There were 516 of us, all lined up in ten rows. The Germans, with their precision, had ten cattle cars and figured fifty kids per car, so they had to cull out sixteen, and the *Oberschefkapo* went out to pick the sixteen. At this point everyone knew this was not good. As the *Oberschefkapo* was picking out the people he wanted, kids were standing on their toes to look taller. I was in the last row. I was tall. After he had picked about fourteen and had still a few rows to search from, he looked around and saw me. He waved to me to come out. But I didn't have my glasses, so I was not quite sure he meant me. Everyone in my area started to run toward him, but he said, 'No, no. This one there,' and he got me out. I was the fifteenth or sixteenth picked. We found out a day later that they all went to Auschwitz and were gassed. I never saw that *Oberschefkapo* before or after.

"Luck had so much to do with survival. We were like birds, the birds that come to my birdhouse here in the winter. They're so nervous, constantly pick, pick, pick, look around, take one pick more, and fly away. This is very much how the prisoners were. You had constantly to be on your guard. The only problem was that we could not fly away.

"By this time, we didn't have names anymore. We had numbers. My number was 72788."

# ⚔ 15 ⚔

# Rastenburg
## 1944
# Madness, Assassination, Honor

*Today I became a general.*
—Colonel Claus von Stauffenberg, July 20, 1944

A FORLORN ASSEMBLAGE of ice cream shacks and snack bars remain boarded up in the springtime chill of an early morning. The parking lot, of modest size, is empty except for one large motor bus, from which a group of German tourists in their sixties and seventies file out under the direction of a jovial guide, whose banter and raucous laughter does little to lift the soggy and dripping atmosphere of this dank stretch of forest. Certainly there are few smiles among these visitors. Their naturally high spirits may well have been chilled by this spot, which Field Marshal Alfred Jodl called a cross between monastery and concentration camp. And few places so gloomily reflect the personality of its chief inhabitant, Adolf Hitler.

In my travels I have come across or visited many sites associated with Hitler: the environs of Linz in Austria, where the restless Alois Hitler (née Schicklgruber), former customs clerk, moved about the neighborhood from address to address, his family in tow; the streets of Vienna, through which his son, a demoralized and penniless Adolf, wandered from flophouse to flophouse, soup kitchen to soup kitchen, a dreamy sort of youth who spent what little money he had to stand in the rear of the opera house listening, it is said, to *Tristan und Isolde* thirty to forty times; the battlefield of Ypres, where Hitler was gassed in October 1918; the bustle of Munich, with its famous Hofbräuhaus, site of many Hitlerian harangues, where I have a photograph of myself drinking beer, as a boy of fourteen, from a stein bigger than my head; Berchtesgaden in the Bavarian Alps, the purity of whose marvelous and pristine atmosphere can obliterate any crime or nefarious association; the ruins of Berlin in 1960, a tour of the Reichstag's empty shell. But none of these places gives you a picture of Hitler. Rastenburg somehow does.

The forests here were part of the Steinort estate, what Marion, Countess Dönhoff, called "the great wilderness on the lake." It was inherited in 1936 by her childhood friend Heini Lehndorff, one of many hundreds of aristocrats who were flushed from hiding and executed for their role in attempting to assassinate Hitler here in East Prussia on July 20, 1944, the so-called Operation Valkyrie headed by Count Claus Philip Schenk von Stauffenberg, a plot as valiant and high-minded as it was inept. Countess Dönhoff recounts with delight her cross-country riding expeditions with the Lehndorffs through this lake-studded environment during happier times, but the deep fastness of wood and undergrowth seems terminally claustrophobic to me.

Hitler christened his eastern headquarters Wolfsschanze, or the Wolf's Lair. He had a Wagnerian penchant for giving such melodramatic nomenclatures to his military quarters, other command posts being code-named Wolfsschlucht (Wolf Gorge), Werwolf (Werewolf), and so on. Psychiatrists, who have written some of the weirdest babble of all on Hitler's admittedly neurotic personality, trace this affection to a sexual source, not surprisingly.* They pinpoint the future dictator's youthful dependence on older mother figures for nurturing and support, women like Helene Bechstein, who freely bankrolled the first National Socialist newspaper from her husband's business funds (he manufactured pianos). Hitler used to lie on Frau Bechstein's divan, his head on her chest. She would stroke his hair and whisper in his ear, "Mein Wölfchen"—"my little wolf."

---

*I particularly remember as a schoolboy in the 1960s reading about the release of a confidential assessment of Hitler's personality written during the war by a U.S. army doctor, suggesting that the Führer encouraged his mistresses to urinate or defecate on his face, the result of his "unresolved Oedipal complex." However farfetched, it is true that Hitler had difficult associations with women. Six of seven with whom it is generally believed Hitler carried on affairs either committed suicide or attempted to.

Wolfsschanze consisted of about 30 acres and was divided into three compounds, all connected by a single entryway. The outermost camp was garrisoned by troops and workers and included an airstrip and railway yard where at all times a steam engine was maintained at full pressure, ready to go at a moment's notice. The middle enclosure housed various offices of the high command, among them the soon to be infamous communication and signals fiefdom of General Erich Fellgiebel, a key member of the July 20 plot, along with ancillary underground facilities housing quarters, cinemas, a casino, and other recreational amenities. The innermost zone of Wolfsschanze, separated from the rest by two rows of barbed wire and patrolled by dogs, was Hitler's camouflaged bunker. Various cronies and party officials commandeered every stately mansion for miles around as their local headquarters. Joachim von Ribbentrop, for instance, moved into Steinort, and Hermann Göring's entourage, preceded by crates of fine wine and fancy foodstuffs, took over a rustic hunting lodge. But Hitler lived alone in spartan quarters, like a hermit, as some observed.

I tag along with the tour group. A map crudely painted on sheets of plywood gratuitously misidentifies the various ruins, pulling Nazi rabbits out of a hat as it were. Thus Wilhelm Keitel's offices are randomly assigned to Göring, Jodl's to Martin Bormann, and so forth. Bormann, Göring, Goebbels, and Himmler, after all, are infinitely more sinister associations than the run of more or less anonymous army officers who filed in and out of here in a continuous stream between 1941 and 1944. In a way this is all immaterial. People come here to see Hitler's bunker.

This building is in ruins. What the retreating Germans failed to destroy—their demolition charges miscarried, yet another chink in the German reputation for master efficiency—the Soviets largely finished off. Hitler's quarters are completely gone, a pile of masonry chunks and rubble. A very moving memorial to the martyred von Stauffenberg graces the site. Several tourists flock about it, taking pictures with camcorders and Polaroids. Ten severe gentlemen from the group stand purposely off to one side and smoke cigarettes. There is no way on earth they will honor this traitor von Stauffenberg, no matter how hideous a figure Hitler may have been. After a few minutes the cheerful tour guide leads them off to inspect other decrepit bunkers. Half an hour later I hear the bus depart. All is stillness here once again.

Hitler found this place profoundly depressing. He was not a Prussian, after all. He had no roots here; nothing in the scenery or geography held his attention or assuaged his nerves. Von Manstein had called this bit of earth "the beautiful province," but everything about it, reinforced by the increasingly disastrous tidings from the Russian front, put Hitler on edge and frayed his temper. Indeed some of the Führer's most volcanic tantrums were reserved for this patch of wet and featureless forest, a frigid wasteland in the snowy winter (Hitler hated snow) and a mosquito-ridden oven during summer. It could well be that Hitler lost his sanity in the few years he lived here. He seemed to General Franz Halder like a dog, foaming at the mouth and "barking."

Certainly most everything he had achieved through his eventful career came to ruin during this short span of time, at first slowly, then in dreadful rush. Along the way, living underground in his bunker, following what one historian called a "troglodyte existence," he lost his zest for life, his appreciation for the few things that gave him joy. He stopped listening to music, took meals alone with his dog, could barely sleep. He complained when the SS, attempting in their leaden way to eradicate the mosquito population, poured oil on the surrounding ponds and lakes and set fire to them, killing all the area's bullfrogs. Hitler missed their soothing croaks, and the frogs were reintroduced the next year. He also became a drug addict here at Wolfsschanze. It is said that his quack physician, Dr. Theo Morell, prescribed over seventy medications for the Führer between 1941 and 1945, some directly injected (with dirty needles), many of a fairly serious narcotic composition. Hitler's hours, irregular to begin with, grew stranger. He often remained awake until 8 a.m. after boring his retinue of secretaries and hangers-on with all-night discourses on early party history and memories from long ago. Many visitors saw Hitler change before their eyes.

Although von Stauffenberg's plot and its near miraculous denouement (from Hitler's standpoint, anyway—it was incredible he survived) is the most melodramatic draw for tourists here, the more substantial undercurrent of the place lies elsewhere. From Wolfsschanze Hitler directed the most daring, ambitious, foolhardy, and cataclysmic venture of his entire life, the invasion of Russia. From the perspective of German history and attitude, this incredible enterprise can perhaps be seen as inevitable, the logical extension of what the Teutonic Knights more than seven centuries before had set out to accomplish in the first place. However turgidly expressed in *Mein Kampf* and elsewhere, Hitler's desire for *Lebensraum*, or living space in the East, is precisely the motivation that impelled many a German before him to mount a horse, unfurl the banner, unsheathe his sword, and move off into the face of a snowstorm for new lands and new glory at the expense of Slavic enemies pushing west to meet him. The only surprising aspect of Hitler's obsession was that his genes and origin as a southerner would not ordinarily have led him in such a direction. But as he frequently remarked, he was fascinated with history and knew all there was to know about Germany's destiny.

As many commentators have noted, he made no secret of his views regarding expansion into Russia. All you had to do was read *Mein Kampf* and everything was there: every step of his life, every dream, every objective laid out in blueprint form, from the Jewish problem to dealing with France, from party politics to dealing with Bolsheviks. This assessment is both true and false.

Should Stalin have realized that Hitler would attack him? Probably so, if he had read *Mein Kampf*. But Stalin, like everyone else, had never waded through the often impenetrable morass of Hitler's dictations to the faithful Rudolf Hess during his imprisonment of 1924. Every German household may have had a copy on its bookshelf, but few ever took the time to plow through it. "I never read *Mein Kampf*," said a high-ranking German politician of the times, "and what is more I don't know anyone who has." *Mein Kampf*, it seems to me, was the equivalent of what gets published every four years in the United States by aspiring candidates for the presidency. I have never read anything ghostwritten for Jimmy Carter, Ronald Reagan, George Bush, or Bill Clinton, and what is more, I don't know anyone who has.

But just the scan of a few pages of Hitler's autobiography is sufficient to see the general military plan: avenge Versailles, humiliate France, overawe Britain, then turn to the principle objective, the eastern frontier. Far-flung colonies, oceanic trade routes, islands of any sort—none of these held Hitler's primary attention. As the English historian H. R. Trevor-Roper commented, Hitler was a man of continents: He came from the center of the European landmass, and he thought in terms of earth and soil, cities and highways, borders and migrations. Either Germans had to resort to emigration or birth control, stifling both its growing population and its industrial progress, or the people must push back their land frontiers and expand. The logical direction was eastward, where German custom, language, even populations still existed, though under foreign flags. In Hitler's mind India was the logical comparison. "What India is for England, the territories of Russia will be for us. If only I could make the Germans understand what this space means for our future! Here in the Wolfsschanze, I feel like a prisoner in these dugouts, my spirit can't escape. In my youth, I dreamed constantly of vast spaces."

Hitler saw this movement in revolutionary terms. He could mention the Teutonic Knights in his speeches, he could pay reverence to Frederick the Great and Hindenburg, but he did not see the Junker example as anything but the fusty past. Proletariats of national socialism would lead the new advance and lock horns with that equally revolutionary movement of the people, Bolshevism, which, as Göring so delicately put it, was merely a mask "for the dirty Jew devil."

Hitler was smart enough to admire the growth of communism, as indeed he grudgingly admired Stalin. No other philosophical movement caused him more unease, and he saw that one or the other ideology must at some near point in the future emerge from conflict as supreme. Hitler was too restless and too dogmatic a spirit ever to believe in anything so congenial as peaceful coexistence. Life was a march from one goal to another. His thoughts—wild in cadence, intemperate in scope, inflamed by rhetorical vehemence and skill—always reached, always went that one step too far, frequently leading their expounder to the very edge of the abyss, over which he too often quailed. The historical record is full of instances where Hitler lost his nerve.

The dogma of national socialism was often gibberish, spread about in murky detail by a few clever men, such as Goebbels, but more often than not by imbeciles like Alfred Rosenberg, Julius Streicher, Hess, and any number of other uneducated street boors. Yet its core beliefs were clear: anti-Communist, anti-Jew, anti-Catholic, antimonarchial, and antiaristocrat. It was also to some extent antiarmy, a distinction many in the West misunderstand.

Hitler conveniently forgot that Frederick the Great, his idol, relied exclusively on the Junker caste to supply the army with steadfast, sure, reliable, nationalistic, and loyal officers. Hitler, on the contrary, wanted nothing to do with them.

This, of course, presents a considerable paradox. The essence of the Prussian army, that unparalleled instrument of military excellence, had always been its Junker officers, and the officers, by their oaths, had always given their allegiance to the king before all. Bismarck may have scorned those he served, but Hindenburg, no matter his disregard for the king as a military influence, sincerely meant all the obsequious flattery that he sprinkled in his memoirs to the otherwise odious and unworthy Wilhelm II. Adolf Hitler, happiest in his younger days only when in uniform and living the ghastly life of a frontline soldier in the trenches, was equally in love with all things military, with one enormous exception: He had no use for the very lifeblood of the army, its aristocratic officer corps.

Hitler's animosity toward what he contemptuously referred to as "our upper ten thousand" was violent, crude, and physical. "A hereditary monarch," he once said, "is a biological blunder." "The boundary between throne and mad house," he declared on another occasion, "is a very slender thread," and on a third, "The last support of an inadequate monarch is the army." "Royal idiot," "blockhead," "dwarfs," "slobbering pig dog aristocrats"—he used all the usual epithets. The old officer class was addicted to Christian values (the worst, indeed, were Catholics!); honor (the very notion was absurd); and the cavalry (the only things Hitler liked about the equestrian "art" were boots). The trick to national socialism, its truest deviation from the past, was to provide, in Hitler's words, "a shortcut" around the German people's traditional reverence for crown and "epaulets." The people would continue their love affair with goose steps, blood, and iron, but the army would revert from a royal entity to a Nazi one. "The army belongs to the Party," Himmler would boast, "and not the other way around. The army does not belong *even to itself.*"*

Of course these were brave words. When Hitler first came to power, he needed the army, and the army, to its enormous regret, succumbed to the allure of rearmament that Hitler promised, along with the promotions and gaudy decorations, batons, and insignia that came along in its wake. "Their mistake," as the panzer veteran said to me, "was to take Hitler too casually, to underestimate him because he was not their equal socially. You know what Hindenburg called him: 'the Bohemian corporal.' What a mistake! It's hard to explain, but those Prussian field marshals, they expressed nobility, even in their body language. They were fine people. To them, honor and ethical standards meant so much. If they would mess up, they would take their own lives. It's happened many times, and you can think of this as you want

---

*The exigencies of two world wars had diluted the blue blood of Germany's officer corps. In 1860 fully two-thirds of all officers were aristocrats. By 1932 the figure had dropped to 24 percent, and the Nazi era saw further erosion. The hearts and minds of the old nobility were never truly won, as Himmler ruefully noted: "You have to admit the Party has not won over this good blood. This is a sober statement of fact."

to. At least you must say they were very special people, and Hitler, in this way, couldn't match them. But they always said, 'We can handle this man,' and in the end they were so wrong. They misjudged him completely. Hitler was a powerful guy, very dangerous. He didn't shrink to take their lives, and after a while they knew this."

Never was this more true than in the 1930s. The days of groveling to the Hohenzollern past were over: no more ceremonial and obsequious homage to the army and its antique virtues, as Hitler had endured at the famous Potsdam garrison church in 1933 when von Hindenburg had saluted Kaiser Wilhelm's vacant pew, a humiliating slap at the new chancellor. Hitler had been in power over a decade. He had the people behind him, insofar as jobs and bread could buy their affection. He had built organizations to parallel those of the army and state, some of which (such as the police and security systems) were clearly ascendant over their "civilian" counterparts. Although the Wehrmacht had forced Hitler to curb his storm troopers (the *Sturmabteilung*, or SA), the SS, originally created as a bodyguard, was fast replacing them. And Hitler by now had lost whatever awe he may have had for generals and field marshals. German officers, he noted, were "fossils and idiots." He would break them down.

The von Blomberg and von Fritsch affairs were Hitler's opportunity. Though mentioned in most histories of the Third Reich, they are not generally given the prominence they deserve, for in these two instances the officer corps of Germany had its last practical opportunity to remove Hitler from power and avoid war, for certainly the provocation with which to justify action had been amply provided, as the Führer's assault on its honor was extreme and straight from the gutter.

The fall of Werner von Blomberg was his own doing in many respects. The war minister, a widower, had made the mistake of falling in love with a woman of dubious reputation. Hitler had attended the wedding, after which Himmler and Göring gleefully presented evidence that the new Frau von Blomberg had been a registered prostitute, once arrested for selling dirty postcards. Accusations against Freiherr von Fritsch, head of the general staff, were even more dire, a third-rate homosexual blackmailer being hauled out from a hallway to accuse him of unnatural vice in the chancellor's own office, a production as cheap and tawdry as the charge itself. Von Fritsch in particular never realized what was happening to him. A soldier of the old Prussian variety, he had publicly ridiculed Hitler in language that even William Shirer, then a reporter based in Berlin, found indiscreet.

Never in this soldier's dreams could he have imagined a disgrace so contrived, illegal, and bereft of truth and dignity. The charges, patently false (the "informer," like so many other Nazi pawns used to foment crisis or scandal, was quickly shot by an SS firing squad), nonetheless were widely spread, sapping the officer corps of the high ground and exposing its values as corrupt.

Generals and colonels were torn. The rowdy, street fighting, amoral Nazi tactics were now invading the inner sanctum, and its members found themselves caught in a peculiar quandary. Germany was rushing to war—too fast, in their opinion. They were enjoying the reestablishment of their military strength, for they, too, wanted the disgrace of Versailles eliminated and socialism restrained. But German military historians have argued, convincingly, that most of these officers did not want a repetition of 1914–1918; they did not want another European conflict that would end, perhaps inevitably, with another crippling defeat. Was Hitler just saber rattling, or was he a madman?* Could they have their magnificent army and peace as well? Was it worth throwing away all they had gained to date in order to protect two wayward officers? Surely those who replaced them would be from among their own and would continue to look after their privileged position. And so amid such dithering did the officer corps acquiesce in the disgrace of von Blomberg and von Fritsch. Yet far from solidifying their position in this tepid display of support for the state, they in fact fatally weakened it. Hitler, fearing their response, slapped his thigh with glee when he saw nothing but grumbling and no reaction. This confirmed his contempt for "all the little men"; they were now seen to be "either fools or cowards." Von Blomberg, in the final masochistic chapter of this story, suggested to the man who had destroyed him that Hitler take his portfolio himself. It was then but a logical step for Hitler's full assumption of power over the Wehrmacht when he declared himself commander in chief four years later.

By then the fatal, dour, intractable oath that every German officer took to his head of state, "a consideration [that] must in no wise be left out of account," according to Walter Goerlitz, had locked into

---

*General Franz Halder thought he was insane, the drive for conquest a manifestation of Hitler's "pathological sexual impulses." So did Field Marshal Walther von Brauchitsch, who, when an associate mentioned the word "war," "tapped his temple with his index finger."

place, the projected violation of which tormented the conscience of every soldier disgusted with nazism. Von Stauffenberg sought release in the confessional, and even his priest refused to free him from this vow. Hitler's mastery of the Wehrmacht grew more complete with each passing day, especially as victories mounted.*

There is no doubt at all that Hitler's incredible good fortune during the early years of the 1940s both exhilarated and humiliated the upper levels of Germany's officer corps. "What can we do?" raged an exasperated Halder. "He succeeds at everything he does!" Bloodless triumphs in the Rhineland, Austria, Czechoslovakia, and Memel—operations the generals had bewailed beforehand—both diminished whatever influence they had left with Hitler and destroyed their ability of appeal to a crazed population now flushed with easy victory. Another headlong push into Poland, again despaired of by many of the officers, and then into the Lowlands and France sealed their fate. The general staff in its various manifestations became a technical resource, planning, implementing, and supplying whatever ventures Hitler independently dreamed up. "He's playing warlord again," Halder wrote in his diary, which did not prevent this general from doing all he was told, sitting in the "ice age" of Prussian values, trying to preserve the "holy grail" of tradition within the great general staff. But Nazis were everywhere, and the Führer, "inspired tinkerer" that he was, thought only of war.

It is strange indeed to think of German generals who did not want war. Let us not confuse this stance with morality, however. Men like Halder, Ludwig Beck, von Fritsch, and Erwin von Witzleben thought more in terms of inadequate munitions, tanks, men, and training than they did of justification and right or wrong. But they did have a sense of restraint; they believed the famous dictum of von Clausewitz that war was an extension of policy. With Hitler, however, war was not an extension of anything—it was the policy itself.

No ruler in modern European history has been as much a liar and dishonest broker as Adolf Hitler. Stalin may indeed have murdered

---

*The officer's oath proved no defense at the Nuremberg trials held after the war by the victorious Allies, nor did it escape the microscopic attention of fellow Germans such as the existentialist philosopher Karl Jaspers, who called it "the good conscience in evil deeds" and professed surprise at the "curious sanctity" that Germans gave it (particularly Prussians). Jaspers, however, did not come from a military background.

millions more of the innocent during the course of his long and amoral career, but he rarely blustered in public or pledged his word of honor on much of anything.* Hitler could refrain from neither, and the continuing surprise of these tension-fraught years is how persistently men of honor refused to admit what their eyes and ears so clearly recorded. "I don't believe in idealism," Hitler said, but Prime Minister Neville Chamberlain of Britain and a long line of others could not bear such a thought.

The "phony war" and then the real thing had tested Hitler's nerves several times, and many witnesses record how poorly the Führer often stood the test, veering off to defeatist despair and hysterical explosions of foaming temper. "Excitement terrible" and "chaos in command" Jodl and others frequently noted in their diaries. But success breeds confidence, then contempt, and Hitler's excitable personality soon adopted the notion of infallibility. German soldiers—not their officers—had provided the Reich with triumph, ergo the Führer now took it upon himself to provide the required generalship. The Russian campaign, more than any other, according to Halder, was "his" war.

⚎

Very few of the German generals who wrote their memoirs after 1945 ever denied their Führer a certain competency in the military field. Guderian, though offended by his coarseness, conceded to Hitler "a fertile imagination," and Halder, mystified by the train of constant success, kept searching for signs of genius that he felt *must* be there.

But von Manstein, perhaps the finest strategic mind of the entire war no matter the army, presented I think the most thoughtful appraisal of all. "When considering Hitler in the role of a military leader," he wrote, "one should certainly not dismiss him with such cliches as 'the lance-corporal of World War I.' He undoubtedly had a certain eye for operational openings . . . and could quickly seize a chance when it was offered him. He possessed an astoundingly retentive memory and imagination that made him quick to grasp all technical matters and problems of armament. He was amazingly familiar with the effect of the very latest enemy weapons and could reel off whole columns of figures on both our own and our enemy's war production. [But] what he lacked, broadly

---

* "Stalin owes nothing to rhetoric," as Hitler observed.

speaking, was military ability based on experience—something for which 'intuition' was no substitute."

As a "military amateur," of course, Hitler was attracted to new theories of warfare, particularly if innovative methodology had previously found disfavor in the stodgy Wehrmacht. Hence, as von Manstein suggested, Hitler's support of mavericks such as Guderian and Erwin Rommel, both men of nonaristocratic origin, was a plus. But what Hitler's character could not compensate for was the lack of "a real training in strategy and grand tactics."

Ominously, in von Manstein's view and certainly Guderian's, Hitler made up for any inadequacy he may have felt as a commander of Napoleonic proportions by his prodigious reservoir of determination and obstinacy. "His overestimation of the power of the will," as von Manstein saw it, "probably did more than anything else to determine the character of Hitler's leadership. This *will*, as he saw it, had only to be translated into *faith* down to the youngest private soldier for the correctness of his decisions to be confirmed and the success of his orders ensured."

However—and ironically—Hitler's immense inner strength "was not matched by a corresponding boldness of decision." As in the past, Hitler was capable of dithering and irresolution, of uncoordinated action on several fronts at once as a means of avoiding resolution on the main theater that counted. Hitler despised the risks associated with truly radical panzer strategy, the "elasticity of operations," in von Manstein's words, that could "be achieved only by a voluntary, if temporary, surrender of conquered territory"—"Your operations always hang by a thread!" Hitler told Guderian. Whenever in a fix or uncertain what to do, Hitler would therefore fall back on his order to stand fast. "I am the only one who knows what has to be done," Hitler said. "I know the generals don't understand me. All they have to do is obey my orders." And again, to Guderian: "There's no need for you to try to teach me. I've been commanding the German army in the field for five years and during that time I've had more practical experience than any gentlemen of the General Staff could ever hope to have. I've studied Clausewitz and Moltke and read all the Schlieffen papers. I'm more in the picture than you are!" And so, to Russia.

By the time Hitler moved his headquarters to Wolfsschanze, plans for Operation Barbarossa were complete. Many in the general staff were now infected with Hitler's optimism, envisioning a campaign of eight to ten weeks. Others, such as Guderian, claimed they were appalled when appraised of the coming campaign. "When [my staff] spread out a map of Russia before me I could scarcely believe my eyes." Reading Clausewitz on Napoleon's campaign of 1812 and meditating on the fate of the Swedish monarch, Charles XII, gave him little solace either. But strategists of the grand tradition such as von Manstein saw little but glory ahead of them on a terrain ideally suited for mobile warfare, the great Asian steppe.

Yet without a doubt the magnitude of their task was daunting. Russia was a landmass some forty-six times greater than that of the prewar Reich, with a population of 190 million, 16 million of whom were of military age. At one point the German line would stretch more than 1,200 miles, a logistical burden of nightmarish proportions. The roads, infrastructure, weather, railway gauge, and strength and composition of the Russian army—all manner of obstacles—were either underestimated or barely known. One hundred and forty-five German divisions would join in the attack, an initial force of over 3 million men, or 70 percent of the Wehrmacht's total strength. In five months 23 percent of this figure would be wounded or killed, the first casualty coming within one minute of jump-off, when a Lieutenant Weinrowski was cut down by machine-gun fire in Memelland. He would be followed by some 10.8 million compatriots, either dead or captured on the field, but only after they themselves had killed the astounding total of 27 million Russians, both military and civilian.

These kinds of statistics scream from the page and take on an importance that few Western historians wish to bestow. D day was an immense operation, the largest amphibious landing ever undertaken in war, with over 175,000 Allied troops offloaded to the Normandy beachhead. On the dunes overlooking this battlefield, 10,000 Americans lie buried, a bloody but essential price for the opening of an effective second front. But Germany did not lose this war on the French coast in June 1944. It had already lost it in Russia. Eighty percent of all battlefield casualties suffered by Germany occurred in the East, the Soviet army having ground up a total of over 500 German divisions, along with another hundred supplied by Italy, Hungary, Spain, Romania, and others from Hitler's "sullen satellites." Stalin sneered when U.S. general George Marshall described the western front's meager dimensions. A single Russian offensive had opened a gap of 25 miles in the German line. Now that was prodigious!*

If Verdun bled the French in 1916, the Russian front indisputably did the same to the Third Reich, "tearing out the life of the German military monster," as Churchill graphically put it. The immense scope of its theater, the numbers of men and materiel involved, and the breadth of some of its maneuvers and engagements dwarfed anything ever seen. In its initial stages, moreover, the string of German triumphs turned even Hitler's egotistical head, who from October on "lived in a world of fantasy," according to Guderian. Never before such advances—Wolfsschanze lay 900 miles behind the fighting in a matter of weeks—never before such encirclements, never before such numbers of the enemy killed or captured: half a million Soviet dead, half a million POWs, over 7,000 tanks, 6,000 airplanes, 12,000 pieces of artillery either destroyed or taken in the first five months alone. Reading accounts and diaries of German soldiers involved reminds one of Edward Gibbon's *Decline and Fall of the Roman Empire*, where he describes Germanic warriors who grew positively fatigued from killing so many of the enemy. This was "preventive war" at its best.

After 1945 and many, many times at the Nuremberg trials, German officers repeatedly defended their invasion, even while discounting the ideological tone that Hitler gave it as a racial fight to the death (which many of the generals did). Telford Taylor, the noted legal scholar and a prosecutor at the trials, ridiculed Jodl when that officer called Barbarossa "undeniably defensive." "Wiser men than I find [that] preposterous," wrote Taylor, with an insouciance that most Germans, today or tomorrow, would find appallingly jejune. No student of the German psyche should ever underestimate the quandary that so many thoughtful Germans felt regarding their geographical position as "cultural Christianity's" eastern bulwark. As Spain's foreign minister noted in 1943, "If Germany did not exist, Europe would have to invent her."

Most geopolitical Germans have always regarded their French and British counterparts as hypocrites. "You saw that pretty quickly after

---

*American, British, and Canadian casualties on D day numbered 4,900 dead, and 12,000 more American soldiers would be killed in the next few months expanding the beachhead further inland. By contrast, and to give some consideration to issues of scale, the Wehrmacht executed approximately this same number of individuals *from its own army* on the eastern front alone for a variety of offenses: dereliction of duty, self-inflicted wounds, desertion, cowardice, drumhead justice, and so on.

World War II," Count Otto Grote said to me. "When Stalin decided he hadn't gotten enough of Eastern Europe, that he wanted Germany, too, well, he got tough just at a time when the United States had a president who wouldn't be pushed around, Harry Truman. That was the very beginning of the cold war, and it wasn't but a few months thereafter that the Allies decided, 'We better not de-Nazify these people anymore; we better get them back on our side, get them rearmed so that we have a strong barrier between us and Russia.' People have always needed Germany."

"Europe is now one family," wrote von Schlieffen. "When discord breaks out in the house it is hard for any member of the family to stand aloof, particularly if he lives in the middle of the house." The German raison d'être since the Teutonic Knights had been to stand firm, to provide a wall, to push harder against forces of Slavdom pushing back. The frontier mentality, moreover, has always been, no matter the culture, one of morbid suspicion—What were the heathens planning? What was happening across that river, on the other side of these woods, in the minds of your merciless foe? And then of course the notion creeps in to find out, to crawl into the no-man's-land to observe, parry, perhaps hit hard before the blow seen being prepared falls on you. In the West we prefer to label such goings-on warmongering. To many in Germany it was common sense, though the element of paranoia made them more willing perhaps to strike than other, overly placid personalities. The Germans were irked by the Slavs, a German academician wrote in 1925: "They provoke [us] with their mistrust until, in the end, all our national penchant for overreaction, for striking out, for fatalism, once more gets the upper hand. . . . The inclination toward extreme solutions is a German characteristic." Frederick the Great called this "*le tout pour le tout*," Günter Grass, among other observers, the "all-or-nothing principle."

Who was fooling whom in 1941? Hitler, clearly, was looking to wage war on the Russian colossus, but who is to say Stalin wasn't thinking the same thing in return? To many on the general staff it seemed only a matter of time. Stalin's greed matched Hitler's. He did not hesitate to grab Polish land, annex the Baltic states, or invade Finland. Who is to say that Germany, still at war with Britain, might not tempt Stalin at some convenient moment in the future? Soviet troop concentrations along the German border were certainly worrisome (and mysterious—to this day historians argue over their mission). To many on the staff, unswayed by the Nazi doggerel churned out by Goebbels, the military situation alone called for action. "Unpopular though this view may now be," wrote the intelligence expert Reinhard Gehlen in 1971, "I must state that Hitler's decision to invade the Soviet Union was correct. It was clear that Stalin had resolved to postpone his attack on [us] only so long as was necessary to see his former ally bleeding to death and exhausted after a conflict with the western allies. Then he would have grinned and attacked us as well, in the knowledge that the capitalist powers had meanwhile torn themselves to pieces too. He might have waited until 1943 or 1944, but my colleagues and I were convinced he was going to attack sooner or later." As von Moltke had said, "Genius is diligence."

Prior to June 22, 1941, all the parties involved were certainly plotting and maneuvering against each other in a diabolical charade. All thought, or allowed themselves to believe, that they were fooling their adversaries to the quick. Stalin saw the Allies, and particularly a desperate Great Britain, trying to turn the Soviet Union against Germany to save their own battered countries. This, of course, was quite true, and Stalin congratulated himself (according to Nikita Khrushchev) with turning Hitler's attentions solely on the West by guaranteeing Russian neutrality with their nonaggression pact. "He presented the arrangement as a game of who was tricking whom," wrote Khrushchev, but "Stalin understood that war was inevitable. The basic elements of Hitler's plan to attack the Soviet Union were well known. As the saying goes, sparrows were chirping about it at every crossroad." Nevertheless, when the blow came, Stalin "walked around like a wet hen. He was so depressed that it was pitiful to look at him."

Wolfsschanze was the nerve center of this unprecedented effort, one that witnessed an initial rush of success, followed by checkmate, then total disaster, all in the span of but twenty-eight months and two winters. The anvil was Stalingrad.

At first the atmosphere at the Wolf's Lair was almost convivial. It was at this stage in the proceedings where Hitler entertained most every evening. Though the notion of love and intimacy were utterly alien to the middle-aged Hitler, he enjoyed company and could complain of too much solitude and loneliness—yet another contradiction in his character. As Streicher was to testify at Nuremberg, "Anyone who had occasion to make Adolf Hitler's acquaintance knows that I am correct in saying that those who imagined that they could pave a way to his personal friendship were entirely mistaken. Adolf Hitler was a little eccentric in every respect and I believe I can say that

*Bormann's bunker*

friendship between him and other men did not exist—a friendship that could be described as an intimate friendship."

This did not exclude from Hitler's sense of comfort the desire for an entourage of eager listeners, and during the days of glory in 1941 there were plenty of them in these remote and depressing woods of East Prussia, a headquarters purposely devoid of ostentation and glamour. (Albert Speer, Hitler's architect, had learned long ago that Hitler despised chateaux, manor houses, and lineaged castles as manifestations of decadent aristocratic taste.) After a long day of studying reports, attending briefings, hearing assessments, going over maps of campaigns, and issuing his directives to frontline generals, Hitler would while away the evening hours over tea and cakes, rambling on in casual conversation with guests and cronies. These monologues, known to historians as Hitler's "table talk," or *Bormann-Vermerke* (i.e., "Bormann notes," after Hitler's secretary, who arranged their transcription), are perhaps the most intriguing view we have of the intimate personality of this strange, morbid, and essentially lonely man.

They amount to some 1,045 typewritten pages and were clearly regarded by those who labored to produce them as a collection of Christlike homilies and sermons, something of a human dimension to contrast with the more formal speeches and papers that were the hallmark of the Führer's official career. This reflects damningly, of course, on the intellectual level of Hitler's associates, for the "table talk" is mercilessly deficient of any saving grace. Coarse, simplistic braggadocio without solidity in any of the topics discussed (including such benign subjects as vegetarianism), these digressions can only be taken as a devastating slight on German perception and judgment. How could any nation or people fall prey to such a person? The taste-lessness of expression aside—the continual reference to "Yids," "nig-gers," "Holy Joes," and so on—one is struck by the sophomoric qual-ity of Hitler's opinions: "Nero didn't set fire to Rome. It was the Christian-Bolsheviks who did that"; "Mark my words, Bormann, I'm going to become very religious"; "I'm convinced the soup of Holstein is the origin of Spartan gruel"; "I shall be interested to see whether my dog becomes a complete and confirmed vegetarian"; and so on. No-ticeable, too, is the complete lack of moderation in the Führer's repar-tee, no shades of gray or middle ground. Art he doesn't like is "worth-less," Brahms a celebrity only because the Jews made a fuss over him, Christianity "a farce," Russian civilization held together by vodka, and their soldiers mere "brutes in a state of nature." Dimly articulated mongrelizations of Nietzsche and Arthur Schopenhauer abound: "Suc-cess justifies everything"; "Terror is a salutary thing"; "All life is paid for in blood"; "Fanaticism is a matter of climate"; "It is bloodhounds people follow"; "Blood doesn't matter to the builders of an Empire." If Leni Riefenstahl's documentary film *Triumph of the Will* had been shot here at Wolfsschanze rather than the podium at Nuremberg, surely Hitler would have been laughed off the stage as a crackpot.

Historically, of course, the transcripts are fascinating and full of in-sight into Hitler's opinions and precepts. These, again, are marked by their lack of reflection. Hitler admires Stalin—"a hell of a fellow"—because he slaughtered his generals in the great purge of the 1930s, lit-tle connecting this absence of professional soldiery in the Soviet army to its abysmal performance in the summer and fall of 1941.* His ap-

---

*"A reign of terror without parallel," wrote the Harvard historian Merle Fainsod. Eight million people were arrested and either imprisoned or executed: three out of five marshals of the Soviet Union were shot, thirteen out of fifteen army commanders, thirty out of fifty-eight corps commanders, 110 out of 195 division commanders, and 211 out of 406 regimental commanders. Khrushchev called the purge "a meat grinder." Three times as many senior officers fell to Soviet firing squads than were killed by the enemy. In the early days of the German invasion, many officers found themselves trans-ported from chains in the gulag to battlefront command in a single day without expla-

praisals of Churchill and Franklin Roosevelt are likewise skewed, and he demonstrates an almost complete naiveté about America's strength and character. When Hitler nonchalantly opened hostilities with the United States in December 1941, Guderian despaired, "This war is now 'total' enough for anyone."*

Perhaps the only humanity to be found here is in Hitler's thoughts on the past, particularly the early days when national socialism was a street-fighting gang of SA men and disgruntled veterans. Hitler revels in the memory of the brawls, rallies, and political upheavals that paved his way to power. That "National Socialist brew," he chortles, "was a little strong for delicate stomachs." A few Reds in the way? "We beat them up, in the hopes of getting a bigger row started." What a contrast to the refined conversation of the officers' club in Berlin!

Hitler reveals in this mental scrapbook how pedestrian his movement's origins indeed were and how little perspective he had gained in the many years since. The highly personalized rough-and-tumbles he enjoyed as a young man had merely been extended to a front some hundreds of miles in length. The Jews and Bolsheviks he had hunted through the alleyways of Munich, Frankfurt, and Berlin, breaking their noses and stomping their heads, he was simply pursuing in greater numbers and with greater killing power. It was a fight to the death in either case.

Yet for all this bombast, his invasion of Russia faltered in the face of a full Soviet counterattack launched in early December 1941. What Himmler called "an open road to the East" grew buried in the snow-drifts of a Russian winter, where temperatures fell to $-50°C$ and men's rectums froze as they tried to defecate. In Guderian's phrase, "the gigantic drama of our destruction" began.

Many theories have been offered as to why the German army failed in Russia, and most point to Hitler's irresolution in those early, heady days of the offensive. Against his generals' advice, the Führer ordered the great pockets of overrun Russian armies to be enveloped and marched off into captivity, a waste of time and effort to many soldiers

---

nation. "Why haven't I seen you for so long?" Stalin asked one of his generals in exasperation. "Where have you been?" "In prison, Comrade Stalin," came the reply. "A fine time to be inside," Stalin grumbled. When Russia turned the tide in 1944, he ordered State Defense Committee member Nikolai Bulganin to begin assembling paperwork "to purge the heroes" all over again.

*A play on one of Goebbels's propaganda lines: "Totaler Krieg—kurzester Krieg!" ("Total war—shortest war!").

when Moscow stood there for the taking. But Hitler relied on Napoleon's experience, wherein Moscow proved an empty prize. Not so in 1941. Most historians believe that the fall of Moscow would have significantly damaged Stalin's ability to hang on, to say nothing of Russia's. Political, economic, military, and psychological nerve center of the entire country, Moscow was indeed the hub of Russian life. The failure to take it was, unlike failure before Leningrad, a tremendous setback to the German effort, and most of the generals realized it. Russia regrouped and struck back, and the long drain of German manpower and resources commenced.

The "table talk" reflects this demise in fortune. Hitler curses "this damnable winter" while at the same time justifying the attack on Russia since its opposition had stiffened: See how they are improving? What if we had waited? The professional soldiers are increasingly infuriating him with their defeatist babble. "I have never lost confidence in the German soldier. It is the generals I'm worried about—I will smash the General Staff!" he tells Guderian petulantly. As if to put iron in every backbone, he personally sacrifices the Sixth Army at Stalingrad.

⚜

"I still see Stalingrad before me," the panzer veteran continues. "That was tough fighting. It was a battle to the end, because if you survived and were captured, it was worse than being dead. My brother, the one who had fought the Spartacists, he was drafted again in 1941, and he was captured by the Russians and made a POW in the Urals. For seven years, we didn't even know if he was alive or not. Because he was an officer, he had a terrible, terrible time, came back skin and bones. But he survived, and he's still alive now, eighty-eight years old. He was lucky. A tough man, of course, but lucky, too. My attitude was, under no circumstance was I going to be taken prisoner by the Russians.

"So I was in the famous tractor plant. The smoke, the cold, the death of your comrades—I can tell you, through all of this our comradeship is what was so special, and something that you, a civilian, will never understand. It made you go on.

"We were using all our heavy guns in Stalingrad, and I was forward observer. One day the Russians were able to get an artillery barrage on our building, and that was the end of me. I was knocked unconscious, and I got a shell particle wedged in my spine, my fifth wound. I got two more in the war, but they weren't serious. The doctor says to me—he's the same one I've had for twenty-five years—this shrapnel is still here, tapping my back, still in the same place.

"When I woke up I found myself all wrapped up in fur, like a Persian rug, and all my belongings, they were tied to my body, I don't know to this day who did that. I got one of the last planes out of there."

I ask the veteran, "Should von Paulus, the Sixth Army's commander, have disobeyed Hitler and tried to break out of the pocket on his own? Many commentators, such as von Manstein in his memoirs, suggest that Stalingrad was suicide."

"I don't really know what goes through your mind when you make statements like this. We were not robots, but I had in my military life, especially as a combat officer, many times experiences where things would have been terribly costly in lives and so on when you question your commander's orders. We would in some cases naturally question orders in our minds, but it was a duty to obey them first. In these American films that I see where an officer in Vietnam gives an order to his noncommissioned officer, and he replies, 'No, I don't go this way,' or some things I read in Schwarzkopf's book, which disgust me very much—we would not do this. Maybe we would have an opportunity to go over this later. Sure, you would confront them. We weren't sissies. I had cases where I would argue later with a superior officer— 'That was stupid'—and he would take this. It's not like in some of these dumb movies and war books. We were human beings, and we had all kinds of backgrounds and our own ideas. But during wartime, in many instances I believe it is very important when you give an order you know it will be obeyed. Otherwise it could cost plenty of lives when you have doubts that the order isn't taken.

"Von Paulus went to the Führer headquarters. He told the Führer, 'We are still able to break out.' Hitler at this time, I believe he was insane. He wanted to relieve Paulus, change the command, but Paulus decided to obey the order, and he said, 'No, I go back to my troops.' I am sure that was the case.

"Sometimes I have to bite my tongue. People are so ignorant. Writers and professors, they put out such nonsense: All Germans are robots; all Germans killed the Jews; all the SS were criminals. Let me tell you something: I came from a background where you wouldn't expect to have a Jew in your family, but my brother, an army officer like me, married one in 1931. I even fell in love with her sister, a girl named Ulla. A wonderful, wonderful family, real Orthodox Jews, just wonderful people. The Nazis gassed the mother, and soon afterwards they found out that my brother was married into them. They said fine, everything will be fine, just divorce her and we'll forget about the whole thing. Otherwise, we send you to a labor camp. Well, if you can believe it, he wouldn't do it. They arrested him and put him in a camp, just at a time when Germany needed good officers! They never arrested his wife, but him they put away in a labor camp. The Americans freed him after the war. Through the influence of my other brothers, the wife was never taken away. She had courage. They wanted her to run away to Stockholm, but she said no. She said, 'I want to be around. My family's here.' And her sister lived on a small island in the River Havel for the entire war. German farmers who knew them supplied her family with food and kept them alive.

"All these Holocaust stories. . . . I have never had anything against the Jews. We did not know—and I realize for you Americans, you do not believe this—that people were in danger. We knew that people were in labor camps, but nobody in my family saw that things had gone out of control. I believe this was so until the last year before war ended that anyone knew they treated them so terribly. I never even heard that my own brother was in a labor camp!*

"Do I feel guilt? I would not be a Christian if I did not. But shouldn't we human beings all feel guilt? It's a disease we have in us. It's a human fault. Look everywhere in human history. What have the Jewish people really learned from all this? They still bomb villages now, they use all kinds of excuses, but the bombs fall in many areas where people are innocent—women, children, for God's sake, the whole ugly picture. Is there ever a rationale for killing a baby?

"We can differ on the Waffen-SS as well. What could some of these poor soldiers do, let's say they were well-built fellows like you? They were just taken up and put in SS divisions, and this crazy political system used them in this master race, elite, Nordic army. There was not a lot of glory for them on the battlefield, especially in Russia. When things went wrong, they were thrown in first, and those regiments,

---

*Von Manstein, convicted himself of war crimes in the eastern theater (though Churchill contributed to his defense fund) may not be the most reliable of witnesses, but he states that "rumors of the kind that circulated at home hardly penetrated to the front." But in her memoirs, Christabel Bielenberg repeats the remark of an American GI that he would like "to meet the Kraut who knew anything about anything."

well, they came back in pieces.* It was crazy. They were just people like anyone else for the most part. And like in old wars, when you lose, then naturally everyone looks for villains, and those SS were it. How many times in 1945 at the POW camps did they check me over for tattoos and other marks? They were always looking for SS people. And don't mistake me: I'm talking here about the Waffen-SS, the combat units, not those camp guard people. To me, I had a feeling that Himmler was a real instrument of the devil. Many of them were, but many of them were not."

At Stalingrad the Sixth Army ceased to exist on February 2, 1943. When Hitler heard the news, he burst into tears. Beethoven was played over state radio. Göring went hunting and bagged 300 hares.

꙰

At Wolfsschanze the "table talk" sputtered to an end. Hitler ate alone, vegetarian meals for the most part, which he shared with his dog. Dr. Morell (nicknamed *Reichsspritzenmeister,* or "Reich Record Holder for Injections") and other doctors alternated his regimen of drugs: depressants to put him to sleep, stimulants to get him going—strychnine, belladonna, Cardiazol, Pervitin, caffeine, Eukodal, Percodan, among many others. Starting in 1944, Hitler's nostrils were swabbed with a cocaine-based solution ten times a day, to go along with twice-daily inhalations of the same drug, straight. His rages and tempers, while always explosive and mercurial, seemed to observers even more extreme. In retrospect, physicians have wondered if the Führer did not suffer one or two mild strokes. The variety of his drug injections and the seemingly random, even cavalier crossover from one narcotic prescription to another may also have induced withdrawal symptoms, further decreasing his capacity for rational thought. "Truly," said an astonished Speer, "he came from a different world."

News from the East, of course, was now all somber. War novelists from what we might call today the East German persuasion—Günter Grass, Theodor Plievier, even the pulp writer Willi Heinrich—all seem to present characters with a stoical turn of mind as the remorseless Russian front engulfs them. Not so the more Catholic, southern school represented by a Heinrich Böll, to whom the forbidding East

---

*In the early months of the campaign, the SS absorbed almost 20 percent of all German battle deaths, "a toll in blood incommensurate with its actual gains" (von Manstein).

was synonymous with agony, unspeakable angst, and destruction. Böll's novella *The Train Was on Time* reverberates with a soldier's single melancholic thought as he heads for the incinerator, "Soon I shall be dead. Soon. Soon. Soon."

Certainly an element of the macabre and surrealistic enters into the recollections of those who visited Wolfsschanze to report on the worsening rout in Russia, their reminiscences being more reliable, I think, than those of the people who never left. Guderian and von Manstein, for example, both intimately involved in eastern operations, seem more trustworthy witnesses than Jodl and Keitel (both hanged in 1946), who rarely left the Führer's side.

Von Manstein, relieved of his command in March 1944, believed at one time that Hitler was capable of "being a man of reason, even if he had no human feelings," but those days had long gone. Hitler's "intolerable interfering" had destroyed what could have been the greatest turn of arms the world had ever seen. Instead Moscow was gone; followed by the Stalingrad debacle, where the once powerful Sixth Army was thrown away; then 1,300 German tanks lost at Kursk just nine months later. The only hope lay in stalemate, but Hitler's obsession with never yielding an inch proved the ruination of any sound and mobile military policy, a direct violation of Frederick the Great's maxim that "he who defends everything defends nothing." Interminable discussions, rambling discourse on secret weapons, irrelevant analyses of projected landings in Sardinia as the great eastern front disintegrated—these became the day-to-day schedule of Wolfsschanze, scenes all enlivened by the parade of lackeys, led by Göring (usually dressed as though for a "masked ball"), who still fawned on the Führer "in credulous adulation." As Ian Buruma astutely observed, Hitler wanted to know everything except the truth.

Guderian, relieved twice of command (Christmas Day 1941 and March 1945), reported the same air of unreality, though he, as a soldier indebted to Hitler, might have been thought a man who would toe the line.* Goebbels ("clever"), Himmler ("impenetrable, oblique—he

---

*Heinz Guderian, panzer specialist, was from a good though hardly regal East Prussian family. He was a modern soldier through and through. Ludendorff and even Charles de Gaulle never flinched when a shell landed nearby—"Gentlemen, behave yourselves," a white-gloved de Gaulle admonished his staff, flattened on the ground after a close miss, while he remained erect and unblinking. Guderian, not a stuffy Prussian by any means, never hesitated to dive for a ditch, nor did Hitler. "I'd get down on my belly too," he once said. Stalin did not consider Guderian a first-class general, merely "an adventurer."

seemed like a man from some other planet"), Bormann ("a gutter-snipe"), and Göring, prancing about in lipstick and makeup ("incompetent and idle")—all these lickspittles had optimism of an almost hallucinatory nature that counterbalanced the assessment of professional soldiers. Tremendous shouting matches ensued, after one of which Göring pulled Guderian out of the room by tugging the back of his uniform. Many generals took to omitting "Heil Hitler" from their repertoire of salutes. "The Eastern Front is a house of cards. . . . All will collapse."

---

Changing into waterproof rubber boots, I head through the woods for a huge clearing of several pastures that stretch beyond the once barbed wire enclosure. In the midst of this, somewhere, is Wolfsschanze's landing strip. I assume this to be by now a long and derelict slice of concrete, something existential standing alone in the middle of green fields with no function, no role to play, little if any glamour attached to it as an "antiquity," irrelevant to the passing Pole on his tractor or slogging on through to a hunting blind. Certainly a parade of officers flying back and forth from the eastern front would be an anachronism today, though the notion of assassination is still alive and well in these parts.

Claus von Stauffenberg landed here on July 20, 1944, placed his bomb at the Führer's feet at Wolfsschanze, saw and heard the explosion, then took off again from this strip for Berlin to spread the joyful tidings—"the pig" was dead!

The minutiae of von Stauffenberg's famous day have been recounted almost to the second by scores of writers and historians. Many plans, trials and errors, even actual "bomb runs" had been hazarded before that hot and airless day in July, but always a glitch, a rescheduling change, or some other inopportune circumstance had prevented the plot from clicking into gear. In March 1943 a bomb had been placed on the Führer's airplane, but the fuse malfunctioned and the explosive did not detonate. Some anxious moments ensued afterward as conspirators removed the device. After all was said and done, Colonel von Stauffenberg took matters into his own hands and decided to carry out the assassination himself. "If generals won't do it," he is alleged to have said, "then colonels must."

Von Stauffenberg, a mutilated war veteran—one eye missing, no right hand, only three fingers on his other—had been named chief of

*Hitler's bunker*

staff of the replacement army, German cannon fodder for decimated
units on the eastern front. As such, he had occasional access to Führer
briefings at Wolfsschanze, as well as a desk in Berlin at the War Ministry, from whose telephones he planned to arrange the takeover of
key installations in the capital by Wehrmacht units and the arrest of
people like Goebbels. Success in the latter field depended entirely on
success in the former.

The conspirators, fatally it seems in retrospect, were far too loosely
organized and far too junior in rank to guarantee success should any
element of their plan go astray. The German Resistance Memorial
Center, located in the former War Ministry, a group of buildings
known as the Bendlerblock in the Tiergarten section of Berlin, has a
long row of photographs showing all these youthful men. Most depressing is to see them with wives and adolescent children, perhaps on
their wedding days, christenings, or other occasions of celebration.
Von Stauffenberg is caught in a poignant though oddly complex snap-
shot, walking down the aisle of Bamberg's ancient St. Jakob's church,
bride on one arm, sword on the other, wearing his everyday steel helmet.

The museum, with utter scrupulousness, lists those officers of real significance who waited upon results: Rommel,* Günther von Kluge, Gerd von Rundstedt, Friedrich Fromm, many others. Only one, General Karl Heinrich von Stülpnagel, had the nerve to move early, according to plan. He arrested 1,200 SS men in Paris on July 20 and was prepared to shoot them all, a move that would cost him horrible torture and a horrible death. The others did nothing, especially when they heard Hitler had survived.

"The Nazis called it a miracle," a German veteran said to me, "but we felt it was an unbelievable disaster that it didn't work. Our high command officers in Russia, they talked about Hitler quite openly; they said we have got to get rid of him as fast as possible. This stupid oak desk, it saved his life! I think the devil had a hand in it."

The oak desk . . . Von Stauffenberg had originally set his deadly briefcase just 6 feet from the seated Führer. He had activated the acid drip that would trigger the bomb six minutes before (while allegedly changing his shirt in Keitel's bunker). A special set of pliers that accommodated his mangled fingers had been devised for working with the bomb. With four minutes to go before detonation, he slipped away from the briefing room. Together with Fellgiebel, communications chief at Wolfsschanze and a key member of the plot, he nervously paced and waited.

At 12:42 the briefcase exploded. All ten windows of the barracks-style building blew out in pieces. Some witnesses saw bodies hurled about amid planks of wood and a barrage of splinters. Neither Stauffenberg nor Fellgiebel could believe anyone inside was still alive. Fellgiebel signaled Berlin to activate the coup d'état then jammed all the equipment, effectively isolating Wolfsschanze. Stauffenberg coolly bluffed his way through three checkpoints, drove to the landing strip, and took off for Berlin. In the three fateful hours it took him to arrive at the Rangsdorf aerodrome, however, the entire enterprise had unraveled inexorably. Hitler, as it turned out, had walked out of the wreckage alive.

By one of those grotesque twists of fate that seem to influence so many pivotal events in history, an officer at the briefing had found Stauffenberg's briefcase in his way and shifted it to the other side of a

---

*To his credit, Rommel, severely wounded three days before, was in hospital and incapable of action.

*Hitler's trousers,
July 20, 1944*

heavy oak stanchion that supported the conference table. This effectively shielded Hitler from the bomb's blast, though not four others,
who were blown to pieces or mortally injured. Marshal Keitel, one of
Hitler's more fawning advisers, had been among the first to emerge
from the ruins. In a scene worthy of any Wagnerian opera, he was also
the first to sight his Führer walking out of the smoking debris in a
daze, staring straight ahead, his trousers in tatters, blood streaming
from his ears. "You are still alive!" he is said to have yelled. That bare
fact doomed von Stauffenberg.

A relation of the von Richthofens, an eminent German family that
gave us both the Red Baron and Frieda Weekley, D. H. Lawrence's tempestuous wife, recalled for me a remark his mother had made. "She
called Stauffenberg a coward. Why hadn't he stayed and seen the job
done properly? Why hadn't he strapped the bomb to his body and just
stood there next to Hitler? He ran off instead before the bomb went

off." I remember the gist of my reply: Lack of courage was never a fault anyone found in Stauffenberg. If he was guilty of anything, it was being too central an element to the coup's success or failure. Requiring him to be both at Wolfsschanze and Berlin put too much importance on a single person.

Stauffenberg had been the heart and soul of this current effort to rid the stage of Hitler. Officers and civilians alike had grumbled for years about Hitler and had formed a loose cabal of conspirators to eliminate him. Between 1934 and 1945, in fact, some forty-two attempts had been fomented against the Führer, some of a pathetically half-baked nature but others, like Stauffenberg's, the result of endless thought and planning. But Germans are not successful plotters. As an exasperated Lenin had said waiting in a sealed railway car for his return trip to Russia, "If Germans want to start a revolution, they buy a train ticket first."

In Stauffenberg's case, too much authority had too willingly been placed in the eager colonel's hand. He had access to Hitler, and he also served as General Fromm's chief of staff, Fromm controlling the troops in and around Berlin. But Fromm, yet another of the hesitant generals, dared not act. Instead, Stauffenberg wrote up orders and directives using Fromm's name that he, Stauffenberg, took upon himself to activate and issue. As a partial result, the coup barely inched ahead during his three-hour flight to Berlin. Two prominent though retired generals, Beck and von Witzleben, had agreed to take control of the armed forces once the coup began, but since neither was on active service they brought no troops with them. In effect, they needed the army delivered into their hands, and Stauffenberg could produce nothing but a few minor officers, especially as word filtered through from East Prussia that Hitler, though not well, was certainly alive.

Fromm took advantage of this information to hand Beck a pistol. The old general, riven with cancer, botched his suicide. A sergeant finished him off. Von Witzleben, disgusted with the wretched shambles of this wretched day, stalked out of the Bendlerblock waving his field marshal's baton and went home to await the Gestapo, whom he knew would come. They did, and he died. Von Stauffenberg, with three others, was taken to the courtyard and shot under the glare of headlights, Fromm's attempt to both demonstrate his loyalty and silence those who might incriminate him. The Gestapo came for him anyway, and he was executed a few weeks before war's end.

That early evening at Wolfsschanze, Benito Mussolini witnessed one of the oddest displays of interpersonal misbehavior ever seen at the

*Nerve center of the coup, July 20, 1944: Stauffenberg's office and telephone, Bendlerblock, Berlin*

Führer's headquarters. Hitler's euphoria at having escaped death once again had given way to lethargy. He sat morosely in an easy chair, sucking lozenges prescribed by Dr. Morell, the contents of which would be interesting to know. A parade of Nazi officials and political officers filed in and out to offer the Führer their congratulations on his survival, but the dismal train of news from various theaters had eroded their faith in a successful outcome. People began pointing fingers at one another, losing tempers. Admiral Karl Dönitz heaped imprecations on the fat, bejeweled Göring, accusing him of gross incompetency for the Luftwaffe's disintegration. Unable to deal with a true professional, Göring turned on the hapless Ribbentrop, screaming at him, "You lousy little champagne peddler" and threatening to strike his face with his field marshal's baton. Ribbentrop in turn yelled out something to the effect that he, at least, was not some cheap scoundrel from the wrong side of town:

"I am *von* Ribbentrop!"—words that could hardly endear himself to the Führer. Hitler, semicomatose, lost in his own reverie, came to life for a brief titanic moment when someone let slip the words "Roehm," "revolt," and "plot," which struck a responsive chord in his memory from long ago.* He catapulted from his seat and put on a display of temper and blood lust the likes of which few had ever seen. To put it simply, he vowed to extirpate anyone even remotely connected with the traitors, a pledge he both kept and broke. Seven thousand arrests were eventually made, 200 executions carried out by drumhead courts, any number of careers and lives brought to an end—suicide pills, strangulations, meat hooks, and coups de grâce from pistols were the order of the day. At the top of the ladder, Rommel, von Kluge, Stülpnagel, and Halder all paid a heavy price. But at the bottom, some escaped. Von Stauffenberg's wife and children were arrested, separated, and placed in concentration camps. Few expected to see them alive again, but none was murdered. This was about as miraculous an outcome as Hitler's survival of the bomb itself.

It is said that Mussolini was profoundly shaken by what he saw and heard that afternoon at Wolfsschanze. He had cause to wonder if everyone had gone mad.

⌗

Walking back through the woods of Wolfsschanze gives me pause for thought. Some of the eeriest aspects of life at headquarters—especially for the secretaries, stenographers, and phone operators—were the random explosions that took place at all hours of the day and night. Deer, it seems, had a habit of wandering through the minefields, triggering one device after another. I am hoping the Poles have cleared all these dreadful things out of here. It makes me nervous.

Hitler decamped from the Wolf's Lair on November 20, 1944. He had spent the majority of the last three years in stubborn residence, but the change of scenery offered little in the way of reinvigoration. He simply replaced one bunker with another. In Berlin, underground, he shot himself five months later. The final official sentence recorded from his mouth was, "The aim must still be to win territory in the East for the German people."

---

*Ernst Roehm, one of Hitler's early comrades and head of the paramilitary SA, was executed on Hitler's orders in the great purge of June 30, 1934. Hitler alleged at the time that Roehm was planning a coup.

On April 20, the 105th anniversary of Hitler's birth, I wander over the rubble of his last address on earth, the Berlin bunker. Newspapers today are full of the news that Britain's football squad has canceled its "friendly competition" against Germany scheduled for this afternoon in Frankfurt, fearing some neo-Nazi demonstration. The German press, happy perhaps to be spared the attendance of rowdy British fans, wishes them godspeed as their plane diverts to the United Arab Emirates. As things turn out, there is (some would say predictably) no cause for alarm; the day passes for any other in this great nation. There is even in some quarters a sense of good-natured "nostalgia" for the old days, as expressed by one eastern German entrepreneur who recently proposed a theme park that would recreate the atmosphere of police state Germany, featuring endless queues for groceries, military parades, and unmarked vans that would swoop down on unsuspecting customers in mock arrests and detentions.

This entire sector of the former East Berlin is little better off than it was in 1945. Plans to rebuild the ancient heart of the old capital are mired in architectural controversy, and no one seems happy with anything anyone says. The city still seems dead on this side of the old Wall, busy and congested on the other. The courtyard of the former Bendlerblock is not particularly crowded, however. A group of twenty or so French teenagers file through the Resistance Museum, which shares its office block with a governmental agency on AIDS. A few German kids lounge on the memorial wall erected to the memory of Stauffenberg, which is dominated by the sculpture of a nude male, his arms in broken shackles. The symbolism, I would suppose, is that as futile as the July 20 plot may have been, the effort alone did at least preserve the honor of Germany. This was certainly the idea that many officers carried to their deaths on the gallows or in front of firing squads. They realized, or should have, that killing Hitler at such a late stage in the war would have had little effect on the Allies and their avenging sweep into Germany.* Still, it must be recognized: A few recklessly brave individuals did try, and they paid a terrible price for their failure.

A plaque is set in the wall where Stauffenberg and the others fell. There are shreds of flowers lying about it, along with several cigarette stubs ground into the sacred soil of Germany.

---

*General Eisenhower's naval aide records indifference to the attempt: "I'm excited about it, but Ike isn't."

# ⊰ 16 ⊱

# Ostpreussen
## 1945
# Along Country Roads

*Kill! Kill! In the German race there is nothing but evil.*
*Stamp out the fascist beast once and for all in its lair!*
*Use force and break the racial pride of these German*
*women. Take them as your lawful booty. Kill! As you*
*storm onward, kill! You gallant soldiers of the Red*
*army.*

—Red Army propagandist Ilya Ehrenburg,
in a leaflet distributed to Russian soldiers

DRIVING ABOUT THE EAST PRUSSIAN countryside, one passes the
occasional military cemetery—not German, of course, because these
have been, as a matter of policy, bulldozed and obliterated, their rubble often used as the foundation for apartment blocks or commercial
development. No, the majority are Russian, either the anonymous
mass graves of POWs or, less customary, the individual interments of
officers who died by the thousands in the storming of Prussia. These
sites are usually forlorn and neglected, about as sorry a contrast as can
be imagined to the manicured graves of Allied casualties that lie scattered in the shadows of appropriately funereal architecture throughout
France, Belgium, the Netherlands, and Luxembourg. Here in the East,
it's quiet enough, to be sure. The wind is just as mournful, the patter-
ing rain as melancholy. But the memorial plinths are all a crumbling
mess of cheap concrete. Flagpoles lie splintered or hanging askew;
tombstones are toppled in various mutilated poses; the greenery hasn't

*Grave of Youain Mikolai Semenovich*

been attended to in years; graffiti and broken vodka bottles lie everywhere. The American notion of tracking down a single soldier missing
in action seems ludicrous in the face of such massive and sloppy indifference. In one shambles of a graveyard, I jot down the obituary of one
Youain Mikolai Semenovich, killed on February 20, 1945: "The bright
memory of you will stay in our hearts." In a few years this enclosure
may well be torn apart and converted once again to a place for cows
and routing pigs.

The Russian plunge into Prussia was an operation devoid of subtlety. Overwhelming numerical superiority, immense artillery
strength, supremacy in the sky, and tanks beyond counting battered
the dwindling Wehrmacht. The maniacal Führer ordered futile last
stands, designating cities and towns as "fortress" sites for suicidal last
stands, whereas their abandonment would have made far greater tactical sense. As a result the Soviets were able to surround and isolate significant numbers of German troops, generally in pockets ringed by the
Baltic on one side, the Red Army in siege positions on the other. In
Kurland in Latvia, twenty-six German divisions were thus cut off and
rendered ineffective to the defense of interior Germany. When fortress

Königsberg was blocked, another twenty-five divisions were essentially squandered. Danzig found itself marooned in late February 1945. Its commander disobeyed orders and managed, with the connivance of the German navy, to evacuate nearly a million soldiers and refugees in an operation more fraught with danger than even Dunkirk. He refused to leave his holding guard behind, however, and surrendered with them on May 9.

The fighting, as most readers might expect to hear, was fearsome, a wintry replication of the horror at Stalingrad played out a hundredfold in city squares and village markets throughout East Prussia. Quarter was not expected and rarely given except in cases of formal surrenders. Soviet soldiers, incited by their own gruesome experiences and by an especially virulent species of propaganda, were released from any formal restraint as they entered Germany. "Yes," as Solzhenitsyn wrote in *The Gulag Archipelago*, "all of us knew very well that if the girls were German they could be raped and then shot. This was almost a combat distinction." Wehrmacht defenders, in contrast, were harassed by their own as much as by the enemy. Execution squads of Nazi diehards hanged malingerers from lampposts or shot retreating men against any convenient wall. The civilian population, numb with horror, ran for its collective life.

As befits a professional writer and editor, Marion, Countess Dönhoff, has left for posterity the most literary and affecting description of what came to be known as the Great Trek, a time of such terror and dislocation that it seems incredible how few people in the West know anything of its detail. The countess, then a young woman in her twenties, left her family's regal estate of Friedrichstein by horseback in the frigid January of 1945, a winter whose unprecedented ferocity added yet another fatal element to the already destructive mix of military collapse and the Soviet hunger for revenge. It is estimated that almost 1.75 million German people left home and farm from January to May of that year, heading for the River Elbe and the supposed magnanimity of British and American armies. Of these, perhaps half died on the road. Invariably, treks were organized and led by the only people left, wives and daughters, hence the sobriquet of these months as "the time of the women."

At the same instance, ironically, the roads were clogged with other women on the march, mostly Jewish, inmates of Nazi death camps driven cruelly westward with no winter clothing, food, or shelter to sustain them. In one of the oddest contradictions of the entire war,

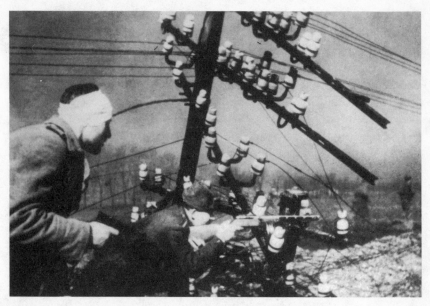

*Soviets storm Königsberg*

these disparate stragglers often found themselves mingling on the same desperate country lanes. The Jews, however, had largely lost their hope, inured from years of privation and senseless loss. "Herr Sentry, I'm still alive," one Jew cried out after the indiscriminate machine-gunning of her column by panicked SS guards, who then shot her through the head. German refugees, by contrast, were often newcomers to the harsh realities of flight and wartime panic.

Most every German originally from the East will have some documentary record of what happened to his or her father or mother or siblings during these evil days. Though very rarely of a polish that Countess Dönhoff gave her story, these diaries and recollections are nevertheless extraordinarily moving in their evocation of the sudden and unprecedented chaos that befell them, often with tragic results. Although it is easy to scoff or ask, as one Pole put it to me, "What in the world did Germans expect? Who started this war anyway?" one cannot question or denigrate the fact that these people, too, were victims who lost all of what they had. To claim their individual bereavements were pretty much what they collectively deserved is beside the point.

*German refugees, Königsberg, winter 1945*

Katharina von Negenborn was twenty years old in 1945 and is today an extraordinarily handsome woman of seventy. We have just finished an excellent luncheon of roast pork and white Rhenish wine, looking out on her spotless garden and a low ridge of verdant hills beyond. This German landscape is over 600 miles from her family's former estate in East Prussia, located near the ancient battlefield of Tannenberg. She reaches for a leather-bound journal.

"We had buried most of our valuables—the silver, porcelain, antique weapons, and such—and we left with our farm people in thirty-two wagons plus the two tractors, the kind with iron wheels, no rubber. They broke down immediately. Some of our things were on sleds; there was so much snow. After only 18 kilometers or so the bottleneck on our little road was so bad that some of our people gave up and returned home. But we could not. We knew the Russians were violent and gruesome. We knew the first thing they'd do is take care of the capitalists, the Junkers. We heard later you had to show them your hands. If they were soft or not the hands of a worker, you'd be separated from the rest.

"Because the Russians were coming up so fast, we had to detour constantly, but many of the rivers had only a single bridge going over, so everything was completely clogged. At Saalfeld in eastern Prussia, we had only two horses and one wagon left, and now there were only five of us—father, mother, our cook, myself, and a French POW we had working for us on the farm. Rumors were everywhere. At the Weichsel River we heard the Wehrmacht was going to blow up the bridge. You can imagine the panic.

"Crossing the old Polish Corridor was very dangerous. There were partisans everywhere. Once the Poles came and they opened up my mother's bag. We were all very scared. But she had packed a crucifix with her clothes, it was on top. When the Pole saw that, he closed the bag, didn't take a thing, and let us go.

"By February we had reached an estate of our family's in Pomerania, but we stayed there too long and the Russians overtook us. We were in the house when they came up. They set it on fire and shot at us when we fled out the back. The POW was gone by this point. When he saw the Russians, he went over to them. He told them where we had buried things back home.

"Out in the woods, a Russian detachment found us and we were arrested. I was put on one side of the road, the rest on the other side. They beat my father and drove me off alone. I was terribly frightened, to death. I thought, this is the end. It was awful, awful, awful.

"We were lucky, though. They didn't shoot my father, as we feared, but put us to work. We foraged food for them from slaughtered animals. We would work for them by day and at night we disappeared into the forest, smeared your face with dirt and hid out until the next day. All this time Goebbels was dropping leaflets on us saying, 'Hold out. We will come back.' Isn't that wonderful?

"After capitulation on May 8, we made our way to the West. As I said, we were the lucky ones. We survived."

An older gentleman, a former East Prussian neighbor of Katharina, nods his head in agreement. "Of our thirteen friends around us, ten died and only three lived. One good friend tried to save his daughter from the Russians. They crushed his skull. When they were finished with the daughter, they killed her, too. She was twenty-five."

Many treks disintegrated almost as soon as they began. Well-organized itineraries with projected destinations and timetables simply collapsed as order disappeared on the roadways. Trekking families became divided as wagons broke down; air raids scattered people

Snapshots from the scrapbook of Katharina von Negenborn

*"This is my husband on his family's East Prussian estate. He's the boy on the horse— harvest time."*

*"Otto, the foreman. He assembled all the wagons for the trek."*

*"My wedding day in 1946. My husband borrowed the tuxedo from his uncle. My dress was made from parachute silk, and we drank sugar beet alcohol at our reception."*

*"This was our first home in the West."*

hither and yon; sickness or wounds required delay and often the abandonment of various members of the party. Many families discovered
themselves traveling in circles, the idea no longer to head west but to
avoid, at all costs, the various Russian spearheads and encirclements
that blocked off various routes of escape. Hans Ulrich von Klitzing
shows me the diary of his mother, Dorothee, who died in 1982, which
describes in harrowing detail the exponential hopelessness that engulfed so many of the trekkers. "On January 19 we decided to leave
our farm even without permission.* Hans (my husband) and I, we saw
the flickering lights of Russian tanks coming closer, and packed fever-
ishly by candlelight. It was the beginning of the end. On the twentieth, at three o'clock in the morning, we left. All the animals were let
loose—our hearts were torn."

---

\*Erich Koch, *Gauleiter* (area commander) of East Prussia, had forbidden civilian families, under pain of roadside execution, to flee their homes. This did not prevent him
from later importuning Grand Admiral Dönitz for a submarine to convey him to South
America. Koch recently died in a Polish prison.

The former *Gauleiter* was fortunate not to have been executed for war crimes by the
Poles after his capture in 1949 by British military police, a reprieve allegedly the result
of his "insider information" on the fate of the spectacular Amber Room of Frederick I
after World War II (see the note on this room in Chapter 7).

The 1941 German invasion of western Russia had been so swiftly achieved that Soviet art custodians had time only to wallpaper the Amber Room before fleeing themselves from the Leningrad suburbs of the Catherine Palace, a ruse that worked for some
weeks but ultimately failed to fool the Germans. In 1943 Hitler ordered Koch to dis-
mantle the amber panels and reassemble them in the royal palace of Königsberg. But
Königsberg in its turn fell to Russian forces two years later, in the spring of 1945—
though not before Koch allegedly had the treasure, valued in 1985 at some \$100 million,
packed up into seventy-two wooden crates and driven away to safety. The question then
became, of course, to where? The Amber Room disappeared and has never resurfaced.

The Russians in particular mounted a vigorous search for the whereabouts of the
seventy-two crates, even going so far as to send teams of divers to scour the hulks of
refugee ships torpedoed or bombed as they fled the quays of Königsberg. Bodies by the
hundreds were found, but no amber. When Koch was extradited to Poland, he found
himself deemed the key to this mystery. Although sentenced to death for the mass murder of 400,000 Poles, he was regularly reprieved, under pressure from Moscow, in the
hopes that some scrap of information might lead to the whereabouts of the amber treasure. Realizing that his life hung in the balance, Koch maintained his silence until 1965,
when a formal suspension of his death sentence was promised in return for information.
His testimony, however, proved disappointingly vague. Experts now agree that the panels were probably hidden in Austrian or Czechoslovakian mine shafts, many of which
were dynamited by retreating German army groups. Amber does not satisfactorily withstand adverse climatological conditions, so the state of this historic assemblage, if ever
found, might well be disappointing.

The week of trekking that followed, in which the von Klitzing party with their farmhands and families traveled 44 miles, was described by the diarist as "a walk of horror." Sullen and dejected German troops meandered aimlessly on the roads, banked on either side by high drifts of snow. Russian aircraft strafed the refugees, killing a child and wounding several stragglers.* Artillery fired back and forth, shooting could be heard from all directions, but the hopelessness of the military situation was obvious to all: "no order, no command." This did not prevent SS zealots from setting up roadblocks and essentially press-ganging men and boys for ditch work and actual fighting on what was euphemistically called the home front. "One of our neighbors died. He was given an anti-tank launcher that was supposed to stop the Russians. Hans and Preuss, our tractor driver, had to stay too, but they met up with us later, as we were waiting for them."

Congestion on the roadways was unbelievable, especially at river crossings. Oftentimes the heavy equipment of the retreating German army simply ran over civilian wagons in their way. "Our young cook was almost crushed to death on a bridge when a tank drove into our wagon. She remained lying on the side of the road, a picture of misery. Hans waited all night for the disbursed caravan to come together again at the exit of the town. I wandered through the city and tried to get help for the injured young woman—in vain! Dissolution, confusion everywhere. Only two of the caravan wagons appeared. We had to give up our fateful waiting." The cook was left behind.

Evening of the next day brought no respite, only disaster. The family barely reached the projected stopover, a nearby farm, the horses at the end of their stamina. The estate managers, old friends of the von Klitzings, warned them off. "At nine o'clock the Russians will be here! You have to go on. We are determined to set the house on fire and take our lives. Take and do whatever you want. If you want to do the same as us, we will help you."

"It was a very dark, very desperate hour," Dorothee von Klitzing writes. "One only saw an end full of horror, not beyond it, no solution, no hope.

"Everything happened with immense speed. Anta (our daughter) wanted to assist our driver in unharnessing the horses, but when we

---

*Strafen* is a German word meaning "to punish."

looked through the window, we recognized a long column of Russians advancing, tanks and many infantry amongst them. They were about to flood the farm. Soon the house was full of smoke and flames. The couple took their lives in front of our eyes.

"For us, there was only one way out, leaving through the back by a high window into a hiding place, a deep trench in the snow, previously described to us. Anta found a way for us, she kept a clear head in any situation. We did not dare leave the trench until night had set in. But then it had to be. We were insufficiently dressed, Hans without even a coat. We did not have anything to eat and were hallucinating at times. It was at least 20° below zero and we had deep snow as well. But with all the excitement one did not feel any of that." The von Klitzing party slipped away into the night, eventually finding shelter in a barn. Russian tank soldiers rousted them the next morning, and perhaps due to the early hour their daughter Anta was not molested. Hereafter she dressed as a pregnant woman to avoid unwelcome attentions from the usually intoxicated soldiery.

Everywhere around them the von Klitzings witnessed nothing but misery. "We saw terrible things. Carts of refugees turned over, plowed through, corpses and dead horses along the roads. In the village of Warweiden there was a large gathering of raging, drunken Russian tank troops and many refugees. If carriages were in the way, soldiers toppled them from icy highways down the steep slopes, with men and horses. Again and again we met the Russians, unbelievable numbers of Russians. They demanded gold and hit us in the face. But they also gave us a sausage and a partridge. Our hearts were heavy—we did not see a way out."

By this time, about thirteen days after leaving their home, the von Klitzings found themselves circled back into their own familiar environs, crowded with other refugees into the upper rooms of a farmhouse. The Russians then began rounding up landowners and estate agents. Hans was taken away. "Come along, *documenta*, back soon, put coats on," an officer ordered. Dorothee accompanied her husband through slush to the town of Osterode, a smoldering shell after several nights of drunken looting. "We had to wait in a crowded guardroom. When Hans was called into the Soviet secret police interrogation, I went along but had to wait in front of the door. Because he was on a blacklist they wanted to portray him as a slave-driver and Nazi. He was beaten. I could not take it and stormed into the room. A red-haired fanatic devil, the lady interpreter, and the dark man with his *nagaika*.* We were released to go into the guardroom.

"This night of deepest worldly misery was a legacy that accompanied me on all the difficult routes that followed. The morning came and Hans and many others were called. I still saw him outside for a moment. He seemed to call out to me, in a cheerful manner. 'We will get some food now. Greetings to Anta!'"

That was the end for Hans von Klitzing. Four years later it was discovered he had been starved to death.

Dorothee and Anta lived in an attic with other stragglers. No farm animals had been left; they lived on a few potatoes and bread made from grain ground up in a coffee mill. At night they were subjected to the appraisal and groping of wandering servicemen. "The Russians came and went, always different ones, once nine times in a single day. All the doors remained unlocked. We peered onto the road, looking for light shining in other houses, listening to steps, to the shooting and screaming of girls in the lower rooms. With burning newspapers as torches, they checked the beds and one was not allowed to move. They were looking for *paninkas*, girls, looking for anything that could be taken along. The worst were the single officers who were accompanied only by one orderly. We used to hide the girls in heaps of straw."

An old prayer book sustained them. "When we read in the evenings, 'Bless the Lord, ye His angels, that excel in strength, that do His commandments, hearkening onto the voice of His word,' we fell asleep without worry. 'Who are you that you are afraid of man, who dies.' Never was I allowed to experience God being so near, Him hearing our prayers and His taking away all the fear."

Polish refugees, uprooted from the East, now were herded into old Prussia. To Dorothee they seemed "as unhappy as we were." For want of any other viable alternative, mother and daughter decided to head for home, a trek of some 20 miles. The hope that their husband and father might somehow be there waiting drove them on. "Our few belongings we carried with us in an old rice basket on wheels. Again and again it would almost tip over. Would we finally have any connection with the outside world? Whom would we find there?"

---

*A *nagaika* is a whip.

*German civilians flee the Soviets*

At the old estate, they were greeted by their former employee, the accounts manager. War and devastation had obliterated class distinction, however. This individual had been named a commissar for the farm, and he dutifully reported the reappearance of his former superior. "This was naturally undesirable," Dorothee dryly observed, but nonetheless he at first successfully protected them from unwarranted accusation—"You stay with me." Farmworkers and dairymen welcomed the von Klitzings back. "Now we are all equal," they would say. "Now we are all 'Refugees on Earth.'" Dorothee forgave those who had taken various items from their home.

"All the stables were devastated and empty. In the courtyard and in the garden, there was furniture standing about. Soon after our arrival the manor was left by the Russians; the Polish *woijd* was supposed to move in. Women were ordered to clean and tidy up the house. I, together with Anta and Elisa Thal, went along voluntarily. We found a jumble of our own and other furniture there. Hans's room was passably tidy. Some of our furniture had been thrown out of the window. We were up to our knees in letters, pictures. I just cannot describe everything here. On the floor, our big brass kettle, full to the brim, used as a toilet. A chaos impossible to imagine if one has not seen it oneself. I do not need to describe how we felt."

At first the house remained empty. The two von Klitzings rummaged through debris, saving what photos and family memorabilia they could. But their protector soon fell from grace. Russians had reactivated the farm distillery, and as a joke they forced the old man to drink cup after cup of wood alcohol straight. His liver failed and death soon followed. Successive waves of Poles and Russians commandeered the manor house, drunken parties and revels, usually accompanied by vandalism and rape, were the order of the day. Even working in the fields did not offer the women any respite. "The elegant, obviously cynical officer in his brand new uniform placed himself next to us and threatened to lash us with his whip if we did not work fast enough. Then he examined us and whispered with his driver. There were only two young women with us, Anta and another girl. I heard the driver ask, 'Both?' The officer: 'No, one is enough.' I whispered to Anta, 'Be careful.' She disappeared behind a pit. And when she came back with the next basket full of potatoes, she was dirty all over, her hair let down and her face contorted. You could not recognize her. My heart was trembling and begging. And suddenly this terrible man said, 'You all go home.' That was one of those moments in which we experienced that there is a higher force, beyond all reason."

The word soon filtered down, however—"You have to go." The von Klitzings by now were no better than field hands, but as German field hands they remained the subject of intense suspicion. Scrounging about for a few pennies and travel papers, the von Klitzings managed to board a train for the West, carrying a single backpack apiece with one loaf of bread. Ironically, their last train was a long string of open coal cars. During the night, they were looted by Polish partisans combing through the passengers. In October 1945 the von Klitzings reached safety. Dorothee's son did not at first recognize her when they met.*

-ᢙ᠊

Aronek Kierszkowski knew a thing or two about coal cars, but his fate in that bitter winter was even harsher than being shuttled about the German railroad system, or what was left of it. Along with an estimated 250,000 others, he was condemned to the infamous death marches, a strangely disjointed effort by the SS to clear their concentration camps of inmates in the face of Soviet advances. If the spirit of early camp life at Stutthof was death from work, that of its later stages was death from exposure and tramping about the countless futile miles of German countryside without food. It is not known how many prisoners perished in those frigid months of 1945. But for the many thousands that did, it was a doubly cruel fate because deliverance seemed so close at hand. Many were marched straight to the Frisches Haff from Stutthof and its satellite camps, with the front only a few miles away, and machine-gunned on the shore or driven into the water to freeze. Others, like Aronek Kierszkowski, were set out on the road west to God knows where.

"It was snowing; it was cold; it was miserable; it was a death march. We had no blankets; we were in ragged striped pajamas. Any place they could drag us to they did. Two events saved my life. I had lined

---

*In 1946 nearly 5 million Germans remained in the former Ostpreussen, the Baltic coastline, Poland, and Russia. The Poles expelled 1.6 million of them in the twelve months after Armistice Day. By 1950 another 2.75 million had been pushed along west from what the Poles called "recovered territories." George Orwell labeled these largely unpublicized evictions "an enormous crime."

up a pair of military boots in Stutthof. Some fellows worked as shoe-makers repairing army boots, and I told one of them that I'd give him two slices of bread I had saved if he could get me a pair of boots. No socks, of course, I had to wrap my feet in rags. And the second took place in January of 1945 before we were driven west. The SS came and said there's a derailed train and we have to put it back on track. We were used to being turned out for work like that. We went there and realized that these cars, derailed and turned over, were full of goods sent west by refugees from East Prussia. There were sacks of sugar and sausages and clothes all over the place. Now, the clothes we didn't know what to do with, because we were in stripes, but the sugar and the sausage! In the wreck I poured a lot of sugar down my boots, it must have come to about two pounds worth. If the SS had caught me doing this, they probably would have shot me on the spot, and in the camp there were other inmates who tried to get it away from me—dog eat dog—but I managed to protect my food. During the march I used to take a spoonful of sugar in the morning and another at night. Later on when I started running out, I had one a day. When liberation came, I still had some left. I wish I had preserved it, really, because the sugar saved my life. That and the boots, marching through the snow, made the difference.

"They drove us for three days through the Polish Corridor into Pomerania, and that was during a tough winter. They didn't give us any food. At night we used to sleep on church floors, very holy places! Our guards were Ukrainians. They wore black uniforms, they were enthusiastic shooters, and they were *terrible*. We ended up in a place called Rieben in West Prussia, apparently a work camp for Poles. There they hardly fed us. In six weeks barely 300 out of 600 were still alive. The commandant, Meisel, used to say, 'Still so many Jews around?'

"We could tell, though, that something was happening. This was at the beginning of March 1945. The Ukrainian guards, as long as they had the German army to back them up, they were heroes, but once they were on their own they didn't know what to do. We just sat around, and once in a while they'd take us out to work. But some inmates saw them wearing civilian clothes under their uniforms, so we said, hmm, the end is coming.

"But the situation for us, you have to understand, was progressively getting worse. Some people asked me later, 'When did it start getting better?' It didn't start to get better. The misery curve kept falling, and as liberation approached it just shot straight down, bang. Corpses were everywhere, people eating bark, grass, anything. A group of inmates was supposed to drag the bodies to a hill beyond the wire fence, but as time progressed they were getting weaker and the death count was rising. They could do ten, maybe twenty corpses a day, but even though the bodies were very light—skin and bones, really—they couldn't move them all towards the end, so they piled them up against a wall in our barrack.

"For food, we were lucky to get a cup of watery soup a day, so I remember well the big celebration when once they found a dead horse outside the camp. They dragged it inside and began making soup out of it. But the cooks were Poles, and the meat they were giving to the Polish inmates in the other barracks, and we got water and bones. They would throw a bone into our big room and the Jewish inmates would start fighting over it like animals. Ah, the Poles! They would look in and kind of enjoy the show.

"At this point someone should have taken over, some Jew. As I look back from a rational point of view, someone should have told the people, 'Liberation is coming. We may as well resort to cannibalism. What the heck? These people are dead in any case. Why should the rest die? They are meat. They'll just rot away in another few weeks.' I heard that some people did it. I did not, but to tell you the truth I have no bad feelings about it. I think if it had been organized, if someone had taken the step and been a leader, we could have saved fifty out of our group during those last few weeks. Sure, it's not very much fun, but you don't have to know what you're eating. We ate a dead horse found at a road site and we didn't care it was a horse. This was a resource. But there were no leaders, only chaos.

"In any case, March 8, 1945, the day before my seventeenth birthday, we knew that things had come to a point. The commandant, Meisel, a fat fellow, he came over to our barrack and gave a speech. He told us that when the Russians find out that we, the Jews, had worked for the SS, they wouldn't like it, so he suggested to us that we should follow him to the West. The next morning he rode up mounted on a horse, and about a hundred inmates followed him. It was sort of a voluntary thing. They could barely get up, but they decided to go with Meisel and the Ukrainians. Imagine how quickly they went. These people could hardly walk, but this was the only thing Meisel could think of to save his skin! He was so damned confused he didn't know what to do.

"It only dawned on me years later what was going through his mind, because I realized that this was a pattern that other SS *Einsatzkommandos* followed. You see, basically, they were cowards. They felt as long as they had Jews they had a mission. At Rieben Meisel had a horse. He could have made 150 kilometers a day and stayed ahead of the Russians. But as a German officer he would certainly have been stopped by the regular army, and they would have said, 'Well, join us. We are fighting for the fatherland.' But as long as he had Jews, he didn't have to do that—he had 'his orders,' 'his mission.' The SS, they were always dragging the few Jews left with them. Meisel needed the Jews for his safe conduct through his own lines. He didn't want to fight!

"I was told by people I met after the war that the Russians caught up with the column a day or two later. The inmates told the Russians who Meisel was and they hanged him from a tree.

"Me and my friends, we took a chance and didn't go with Meisel. We decided we aren't going. It was a risk. They could have machine-gunned all of us who stayed, but they didn't. After a while, we realized we were not supervised anymore: Everyone had gone—the SS and their Ukrainian guards, all gone. The next morning we heard people yelling, 'The Russians are coming!' and these five scouts came in, two women and three men. They stood there and looked at all these dead people piled up along the walls and looked at the survivors. And the smell, it must have been horrendous to them. This would be like when you go to some of these enormous Polish outhouses; they have tremendous smells, but after you sit there for a while, you don't notice it at all, and in a way, neither did we. The two Russian women scouts, they started to cry. They couldn't take it. They said things like, 'Please, get out of here! It stinks here. It's terrible. You're free—go!'

"It was salvation, really. Imagine you're in hell, and a few angels come in and say, 'You don't belong here. You may leave.'

"A few of our group soon located the warehouse that the SS and Ukrainian guards had left behind, and they brought food in. Some of the older fellows who were in their thirties said, 'Just eat one bite once in a while. Don't start feeding yourself with all that food because your stomach will not be able to digest it.' It was the best advice we could have in the circumstances. A number of people who overate died. We rationed ourselves.

"The Russians, of course, they were not as organized as the American army. They just said to us, 'Get out of here, quickly.' So all the people who could walk started to get out of the camp. Which way? Anywhere! Me and my friends, we went in one direction, and we stopped at a German farm. There was a house on a hill, a barn nearby, these fantastic fields. And it was a very interesting feeling because the Germans there were afraid of us. There we were in this striped clothing, so weak we could barely walk, and they were afraid of us. They asked, What did we need? We said we want some warm water to wash up. Can you imagine, this German kid went out to get water for us, heating it up, giving us food, and we are looking at each other thinking, what a turn of events!

"Next day in the morning when we woke up, we came out from the house and all around us was the Soviet army: tanks, artillery, and trucks, and after a while a few German planes came and tried to bomb them, so we got back into hiding. I thought we've survived all this and now to get killed by the bombers! As we stood there a young man stuck his head out of the barn and said to us, 'Hey! Get me out of here! I'll give you a lot of money.' Do you know who it was? It was the second in command at our camp, an SS man, maybe nineteen years old, and here he was, in civilian clothes. Well you know, a couple of days earlier he had decided, since he had nothing to do, to take a group of us to a bathhouse nearby. We hadn't had a bath for months and months. There were maybe fifty to a hundred of us, all kids. Well on the way back he didn't like how one of us was walking, so he shot him dead. Imagine! And here he is telling us he'll give us money! So we said, 'Just wait, just wait a moment.' We then told a Russian officer who came by, 'Here's an SS man. He just shot one of our kids a few days ago.' The Russian went over to the barn and called him out. He asked the man for his papers, and after checking them, he threw them on the ground and shot him on the spot. This is the way to treat people like this! An American officer would have made a big fuss, tried to intern him, treated him like a human being, fed him, and possibly let him go.

"What was interesting about the whole thing is that although we had nothing, we didn't even go over to him to get his suit or his shoes or to see if he had any money. We didn't even look behind the barn door to see if he had a suitcase. We were tired of dead people. We just left him and walked away.

"So we were on the road, and those Germans, they were scared stiff. I never saw anything like it. They were saying, 'Don't kill us. Don't kill us.' Some of them, as soon as they saw us in our striped suits, would jump off their wagons and run away. They probably thought we were ghosts. And we would take over their wagons. After a while we had four of them, and we just went in the same direction as the wagons were going. We always stopped for food—you collected food. That's all you were concerned with."

Kierszkowski and his group occupied an empty house on the main street of Lauenburg and were joined a few days later by liberated Jewish girls from other camps. After a few months' recovery, they eventually headed east for Poland and home. Mistaken for liberated Russian POWs—a status, given Stalinist paranoia, that could easily have led to summary execution or deportation to Siberia—they were deprived of their wagon train and arrested by the Soviet NKVD.* Amid the confusion of that early fall, he escaped and made his way to Berlin.

⇥⇤

All along the shores of the Frisches Haff, German civilians from Königsberg to Elbing saw but one route of escape, a perilous and desperate journey over the ice floe of the half-frozen lagoon to the narrow sand spit Frisches Nehrung, and from there to Danzig. German sources are vague as to how many people attempted the passage, but over a million seems plausible. A rough guesstimate usually given is that half those who set out on foot never made it to the other side. Shifting bergs, splintered and cut adrift by Russian artillery fire, thin ice cover and treacherous soft spots, and mini tidal waves a foot or more in height, whipped up by the fierce winter winds, devastated the horde of refugees, many hauling sleds holding children or wounded relatives. Tales of unimaginable horror permeate the testaments of survivors, brothers or sisters or aunts suddenly disappearing through the ice to a frozen death below, dead animals and humans littering the ghastly reach of twisted, slushy ice, the cries of pain as mothers gave birth to children in open weather on the frigid wasteland. For those who survived, it was a moment of hell never forgotten. For those who died, it was an open graveyard that took three months, until the springtime thaw, for closure, for only then could the bloated corpses sink below the water, some never to reappear, others to wash up onto shore in one great charnel heap.

---

*Stalin's order number 270 stated that all Russian soldiers captured by the enemy were "traitors to the motherland."

In Danzig over a million and a half refugees and wounded soldiers clogged the city, and many of these were unwelcome. "When they heard we were from the old German territories, they called us Nazis and blamed us for everything," related one of these. Another refugee wrote later that

> just before I left Danzig I was queuing in a butcher's shop to collect my ration. A Reich German was also there and the assistant was slicing him some sausage. He watched her precise cutting and measuring, and finally lost patience with her: "Come on, don't be so stingy. Don't forget we Reich Germans pulled you Danzigers out of the shit in 1939." The assistant pointed at the sausage with her knife and said: "Reich German, I would have given you three whole sausages just to leave us in that shit in the first place."

Thousands of these stragglers were to die as Russian submarines, lurking about the Danzig roads, torpedoed Red Cross ships seeking to evacuate them west. Even the Royal Air Force joined in, bombing and strafing at will. "In the West you often see newsreels of our Stukas shooting down civilians as they fled from the front in 1939," one older German said to me. "What you won't see is footage from Danzig in 1945, even though it was much the same thing. I know you all think we deserved it, but all the same, misery is misery, and I wish the West knew more of what we endured in those times."

⸛

The last and certainly most valiant military effort of the Wehrmacht during World War II was the maintenance of a corridor west through the countryside of northern Germany that served to funnel the vast and panic-stricken rabble of refugees to safety beyond the River Elbe. Hitler by now was dead, the high command structure in shambles, and resistance to Anglo and American forces surging toward Berlin almost nonexistent. Local initiative by local officers, often of junior rank, continued the fight against Russian forces, whether from zealotry or nihilism depended on the personalities of those involved. On the large estate of Varchentin, just two hours' travel from the Elbe, the fourteen-year-old Otto Grote watched the horde of trekkers with fascination.

"The Russians came quicker than the population could move, but we saw as early as January of 1945 all these Conestoga-type wagons coming into our village, people who had left early, all the way from East Prussia. It was snowing like mad, and an unbelievable sensation to see, these first waves of carts, each with a couple of horses drawing them and the horses in bad shape. These people really had nothing but their clothes.

"The best shape of anyone in the general population, ironically, were the thousands of POWs that the Germans were moving off. We had these huge barns on the estates, all of which were requisitioned, and these guys who were air corps people from England and America who had been shot down, they were all put up in the barns. They had these Red Cross packages from Switzerland, so they were fine. My mother, she couldn't be seen with any of them, used to send me out in the pitch darkness of night to try and make deals with them, because they didn't have any fresh bread and we did, though it was barely digestible, something like 25 percent potato meal. I'd trade it for some coffee or cigarettes."

"Were these men guarded?" I ask.

"Barely. They knew that they had to get out, too. I mean, everyone was moving in the same direction, west, and history has shown that the Russians kept a lot of these airmen prisoners forever. So the atmosphere was pretty casual for them, though certainly not for us or the trekkers. The Nazi Party was still in charge locally, and it was drumhead justice. You opened your mouth and they could just walk in and boom, you're dead. I was hiding in some bushes in front of our place one night because my mother had sent me out. We didn't have any electricity at that point, so it was really dark. And I heard the local political leader talking, who was basically an employee of ours; he was the so-called *Ortsgrupenleiter*, the political guy in charge of the community for the party, and I heard him say to one of his henchmen, 'We're going in with our pistols drawn and find out if the countess has moved anything. And if she has moved out anything, she's violated the trek restriction, and we'll shoot her on the spot.' Those were the conditions! If you were caught packing up, you could be executed. They called it *Treckverbot*—the word *Treck* an expression from the Boers in South Africa.

"The most peculiar part of it was the power we kids had. We were dangerous. What we heard was that victory was just around the corner. There are secret weapons and all kinds of things. But here you have this flood of refugees coming in; nobody says anything; you're on your own in terms of figuring out what's really going on. For an adult to discuss this situation with you, well, he took a chance. We were all in the Jungvolk, which was the equivalent of Germany's Cub Scouts—it was absolutely mandatory to be enrolled in that through your fourteenth birthday—and we could turn people in, call our superior over and say, 'Hey, this old fart up there is telling us the war is lost.' Well, they'd just cart him off. We were basically the only men left. We had a kind of power you just can't appreciate.

"By February, early March, you began to see slivers of red on the eastern horizon every night. Boy, it was frightening to see that. Jesus, it was depressing. And that little sliver got to be wider and wider every week, and eventually it was up to here and you saw this thing—it was like a giant, like one of those cheese covers you put over cheese. It just came over you. You couldn't help but be frightened by this, and as it came closer and as it got higher and higher up in the sky, you began to see yellow and white lights flaring up in there but still you couldn't hear anything. I've never known anything more terrifying as that slow death that was coming up on you, and we all knew what the hell it was.

"By the second half of March, you began to hear the rumbling of the front, and by the time April came, it was very loud. This was basically the time of the Wehrmacht's last stand when they tried to keep this corridor going to the west. The next major town to the east of us, between us and the Oder, was a place called Neubrandenburg. It was a wonderful old Gothic town that still had a lot of churches and the defensive wall constructed in the twelfth century by Henry the Lion. And there what was left of the Leibstandarte Adolf Hitler [or LAH; Hitler's bodyguard] put up a defense. They were probably the last elite outfit in the German army, and they fought there for a long time because Neubrandenburg is the key position to getting out to the Elbe; there were only two roads you could use going west, and that place controlled them both. As a result those roads were completely jammed with army units, eventually joined by retreating treks. It was total chaos, but they held on there, oh, I guess it was three weeks, until it was all over.

"Then I got a phone call, which was incredible. I mean, here I was just a kid in the Jungvolk and I mean, the telephone! This is the first time I can ever remember using one! Today, it's nothing, but in those days for me, this was a big deal. It was the local party office, and they said the following: We want you to burn all the papers of the Jungvolk in the file cabinets—right now, burn them; secondly, we want every-

Awaiting the inevitable: German troops in East
Prussia, *1945, by A. Hierl*

body that can walk and is in good health to appear in Malchin, which
is the county seat, and Malchin was to be defended by what was left of
this LAH outfit and us, the local youth. This is something the Communist regime has never said anything about, but there must have
been hundreds if not thousands of kids who died there in Malchin,
which I think held out for three days, and they either were killed by
the Russians outright or they were caught up in the battle or shot as
prisoners. No one knows where they're all buried.

"But clearly, thousands and thousands of refugees managed to escape because these LAH guys and the Waffen-SS were all on this suicide mission. I mean, they knew they would either die in a Russian
POW camp or be wiped out in the battle, and I guess they preferred to
go out fighting, this end of the world stuff, this Götterdämmerung. I
sensed that at the time, and speaking honestly, I still wanted to go
with them.

"This is one of those things, if you're writing about Germany, that is very difficult to put in perspective. As a kid, as a member of these youth organizations, we were from the beginning trained that we were going to die for Germany. Today you'd say, Jesus Christ, were these guys ever brainwashed! And it's true, the brainwashing was so effective that death was just an ordinary, accepted thing. It's often occurred to me that it wasn't just the Jews that were in concentration camps; in retrospect all of Germany was in a concentration camp. We were getting slaughtered just as the Jews had been. I mean in our little village, very few men came back from the eastern front. The ghettos disappeared, and so did our village. Death was all over the place. When you look at Hitler's attitude, he said, 'I'm the greatest leader Germany has ever had, and if I go down to ruin I will take all of Germany down with me as a punishment.' The general attitude of the population, it reminds me of Jonestown, all those people taking poisoned Kool-Aid. This element that Hitler had created in Germany, this was as close as any society has come to committing mass suicide. It's hard in retrospect to understand, so you ask yourself, Was Hitler insane, and did he, by the force of his personality, turn all of Germany into an insane society? There is certainly an element of truth in that.

"Now my mother, she was a very forceful personality, and she knew what I was thinking. I'm sure she slipped me a Mickey because I got very sick for a couple of days. I couldn't even walk, so I didn't go to Malchin, thank God. Her attitude was to keep me from doing something stupid, to get me under control.

"My mother, you know, she was an American, from Boston, as a matter of fact. She was extremely good-looking and had all kinds of people wooing her, even after her marriage. She met my father in 1929. She had been going around the world with a very wealthy stockbroker; I mean he must have been far older than she was—'mother's friend' we used to call him—and he had money in October of that year; by November he had none. And money was very important to my mother. Anyway, in the course of going to a cocktail party she met my father, and he pursued her. His wealth and social position were a major consideration to her, and she married him—though this part of the German landscape, you know, the terrible weather up here, unbelievably bad, she must have often said, 'By God, how do I make that decision!' But Varchentin was big, something over seventy rooms, 3,000 hectares. We had four villages, and in 1945 there was only a single thing she was thinking. With my father dead on the Russian front, she was the heir to a very large property, and she said, 'Gee, those god-damned Americans are on the Elbe, and they can be here in a day, so let's not do anything precipitous because the moment I leave here everything is gone.' She said that for weeks, and just held on. There was also a little problem with the *Treckverbot*.

"But one day some big staff car came driving up, fast, you know. The chickens barely had time to get out of the way. You could hear the gravel kick around as he made the turn, came to a screeching halt, just like the movies. And out steps this high-ranking SS officer, his name was Mazuw, and he said to my mother, 'Frau Gräfin, if you don't get your kids out of here in the next twelve hours, you're all going to be gone, you won't live. Why are you still here?' My mother said, 'I don't have anything to worry about. I'm going to hoist a Swiss flag on this tower and an American flag on that tower, and I've got all sorts of Swiss and American papers, and they're not going to do anything.' He suppos-edly replied, 'You've got to be kidding. The Russian frontline troops are coming here. They don't know how to read or write. They don't know one flag from another. You fly a flag and it's not theirs, they're going to blow you to pieces, and that's after they get done with you.' At that mo-ment, my mother said, 'God, we better get the hell out of here.'

"The whole idea of Russians on the loose, well, that was just the ex-tra bit of terror that she needed. You know, that Goebbels, he would have made a great advertising executive, he would have dominated Madison Avenue. No one portrayed an image better than he did. When I was twelve, the time of Stalingrad, he ran these posters with red all over them: the firestorm coming, the Mongolian tidal wave, and you had only to look at that and be terrified. They did all this to stiffen up our resistance. They'd say if you give up to the Russians, they'll cas-trate all of you—and it worked. This sense of horror had been carefully nurtured by German propaganda for years, and believe me, the people in my little village believed it. There was enormous fear of what would happen when the Russians marched in.

"This Mazuw, by the way, I've figured out why he came. After the war my mother married an officer who came over to Germany on Eisenhower's staff, someone she'd known in Berlin as a diplomat. And everyone would write her asking for help or a deposition in the de-Nazification hearings, but Mazuw was the only one she wrote a letter for. His attitude must have been, 'It doesn't hurt to have an American friend. It might help later on.' With Mazuw it definitely did.

"Anyway, we'd had remnants of the famous Sixth Panzer Division stationed with us at Varchentin. These are the guys—I think that was Rommel's unit, either his or Guderian's—that led the breakthrough on the Meuse into France in '41, I mean a famous division. They had been in Königsberg defending East Prussia, and so few of them got out that they weren't allowed to say they were the Black Division. All they had left were a few jeeps and trucks and rifles. There were two lieutenants there that my mother liked or who liked her—with men, my mother could do anything she wanted, click, just like that—so she persuaded these two to get us out. One drove a truck. The other came up in a car for the three of us. We were the last to go. It was Sunday, April 29, just a few days before armistice on May 8. The roads, I mean they were totally jammed, all kinds of people fleeing at this point. The party wasn't there to enforce law and order anymore, only the SS were still on the roads. And wouldn't you know it, but they had set up a roadblock on the only road left out over the river.

"Boy, I tell you, this is the only time in my life when I was really scared. This young lieutenant and my mother in the front seat, I was in the back, and the whole car loaded up with gear. I was so crammed in with stuff I couldn't move, and all of a sudden my left leg cramped up; it was stone cold. 'What's wrong with my leg?' I said to myself. 'The damned thing is paralyzed.' I didn't know what had happened to it. It turned out I had inadvertently stepped into one of those earthenware crocks full of cold lard that we were escaping with, and I had no circulation in my leg. So I was in pain.

"We come up to the roadblock, and there they were, all these SS just standing there with submachine guns. They had a couple of armored cars with them, shoring up the barricade; they had set up some machine-gun nests. So they looked at us, looked over my mother, and they said, 'Over there.' My first thought was they're going to confiscate this car because they want it for the army; but no, they wanted to see papers. Now my mother was always very cool—she always had things under control. She was very dominant. But when I saw the look on her face as she frantically got out all these papers for him and explaining where she got them, well, this guy was unimpressed by anything he saw. And I said, 'OK, shit, this is *bad* news.' I suddenly realized this was going to be life or death. I said to myself, 'I still have my Jungvolk papers. Maybe I can help defend this city with the others, and they won't shoot me with mother.' My other thought was, 'If only

I can get over this river, get over to the other side.' And then, the miracle happened.

"There was this enormous commotion behind us where the roadblock was. Apparently a bunch of German soldiers who had come all the way from Russia in this large piece of equipment, this huge half-track used to pull artillery, just ran right over this roadblock, flattened these SS guys, there were just bodies all over the street. In the confusion everyone who had been pulled over just backed up and took off, and so did we.

"The strangest thing I remember was at the end. The Germans had taken what was left of their big warships with their big guns and moved them into all these river mouths and deltas to shell the access routes to keep the Russian armor away. As you moved west, you could hear these enormous explosions, this coastal artillery sort of thing firing into the interior. I didn't see them, they must have been 15 or 20 miles away, but you could hear these constant explosions going on all the time. That was eerie."

# ⊰ 17 ⊱

# In the West:
# Survivors

*I find it very hard to say what Germany is just now. It is a country without a government, without any definite borders. Germany has no troops, she is broken up into occupation zones. Take this and define what Germany is. It is a broken country.*
—Joseph Stalin, Potsdam, July 18, 1945

KATHARINA VON NEGENBORN shows me a porcelain fruit bowl. "My parents buried this china in 1945 in the back of our house in East Prussia. The Poles who live there now dug it up, they say in 1976. When I visited the place in 1980, they offered to sell it to me, and of course I bought it. It was a very strange experience having it back, but wonderful, too."

Aronek Kierszkowski would like to show me something he could have retrieved, but he missed his chance, and in a way he doesn't seem to mind. "I was seventeen in 1945, going on a hundred."

Kierszkowski made up his high school education by studying with private German tutors from 1946 to 1947. He paid for these tutorials with bags of oatmeal collected in his DP camp. "If you could prove you were a camp survivor, you were entitled to free tuition plus 200 marks a month living money. After passing equivalency exams, I enrolled at the technical university of Munich in November of 1947. I was starving at the time, eating noodles three times a day. A pack of cigarettes was worth 110 marks, so you can figure how far 200 marks

*Katharina von Negenborn with recovered china*

went. I lived in a little room, rented out from a German family. Some of the windowpanes were broken. It was pretty cold.

"Well, after living there for a few months I was talking with my landlady. She was around forty, I'd say, and she was kind of an unattractive woman, and her husband wasn't very good-looking either. But they had this beautiful little blond daughter, maybe four years old. So I asked, 'How did you come by this child?' And she told me that she had been a guard at Dachau, the concentration camp near Munich. A Russian woman had got pregnant at the camp and had to give up her child after birth. My landlady then took her, raising her as her own. This was her story, anyway.

"Then one day, looking for something, I found many bars of soap in a little closet near my room, bars and bars of it. And you know, I sometimes wonder about this. I wouldn't be surprised if this was the soap they made out of humans. It looked very much like military-type cubes, all dark colors. It didn't look like regular soap to me, but I didn't realize at the time that this was a possibility. The curious thing is, she knew I was a Jew. This is really the peculiarity of the situation for many Germans. She wanted to show me that she was a 'good' guard."

Otto Grote spent his first months in the West living in ditches and barns. "After crossing the Elbe, we found our way to some relatives. We watched the British army march through. My mother, she didn't have any money, no Swiss francs or dollars; what money she did have was worthless, wouldn't buy anything. Her bank accounts in Berlin had all been destroyed, so all she had were a few possessions she had sent west earlier, and these she bartered for food.

"We did have horses and a wagon, and in June we made the trip from northern Germany all the way down to cousins we had in Swabia. It took almost five or six months to do it, and I mean, I loved it. Sleeping outside or in barns, tending the horses—it was a wonderful adventure from my point of view. My mother, though, she was terrified most of the time. How can she keep five kids alive on the road?

"I remember once taking the horses out and driving my mother to some farmer in a village on the Neckar near Stuttgart, and she traded a beautiful silver platter for a liverwurst. I loved the liverwurst, but can you imagine! She organized everything. Special rations, coal in the winter, everything. Organization meant buying, stealing, bartering, getting your hands on food or clothes, whatever you needed, any way you could. It was *organisiert*—that was the classic term of this era—it meant something like, 'anything you need to do.'"

The panzer veteran ended up in POW camps in France and Britain. "I was captured by Patton's forces on the Rhine. It's a lucky thing we had no heavy weapons because then we would have had to fight to the end. As it was, we had nothing left; we had no choice but to surrender. By that time I hated war anyway. They ripped my shoulder pieces off, they took my watch, my medals, everything from me. Usually they went for leather coats, but for some reason they didn't take that away from me, which was very lucky. I found a scrap of paper in one of the pockets, a note from a girl in the Rhineland I had met, with her address on it. After the war I went back to see her, and we were married.

"I was in a French camp for the first couple of months; they had almost 30,000 German officers in it. They treated us terribly, just as bad as the Russians. Whatever we got for food they sold on the black market. Then English officers came in, gave out questionnaires, then interviewed us. The intelligence officer who spoke with me was a Jew, as I recall. I convinced him I had never been a Nazi, that my family was against Nazis, that I had been wounded at Stalingrad fighting the Russians. He was a very nice man, and he believed me.

"They took ninety of us out of the camp and brought us to Oxford, where they treated us like gentlemen, I must say. We were mostly regiment and battalion commanders, all kind of young, and they were training us to take over POW camps. I was assigned to a camp in Bristol, oh, it must have been for a year, and that was very hard. There were many officers in that camp who worked against me. A German doctor there— he was from East Prussia; his parents took their lives when the Russians came in—he warned me, 'You better watch out. They possibly kill you. They claim you are a turncoat'—that sort of thing. They came mostly from the navy. We had quite a few submarine commanders there, and they just couldn't take it. That's a real sad story, too.

"When I got out, I smuggled myself east to see my parents in Erfurt. My father's business, of course, had all disappeared, and people like us . . . well, in Erfurt, we are not liked, as you can well imagine. The Communists had my father doing manual labor, that sort of thing, but he wasn't a person who would give in. He was tough. I was home only two days before a neighbor came and said, 'You have to get as fast as possible away. They come get you.' Just like the Nazis, they had on each block someone to spy on you. My parents took me to the railroad station with my suitcase. That's the last time I saw either of them. They lost everything.

"So now, here we are, fifty years later, and I still have nightmares. So does my brother, and he's eighty-eight years old. Only a few months ago I slept with him and I had to get out of the bed, otherwise he would hit me and kick me. I watched him for a while, then I woke him up and said, 'What are you doing?' It took him quite a few minutes to come back, and that's when we talked about war and the experiences we had. It comes back to him in the night, in his nightmares, just like me."

In a new housing development on a bluff overlooking the Rhine near Koblenz, I walk once again through another immaculate garden that features not a single weed or agricultural blemish of any kind, the very blades of grass almost willed into perfect order. Beyond the tidy rectangular plot of flower beds and vegetables, a long stretch of brilliant green fodder lies ready for the scythe. "I still do it by hand, for the exercise," an octogenarian says to me as we stroll along a neat pebbled path that parallels the border fence. "The land here is more fertile than my parents' estate, which was about 40 kilometers west of Königsberg. I've been back there four times in the last five years." We come up to several small pine trees. "I dug these up on the old farm, one each trip, and brought them back here. One almost died, but I nursed it back to health. I'll dig up another one this summer when I visit. The Russian who lives on the place is very, very proper, and he helps me with the digging. They're a very sentimental people."

"What about you? Are you sentimental?"

"Yes, in my soul I am, though I keep sentiment to myself. People here in Germany miss the point of reunification completely. They say now, once again, Germany is united. This is not correct. There can be no historical Germany without Prussia. We have a single large country now where for fifty years we had two. This may be a Germany of the future, but it is not the Germany I grew up with and still remember best. What makes the Germans happy today makes me very sad."

The Germany of the past, of course, is redefined daily throughout this country. Every event, every occurrence, every personality is judged according to the lens of a gruesome history, a history that many exploit to make their message larger than life. "Why call a person an 'asshole' when you get more effect by calling him a 'Jewish asshole'?" one middle-aged lawyer said to me. "Vandalizing a Jewish cemetery is far more interesting than doing the same thing in a Catholic cemetery—who cares about that?"

"Are you saying anti-Semitism is a cured disease?" I asked.

"I think it is. We are 80 millions now in Germany; only 20,000 Jews live here today. That's not enough to make a difference. I think the skinheads' Jew-baiting is rhetoric. We have no way of controlling our young people. It's so easy to demonstrate your uneasiness and your opposition to what is happening, such as unemployment, for example, by yelling things like 'Jews out.' It's natural, certainly historical, but it is not like the deep-seated anti-Jew thing of the 1920s. I don't believe for a moment that we have a sentiment for this."

"Well, there are no Jews in Poland either, but I have the feeling they really do hate Jews."

"The Poles are different. They are a nineteenth-century people preoccupied with their 'victim' status. By the time we are finished reinvigorating their economy, which will happen in the first quarter of the twenty-first century, they will be free of that attitude. It is too primitive, and smart Poles know this."

What about "smart" Germans? Will they bury the notion of Prussia along with their anti-Semitic prejudices? "I think so, yes," he continued. "At one point after the war, 20 percent of our West German population were Germans from the east, and naturally enough we, as their children, always are interested to go back to our roots, nostalgia and that sort of thing, to see what your parents have been talking about. That's far removed from saying, I have a 'right' to that place, a 'right' to take it over. It gives you the 'right' to return and to invest—we have tried, for example, to buy back our property in the east—but I don't think that's an aggressive spirit per se."

Talking to a businessman, however, such as Count von Schulenburg, suggests steel just beneath the surface. The count, as a cosmopolitan man (and a shrewd one, investing both in chocolates and dental supplies, a cause-and-effect equation that fairly corners a market) repeats the usual comforting bromides of "cooperation" and "communication," though readily admitting that "Germany will look east and prosper east. It's not a matter of a year or two, but I think within five there will be a certain approach to the east that will result in profit. This approach I would call 'Prussian'; it suggests a certain thoroughness and attention to detail and finance that many of our competitors lack. I don't think some people feel it is an aggression. It is really that just to survive, just to fulfill the demands of our social welfare system, we need business."

Certainly von Schulenburg thought reunification would bring more immediate benefits, both personal and national. "The opening of the [iron curtain] was on the twenty-third of December in 1989. I crossed the border three days later, and at the time I was happy. I said to myself as I drove around, 'This is my property. I will have it back.' As you know, this never happened. The state decided to act like a criminal, to own what the Communists took from us after the war, and to sell it to pay for reunification. They acted, as you say in America, as a 'fence.' And the GDR! Well, for forty years we've been talking about reunification, and then it happens and we're horrified. One hundred billion a year for four years have been invested. We're developing an undeveloped country. We believed we were taking over a decent economy, but what we've got was a deathbed patient.*

"The other problem we have is the feeling of not being finished. The territory we recovered through reunification is called by us the 'Mid-

---

*Another famous German family thwarted in its efforts to recover lost property are the Mendelssohns, whose former estate lies 20 miles east of Berlin. Despite their status as Jews, and famous Jews at that—Felix, the composer, and Moses, the philosopher, are only two of the better-known—the Mendelssohns managed to save their property from the Nazis, only to lose it under the GDR. Descendants are now locked in a legal battle with an ex–Communist Party official over ownership, a case they are expected to lose.

dle Deutschland.' The real East Prussia is still under Poland and Russia, however. Reunification is a step in the right direction, but as a process it is not complete."

Many observers believe the tinder is dry enough that a certain type of leader with a certain type of message could set it afire. As Otto Grote said to me, "East Prussia is an emotionally charged issue. It is not economically important in and of itself, and many Germans, having seen what the GDR was like, don't want to touch anything east of the Oder. Those are the 'comfortable' Germans. But you do have very influential people—you have Graf Dönhoff, for instance—who without meaning to at all can get otherwise very sober people very sad and melancholy about 'the lost province' or, to use something from American history, the sort of feelings associated with the Alamo.

"In many ways, I have to tell you, Germans have not changed and their feelings about Prussia have not changed. Take music, for example. Both my brothers were professors of music, my grandmother was an opera star, and it turns out that I have a very musical ear, too. It had been my job in the Jungvolk to instruct people in singing these songs—I must have known as a boy over one hundred songs. I knew their melodies, oh, absolutely by heart. Even today, I hear a bar or two of this music, and even today, fifty years later, I could recite it to you.

"Now Hitler and this very basic, almost guttural language that he used, these are the kinds of words that came up in this music. The words meant nothing. I didn't know what any of these words meant. I only remembered the music. But as soon as the melody comes out, I remember exactly the words. It's really just an enormously powerful form of memory and national identification.

"Well, this summer I was at a wedding, drove through the neighborhood, and there was the local village, and the fire department had staged a cookout. What do they have there but the classic band, and what are they playing, what are they playing? I tell you, it was the same as fifty years ago. Nothing has changed. Nothing has changed. They played it under the kaiser. They played it under Hitler. They played it under the Communists. They're playing it now. They may be rural, they may be against the past, down on everything they may have done in history, but here they are doing exactly what they did then.*

---

*A German literary critic once noted "the four quarters of the riven German soul: murder, bureaucracy, theology and music."

"Nothing, nothing compares to what they did to how many thousands of people, the brainwashing and all. You remember what Hitler said, I can't totally recreate it: 'You give me your kids six to ten, and we'll get them oriented this way; and you give them to me after they're ten and we'll put them in this and they'll be even more inculcated; and by the time they get to be twenty-one [slaps his hands], you'll never get 'em back. And that is not just a hollow boast. Those 6 million who were in the Hitler Youth and saw Germany go under, they in their souls haven't given up. They're still there, and until all of them are dead, you're not safe, because they can be triggered just like that, and they are being triggered by the right wing. They are still there.

"If some demagogue in a new Germany—a new, powerful Germany—starts yelling about East Prussia, it will rouse people up who never saw the place, who previously had no connection with it."

This seems to me a reasonable hypothesis. As Edmund Wilson wrote in *Patriotic Gore*, people commonly behave irrationally, in ways that perfectly objective observers find incompatible with logic and good sense. Germany has no formal tradition of democratic inclinations. In Grote's words, "They do not understand the first thing of what Jefferson represented." Germans dutifully go to the polls, they dutifully pull the proper levers, and they dutifully turn their backs on extremist parties like the REP (Republikaner), which garnered a ludicrous 1.9 percent in the 1994 elections. This only means, according to some, that they haven't been pushed enough in some primal way that would cause them to break ranks en masse with respectability. "Germany is a socialist country," an American businessman with extensive connections in the east said to me. "People who think the Nazis were right-wing, for example, have it quite wrong. When Germans say the Nazis were right-wing, they only mean that Nazi deputies sat to the right in the old Reichstag assemblies. It is not the same thing as right-wing in the United States, whereby you say that a Patrick Buchanan or a John Birch is right-wing, meaning conservative. No, no! The differences between the Nazis and the Communists were paper thin; the war between Nazi and Communist was between two rival socialist systems. Nowadays the broader picture is quite similar. Germans are either employed in very large companies that are run in a very dogmatic way, or they work [for] or are dependent on the state, which also runs in a dogmatic way. Look at the former GDR: Talk about a state-run economy! I do not believe that structurally or psychologically they have changed enough for us to be relaxed about it. They are capable, like a herd, of veering off in stampede and going over the edge."

"What about militarily?" I asked. "I see no resurgence in the military of what the situation was during Weimar. I didn't see an army eager to join us in the Gulf War or to contribute troops to Yugoslavia."

"Quite true—they don't want to be tempted! And Weimar was different: The military caste of the 1920s and '30s was still intact, still intent on perpetuating the myth they hadn't been beaten, something they couldn't do in '45 when the country lay completely ruined. Their credibility was finished, to say the least. What I refer to here is not necessarily a military threat. The army will not roll out of its barracks and occupy East Prussia, but the deutsche mark will. Listen to the Lufthansa advertising campaign: 'We'll take you to Vilnius. We'll take you to Minsk. We'll take you to Riga and Tallin'—all these cities most people have never heard of. And what's their tag line? 'We're the only ones there!' The German economy will swallow those places up. It's both a promise and a threat. The promise is economic. The Kaliningrad *Oblast*! If any place needs help, there it is: something like 800 percent inflation, the *mafiya* running wild, protection rackets and petty crime out of control, the place completely bankrupt. They need and want German help. But the threat is there, too, and it's a racial one. Eastern Europe is not a melting pot like America. In America you have, what, 100 million people of German extraction, but they want to be known as Americans, not Germans. That's not the way it is in the east. I mean, just look at the Balkans. Does anyone there want to be known as Yugoslavian? So you have the potential for a great deal of tension."

"And if Russia disintegrates, blows up, or self-destructs?"

"That would be a disaster. There are Germans who would see in that the proverbial window of opportunity, and once again, 'Poland be damned. We're on our way.'"

⟜⟝

Hamburg, a capitalist dreamscape, unfolds its gleaming dockside of boundless ships and freight yards and heavy cranes before my eyes as I speed along the spotless autobahn toward the skyscrapered city center. Danzig, Königsberg, Warsaw—these are old dead mares in comparison. The free-market economy of the West, though brash and materialistic to a degree of coarseness despised by so many, still emits a vitality and spring in the step that most eastern vistas sorely lack. But in the editorial offices of *Die Zeit*, overlooking fashionable arcades and shops, I am nevertheless brought back to Prussia once again.

Marion, Countess Dönhoff, sips coffee as we chat, the paper just having bedded down for the week. We are discussing *Schindler's List* and its impact on Germany. She informs me that something like 4 million German schoolchildren, an extraordinary figure, have seen this film. "Everyone is talking about it." I leaf through some of my own notes, especially a conversation I had the day before with a schoolteacher who had taken her entire class to the movie. "Kids not moved," she said, then "couldn't see beyond the fact it was a horror picture. It showed cruelty, but the kids can see that on evening television, live from Yugoslavia. Movie counterproductive; it would be better to read about the horror—you must not see it—otherwise it becomes ordinary. There was no person in the film who I [the schoolteacher] could identify with as a woman and a wife. No differentiated German characters: They're all the same, always shouting or killing. It would be better for the children to see the Auschwitz showers in person than in a film."

"I can agree with that assessment completely," says the countess, "but if you look at the slightly larger picture, its value as an educational tool cannot be denied, especially when you consider who made it. This is not propaganda. It is not a classroom textbook. It is 'entertainment,' if such a word can be used, but 'entertainment' with a strong and worthy message, like any good book or play. I am so glad so many young people have been able to see it. I was very moved myself."

I ask her if people like Zhirinovsky or right-wing German groups might seek to exploit the Ostpreussen card should Russia continue to waver internally. "No, no. Hysteria from the right has nothing to do with Prussia. It has more to do with worries over jobs and foreign immigrants, what you see in all the countries of industrialized Europe. We have now more than 4 million unemployed, and we have about 6 million foreigners here, and each year more and more are coming. No wonder people get scared. This has nothing to do with some kind of special nationalism."

"There are writers who think the German situation right now is similar to Weimar," I observe, "with very similar popular notions running through all strata of society that might tend to undermine it. Instead of the 'stab in the back,' we have the 'Auschwitz lie,' for exam-

*Marion, Countess Dönhoff*

ple; instead of inflation we have high unemployment and recession; instead of Jews we have immigrant workers and so on."

"No, no, I cannot take that seriously. I have *never* heard that. I mean, I know there are these groups. I know there are completely crazy people here who deny the Holocaust and who are not allowed to speak here anymore, which is a triumph of our law, not to tolerate that. But it is absolutely senseless to my mind to compare the Weimar epoch with today. There are lots of people who say, 'Aha, this is how Weimar began in the '20s: the monarchy gone, the war lost, inflation out of control, Weimar in charge.' Is it a wonder that everyone was against democracy? Germans were unprepared for it, just like some of the eastern countries today. If you want to compare Weimar conditions, compare them with Russia or Poland, but not Germany.

"When Hitler came, we had 7 million unemployed. There was not a factory chimney with smoke—everything was out. The whole middle class was deprived of everything they had in the banks. The French had taken over the whole Ruhr area, had shut down all the plants that competed with their own—no wonder the people cried for a strong man. But today people don't want a strong man; it would be impossible for a Hitler to appear on the scene. Germans want a certain order, they want a situation where a million strangers do not come into our tiny country each year to compete for jobs.

"I am always fighting against this completely wrong conception that the Prussian spirit was always the military spirit, the 'strong man' spirit. Here is World War II and here is Adolf Hitler, all Prussian. This is not so. We all know Hitler was an Austrian, not a Prussian. We know that Königsberg was not Berlin. Really, Hitler had no idea, no raison d'être as far as Prussia was concerned. In many important ways Prussia has always been a backbone and Königsberg the most liberal part of Germany in the north."

"Does the notion 'Prussia' mean anything today?"

"It changes now. First of all, the young people are so disgusted at what is happening here all over, not just in West Germany, but Italy, France, England, too: this criminality and corruption. So they look for something finer. Isn't there something which is more than just money? They look at society and see everyone running behind money. And then automatically they come to what we would say is German, *Geist.* I do not know quite what the English equivalent is. 'Intellect' is not the right word, 'spirit' neither, but they see a national life is only about GNP, gross rate, God knows what. Nobody talks about cultural things, spiritual things, literature, art. The whole world becomes more and more dull, uninteresting. And therefore people turn back to former days, and it's quite amazing. Prussia means integrity, a special kind of integrity, an unselfish attitude. People seem to want that today, and this is the model."

"Have you returned to your ancestral home since the Wall came down?"

"Last year. I didn't want to go, but the Russians invited me to a conference. They were very nice. They provided me with a car and a translator. But Friedrichstein is nothing. Everything was mutilated. No agriculture, no administration, no nothing. It looks like nothing. There was a huge formal lawn; today there is only a tiny fragment left that is not woods, overgrown, finished."

"What were your feelings, if I may ask?"

A dismissive wave of the hand and a frown: I have trampled the line of good taste. "That you must imagine."

Editors come in with futile, wished-for changes in final copy. The countess must go, but she offers me a chocolate first. I notice a painting of a formal lawn with statuary on her wall. "Yes, it is Friedrichstein. Tourists—people I do not know at all—they send me photographs, sketches, and even paintings of the place when they visit. It is quite touching." Looking wistfully out the window, she says, "I want only one thing for Prussia. I want this country, which is my old beautiful country, to be fruitful again." She walks me to the elevator.

※

The future and what it holds no one can say. Speeding down the autobahn for Frankfurt and my flight home, I keep one eye open for castles, church towers, the quaint and manicured fields of an almost medieval landscape and the other for Mercedes and BMWs flying up behind me, lights flashing, roaring by. Ostpreussen seems to be the past, but the dark furnace of emotion promises the heat and invincibility of a powerful German engine bent on its will. What direction that will take is an open question.

I am in many ways exhausted by the people and places I've seen, and most particularly affected by the melancholia and sense of loss that so permeate the memories of a generation now dying away. Will their last thoughts on earth be of walking hand in hand with a mother or father over the hay fields of a homeland lost long ago? Our world, both past and present, has enough woe for all, it seems.

Otto Grote returned to Varchentin in June 1989. "When I first saw it, my attitude was, 'My God!' It was like I was fourteen again. I had to pinch myself. Everything was there. My next set of impressions were very different; it was like, everything's there but it isn't there. Do you remember when the French discovered the wreck of the *Titanic*, they sent cameras down in the Atlantic to photograph it underwater? What you saw was [that] all organic matter had been etched away; there was only the hulk of steel. Varchentin was like that. Our old home and grounds had become a quarry, stripped away just like the *Titanic*. It was naked. Every fence of wrought iron, every structure—the icehouse, the boathouse—every brick that was in the steps, every brick that was in a wall, all the latticework . . . all of it had disappeared and only nature remained, nature and this huge, gutted house.

"I wanted it back. I mean, property rights, I thought they were sacred. I spent nearly all of my savings on lawyers and lawsuits to get it back. But they had seen me coming a mile away—the Communist politicians and would-be future owners. They had been prepared for us for a long time in advance. We were barred at every turn by enormous efforts, and it all came to nothing.

*Count Otto William
Frederick Grote and
law files*

"Not to allow us to come back, that is a disaster. They were afraid I was a Junker, one of these arrogant aristocrats! They thought I was going to walk around the place in black boots. This is a good way to lose everything. You watch what I say."

About the same time that the aptly named Kaiser-Nostalgie-Express pulls out of the train station in Frankfurt for points east, my jet takes off from the international airport here, bound for New York. I pick up some reading matter and see an interview with the Nobel Prize winner of 1986, Elie Wiesel, in which he complains that for Germans, "forgetting is a national philosophy." That may be true for the ugly things that have, in truth, disfigured their past, but as the plane banks sharply and I stare into the rising sun shining that same moment over Vienna, Warsaw, Königsberg, the Frisches Haff, Stutthof, and Danzig, I see all too clearly that remembrance is a selective exercise at best. Prussia, geographically, can be willed out of existence. The Poles have proven that, along with the Russians, the Lithuanians, the Estonians, and the Latvians, all with enormous energy and resolve. But can they eradicate its memory? Can they eradicate desire?

# Notes

## Front Matter

p. vii   *"To be German and have character . . ."*: Johann Gottlieb Fichte, as quoted by Erich Ludendorff, *Ludendorff's Own Story: August 1914–November 1918* (New York: Harper and Brothers, 1920), vol. 2, p. 434. For Fichte, see Eugene N. Anderson, *Nationalism and the Cultural Crisis in Prussia, 1806–1815* (New York: Octagon, 1966), pp. 16–63.

vii   *"Ease is inimical to civilization"*: Arnold J. Toynbee, *A Study of History* (New York: Oxford University Press, 1958), vol. 1, p. 88.

vii   *"Besides you, only your colleague is kept awake at night . . ."*: Günter Grass, *Two States—One Nation?* trans. K. Winston (New York: Harcourt Brace Jovanovich, 1990), p. 26.

## Chapter 1–Old Prussia

25   *"Our Baltic families . . ."*: *Hitler's Secret Conversations: 1941–1944*, trans. N. Cameron and R. H. Stevens, ed. H. R. Trevor-Roper (New York: Octagon, 1953), p. 527.

27   *Heine's poem* Die Loreley: *The Complete Poems of Heinrich Heine*, trans. H. Draper (Boston: Suhrkamp/Insel, 1982), pp. 76–77.

29   *"Dead Warrior! Go now to Valhalla"*: Heinz Guderian, *Panzer Leader*, trans. C. Fitzgibbon (New York: E. P. Dutton, 1952), p. 34.

30   *Hindenburg a self-professed "Old Prussian"*: *Out of My Life*, trans. F. A. Holt (London: Cassell, 1920), p. 5.

31   *"Where is Germany?"*: Personal communication, Julie Roy Jeffrey, Department of History, Goucher College. "Germany? But where is it? I can't find that country. Where it starts as a land of scholars, it ends as political entity."

33   *"Drang nach Osten"*: Jonathan Riley-Smith, *The Crusades: A Short History* (New Haven, Conn.: Yale University Press, 1987), p. 163; Heinrich G. Treitschke, *Origins of Prussianism: The Teutonic Knights*, trans. Eden Paul and Cedar Paul (London: G. Allen and Unwin, 1942), p. 63; A. P. Vlasto, *The Entry of the Slavs into Christendom* (Cambridge: Cambridge University Press, 1970), p. 152.

p. 37    *"Russia's Hitler"*: Craig R. Whitney, "Russian Nationalist Stirs Up a Storm in Germany," *New York Times*, December 23, 1993, p. A8. See also Vladimir Solovyov and Elena Klepikova, *Zhirinovsky: Russian Fascism and the Making of a Dictator*, trans. C. Fitzpatrick (Reading, Mass.: Addison-Wesley, 1995), and Vladimir Kartsev, *!Zhirinovsky!* (New York: Columbia University Press, 1995).

38    *Prussia has been a war cry before, feeding into "the dynamic strength of German national feeling"*: Adam Michnik, "More Humility, Fewer Illusions," *New York Review of Books*, March 24, 1994, p. 24.

38    *"If you look at the German elite . . ."*: Jürgen Habermas, quoted in ibid., p. 27.

38    *"The desire among modern German politicians . . ."*: *The Downing Street Years* (New York: HarperCollins, 1993), p. 748. See also pp. 783–784, 790–796, 812–815.

38    *Polityka*: "Back to the Future," trans. R. Livingstone, reprinted in the *New York Review of Books*, November 17, 1994, p. 42.

38    *"Should we fear Germany? . . ."*: Habermas, op. cit., p. 26. Umberto Eco had this to say on the topic: "Even though I am much concerned about the various Nazi-like movements that have arisen here and there in Europe, including Russia, I do not think that Nazism, in its original form, is about to reappear as a nationwide movement. Nevertheless, even though political regimes can be overthrown, and ideologies can be criticized and disowned, behind a regime and its ideology there is always a way of thinking and feeling, a group of cultural habits, of obscure instincts and unfathomable drives. Is there not another ghost stalking Europe (not to speak of other parts of the world)?" "UrFascism," *New York Review of Books*, June 22, 1995, p. 12.

38    *"Germans have not reformed . . ."*: Quoted in "The Fourth Reich: The Menace of the New Germany," *Argonaut*, new series 2, vol. 138, no. 4213, 1993, p. 44.

39    *Bismarck's niece*: Edward Crankshaw, *Bismarck* (New York: Viking, 1981), p. 414.

39    *German unemployment figures*: Timothy Garton Ash, "Kohl's Germany: The Beginning of the End?" *New York Review of Books*, December 1, 1994, p. 24; Amity Shlaes, "Annals of Money: Loving the Mark," *New Yorker*, April 28 and May 5, 1997, pp. 188–193.

40    *"Rubble women" or "Trümmerfrauen"*: Christabel Bielenberg, *The Road Ahead* (New York: Bantam, 1992), p. 104.

42    *"The new instrument of torture . . ."*: Grass, op. cit., p. 3.


## Chapter 2–Marienburg

43    *"They robbed and burned wonderfully . . ."*: William Urban, *The Baltic Crusade* (De Kalb: Northern Illinois University Press, 1975), p. 159.

p. 46    *Prussian alphabet:* Hermann Schreiber, *Teuton and Slav: The Struggle for Central Europe,* trans. J. Cleugh (New York: Knopf, 1965), p. 20.

48    *Jeremiah 48:40:* Cited in Robert Bartlett, *The Making of Europe: Conquest, Colonization and Cultural Change, 950–1350* (Princeton, N.J.: Princeton University Press, 1993), p. 260. See also Luke 14:23: "Go out into the highways and hedges and compel them to come in," cited in A. P. Vlasto, *The Entry of the Slavs into Christendom* (Cambridge: Cambridge University Press, 1970), p. 152.

48    *Pagans must "convert or be wiped out":* Eric Christiansen, *The Northern Crusades: The Baltic and the Catholic Frontier, 1100–1525* (London: Macmillan, 1980), p. 51. A typical crusader appeal from Bernard can be found in his letter "To the English People," *St. Bernard of Clairvaux Seen Through His Selected Letters,* trans. B. S. James (Chicago: Henry Regnery, 1953), pp. 265–269. See also Jonathan Riley-Smith, *What Were the Crusades?* (London: Macmillan, 1977), pp. 18–21. Theologians and church officials were aware of the moral contradictions in preaching crusades, often quoting St. Gregory the Great's remark, "Much evil must befall ere the coming of eternal life be proclaimed." Schreiber, op. cit., p. 54.

48    *Most fighting men who took the cross were "a little while ago, robbers":* Riley-Smith, *What Were the Crusades?,* p. 31.

48    *Push your sword "as far as it will enter":* Joinville and Villehardouin, *Chronicles of the Crusades,* trans. M. R. B. Shaw (Harmondsworth, UK: Penguin, 1982), p. 175.

49    *Lübeck:* See Wilson King, *Chronicles of Three Free Cities: Hamburg, Bremen, Lübeck* (London: J. M. Dent & Sons, 1914).

51    *"Pagans are the worst of men . . .":* Bartlett, op. cit., p. 136.

52    *"Dog heads":* ibid., p. 224.

52    *The knights established fifty-four towns, and following statistics:* Carl Tighe, *Gdańsk: National Identity in the Polish-German Borderlands* (London: Pluto Press, 1990), p. 15.

52    *"Ordensstaat":* ibid., p. 307.

53    *God had gloriously "reserved for them enemies":* Christiansen, op. cit., p. 118.

53    *Pagans inhabited territories "where no apostle ever came":* Bartlett, op. cit., p. 98.

53    *The famous notion "dilatio et defensio":* Riley-Smith, *What Were the Crusades?,* p. 25. This point of view was expressed and justified in many ways over the years by German generals and politicians: *Si vis pacem, para bellum.* See Walter Goerlitz, *History of the German General Staff, 1657–1945,* trans. B. Battershaw (New York: Praeger, 1953), p. 100.

53    *"Because of its central position . . .":* George Bailey, *Germans: The Biography of an Obsession* (New York: World Publishing, 1972), p. 430.

55    *Amber:* Patty C. Rice, *Amber: The Golden Gem of the Ages* (New York: Van Nostrand Reinhold, 1980); Lynn H. Nicholas, *The Rape of*

*Europa: The Fate of Europe's Treasures in the Third Reich and the Second World War* (New York: Knopf, 1994), pp. 190–192, 361; Michael Glenny, "The Amber Room," *Art and Antiquities*, March 1989, pp. 108–111, 143–149; John F. Ross, "Treasured in Its Own Right, Amber Is a Golden Window on the Long Ago," *Smithsonian*, January 1993, pp. 30–42.

p. 58    *Marienburg as Germany's "old bastion in the East . . ."*: *Der Letzte Kaiser* (Berlin: Bertelsmann Lexikon Verlag, 1991), p. 314, as quoted by Amos Elon, "The Nowhere City," *New York Review of Books*, May 13, 1993, p. 29.

58    *"Un poseur ridicule"*: Wilhelm also dressed up as Frederick the Great on occasion. For photographs of the kaiser in his impersonations, see John C. G. Röhl and Nicolaus Sombart, eds., *Kaiser Wilhelm II, New Interpretations: The Corfu Papers* (Cambridge: Cambridge University Press, 1982), p. 49; Alan Palmer, *Frederick the Great* (London: Weidenfeld and Nicolson, 1974), p. 218.

59    *"Sergei Mikhailovich, you are a good Bolshevik after all"*: Marie Seton, *Sergei M. Eisenstein: A Biography* (London: Dennis Dobson, 1978), p. 386.

60fn    *A typical torture*: Schreiber, op. cit., p. 50.

61    *"4 marks to 2 serving men for hawks . . ."*: ibid., p. 79.

61    *"Undismayed heroes fall into grim death . . ."*: Bartlett, op. cit., p. 100.

61    *Mary as patron saint of order*: See Mary Ellen Goenner, *Mary-Verse of the Teutonic Knights* (New York: AMS Press, 1970).

61    *"Jubilant monsters . . ."*: Wilfrid Ward, "Prussianism, Pacifism and Chivalry," *Dublin Review*, vol. 157, no. 314, July 1915, p. 212.

62    *Teutonic Knights compared with SS stormtroopers*: Christiansen, op. cit., p. 4; Seton, op. cit., pp. 397–398.

62    *"The ideal of the well born man without possessions . . ."*: William James, *The Varieties of Religious Experience* (Cambridge: Harvard University Press, 1985), p. 255.

62    *"Look at my works, ye Mighty, and despair"*: Christiansen, op. cit., p. 99.

63    *Jacques de Molay and the Templars*: Malcolm Barber, *The Trial of the Templars* (Cambridge: Cambridge University Press, 1978).

## Chapter 3–Danzig

65    *"At last, Far in th' Horizon to the North . . ."*: John Milton, *Paradise Lost* (New York: Odyssey Press, 1962), book 6, 78–86, p. 140. Sergei Eisenstein was enormously influenced by this English poet's war scenes. Milton "frequently described the heavenly battles with such strongly earthy detail that he was often the subject of serious attacks and reproaches." This poem had a direct bearing on Eisenstein's portrayal of the Teutonic Knights in the climactic confrontation of

*Alexander Nevsky.* See Sergei Eisenstein, *The Film Sense* (New York: Meridian Books, 1957), pp. 57–65.

p. 67fn   The Tin Drum *not published in Polish until 1983*: Tighe, op. cit., p. 278.

67fn   *"Do something"*: Pawel Huelle, *Moving House*, trans. M. Kandel (New York: Harcourt Brace, 1995), pp. 6, 8.

69fn   *Closure of Gdansk shipyard*: Jane Perlez, "Ship of Dreams Goes Under in Poland," *New York Times*, March 29, 1997, p. 4.

69   *"Wrath kindled gentleman"*: William Shakespeare, *Richard II*, 1.1.152.

69   *"Full often time he had abroad bygonne . . ."*: Geoffrey Chaucer, "Prologue," *The Canterbury Tales*, part I: 52–55, as quoted by Lucy Toulmin Smith, *Expeditions to Prussia and the Holy Land Made by Henry Earl of Derby (Afterwards Henry IV), in the Years 1390–1 and 1392–3. Being the Accounts Kept by His Treasurer During Two Years* (London: Camden Society, 1894), p. xviii.

71   *Gauls "most greatly admire . . ."*: *Bellum Gallicium*, as translated in J. J. Tierney, "The Celtic Ethnography of Posidonius," *Proceedings of the Royal Irish Academy*, vol. 60, 1959–1960, p. 274.

71   *"Trapped in steel"*: Chaucer, "The Knight's Tale," part I: 2157, as quoted by Albert S. Cook, "The Historical Background of Chaucer's Knight," *Transactions Connecticut Academy of Arts and Sciences*, vol. 20, May 1915, p. 167.

71   *"He goes into the wilderness . . ."*: Christiansen, op. cit., p. 167.

72   *"Pestilential enemies of Christ"*: ibid., p. 150.

72   *"Huge route of knights"*: Chaucer, *Troilus and Criseyde*, part V: 65, as quoted by Cook, op. cit., p. 172.

73   *Lawrence "of the kitchen and scullery"*: Smith, op. cit., p. xxiv.

75   *"Common souldiers" and "annoyed"*: Thomas Walsingham, *Historia Anglicana*, as quoted by Cook, op. cit., pp. 198–199.

75   *"Sigh my English breath in foreign clouds"*: Shakespeare, op. cit., 3.1.19.

75   *"Manhunts of the peasantry for sport"*: Barbara Tuchman, *A Distant Mirror: The Calamitous 14th Century* (New York: Knopf, 1978), p. 69.

75   *"Safaris"*: Christiansen, op. cit., p. 151.

77   *"Assassins"*: Joinville and Villehardouin, op. cit., p. 277.

77   *"His nose was heigh"*: "The Knight's Tale," part I: 2167, as quoted by Cook, op. cit., p. 170.

77   *"Elevated"*: ibid.

77fn   *Kant's skull*: Ronny Kabus, *Ruinen von Königsberg: Bilder eines Kaliningrader Architekten* (Husum: Husum Druck- und Verlagsgesellschaft, 1992), pp. 120–121.

77fn   *Einstein's brain*: Scott McCartney, "The Hidden Secrets of Einstein's Brain Are Still a Mystery," *Wall Street Journal*, May 5, 1994, p. 1.

78   *Provocations between the two world wars*: Tighe, op. cit., pp. 111–128.

p. 78fn    *"A farce"*: Nikita Khrushchev, *Khrushchev Remembers: The Glasnost Tapes*, trans. J. L. Schecter and V. V. Luchkov (Boston: Little, Brown, 1990), p. 49.

79      *Polish cavalry attack German tanks*: Richard M. Watt, *Bitter Glory: Poland and Its Fate, 1918 to 1939* (New York: Simon & Schuster, 1982), p. 422.

80      *The Germans were "embarrassed"*: See Nicholas Bethell, *The War Hitler Won: The Fall of Poland, September, 1939* (New York: Holt, Rinehart & Winston, 1972), p. 134.

## Chapter 4–Grünwald

81      *"Our order will never lack wealth . . ."*: Schreiber, op. cit., p. 92.

84      *"They conquered the town and burnt it . . ."*: Michael Burleigh, *Prussian Society and the German Order: An Aristocratic Corporation in Crisis 1410–1466* (Cambridge: Cambridge University Press, 1984), p. 73.

84      *Townsmen and gentry complained "of a multitude of oppressions"*: ibid., p. 140.

84      *Burghers and landowners "hoping to enjoy the practical liberty . . ."*: Ernest Barker, "The Teutonic Order," *Encyclopaedia Britannica*, 13th ed., 1926, vol. 25, p. 678.

85      *"Commanders shall only admit . . ."*: Burleigh, op. cit., p. 41.

85      *"Undress . . ."*: Treitschke, op. cit., p. 63.

85      *Teutonic Order overly "corporate"*: Burleigh, op. cit., p. 2.

87      *The order "will have us as serfs"*: ibid., p. 168.

87      *"My lord should visit the unbelievers . . ."*: ibid., p. 163.

89      *"For each forty hides of land . . ."*: *Before the Storm: Memories of My Youth in Old Prussia*, trans. J. Steinberg (New York: Knopf, 1990), p. 110.

## Chapter 5–Frauenburg

93      *"And new philosophy calls all in doubt . . ."*: "The Anatomy of the World," *The Complete Poems of John Donne*, ed. R. E. Bennett (Chicago: Packard, 1942), l. 205, p. 206.

95      *George Kennan*: Marion, Countess Dönhoff, *Before the Storm: Memories of My Youth in Old Prussia*, trans. J. Steinberg (New York: Knopf, 1990), p. viii.

96      *Copernicus "was a German canon"*: Treitschke, op. cit., p. 151. See also Hermann Kesten, *Copernicus and His World* (New York: Roy Publishers, 1945), p. 11: "Many Germans also claim him for their fatherland. It is not the most inglorious imperialism to want to worship great men of other counties as your own. How many nations

have made a Jew their savior?" See also Andreas Dorpalen, *Heinrich von Treitschke* (New Haven, Conn.: Yale University Press, 1957).

p. 96   *Painting of Copernicus by Matejko*: Juliusz Starzyński, *Jan Matejko* (Warsaw: Wydawnictwo Arkady, 1962), plate 43.

97   *"Mathematics are written for mathematicians"*: On the Revolutions of the Heavenly Spheres, trans. A. M. Duncan (New York: Barnes & Noble, 1976), p. 27.

100   *"Hypothetical" and "factual"*: On the Revolutions of the Heavenly Spheres, trans. R. M. Hutchins, *Great Books of the Western World*, ed. Robert Maynard Hutchins (London: Encyclopaedia Britannica, 1955), vol. 16, p. 505. On the controversy of Osiander and his introductory remarks to *De revolutionibus*, see Bruce Wrightsman, "Andreas Osiander's Contribution to the Copernican Achievement," *The Copernican Achievement*, ed. R. S. Westman (Berkeley: University of California Press, 1975), pp. 213–243.

100fn   *"I, for my part, believe the sacred scripture . . ."*: B. A. Gerrish, "The Reformation and the Rise of Modern Science: Luther, Calvin and Copernicus," *Calvin and Science*, ed. R. C. Gamble (New York: Garland Publishing, 1992), vol. 12, p. 6.

100fn   *Copernicus "a fool"*: Gerrish, op. cit., p. 168; Bertrand Russell, *A History of Western Philosophy* (New York: Simon & Schuster, 1945), p. 528.

100   *Albrecht and Martin Luther*: See Heinrich Bornkamm, *Luther in Mid-Career, 1521–1530*, trans. E. T. Bachmann (Philadelphia: Fortress Press, 1983), pp. 317–336.

## Chapter 6–Grosse Werder

107   *An aristocratic "ant heap"*: C. V. Wedgwood, *The Thirty Years War* (New York: Random House, 1995), p. 40.

111   *"I hear nothing but lamentations . . ."*: Letters Relating to the Mission of Sir Thomas Roe to Gustavus Adolphus, 1629–1630, ed. S. R. Gardiner (London: Camden Society, 1856), p. 38.

112   *Frederick William watched with "gloomy bewilderment"*: Wedgwood, op. cit., p. 281.

113   *"Politics and villainy . . ."*: The Confessions of Frederick the Great, trans. S. Sladen (New York: G. P. Putnam's Sons, 1915), p. 70.

## Chapter 7–Neudeck

115   *"In general my subjects are hardy and brave . . ."*: ibid., p. 38.

116fn   *Neudeck estate*: Andreas Dorpalen, *Hindenburg and the Weimar Republic* (Princeton, N.J.: Princeton University Press, 1964), pp. 135–137; John W. Wheeler-Bennett, *The Nemesis of Power: The German Army in Politics, 1918–1945* (New York: St. Martin's Press,

1954), p. 27; Harry Kessler, *In the Twenties: The Diaries of Harry Kessler*, trans. C. Kessler (New York: Holt, Rinehart & Winston, 1971), p. 469; William Shirer, *The Rise and Fall of the Third Reich* (Simon & Schuster, 1960), pp. 179–181.

p. 118fn    *Frederick learned no history prior to that of the sixteenth century*: Nancy Mitford, *Frederick the Great* (London: Hamish Hamilton, 1970), p. 23; Heinrich von Treitschke, *The Life of Frederick the Great*, trans. S. Sladen (New York: G. P. Putnam's Sons, 1915), p. 165.

119    *"My All-Highest War Lord"*: Hindenburg, op. cit., p. 67.

119    *The Great Elector seeking to build an army "to make me considérable"*: Hajo Holborn, *A History of Modern Germany* (New York: Knopf, 1964), vol. 2, p. 65.

120    *The Junker class Frederick's "machines"*: James W. Whitthall, *Frederick the Great on Kingcraft* (London: Longmans, Green, 1901), p. 46.

120    *"War, it is a trade" and following*: *Confessions of Frederick the Great*, pp. 41, 40.

120    *Frederick I's coronation characterized by its "inflated grandeur"*: Arthur W. Holland, "Prussia," *Encyclopaedia Britannica*, 13th ed., 1926, vol. 27, p. 523; Mitford, op. cit., pp. 83–84.

122    *Frederick the Great's goal of "making noise in the world"*: Whitthall, op. cit., p. 58.

123    *Frederick William's treasury of seven million thalers "a colossal achievement"*: Holborn, op. cit., p. 192.

123    *"I am the King of Prussia's Field Marshal"*: ibid., p. 191; Goerlitz, op. cit., p. 4.

124fn    *Voltaire: Selections from the Writings of Lord Macaulay*, ed. G. O. Trevelyan (New York: Harper & Brothers, 1877), p. 233.

124fn    *"I have sucked the fruit . . ."*: Francis Kugler, *Life of Frederick the Great: Comprehending a Complete History of the Silesian Campaigns and the Seven Years' War* (London: George Routledge and Sons, 1877), p. 275.

124    *"The King" and following from von Clausewitz*: Karl von Clausewitz, *On War*, trans. J. J. Graham (New York: Dorset Press, 1991), pp. 245, 259, 261, 402, 246.

124    *"In the face of storm . . ."*: Mitford, op. cit., p. 211; Shirer, op. cit., pp. 1108–1109.

126    *"Bonapart at Arcole," 1796*: "The Napoleonic School," *The Great Masters in the Louvre Gallery* (New York: D. Appleton, 1907), p. 32. According to Napoleonic biographers, however, Napoleon never rushed across the bridge in question, as depicted by Gros. French troops were inspired that day by General André Masséna, Napoleon having fallen off the road into a swamp during the charge. See Alan Schom, *Napoleon Bonapart* (New York: HarperCollins, 1997), p. 55.

126    *"Dogs . . ."*: See Thomas Carlyle, *History of Friedrich II, of Prussia, called Frederick the Great* (London: Chapman and Hall, 1871), vol. 1, p. 72; Mitford, op. cit., p. 221. Zorndorf, October 2, 1758, was one of Frederick's bloodiest victories, as he wrote to Voltaire: "I am much

obliged to the solitary of *Les Délices* for the interest he takes in the adventures of Don Quixote of the North; the said Don Quixote leads the life of strolling players, playing sometimes at one theatre and sometimes at another, sometimes hissed, sometimes applauded. The last play he was the Thebaide; at the end there scarcely remained a candle-snuffer." *Letters of Voltaire and Frederick the Great*, trans. R. Aldington (New York: Brentano's, 1927), p. 244.

p. 126fn  *Frederick's casualty figures*: Paul Kennedy, *The Rise and Fall of the Great Powers: Economic Change and Military Conflict from 1500 to 2000* (New York: Atheneum, 1987), p. 272.

127fn  *"Kant is a scarecrow"*: Friedrich Nietzsche, *The Will to Power*, trans. W. Kaufmann and R. J. Hollingdale (New York: Random House, 1967), p. 78.

127  *At public functions "it is my German cook . . ."*: *The Confessions of Frederick the Great*, p. 64.

127  *Frederick's eastern province "a desert"*: Mitford, op. cit., p. 71.

127  *Shakespeare, "that vast manure heap"*: ibid., p. 287.

128  *"Make boldly . . ."*: Whitthall, op. cit., p. 45.

128  "It would seem that in Poland . . .": Kugler, op. cit., p. 543; Chester V. Easum, *Prince Henry of Prussia: Brother of Frederick the Great* (Madison: University of Wisconsin Press, 1942), p. 269; S. Fischer-Fabian, *Prussia's Glory: The Rise of a Military State*, trans. L. Stern and P. Stern (New York: Macmillan, 1981), p. 276.

128fn  *"She weeps . . ."*: Mitford, op. cit., p. 277.

129  *"These provinces . . ."*: ibid., p. 273.

## Chapter 8–Eylau

133  *"A day of bloody memory"*: A Lieutenant Krettly, in Jean Savant, *Napoleon in His Time*, trans. K. John (London: Putnam, 1958), p. 189.

136  *Kant's epitaph*: *Critique of Practical Reason*, trans. L. W. Beck (New York: Macmillan, 1993), p. 169. This paragraph, which "the starry heavens" begins, is perhaps the best known of all Kant's formulations. See also Ernst Cassirer, *Kant's Life and Thought* (New Haven, Conn.: Yale University Press, 1981); Frederick C. Beiser, "Kant's Intellectual Development: 1746–1781," *The Cambridge Companion to Kant*, ed. Paul Guyer (Cambridge: Cambridge University Press, 1992), pp. 26–57. Isaiah Berlin wrote that Kant "laid bare categories of a very pervasive, very basic kind—space, time, number, thinghood, freedom, moral personality—and therefore, for all that he was a systematic and often pedantic philosopher, a difficult writer, an obscure logician, a routine professorial metaphysician and moralist, he was in his lifetime recognized to be what he was, not merely a man of genius in many fields but one of the few authentically profound and therefore revolutionary thinkers in human history." *The Sense of Reality: Studies in Ideas and Their History* (New York: Farrar, Straus and Giroux, 1996), p. 17.

p. 136    *Königsberg University "barely more than a glorified high school"*:
          Guyer, op. cit., p. 3.
137       *Mendelssohn's phrase "the all-shattering Kant" was contemporane-*
          *ously well known*: see N. M. Karamzin, *Letters of a Russian Traveler,*
          *1789–1790,* trans. F. Jonas (New York: Columbia University Press,
          1957), p. 39.
141       *"Who remembers Eylau?"*: Hilaire Belloc, *Napoleon* (Philadelphia:
          Lippincott, 1932), p. 260. Victor Hugo did, however. See his 1874
          poem "Le Cimetière d'Eylau," in *La Légende des Siècles* (Paris: Edi-
          tions Garnier Frères, 1962), pp. 654–661.
142       *"We fell asleep . . ."*: Holborn, op. cit., p. 372.
143       *"The French require a prince . . ."*: Savant, op. cit., p. 171.
143fn     *30,000 Napoleonic titles in print*: M. Lincoln Schuster, ed., *The*
          *World's Great Letters* (New York: Simon & Schuster, 1940), p. 191.
143       *"Boney is not a gentleman"*: David G. Chandler, "How Wars Are De-
          cided: Napoleon—The Fall of a Giant?" in David G. Chandler, *On the*
          *Napoleonic Wars* (London: Greenhill Books, 1994), p. 238.
144       *Europe was a harlot*: L. A. Pichon, *De l'état de la France sous la dom-*
          *ination de Napoléon Bonapart* (Paris: 1814), in Savant, op. cit., p. 105.
144       *"Penal institution"*: See Fischer-Fabian, op. cit., pp. 82–86.
145       *"You engage . . ."*: Chandler, "Napoleon: Classical Military Theory
          and the Jominian Legacy," in Chandler, *Napoleonic Wars*, p. 245.
146       *"If the King and Queen want to see a battle . . ."*: General Staff
          School, *The Jena Campaign: Source Book* (Fort Leavenworth, Kans.:
          General Service School Press, 1922), p. 321.
146       *"I feel splendid . . ."*: Emil Ludwig, *Napoleon*, trans. E. Paul and C.
          Paul (New York: Boni and Liveright, 1928), p. 255.
146       *Battles of Jena and Auerstädt*: William O. Shanahan, *Prussian Mili-*
          *tary Reforms: 1786–1813* (New York: AMS Press, 1966), pp. 86–126;
          Francis Petre, *Napoleon's Conquest of Prussia—1906* (New York:
          John Lane, The Bodley Head, 1907), pp. 121–164; Colmar von der
          Goltz, *Jena to Eylau: The Disgrace and the Redemption of the Old-*
          *Prussian Army, a Study in Military History*, trans. C. F. Atkinson
          (New York: E. P. Dutton, 1913).
146fn     *"Glory was what he chiefly lived on . . ."*: Savant, op. cit., p. 183.
147       *Scharnhorst "filled with disgust . . ."*: von der Goltz, op. cit., p. 14.
147       *Blücher a man "of ardent and vivid temperament"*: "Gebhard
          Leberecht von Blücher," *Encyclopaedia Britannica*, 13th ed., 1926,
          vol. 3, p. 90.
148fn     *"General Staff officers have no names"*: Reinhard Gehlen, *The Ser-*
          *vice: Memoirs*, trans. D. Irving (New York: E. P. Dutton, 1952), p. 26.
          Goerlitz attributes this remark to General Hans von Seeckt; Goerlitz,
          op. cit., p. 14. See also Hindenburg, op. cit., p. 55.
148fn     *Officer corps "the work of art . . ."*: Nietzsche, op. cit., p. 419.
149fn     *Polish losses in invasion of Russia*: Tighe, op. cit., p. 43.
149       *Foraging in Poland and East Prussia*: See Otto Springer, ed. and
          trans., *A German Conscript with Napoleon: Jakob Walter's Recollec-*

*tions of the Campaigns of 1806 and 1807* (Lawrence: Bulletin of University of Kansas, 1938), pp. 137–165.

p. 149    *"Any bread? . . ."*: Constant, First Valet de Chambre of the Emperor, *Memoirs: The Private Life of Napoleon, His Family and His Court*, trans. E. G. Martin (New York: Scribner's, 1895), vol. 2, p. 189.

150    *"If I were the Russian commander for but two hours!"*: Henry La Chouque, *The Anatomy of Glory, Napoleon and His Guard: A Study in Leadership*, trans. A. Brown (Providence, R.I.: Brown University Press, 1961), p. 95.

150    *Comparison of battle with wedding night*: Von Clausewitz, op. cit., p. 416.

150    *"Point d'appui"*: Count Maximilian Yorck von Wartenburg, *Napoleon as a General* (London: Kegan Paul, Trench, Trübner & Co., 1902), vol. 1, p. 304.

151    *Murat "that spoilt child of glory"*: J. de Norvins, *Souvenirs d'un historian de Napoléon. Mémorial de J. de Norvins* (Paris: L. de Lanzac de Laborie, 1897), p. 397.

151    *"What news? . . ."*: General Saint-Chamans, *Mémoires du général comte de Saint-Chamans, ancien aide de camp du maréchal Soult* (Paris: 1896), in Savant, op. cit., p. 191.

152    *"The Russians have done us great harm"*: David G. Chandler, *The Campaigns of Napoleon* (New York: Macmillan, 1966), p. 549.

152    *Whoever stands on the field "armored in constancy"*: General Baron Paulin, *Les Souvenirs du général Paulin 1782–1876* (Paris: 1895), in Savant, op. cit., p. 193.

152    *"I have never seen so many dead . . ."*: Saint-Chamans, op. cit., p. 192.

152    *"What a shambles . . ."*: Belloc, op. cit., p. 259.

152    *"What will Paris say?"*: Alfred Vagts, *A History of Militarism: Romance and Reality of a Profession* (New York: Norton, 1937), p. 25; Ludwig, op. cit., p. 267.

152    *Soldiers cry for bread*: La Chouque, op. cit., p. 89; Constant, op. cit., p. 189; Saint-Chamans, op. cit., p. 192.

152    *"Enfin un chateau!"*: Carl von Lorck, *Ostpreussische Gutshäuser: Bauform und Kulturgehalt* (Kitzingen/Main, Germany: Holzner-Verlag, 1953), p. 65, plates 43–47. See also Hans Graf Lehndorff, *Token of a Covenant: Diary of an East Prussian Surgeon: 1945–47*, trans. E. Mayer (Chicago: Henry Regnery, 1964), p. 319.

153    *"That is awful . . ."*: Constant, op. cit., vol. 2, p. 165. For secret liaisons of the emperor in general, see vol. 2, pp. 149–161.

153    For portraits of Walewska and contemporary accounts, see Proctor Patterson Jones, *Napoleon: An Intimate Account of the Years of Supremacy, 1800–1814* (New York: Random House, 1992), pp. 213–224, 429–431; Constant, op. cit., vol. 2, pp. 177–184.

153    *"Kings do not sigh long in vain . . ."*: Constant, op. cit., vol. 2, p. 192.

153fn    *"She is rich . . ."*: Ludwig, op. cit., p. 633.

338 Notes from pages 154–172

154fn On the film Conquest: Barry Paris, Garbo: A Biography (New York: Knopf, 1995), pp. 337–341.

154 *Horses's four legs bathed in blood*: Norvins, op. cit., p. 409.

155 *Prussian king "a blockhead"*: Nigel Nicolson, *Napoleon 1812* (New York: Harper & Row, 1985), p. 22.

155 *"Napoleon knew men well . . ."*: Johann Peter Eckermann, *Conversations of Goethe*, trans. J. Oxenford (New York: E. P. Dutton, 1930), p. 311.

155 *The Frauenkirche*: David Irving, *The Destruction of Dresden* (New York: Holt, Rinehart & Winston, 1963).

155 *The revival of orthodoxy*: See Nathaniel Davis, *A Long Walk to Church: A Contemporary History of Russian Orthodoxy* (Boulder, Colo.: Westview Press, 1995).

# Chapter 9–Cadinen

163 *"You have a little cold . . ."*: Alan Palmer, *The Kaiser: Warlord of the Second Reich* (New York: Scribner's, 1978), p. 121.

163 *Frauenburg "the remotest place on earth"*: Owen Gingerich, "Copernicus: A Modern Reappraisal," *Man's Place in the Universe: Changing Concepts*, ed. D. W. Corson (Tucson: University of Arizona Press, 1977), p. 34.

164 *The kaiser "an extraordinary man"*: Winston Churchill, *Thoughts and Adventures* (London: Thorton Butterworth, 1932), p. 152.

164 *Wilhelm took command of "the Grand Finale"*: ibid., p. 79. For a photograph of Churchill at German military maneuvers, see Röhl and Sombart, op. cit., p. 128.

164 *"Well has it been said . . ."*: ibid., p. 152.

167 *Memoirs of Field Marshal Colmar von der Goltz*: Goerlitz, op. cit., p. 56.

168 *Bismarck considered by many as a traitor to his class*: E. J. Feuchtwanger, *Prussia: Myth and Reality. The Role of Prussia in German History* (London: Oswald Wolff, 1970), p. 204.

168 *January 18, 1871*: The "heroic" 1885 painting of this event by Anton von Werner—*The Proclamation of German Unification*—hangs in the Bismarck museum at his former estate of Friedrichsruh, near Hamburg. See Von Ingeborg Köpke, *Bismarck-Museum Friedrichsruh* (Neumünster, Germany: Karl Wachholtz Verlag, 1992), p. 13.

170 *This resulted in a certain "morbidity" of view*: Goerlitz, op. cit., p. 72.

170 *Von Roon the "King's Sergeant"*: ibid., p. 79.

172 *"Here's a fine recruit . . ."*: Roger Parkinson, *Tormented Warrior: Ludendorff and the Supreme Command* (New York: Stein and Day, 1979), p. 13.

172 *Nature "did not fit Wilhelm for the soldier's life "*: Palmer, op. cit., p. 14.

p. 172   *Wilhelm's wife "the Holstein cow"*: ibid.; Daphne Bennett, *Vicky: Princess Royal of England and German Empress* (New York: St. Martin's Press, 1971), p. 230.

172   *Wilhelm "selfish and domineering" and following*: Palmer, op. cit., pp. 14, 56, 39.

173   *Hitler's contempt for Wilhelm*: *Hitler's Secret Conversations*, p. 526.

173   *"Bismarck was aspiring . . ."*: G. L. Sulzberger, *The Fall of Eagles* (New York: Crown, 1977), p. 391.

173   *Prelude and outbreak of the Great War*: Sidney B. Fay, *The Origins of the World War*, 2 vols. (New York: Free Press, 1966).

174   *Russia, "that mighty steamroller"*: Churchill, op. cit., p. 149.

175   *"Fatty"*: Barbara Tuchman, *The Guns of August* (New York: Macmillan, 1962), p. 270; Winston Churchill, *The Unknown War: The Eastern Front* (New York: Charles Scribner's Sons, 1932), p. 175.

## Chapter 10–Tannenberg

177   *"World history knows three battles . . ."*: *Hitler's Secret Conversations*, p. 21.

181   *"Enough of war on two fronts . . ."*: Gerard E. Ritter, *The Schlieffen Plan, Critique of a Myth* (London: Oswald Wolff, 1958), p. 33.

181   *Hindenburg a man no one "had ever seen before"*: Max Hoffmann, *The War of Lost Opportunities* (New York: International Publishers, 1925), p. 26.

182   *Ludendorff ordered to "prevent the worst from happening"*: Ludendorff, op. cit., p. 49.

182   *Ludendorff's remark that "all I stand for is authority . . ."*: ibid., p. 10.

182   *Ludendorff's "ruthless energy"*: Hindenburg, op. cit., p. 147.

182   *Hindenburg's decorations "the minimum . . ."*: John W. Wheeler-Bennett, "Hindenburg," in *Great Contemporaries* (London: Cassell, 1935), p. 164.

182–183 *Hindenburg drinking beer "with the gravity of a hippopotamus"*: A. G. Gardiner, *Portraits and Portents* (New York: Harper & Brothers, 1926), p. 165.

183   *"I am ready"*: Hindenburg, op. cit., p. 81.

183   *Ludendorff a "robot Napoleon"*: B. H. Liddell Hart, *Reputations Ten Years After* (Boston: Little, Brown, 1928), p. 181.

183   *Hindenburg "calm and almost cheerful" and following*: Margarethe Ludendorff, *My Married Life with Ludendorff*, trans. R. Somerset (London: Hutchinson, 1930), pp. 84, 19.

184   *Diary of British attaché*: Alfred Knox, *With the Russian Army 1914–1917, Being Chiefly Extracts from the Diary of a Military Attaché* (London: Hutchinson, 1921), vol. 1, pp. 59, 39, 45, 50, 60, 70, 71, 73, 78, 79, 86, 90.

p. 185   *Solzhenitsyn remarked "the task of convincing history . . ."and following*: Aleksandr Solzhenitsyn, *August 1914*, trans. M. Glenny (New York: Farrar, Straus and Giroux, 1971), pp. 218, 212.

186   *Wireless messages sent in the clear a "quite incomprehensible thoughtlessness"*: Hoffmann, op. cit., p. 28.

186   *XX Corps was to be "the anvil"*: D. J. Goodspeed, *Ludendorff, Genius of World War I* (Boston: Houghton Mifflin, 1966), p. 80. See also Hindenburg, op. cit., p. 80.

187   *Samsanov's behavior deemed "cowardly"*: Tuchman, *Guns of August*, p. 295; S. L. A. Marshall, *World War I* (New York: American Heritage, 1964), p. 61.

188   *Final operation "the harvest"*: Hindenburg, op. cit., p. 98.

190   *A French officer called this error "our salvation"*: B. H. Liddell Hart, *The Real War* (London: Faber & Faber, 1930), pp. 74–78; Tuchman, *Guns of August*, p. 436.

190   *"Will any German . . ."*: Erich von Ludendorff, *My War Memories: 1914–1918* (London: Hutchinson, 1920), vol. 1, p. 57.

191   *Austria, Germany's ally, "a corpse"*: ibid., p. 117.

191   *The western front "ironmongery"*: Erich von Manstein, *Lost Victories*, trans. A. G. Powell (Chicago: Henry Regency, 1958), p. 63.

191   *An affront to the "art" of war*: Ludendorff, op. cit., p. 47.

192   *Ludendorff became "unapproachable . . ."*: Arnold Zweig, *The Crowning of a King*, trans. E. Sutton (New York: Viking, 1938), p. 137.

192fn   *"The reader will observe . . ."*: Churchill, *Thoughts and Adventures*, p. 155.

192   *"Here is where Hindenburg slept . . ."*: Zweig, op. cit., p. 140. On the same page Zweig recounts Hoffmann's other sarcastic remark: "Since I heard that Hindenburg won the Battle of Tannenberg, I have ceased to believe in Hannibal or Caesar."

192fn   *Hoffmann portrayed as a man possessed of "an inner poise . . ."*: ibid., pp. 126, 133. The Hoffmann figure, Wilhelm Clauss, reflects the tensions and animosities that eastern front commanders felt for their opposite numbers in the west, particularly Erich von Falk and later Ludendorff (portrayed as Schieffenzahn, an "evil genius"). The best summary is book 4, chapter 1, "General Clauss Offers His Condolences," pp. 131–138.

193fn   *Hoffmann died "of overwork and old brandy"*: B. H. Liddell Hart, *Through the Fog of War* (New York: Random House, 1938), p. 226.

192   *"When I won the battle . . ."*: Goerlitz, op. cit., p. 181. See also Admiral Georg von Müller's remark that since Tannenberg Ludendorff "suffered from megalomania." *The Kaiser and His Court: The Diaries, Note Books and Letters of Admiral Georg Alexander von Müller, Chief of the Naval Cabinet, 1914–1918*, ed. Walter Goerlitz, trans. M. Savill (New York: Harcourt, Brace & World, 1959), p. 413.

193   *Kaiser a "crowned observer"*: ibid., p. 167.

193   *"Sergeant major"*: Goodspeed, op. cit., p. 188.

p. 193   "Siamese twin": John Toland, *No Man's Land: 1918, The Last Year of the Great War* (New York: Doubleday, 1980), p. 482.

193      *"Politics demanded a victim . . .":* Hindenburg, op. cit., p. 433.

194      *The kaiser a "byzantine figure":* Feuchtwanger, op. cit., p. 215.

194      *"Military oaths! . . .":* General Wilhelm Groener. See Toland, op. cit., p. 531; Kuno Graf von Westarp, "Das Ende der Monarchie am 9. November 1918," in *From Bismarck to Hitler: The Problem of Continuity in German History,* ed. J. C. G. Röhl (New York: Barnes & Noble, 1970), pp. 84–87.

## Chapter 11–Gross Pötzdorf

195      *"Hitler came from no man's land . . .":* Golo Mann, *Reminiscences and Reflections: A Youth in Germany,* trans. K. Winston (New York: Norton, 1990), p. 287.

201      Junkers *"callous, narrow-minded, conceited": The Peasant War in Germany,* ed. Leonard Krieger (Chicago: University of Chicago Press, 1967), pp. 3–18; see also Tighe, op. cit., p. 67.

201      *Death of Weimar "part murder, part wasting sickness . . .":* Peter Gay, *Weimar Culture: The Outsider as Insider* (New York: Harper & Row, 1968), p. xiii.

201      *The Rise and Fall of the Third Reich simplistic "journalism":* Klaus Epstein, "Shirer's History of Nazi Germany," *Review of Politics,* vol. 23, no. 2, April 1961, pp. 230–245.

202      *"I'll make him a postmaster . . .":* Bert Edward Park, *The Impact of Illness on World Leaders* (Philadelphia: University of Pennsylvania Press, 1986), p. 85.

202      *Oskar von Hindenburg:* Kessler, op. cit., p. 469.

202      *"They say the old man signs anything now . . .":* Park, op. cit., p. 88.

202      *Ludendorff's sanity weighed in the balance, "the solitude in a strange land particularly hard to bear":* M. Ludendorff, op. cit., p. 198.

202      *"I'm at war with myself . . .":* ibid., p. 180.

202      *Count Harry Kessler on "the Kapp farce" and following:* Kessler, op. cit., pp. 121–122.

203      *"Tonight we shall have champagne . . .":* Sigurd von Ilsemann, "Der Kaiser in Holland," in Röhl, op. cit., p. 123.

203fn    *"Though the bluest of East Elbian blood flowed in their veins . . .":* John Wheeler-Bennett, *Knaves, Fools and Heroes in Europe Between the Wars* (London: Macmillan, 1974), p. 181.

203fn    *The Third Reich "a mustard republic, brown and sharp":* Christian Zentner and Friedemann Bedürftig, eds., *Encyclopedia of the Third Reich* (New York: Macmillan, 1991), vol. 2, p. 1048.

206fn    *Hitler "certainly had an extraordinary power . . .":* Ron Rosenbaum, "Explaining Hitler," *New Yorker,* May 7, 1995, p. 60.

## Chapter 12–Suwalki

p. 212   *"Southern fields" and following*: Shmuel Abramsky, "Study of Suwalk Jewry," in S. Abramsky, Ariel, Y. Berelson, B. Kahan, S. Savitt-Zavozhnitzky, and L. Sherer, *Jewish Community Book: Suwalk and Vicinity* (N.p.: Yair-Abraham Stern-Publishing House, n.d.), p. 9.

213      *Suwalki population statistics*: ibid., pp. 12–13.

214fn    *"There is no sense in being offended . . ."*: Józef Grzegorczyk, as interviewed by Miasto Otwarte, "Open City," *Kaleidoscope*, vol. 4, no. 77 (1994), p. 10.

217fn    *Hans Küng*: James Carroll, "The Silence," *New Yorker*, April 7, 1997, p. 60.

219fn    *Sempo Sugihara*: Hillel Levine, *In Search of Sugihara* (New York: Free Press, 1996); Zorach Warhaftig, *Refugee and Survivor: Rescue Efforts During the Holocaust* (Jerusalem: Yad Vashem, 1988), pp. 102–117; Israel Gutman, *Encyclopedia of the Holocaust* (New York: Macmillan, 1990), pp. 1423–1424.

221fn    *Lithuanian statistics*: Gutman, ibid., pp. 895–899.

229      *Avraham Stern*: Kati Marton, *A Death in Jerusalem* (New York: Pantheon, 1994), particularly pp. 16, 45–59; Joseph Heller, *The Stern Gang: Ideology, Politics and Terror, 1940–1949* (London: Frank Cass, 1995); Gutman, op. cit., pp. 910–911.

## Chapter 13–The River Memel

231      *"Hitler wanted to be another Napoleon . . ."*: Von Manstein, op. cit., p. 283.

233      *Guderian gulped*: Guderian, op. cit., p. 142.

237fn    *Russian POW statistics*: John Garrard and Carol Garrard, "Bitter Victory," in *World War II and the Soviet People: Selected Papers from the Fourth World Congress for Soviet and East European Studies, Harrogate, 1990*, eds. John Garrard and Carol Garrard (New York: St. Martin's Press, 1993), pp. 24, 6.

## Chapter 14–Stutthof

242      *Himmler ordered beach facilities constructed "for recreational purposes"*: Konnilyn G. Feig, *Hitler's Death Camps: The Sanity of Madness* (New York: Holmes & Meier, 1979), p. 192.

242      *Jan Bronski shot for "irregular military activity"*: Günter Grass, *The Tin Drum*, trans. R. Manheim (New York: Crest, 1964), p. 237. See also Grass, *On Writing and Politics, 1967–1983* (New York: Harcourt Brace Jovanovich, 1985), pp. 28–29.

p. 243   *Stutthof no longer a detention center just for "antisocial persons"*: Feig, op. cit., p. 197.

243   *Stutthof statistics*: Gutman, op. cit., vol. 2, p. 1421.

243   *No one in the countryside could claim not to have known . . .*: See Daniel Jonah Goldhagen, *Hitler's Willing Executioners* (New York: Knopf, 1996), pp. 313–316, 364–366, 575.

244   *"I don't know whether in this atmosphere . . ."*: Andrzej Zakrzewski, aide to President Lech Walesa, as quoted in Reuter's "John Paul Warns of Hatred That Led to Death Camps," *Boston Globe*, January 30, 1995, p. 7.

245   *"What is truth?"*: John 18:38.

245   *Wreaths, plaques, and flags "sweeten the horror"*: Lawrence L. Langer, *Admitting the Holocaust: Collected Essays* (New York: Oxford University Press, 1995), p. 182. Along similar lines see Ralph Melnick, *The Stolen Legacy of Anne Frank: Meyer Levin, Lillian Hellman, and the Staging of the Diary* (New Haven, Conn.: Yale University Press, 1997); Lawrence Graver, *An Obsession with Anne Frank: Meyer Levin and the Diary* (Berkeley: University of California Press, 1995); and Cynthia Ozick, "Who Owns Anne Frank?" *New Yorker*, October 6, 1997, pp. 76–87.

245   *"Afterwards, Jews were ordered to jump . . ."*: Martin Gilbert, *The Holocaust: A History of the Jews of Europe During the Second World War* (New York: Holt, Rinehart & Winston, 1985), p. 115.

245   *"The process of melting down . . ."*: Feig, op. cit., pp. 200–202.

245   *"Committed or consistent deniers of the Holocaust make up only a small segment of the [American] population, about 2 percent or less"*: Michael R. Kagay, "Poll on Doubt of Holocaust Is Corrected: Roper Says 91% Are Sure It Occurred," *New York Times*, July 8, 1994, p. A10. See also Pierre Vidal-Naquet, *Assassins of Memory: Essays on the Denial of the Holocaust*, trans. J. Mehlan (New York: Columbia University Press, 1992); Deborah E. Lipstadt, *Denying the Holocaust: The Growing Assault on Truth and Memory* (New York: Free Press, 1993).

246   *The Holocaust "being something fundamentally different . . ." and following*: Lucy S. Dawidowicz, *The Holocaust and the Historians* (Cambridge: Harvard University Press, 1981), p. 14.

247fn   *The Eichmann trial*: Hannah Arendt, *Eichmann in Jerusalem: A Report on the Banality of Evil* (New York: Viking, 1993). On controversy within Jewish circles, Irving Howe, *A Margin of Hope: An Intellectual Autobiography* (New York: Harcourt Brace Jovanovich, 1982), pp. 247–282; Amos Elon, "The Case of Hannah Arendt," *New York Review of Books*, November 7, 1997, pp. 25–29.

249   *Musel-men, or Muselmänner*: Primo Levi, *Survival in Auschwitz* (New York: Simon & Schuster, 1993), p. 90.

## Chapter 15–Rastenburg

p. 253   *"Today I became a general"*: Pierre Galante, *Operation Valkyrie: The German Generals' Plot Against Hitler*, trans. M. Howson and C. Ryan (New York: Harper & Row, 1981), p. 13.

253   *Alfred Jodl's remark on Rastenburg*: James P. O'Donnell, *The Bunker: The History of the Reich Chancellery Group* (Boston: Houghton Mifflin, 1978), p. 52; Robert Payne, *The Life and Death of Adolf Hitler* (New York: Praeger, 1973), p. 433. See also Joseph Goebbels, *The Goebbels Diaries, 1942–1943*, ed. and trans. Louis P. Lochner (New York: Doubleday, 1948), p. 130.

254   *Hitler's affection for* Tristan und Isolde: *Hitler's Secret Conversations*, p. 271. See also William A. Jenks, *Vienna and the Young Hitler* (New York: Columbia University Press, 1960).

254   *Hofbräuhaus*: Not to be confused with the Bürgerbraukeller, site of the 1923 putsch, since destroyed.

254   *Berchtesgaden*: Philip Hamburger, "Letter from Berchtesgaden," *New Yorker*, May 1, 1995, pp. 70–73.

254   *"The great wilderness on the lake"*: Dönhoff, op. cit., p. 79.

254   *Wolf's Lair*: Galante, op. cit., p. 145.

254   *"Mein Wölfchen"*: Otto Strasser and Michael Stern, *Flight from Terror* (New York: R. M. McBride, 1943), p. 111; Walter C. Langer, *The Mind of Adolf Hitler: The Secret Wartime Report* (New York: Basic Books, 1972), p. 94; Charles Bracelen Flood, *Hitler: The Path to Power* (Boston: Houghton Mifflin, 1989), p. 192; Park, op. cit., p. 175.

254fn   *Assessment of Hitler's personality*: Robert G. L. Waite, *The Psychopathic God: Adolf Hitler* (New York: Basic Books, 1977), pp. 54, 148–149, 175, 237–243; Langer, op. cit.

256   *East Prussia "the lovely province"*: Von Manstein, op. cit., p. 24.

256   *Hitler hated snow*: Goebbels, op. cit., p. 131.

256   *Hitler "barking"*: Galante, op. cit., p. 92; Mann, op. cit., p. 286.

256   *Hitler's "troglodyte existence"*: H. R. Trevor-Roper, "The Mind of Adolf Hitler," *Hitler's Secret Conversations*, p. xi.

256   *Hitler's drug addiction*: Park, op. cit., pp. 177–189; Guderian, op. cit., p. 341; Galante, op. cit., p. 133.

257   *"I never read Mein Kampf . . ."* : Count Schwerin von Krosigk, in Bailey, op. cit., p. 64. See also B. H. Liddell Hart, *Strategy* (New York: Praeger, 1960), pp. 223–224.

257   *Mein Kampf*, trans. R. Manheim (Boston: Houghton Mifflin, 1943), representative views on the following: pp. 300–308 (Jews); p. 632 (Treaty of Versailles); pp. 618–621 (relations with France and Britain); pp. 659–664 (Russia). See also Andreas Hillgruber, "Hitler's Program," *Germany and the Two World Wars*, trans. W. C. Kirby (Cambridge: Harvard University Press, 1981), pp. 49–55: "If only *Mein Kampf* had been taken seriously."

257   *Hitler was a man of continents . . . and following*: Trevor-Roper, op. cit., p. xvi.

p. 257    *"What India is for England ..."*: Hitler's Secret Conversations, pp. 20, 276.

258    *Göring's anti-Semitism*: Shirer, op. cit., pp. 430–437.

258    *Instances where Hitler lost his nerve*: Guderian, op. cit., pp. 109, 439; Von Manstein, op. cit., p. 78. Hitler felt differently: "I've noticed on the occasion of such events that, when everybody loses their nerves, I'm the only one who keeps calm." *Hitler's Secret Conversations*, op. cit., p. 276. See also *The Goebbels*, op. cit., p. 130.

259    *Animosity toward "our upper ten thousand" and following*: Hitler's Secret Conversations, pp. 494, 312, 480, 100, 480, 311, 38; Paul West, *The Very Rich Hours of Count von Stauffenberg* (New York: Harper & Row, 1980), p. 287.

259    *Reverence for "epaulets"*: Galante, op. cit., p. 133.

259    *Hitler and the equestrian "art"*: John Keegan, *The Second World War* (New York: Viking, 1990), p. 395.

259    *"The Army belong to the people ..."*: West, op. cit., p. 262.

259fn    *Ratio of aristocratic officers*: Omer Bartov, *The Eastern Front, 1941, German Troops and the Barbarization of Warfare* (New York: St. Martin's Press, 1985), p. 43.

259fn    *"You have to admit the party has not won over this good blood ..."*: Jeremy Noakes, "Nazism and High Society," in *Confronting the Nazi Past: New Debates on Modern German History*, ed. M. Burleigh (New York: St. Martin's Press, 1996), p. 58.

260    *German officers were "fossils and idiots"*: Galante, op. cit., p. 97.

260    *Von Blomberg and von Fritsch affairs*: Telford Taylor, *Sword and Swastika: Generals and Nazis in the Third Reich* (Chicago: Quadrangle Books, 1969), pp. 122–174; Robert J. O'Neill, *The German Army and the Nazi Party, 1933–1939* (New York: J. H. Heinemann, 1966), pp. 139–150; Wheeler-Bennett, *Nemesis of Power*, pp. 363–374; Nicholas Reynolds, *Treason Was No Crime: Ludwig Beck, Chief of the German General Staff* (London: William Kimber, 1976), pp. 121–147.

260    *Von Fritsch had publicly ridiculed Hitler*: William L. Shirer, *Berlin Diary: The Journal of a Foreign Correspondent, 1934–1941* (New York: Knopf, 1941), p. 27.

261fn    *Hitler's "pathological sexual impulses"*: Galante, op. cit., p. 69.

261fn    *Brauchitsch "tapped his temple ..."*: ibid., p. 55.

261    *The intractable oath, "a consideration [that] must in no wise be left out of account"*: Goerlitz, op. cit., p. 355; Guderian, op. cit., p. 34; Wheeler-Bennett, *Nemesis of Power*, pp. 363–364.

262fn    *"The good conscience in evil deeds" and following*: Karl Jaspers, *The Question of German Guilt*, trans. E. B. Ashton (New York: Capricorn Books, 1961), pp. 65–66.

262    *"What can we do? ..."*: Goerlitz, op. cit., p. 338.

262    *"He's playing warlord again"*: Keegan, op. cit., p. 193.

p. 262    *The "ice age" of Prussian values*: General Hermann Reinecke, as quoted in Telford Taylor, *The Anatomy of the Nuremberg Trials* (Boston: Little, Brown, 1992), p. 189.

262    *The "holy grail" of tradition*: Franz Halder, *The War Diary, 1939–1942*, eds. Charles Burdick and Hans-Adolf Jacobsen (Novato, Calif.: Presidio Press, 1988), p. 306.

262    *Hitler "an inspired tinkerer"*: Galante, op. cit., p. 219.

262    *"War is a mere continuation of policy by other means "*: Von Clausewitz, op. cit., p. 119.

263    *"Stalin owes nothing to rhetoric"*: *Hitler's Secret Conversations*, op. cit., p. 7.

263    *"I don't believe in idealism"*: ibid., p. 244.

263    *"Excitement terrible" and following*: Goerlitz, op. cit., p. 373.

263    *Russian campaign "his" war*: Keegan, op. cit., p. 193.

263    *Hitler possessed of "a fertile imagination"*: Guderian, op. cit., p. 303.

263    *Von Manstein's assessments of Hitler*: Von Manstein, op. cit., pp. 274–288.

264    *"Your operations always hang by a thread"*: Guderian, op. cit., p. 161.

264    *"I am the only one who knows what has to be done" and following*: Galante, op. cit., pp. 168, 136.

264    *"There's no need for you to try to teach me ..." and following*: Guderian, op. cit., pp. 378, 142.

265    *"When [my staff] spread out a map of Russia before me ..."*: ibid., p. 14.

265    *Russian statistics*: Paul Carell, *Hitler Moves East: 1941–1943* (Boston: Little, Brown, 1963), pp. 30, 74; Garrard and Garrard, "Bitter Victory," pp. 1–2.

266    *Germanic warriors fatigued from killing*: Edward Gibbon, *The History of the Decline and Fall of the Roman Empire*, ed. J. B. Bury (New York: AMS Press, 1974), vol. 3, p. 129.

265    *Hitler's "sullen satellites"*: John Erickson, *The Road to Berlin* (Boulder, Colo.: Westview Press, 1983), p. ix, as quoted in Garrard and Garrard, "Bitter Victory," p. 2.

266fn   *Allied casualties in Normandy and German executions on eastern front*: Stephen D. Ambrose, *D-Day, June 6, 1944: The Climactic Battle of World War II* (New York: Simon & Schuster, 1994); Garrard and Garrard, "Bitter Victory," p. 5.

265    *Stalin sneered*: Erickson, op. cit., p. 481.

266    *Russian front "tearing out the life of the German military monster"*: Martin Gilbert, "Winston Churchill and the Soviet Union, 1939–45," Garrard and Garrard, "Bitter Victory," p. 250.

266    *Hitler "lived in a world of fantasy"*: Guderian, op. cit., p. 244.

266    *Soviet war losses*: Garrard and Garrard, "Bitter Victory," p. 7.

266    *"Wiser men than I ..."*: Taylor, *Nuremberg Trials*, p. 437.

266    *"If Germany did not exist ..."*: Guderian, op. cit., p. 286. See also Clive Ponting, *Armageddon: The Reality Behind the Distortions,*

*Myths, Lies, and Illusions of World War II* (New York: Random House, 1995), pp. 325–343.

p. 267   *Denazification proceedings*: ibid.

267   *"Europe is now one family . . ."*: ibid., p. 461.

267   *"They provoke [us] with their mistrust . . ."*: Carl J. Burckhardt as quoted in Gehlen, op. cit., p. xxii.

267   *"Le tout pour le tout"*: Ernest F. Henderson, *Germany's Fighting Machine* (Indianapolis: Bobbs-Merrill, 1914), p. 16.

267   *The "all or nothing principle"*: Kennedy, op. cit., p. 272; Churchill, *Thoughts and Adventures*, p. 149.

268   *"Unpopular though this view may now be . . ."*: Gehlen, op. cit., p. 26; Ponting, op. cit., pp. 138–147.

268   *"Genius is diligence"*: Von Manstein, op. cit., p. 79.

268   *"He presented the arrangement as a game . . ." and following*: Khrushchev, op. cit., pp. 48, 54, 50, 67.

268   *"Anyone who had occasion to make Adolf Hitler's acquaintance . . . "*: Taylor, *Nuremberg Trials*, p. 378.

269   *Hitler's "table talk"*: *Hitler's Secret Conversations*, op. cit., pp. 3, 32, 34, 53, 72, 73, 167, 214, 222, 236, 264, 292, 476, 494, 498.

270   *"Blood doesn't matter . . ."*: Galante, op. cit., p. 120.

270fn   *"A reign of terror without parallel"*: Merle Fainsod, *A History of Russia* (Oxford: Oxford University Press, 1993), p. 504. See also F. Beck and W. Godin, *Russian Purge and the Extraction of Confession*, trans. E. Mosbacher and D. Porter (New York: Viking, 1951); Leonard Schapiro, "The Great Purge," in *The Red Army*, ed. B. H. Liddell Hart (New York: Harcourt, Brace, and Co., 1956), pp. 65–78.

270fn   *Purge statistics*: Garrard and Garrard, "Bitter Victory," p. 34.

270fn   *The purge "a meat grinder"*: Khrushchev, op. cit., p. 26.

271fn   *"Why haven't I seen you for so long? . . ."*: Genrikh Borovik, *The Philby Files: The Secret Life of Master Spy Kim Philby* (Boston: Little, Brown, 1994), p. 123.

271fn   *Bulganin assembles paperwork "to purge the heroes" again*: Erickson, op. cit., p. 404.

271   *"This war is now 'total' enough for everyone"*: Guderian, op. cit., p. 260.

271   *Himmler's "open road to the east"*: Taylor, *Nuremberg Trials*, p. 203.

271   *Men's rectums froze*: Galante, op. cit., p. 123.

271   *Guderian's phrase*: Guderian, op. cit., p. 415.

272   *Hitler curses "this damnable winter"*: *Hitler's Secret Conversations*, p. 259; Goebbels, op. cit., pp. 130–131.

272   *"I will smash the General Staff . . ."*: Guderian, op. cit., p. 397.

273   *Von Paulus*: Walter Goerlitz, *Paulus and Stalingrad: A Life of Field-Marshal Friedrich Paulus with Notes, Correspondence and Documents from His Papers*, trans. R. H. Stevens (New York: Citadel Press, 1963).

273   *Stalingrad was suicide*: Von Manstein, op. cit., pp. 289–366.

p. 274   *Von Manstein's contention that "rumors of the kind that circulated at home hardly penetrated to the front"*: ibid., p. 104. On the field marshal's trial, see R. T. Paget, *Manstein: His Campaigns and His Trial* (London: Collins, 1951); and John Wheeler-Bennett, *Friends, Enemies and Sovereigns* (New York: St. Martin's Press, 1976), pp. 114–118. Von Manstein, according to Wheeler-Bennett, was "cold and aloof and contemptuous" in the dock.

274      *Christabel Bielenberg's remark*: Bielenberg, op. cit., p. 96.

274      *Waffen-SS*: Distinctions that Germans chose to make on the organizational makeup of the Waffen-SS are not universally understood outside their country and have caused difficulties on many occasions, U.S. president Ronald Reagan's proposed wreath-laying presentation at Bitburg (where six members of the Waffen-SS are buried) being one. In May 1997, controversy concerning governmental pensions to SS veterans, a practice excoriated by Holocaust victims, again caused considerable embarrassment.

The Waffen-(meaning "armed") SS underwent incredible growth with the commencement of war in 1939, from 22,000 more or less elite members to 600,000 by 1945. Although ostensibly a "praetorian" guard devoted in its loyalty exclusively to the person of Adolf Hitler, the majority of its members by war's end were essentially ordinary servicemen barely distinguishable in zeal or proficiency from the Wehrmacht. It is, however, also accurate to say that certain cadres of the SS remained fanatic and true to the organization's original zealotry, which resulted in some of the more bestial crimes of the entire war. So, as in everything else in life, the veteran's comments here reflect a mixture of threads and beliefs. See Zentner and Bedürftig, op. cit., vol. 2, pp. 1011–1012; Von Manstein, op. cit., p. 188; Bernd Wegner, *The Waffen-SS: Organization, Ideology and Function* (London: Basil Blackwell, 1990).

275      *SS "in general paid a toll in blood . . ."*: Von Manstein, op. cit., p. 188.

275      *"Reichsspritzenmeister"*: Zentner and Bedürftig, op. cit., vol. 2, p. 601.

275      *"Truly he came from a different world"*: Park, op. cit., p. 167.

276      *"Soon I shall be dead . . ."*: Heinrich Böll, *The Train Was on Time*, trans. L. Vennewitz (New York: McGraw-Hill, 1970), p. 162.

276      *Reminiscences of Jodl and Keitel*: See Wilhelm Keitel, *The Memoirs of Field-Marshal Keitel*, trans. David Irving (London: William Kimber, 1965). Jodl's diary has not been published, although excerpts have appeared now and then.

276      *Hitler capable of "being a man of reason" and following*: Von Manstein, op. cit., pp. 24, 284.

276      *"He who defends everything . . ."*: Keegan, op. cit., p. 155; Von Manstein, op. cit., p. 410.

276      *Parade of lackeys "in credulous adulation" and following*: Von Manstein, op. cit., pp. 154, 28.

p. 276   *Hitler wanted to know everything except the truth*: Ian Buruma, "Chinese Whispers," *New Yorker*, February 13, 1995, p. 84.

276   *"Gentlemen, behave yourselves"*: Jean Lacouture, *De Gaulle: The Rebel, 1890–1944*, trans. P. O'Brian (New York: Norton, 1990), p. 185. Contrast to Guderian, op. cit., p. 156; Galante, op. cit., p. 240.

276   *Guderian "an adventurer"*: Erickson, op. cit., p. 478.

276–277   *Goebbels, Himmler, Bormann, and following*: Guderian, op. cit., pp. 302, 325, 387, 444, 447, 448, 449.

277   *Hitler commonly referred to as "the pig"*: Galante, op. cit., p. 31.

277   *"If generals won't do it . . ."*: ibid., p. 187.

280   *Hitler's trousers*: There is some debate among historians whether these tattered remains held up for view were indeed Hitler's. Most think they were, and Galante repeats the story that Hitler sent these remnants along to Eva Braun as a memento of his fortuitous escape. A minority view assigns ownership of these shreds to Captain Hermann Fegelein, an SS liaison officer who also survived the blast. Fegelein married Eva Braun's sister in 1944, which did not ultimately save his life one year later, when Hitler ordered him shot on April 28 for deserting the famous bunker as Russian forces closed in. Eva made no attempt to intercede. Hitler married his mistress the next day and took his own life on the thirtieth.

280   *"You are still alive!"*: Albert Speer, *Memoirs: Inside the Third Reich*, trans. R. Winston and C. Winston (New York: Macmillan, 1970), p. 389.

280   *Stauffenberg a coward?*: Michael von Richthofen Jeffrey, personal communication with the author. Wheeler-Bennett, *Friends, Enemies and Sovereigns*, pp. 103–104, makes this argument: "The failure of the conspiracy . . . was simple in the extreme. The conspirators lacked among them a dedicated assassin. This was in no case prompted by cowardice but by the genuine desire of many in the conspiracy to play some part in the rebuilding of the structure of a New Germany. . . . Though a courageous man, [von Stauffenberg] was not the stuff of which dedicated assassins are made."

281   *Number of assassination attempts*: John Weitz, *Hitler's Diplomat: The Life and Times of Joachim von Ribbentrop* (New York: Ticknor & Fields, 1992), p. 278.

281   *"If Germans want to start a revolution . . ."*: Gehlen, op. cit., p. 98.

282   *"You lousy little champagne dealer . . ."*: Weitz, op. cit., p. 312.

283   *Deer trip land mines*: Galante, op. cit., p. 15.

283   *"The aim must still be to win territory in the east . . ."*: Shirer, *Rise and Fall of the Third Reich*, p. 1131.

284   *"Nostalgia" for the old days*: Spurgeon Thompson, "The Romance of Simulation: W. B. Yeats and the Theme-Parking of Ireland," *Éire-Ireland*, vol. 30, no. 1 (spring 1995), p. 18.

284   *The reconstruction of Berlin*: Paul Goldberger, "Reimagining Berlin," *New York Times Magazine*, February 5, 1995, pp. 45–53; Raymond Sokolov, "After the Fall of the Wall, Berlin Puts Itself Together," *Wall*

*Street Journal*, February 1, 1996, p. A16; Peter Conrad, "Rebuilding Berlin," *New Yorker*, April 28–May 5, 1997, pp. 221–226.

p. 284    *"I'm excited about it . . .":* Harry C. Butcher, My Three Years with Eisenhower (New York: Simon & Schuster, 1946), p. 620.

## Chapter 16–Ostpreussen

285    *"Kill! Kill! . . .":* Tighe, op. cit., p. 200. See also Theodore Schieder, ed., *The Expulsion of the German Population from the Territories East of the Oder-Neisse-Line,* trans. V. Stranders (Bonn: Federal Ministry for Expellees, Refugees and War Victims, 1958), p. 49; Carell, op. cit., p. 963–967; Albert Seaton, *Russo-German War* (New York: Praeger, 1971), p. 544; Erickson, op. cit., pp. 508, 746; Gehlen, op. cit., p. 106; Garrard and Garrard, "Bitter Victory," pp. xvi, plate 33; Ilya Ehrenburg and Konstantin Simonov, *In One Newspaper: A Chronicle of Unforgettable Years,* trans. A. Kagan (New York: Sphinx Press, 1985).

287    *"Yes, all of us knew . . .":* Aleksandr Solzhenitsyn, *The Gulag Archipelago,* trans. T. P. Whitney (New York: Harper & Row, 1973), p. 21.

287    *Trek statistics:* George Kennan, foreword to Dönhoff, op. cit., p. viii; see also Tighe, op. cit., p. 216.

287    *These months "the time of the women":* See Lehndorff, op. cit., p. 130.

288    *"Herr Sentry . . .":* Gilbert, op. cit., p. 780.

292    *"On January 19 we decided to leave . . .":* Dorothee von Klitzing, "The Last Days in Grünfelde and What Followed," trans. V. D. Nygren, typescript.

292fn    *Behavior of Koch:* Speer, op. cit., p. 496; Zentner and Bedürftig, op. cit., vol. 1, pp. 506–507.

299fn    *Relocation statistics:* Tighe, op. cit., pp. xx, 205, 216.

299    *Death marches:* Goldhagen, op. cit., pp. 327–371.

304fn    *Stalin's order number 270:* Actually two orders, numbers 270 and 227. Garrard and Garrard, "Bitter Victory," p. 10; Solzhenitsyn, *Gulag,* p. 81.

305    *"When they heard we were from the old German territories . . .":* Tighe, op. cit., pp. 187–188.

## Chapter 17–In the West

313    *"I find it very hard . . .":* Charles L. Mee, *Meeting at Potsdam* (New York: M. Evans and Co., 1975), p. 111.

318    *"The State decided to act like a criminal . . .":* An unlikely ally (though for different reasons) in condemning Bonn for its fire sale of "the peoples' property" in the east was Günter Grass, an impassioned

opponent of reunification. Grass's novel *Ein weites Feld* (*A Broad Field*) provoked enormous controversy.

p. 318  *The Mendelssohns*: Peter Gumbel, "Famed German Family Faces Battle to Regain Historic Estate," *Wall Street Journal*, December 5, 1995, p. 1.

319  *"Germans have not changed ..."*: See also Barbara Marshall, "German Reactions to Military Defeat, 1945–1947: The British View," *Germany in the Age of Total War*, eds. V. Berghahn and M. Kitchen (London: Croom Helm, 1981), pp. 218–239.

319fn  *"The four quarters of the riven German soul"*: Michael Hofmann, in Wolfgang Koeppen, *Death in Rome*, trans. Michael Hofmann (Harmondsworth, UK: Penguin, 1994), p. ix.

320  *"Those six million who were in the Hitler Youth ..."*: See Alfons Heck, *The Burden of Hitler's Legacy* (Frederick, Colo.: Renaissance House, 1988); Gerhard Rempel, *Hitler's Children: The Hitler Youth and the SS* (Chapel Hill: University of North Carolina Press, 1989); H. W. Koch, *The Hitler Youth: Origins and Development, 1922–45* (London: Macdonald and Jane's, 1975).

320  *People commonly behave irrationally*: Edmund Wilson, *Patriotic Gore* (New York: Oxford University Press, 1962), pp. ix-xxxii.

320  *1994 election analysis*: Ash, op. cit., p. 21.

322  *There are writers who think ...* : Friedbert Pflueger, *Deutschland driftet* (Düsseldorf: Econ Verlag, 1994).

324  *Geist*: See Friedrich Meinecke, "The Year 1848 in German History: Reflections on a Centenary," *1848: A Turning Point*, ed. M. Kranzberg (Boston: D. C. Heath, 1959), p. 54.

325  *Varchentin*: Terence Roth, "Costly Quest: Attempts to Reclaim an East German Estate," *Wall Street Journal*, October 8, 1991, p. 1.

# Select Bibliography

Books, articles, and monographs on the long history of Germany, particularly those dealing with the twentieth century, are voluminous beyond comprehension. As the writer Martin Gilbert noted in his history of World War I, for example, the literature he would have been expected to master "defies the reading ability of any one individual." The works listed below are therefore by definition idiosyncratic to some extent. They cannot be expected to present a complete overview or a balanced portrait of what is a very complicated subject. Nevertheless, these are the authorities on whom I relied while researching and writing this book (those I used most extensively are marked with asterisks). Experts will certainly notice omissions.

## General Surveys

Bailey, George. *Germans: The Biography of an Obsession* (New York: World Publishing, 1972).

Barraclough, Geoffrey. *The Origins of Modern Germany* (New York: Capricorn Books, 1963).

*Carsten, F. L. *A History of the Prussian Junkers* (Brookfield, Vt.: Scolar Press, 1989).

Davies, Norman. *God's Playground: A History of Poland*. 2 vols. (New York: Columbia University Press, 1982).

_____. *Europe: A History* (New York: Oxford University Press, 1996).

Dvornik, Francis. *The Slavs in European History and Civilization* (New Brunswick, N.J.: Rutgers University Press, 1962). Useful through the eighteenth century.

Halecki, Oscar. *Borderlands of Western Civilization: A History of East Central Europe* (New York: Ronald Press, 1952).

_____. *A History of Poland* (London: Routledge & Kegan Paul, 1983).

Holborn, Hajo. *A History of Modern Germany*. 3 vols. (New York: Knopf, 1967).

Kennedy, Paul. *The Rise and Fall of the Great Powers: Economic Change and Military Conflict from 1500 to 2000* (New York: Random House, 1987).

Koch, H. W. *A History of Prussia* (London: Longman, 1978).

Pinson, Koppel S. *Modern Germany: Its History and Civilization* (New York: Macmillan, 1966).

Reddaway, W. F., J. H. Person, O. Halecki, and R. Dyboski. *The Cambridge History of Poland.* 2 vols. (Cambridge: Cambridge University Press, 1941, 1950).

Tuttle, Herbert. *History of Prussia* (Boston: Houghton Mifflin, 1884–1896).

Vagts, Alfred. *A History of Militarism: Civilian and Military* (New York: Free Press, 1959).

## Part One: Beginnings

### On the Crusades, Prussia, and the Teutonic Order

Barnes, A. S. "The Teutonic Knights and the Kingdom of Prussia." *Dublin Review,* vol. 157, no. 314 (July 1915), pp. 272–283.

Bartlett, Robert. *The Making of Europe: Conquest, Colonization and Cultural Change, 950–1350* (Princeton, N.J.: Princeton University Press, 1993).

*Benninghoven, Friedrick. *Unter Kreuz und Adler: Der deutsche Orden im Mittelalter* (Berlin: Geheimes Staatsarchiv Preussischer Kulturbesitz, 1990). Interesting bibliography.

Benvenisti, Meron. *The Crusaders in the Holy Land* (New York: Macmillan, 1970).

Browne, Charles. "The Knights of the Teutonic Order." *Transactions of the St. Paul's Ecclesiological Society,* vol. 3, 1895, pp. 1–15.

Brundage, James A. *The Crusades, Holy War, and Canon Law* (Brookfield, Vt.: Variorum, 1991).

*_____, trans. *The Chronicle of Henry of Livonia* (Madison: University of Wisconsin Press, 1961).

*Burleigh, Michael. *Prussian Society and the German Order: An Aristocratic Corporation in Crisis @1410–1466* (Cambridge: Cambridge University Press, 1984).

*Carsten, F. L. *The Origins of Prussia* (Oxford: Clarendon Press, 1954).

*Christiansen, Eric. *The Northern Crusades, the Baltic and the Catholic Frontier, 1100–1525* (London: Macmillan, 1980).

*Cook, Albert S. "The Historical Background of Chaucer's Knight." *Transactions, Connecticut Academy of Arts and Sciences,* vol. 20, February 1916, pp. 161–240.

Dichter, Bernard. *The Order and Churches of Crusader Acre* (Acre, Israel: Municipality of Acre, 1979).

Dollinger, Philippe. *The German Hansa.* Trans. D. S. Ault and S. H. Steinberg (Stanford, Calif.: Stanford University Press, 1970).

Erdmann, Carl. *The Origin of the Idea of Crusade.* Trans. M. Baldwin and W. Goffart (Princeton, N.J.: Princeton University Press, 1977).

*Evans, Geoffrey. *Tannenberg, 1410–1914* (Harrisburg, Penn.: Stackpole, 1971), pp. 3–52.

Giles, Frances. *The Knight in History* (New York: Harper & Row, 1984).

Groenner, Mary Ellen. *Mary-Verse of the Teutonic Knights* (New York: AMS Press, 1970).

Jurgela, Constantine. *Tannenberg (Eglija-Grunwald) 15 July 1410* (New York: Lithuanian Veterans Association "Ramovē," 1961).

Kirby, John L. *Henry IV of England* (London: Constable, 1970).

Krollmann, Christian. *The Teutonic Order in Prussia*. Trans. E. Horstmann (Elbing, Germany: Preussenverlag, 1938).

Lotter, Freidrich. "The Crusading Idea and the Conquest of the Region East of the Elbe: The Tenth- and Eleventh-Century Background." In *Medieval Frontier Societies*, eds. R. Bartlett and A. MacKay (Oxford: Clarendon Press, 1989), pp. 267–306.

Malowist, Marian. "The Trade of Eastern Europe in the Later Middle Ages." In *Trade and Industry in the Middle Ages*, vol. 2 of *The Cambridge Economic History of Europe*, eds. M. M. Postan and E. Miller (Cambridge: Cambridge University Press, 1987).

Nash, E. Gee. *The Hansa: Its History and Romance* (London: John Lane, The Bodley Head, 1929).

Olins, Peter Z. *The Teutonic Knights in Latvia* (Riga: B. Lamey Edition, 1928).

Postan, Michael. "The Trade of Medieval Europe: The North." In *Trade and Industry in the Middle Ages*, vol. 2 of *The Cambridge Economic History of Europe*, eds. M. M. Postan and E. Miller (Cambridge: Cambridge University Press, 1987).

Schildhauer, Johannes. *The Hansa: History and Culture*. Trans. K. Vanovitch (Leipzig: Edition Leipzig, 1985).

Schreiber, Hermann. *Teuton and Slav: The Struggle for Central Europe*. Trans. J. Cleugh (New York: Knopf, 1965).

Setton, Kenneth M., ed. *A History of the Crusades* (Madison: University of Wisconsin Press, 1969), vol. 2, pp. 429–462; vol. 3, pp. 545–585.

*Smith, Lucy Toulmin, ed. *Expeditions to Prussia and the Holy Land Made by Henry Earl of Derby (Afterwards Henry IV), in the Years 1390–1 and 1392–3. Being the Accounts Kept by His Treasurer During Two Years* (London: Camden Society, 1894).

*Stretton, Grace. "Some Aspects of Medieval Thought: Notably Transport and Accommodation, with Special Reference to the Wardrobe Accounts of Henry, Earl of Derby, 1390–1393." *Transactions of the Royal Historical Society*, vol. 7, fourth series 1924, pp. 77–97.

Thompson, James Westfall. *Feudal Germany* (Chicago: University of Chicago Press, 1966).

Treitschke, Heinrich G. *Origins of Prussianism: The Teutonic Knights*. Trans. E. Paul and C. Paul (London: G. Allen and Unwin, 1942).

*Urban, William. *The Baltic Crusade* (De Kalb: Northern Illinois Press, 1975).

———. "The Organization of Defense of the Livonian Frontier in the Thirteenth Century." *Speculum*, vol. 48, no. 1, July 1973, pp. 525–532.

Vlasto, A. P. *The Entry of the Slavs into Christendom* (Cambridge: Cambridge University Press, 1970).

Wojciechowski, Zygmunt. *The Territorial Development of Prussia in Relation to the Polish Homelands* (Toruń, Poland: Baltic Institute, 1936).

Zajaczkowski, Stanislaw. *Rise and Fall of the Teutonic Order in Prussia* (London: J. S. Bergson, 1935).

Zimmern, Helen. *The Hansa Towns* (New York: G. P. Putnam's Sons, 1900).

## On Copernicus

Armitage, Angus. *Copernicus: The Founder of Modern Astronomy* (New York: A. S. Barnes, 1962).

_____. *Sun, Stand Thou Still* (New York: Henry Schuman, 1947).

*Bieńkowska, Barbara, ed. *The Scientific World of Copernicus on the Occasion of the 500th Anniversary of His Birth, 1473–1973* (Dordrecht, Netherlands: D. Reidel, 1973). Excellent summary of local and political issues.

*Bogucka, Maria. *Nicholas Copernicus: The Country and Times.* Trans. L. Szwajcer (Warsaw: Ossolinski Publishing House, 1973).

Corson, D. W., ed. *Man's Place in the Universe: Changing Concepts* (Tucson: University of Arizona Press, 1977), pp. 3–75.

Gingerich, Owen, ed. *The Nature of Scientific Discovery: A Symposium Commemorating the 500th Anniversary of the Birth of Nicholas Copernicus* (Washington, D.C.: Smithsonian Institution Press, 1975).

Gerrish, B. A. "The Reformation and the Rise of Modern Science: Luther, Calvin and Science." In *Calvin and Science,* ed. Richard C. Gamble (New York: Garland Publishing, 1992), vol. 12, pp. 1–16.

Hoyle, Frederick. *Astronomy* (London: Rathbone, 1962), pp. 1–105. A primer.

_____. *Nicholas Copernicus: An Essay on His Life and Work* (New York: Harper's, 1973). Specialist interpretation, but penetrating and worth the effort.

Knoll, Paul W. "The Arts Faculty at the University of Cracow at the End of the Fifteenth Century." In *The Copernican Achievement,* ed. R. S. Westman (Berkeley: University of California Press, 1975), pp. 137–156.

*Kuhn, Thomas S. *The Copernican Revolution: Planetary Astronomy in the Development of Western Thought* (New York: Vintage, 1959). Excellent introduction for the layperson.

Neyman, Jerzy. "Nicholas Copernicus (Mikolaj Kopernik): An Intellectual Revolutionary." In Jerzy Neyman, ed., *The Heritage of Copernicus: Theories "More Pleasing to the Mind"* (Cambridge: MIT Press, 1974), pp. 1–22.

Stimson, Dorothy. *The Gradual Acceptance of the Copernican Theory of the Universe* (Gloucester, Mass.: Peter Smith, 1972).

# Part Two: Consolidation

## General

Beiser, Frederick C. *Enlightenment, Revolution, and Romanticism: The Genesis of Modern Germanic Political Thought 1790–1800* (Cambridge: Harvard University Press, 1992).

Berdahl, Robert M. *The Politics of the Prussian Nobility: The Development of a Conservative Ideology, 1770–1848* (Princeton, N.J.: Princeton University Press, 1988).

Brose, Eric Dorn. *The Politics of Technological Change in Prussia: Out of the Shadow of Antiquity, 1809–1848* (Princeton, N.J.: Princeton University Press, 1993).

*Carsten, F. L. *The Origins of Prussia* (Oxford: Clarendon Press, 1954).

*Craig, Gordon A. *The Politics of the Prussian Army: 1640–1945* (Oxford: Oxford University Press, 1978).

Demeter, Karl. *The German Officer-Corps in Society and State: 1650–1945*. Trans. A. Malcolm (New York: Praeger, 1965).

Dupuy, Trevor M. *A Genius for War: The German Army and General Staff, 1807–1945* (Englewood Cliffs, N.J.: Prentice-Hall, 1977).

Fay, Sidney B. *The Rise of Brandenburg-Prussia to 1786* (New York: Holt, 1937).

Feuchtwanger, E. J. *Prussia: Myth and Reality—The Role of Prussian German History* (London: Oswald Wolff, 1970).

Kehr, Eckart. *Economic Interest, Militarism, and Foreign Policy: Essays on German History* (Berkeley: University of California Press, 1977).

Kitchen, Martin. *A Military History of Germany from the Eighteenth Century to the Present Day* (Bloomington: Indiana University Press, 1975). Useful through World War II.

Krieger, Leonard. *The German Idea of Freedom: History of a Political Tradition* (Chicago: University of Chicago Press, 1972). Good through 1871.

Langer, Herbert. *The Thirty Years' War*. Trans. C. S. V. Salt (New York: Dorset Press, 1980).

Moltke, Helmuth Karl Bernhard von. *Poland: An Historical Sketch*. Trans. E. Buckheim (London: Chapman and Hall, 1885).

*Ogg, David. *Europe in the Seventeenth Century* (New York: Collier Books, 1965).

Ramm, Agatha. *Germany, 1789–1919: A Political History* (London: Methuen., 1967).

Ritter, Gerhard. *The Sword and Scepter: The Prussian Tradition, 1740–1890*. Trans. H. Norden (Coral Gables, Fla.: University of Miami Press, 1969).

Rosenberg, Hans. *Bureaucracy, Aristocracy and Autocracy: The Prussian Experience, 1660–1815* (Boston: Beacon Press, 1966).

Sheehan, James J. *German History, 1770–1866* (Oxford: Clarendon Press, 1989). Good through the ascension of Bismarck.

*Wedgwood, C. V. *The Thirty Years War* (New York: Random House, 1995).

## On the Great Elector and Frederick the Great

Abbot, John. *History of Frederick the Second, Called Frederick the Great* (New York: Harper & Brothers, 1871). Anecdotal.

*Asprey, Robert B. *Frederick the Great: The Magnificent Enigma* (New York: Ticknor & Fields, 1986).

Duffy, Christopher. *The Military Life of Frederick the Great* (New York: Atheneum, 1986).

Dupuy, Trevor. *The Military Life of Frederick the Great of Prussia* (New York: Franklin Watts, 1969).

Ergang, Robert. *The Potsdam Führer: Frederick William I, Father of Prussian Militarism* (New York: Octagon, 1972).

Frey, Linda, and Masha Frey. *Frederick I: The Man and His Times* (Boulder, Colo.: East European Monographs, 1984).

Gawthrop, Richard L. *Pietism and the Making of Eighteenth-Century Prussia* (Cambridge: Cambridge University Press, 1993).

Gaxotte, Pierre. *Frederick the Great*. Trans. R. Bell (New Haven, Conn.: Yale University Press, 1942).

Gooch, G. P. *Frederick the Great: The Ruler, the Writer, the Man* (New York: Knopf, 1947).

Hubatsch, Walther. *Frederick the Great of Prussia: Absolutism and Administration*. Trans. P. Doran (London: Thames and Hudson, 1975).

Johnson, Hubert C. *Frederick the Great and His Officials* (New Haven, Conn.: Yale University Press, 1975).

Jomini, Baron. *Treatise on Grand Military Operations: Or a Critical and Military History of the Wars of Frederick the Great*. 2 vols. Trans. S. B. Holabird (New York: D. Van Nostrand, 1965).

Kugler, Francis. *Life of Frederick the Great: Comprehending a Complete History of the Silesian Campaigns and the Seven Years' War* (London: George Routledge and Sons, 1877).

Macaulay, Lord. *Selections from the Writings of Lord Macaulay*. Ed. G. O. Trevelyan (New York: Harper & Brothers, 1877).

Mitford, Nancy. *Frederick the Great* (London: Hamish Hamilton, 1970).

Palmer, Alan. *Frederick the Great* (London: Weidenfeld and Nicolson, 1974).

Palmer, R. R. "Frederick the Great, Guilbert, Bülow: From Dynastic to National War." In *Makers of Modern Strategy from Machiavelli to the Nuclear Age*, ed. P. Paret (Princeton, N.J.: Princeton University Press, 1986), pp. 91–119.

Reddaway, W. F. *Frederick the Great and the Rise of Prussia* (New York: Greenwood Press, 1969).

Reiners, Ludwig. *Frederick the Great: A Biography*. Trans. L. Wilson (New York: G. P. Putnam's Sons, 1960).

Ritter, Gerhard. *Frederick the Great: A Historical Profile*. Trans. P. Paret (Berkeley: University of California Press, 1968).

Schevill, Ferdinand. *The Great Elector* (Chicago: University of Chicago Press, 1947).

Simon, Edith. *The Making of Frederick the Great* (Boston: Little, Brown, 1963).

Snyder, Louis L., ed. *Frederick the Great* (Englewood Cliffs, N.J.: Prentice-Hall, 1971).

Treitschke, Heinrich von. *The Confessions of Frederick the Great and the Life of Frederick the Great*. Trans. C. Sladen (New York: G. P. Putnam's Sons, 1915).

Whitthall, James William. *Frederick the Great on Kingcraft* (London: Longmans, Green, 1901).

Young, Norwood. *The Life of Frederick the Great* (New York: Holt, 1919).

## On Napoleonic Campaigns and the Finckenstein Interlude

Aubrey, Octave. *The Empress Might-Have-Been: The Love Story of Marie Valevska and Napoleon.* Trans. H. G. Wright (New York: Harper's, 1927).

Barnett, Correlli. *Bonaparte* (New York: Hill & Wang, 1978), pp. 119–135.

Belloc, Hilaire. *Napoleon* (Philadelphia: Lippincott, 1932).

*Chandler, David G. *The Campaigns of Napoleon* (New York: Macmillan, 1966), pp. 441–555.

Constant, First Valet de Chambre of the Emperor. *Memoirs: The Private Life of Napoleon, His Family and His Court.* Trans. E. G. Martin (New York: Scribner's, 1894), vol. 2, pp. 176–198.

Cronin, Vincent. *Napoleon* (London: HarperCollins, 1994).

Delderfield, R. F. *Napoleon in Love* (New York: Simon & Schuster, 1959), pp. 175–191.

Goltz, Colmar von der. *Jena to Eylau: The Disgrace and the Redemption of the Old-Prussian Army, a Study in Military History.* Trans. C. F. Atkinson (New York: E. P. Dutton, 1913).

*Goerlitz, Walter. *The German General Staff, 1657–1945.* Trans. B. Battershaw (New York: Praeger, 1953).

Joachim, Erich. *Napoleon in Finckenstein* (Berlin: Behrend, 1906).

Jomini, Baron. *Life of Napoleon.* Trans. H. W. Halleck (New York: D. Van Nostrand, 1864), pp. 265–271 (Eylau); pp. 306–312 (Friedland).

La Chouque, Henry. *The Anatomy of Glory—Napoleon and His Guard: A Study in Leadership.* Trans. A. Brown (Providence, R.I.: Brown University Press, 1961), pp. 84–89 (Eylau); pp. 97–102 (Friedland).

Macdonell, A. G. *Napoleon and His Marshals* (New York: Macmillan, 1934).

Meinecke, Friedrich. *The Age of German Liberation: 1795–1815.* Trans. P. Paret and H. Fischer (Berkeley: University of California Press, 1977).

Paret, Peter. "Napoleon and the Revolution in War." In *Makers of Modern Strategy from Machiavelli to the Nuclear Age,* ed. P. Paret (Princeton, N.J.: Princeton University Press, 1986), pp. 123–142.

Parker, Harold T. *Three Napoleonic Battles* (Durham, N.C.: Duke University Press, 1944), pp. 3–23 (Friedland).

Petre, Francis. *Napoleon's Campaign in Poland, 1806–7: A Military History of Napoleon's First War with Russia* (London: John Lane, The Bodley Head, 1907).

_____. *Napoleon's Conquest of Prussia—1806* (London: John Lane, The Bodley Head, 1907).

Savant, Jean. *Napoleon in His Time.* Trans. K. John (London: Putnam, 1958).

Simms, Brendan. *The Impact of Napoleon: Prussian High Politics, Foreign Policy and the Crisis of the Executive, 1797–1806* (Cambridge: Cambridge University Press, 1997).

Sutherland, Christine. *Marie Walewska* (New York: Vendome, 1979).

Thompson, J. M. *Napoleon Bonapart* (New York: Oxford University Press, 1952).

Yorck von Wartenburg, Count Maximilian. *Napoleon as a General.* 2 vols. (London: Kegan Paul, Trench, Trübner & Co., 1902).

## On Clausewitz, Sharnhorst, and Military Theorists

Anderson, Eugene. *Nationalism and the Cultural Crisis in Prussia, 1806–1815* (New York: Farrar & Reinhart, 1939).

Aron, Raymond. *Clausewitz: Philosopher of War.* Trans. C. Booker and N. Stone (New York: Simon & Schuster, 1976).

Howard, Michael. *Clausewitz* (New York: Oxford University Press, 1983).

Paret, Peter. *Clausewitz and the State: The Man, His Theories, and His Times* (New York: Oxford University Press, 1976).

_____. "Clausewitz." In *Makers of Modern Strategy from Machiavelli to the Nuclear Age,* ed. P. Paret (Princeton, N.J.: Princeton University Press, 1986), pp. 186–213.

_____. *Yorck and the Era of Prussian Reform, 1807–1815* (Princeton, N.J.: Princeton University Press, 1966).

Parkinson, Alan. *Clausewitz: A Biography* (New York: Stein and Day, 1971).

Simon, Walter M. *The Failure of the Prussian Reform Movement, 1807–1819* (New York: Howard Fertig, 1971).

Sky, John. "Jomini." In *Makers of Modern Strategy from Machiavelli to the Nuclear Age,* ed. P. Paret (Princeton, N.J.: Princeton University Press, 1986), pp. 143–185.

## Part Three: Blood and Iron

### General

Baack, Lawrence J. *Christian Bernstorff and Prussia: Diplomacy and Reform Conservatism, 1818–1832* (New Brunswick, N.J.: Rutgers University Press, 1980).

Craig, Gordon A. *The End of Prussia* (Madison: University of Wisconsin Press, 1984).

_____. *Europe Since 1815* (New York: Holt, Rinehart & Winston, 1974).

*_____. *Germany: 1866–1945* (New York: Oxford University Press, 1978).

Gillis, John R. *The Prussian Bureaucracy in Crisis, 1840–1860: Origins of an Administrative Ethos* (Stanford, Calif.: Stanford University Press, 1971).

Hamerow, Theodore S. *Restoration, Revolution, Reaction: Economics and Politics in Germany, 1815–1871* (Princeton, N.J.: Princeton University Press, 1958).

*MacDonough, Giles. *Prussia: The Perversion of an Idea* (London: Sinclair-Stevenson, 1994). Useful through World War II.

Ritter, Gerhard. *The Sword and Scepter: The European Powers and the Wilhelminian Empire, 1890–1914.* Trans. H. Norden (Coral Gables, Fla.: University of Miami Press, 1969).

Röhl, J. C. G., ed. *From Bismarck to Hitler: The Problem of Continuity in German History* (New York: Barnes & Noble, 1970).

Taylor, A. J. P. *The Struggle for Mastery in Europe, 1848–1918* (Oxford: Oxford University Press, 1977).

Treitschke, Heinrich G. *History of Germany in the Nineteenth Century.* 7 vols. Trans. E. Paul and C. Paul (New York: McBride, Nast & Co., 1915).


## On the Bismarck Era

Blanke, Richard. *Prussian Poland in the German Empire (1871–1900)* (Boulder, Colo.: East European Monographs, 1981).

Bucholz, Arden. *Moltke, Schlieffen, and Prussian War Planning* (New York: Berg, 1991).

Craig, Gordon A. *The Battle of Königgratz, Prussia's Victory over Austria, 1866* (Philadelphia: Lippincott, 1964).

Crankshaw, Edward. *Bismarck* (Harmondsworth, UK: Penguin, 1983).

Dawson, William H. *The German Empire 1867–1914 and the Unity Movement.* 2 vols. (Hamden, Conn.: Archon Books, 1966).

Eyck, Erich. *Bismarck and the German Empire* (New York: Norton, 1964).

Friedjung, Heinrich. *The Struggle for Supremacy in Germany, 1859–1866* (New York: Russell & Russell, 1966).

Friedrich, Otto. *Blood and Iron: From Bismarck to Hitler, the von Moltke Family's Impact on German History* (New York: HarperCollins, 1995).

Holborn, Hajo. "The Prusso-German School: Moltke and the Rise of the General Staff." In *Makers of Modern Strategy from Machiavelli to the Nuclear Age,* ed. P. Paret (Princeton, N.J.: Princeton University Press, 1986), pp. 281–295.

Howard, Michael. *The Franco-Prussian War: The German Invasion of France, 1870–1871* (New York: Macmillan, 1961).

Hughes, Daniel J., ed. *Moltke on the Art of War, Selected Writings* (Novato, Calif.: Presidio Press, 1993).

Kitchen, Martin. *The German Officer Corps: 1890–1914* (Oxford: Clarendon Press, 1968).

Lowe, Charles. *Bismarck's Table Talk* (Philadelphia: Lippincott, 1895).

Moltke, Helmuth Karl Bernhard. *The Franco-German War of 1870–71.* Trans. C. Bell and M. W. Fischer (New York: Harper & Brothers, 1892).

Muncy, Lysbeth W. *The Junker in the Prussian Administration Under William II, 1888–1914* (New York: Howard Fertig, 1970).

Palmer, Alan. *Bismarck* (London: Weidenfeld and Nicolson, 1976).

Pflanze, Otto. *Bismarck and the Development of Germany* (Princeton, N.J.: Princeton University Press, 1990).

Poschinger, Heinrich von. *Conversations with Bismarck* (New York: Harper & Brothers, 1900).

Ridley, Jasper. *Napoleon III and Eugenie* (New York: Viking, 1980).

Robertson, Priscilla. *Revolutions of 1848: A Social History* (Princeton, N.J.: Princeton University Press, 1971).

Rothenberg, Gunther E. "Moltke, Schlieffen, and the Doctrine of Strategic En-velopment." In *Makers of Modern Strategy from Machiavelli to the Nuclear Age*, ed. P. Paret (Princeton, N.J.: Princeton University Press, 1986), pp. 296–325.

Showalter, Dennis E. *Railroads and Rifles: Soldiers, Technology, and the Uni-fication of Germany* (Hamden, Conn.: Archon Books, 1975).

Snyder, Louis L. *The Blood and Iron Chancellor: A Documentary-Biography of Otto von Bismarck* (Princeton, N.J.: D. Van Nostrand, 1967).

Taylor, A. J. P. *Bismarck, the Man and the Statesman* (New York: Vintage Books, 1967).

Tims, Richard W. *Germanizing Prussian Poland: The H-K-T Society and the Struggle for the Eastern Marches in the German Empire, 1894–1914* (New York: AMS Press, 1966).

Wawro, Geoffrey. *The Austro-Prussian War: Austria's War with Prussia and Italy in 1866* (Cambridge: Cambridge University Press, 1996).

Whitman, Sidney. *Personal Reminiscences of Prince Bismarck* (London: John Murray, 1902).

Whitton, Frederick E. *Moltke* (Freeport, N. H.: Books for Libraries Press, 1972).

## On Kaiser Wilhelm II

Balfour, Michael. *The Kaiser and His Times* (New York: Norton, 1972).

Bennett, Daphne. *Vicky: Princess Royal of England and German Princess* (New York: St. Martin's Press, 1971).

Bigelow, Pouttney. *Prussian Memories, 1864–1914* (New York: G. P. Putnam's Sons, 1915).

Cecil, Lamar. *Wilhelm II, Emperor and Exile, 1900–1941* (Chapel Hill: Univer-sity of North Carolina Press, 1996).

_____. *Wilhelm II, Prince and Emperor, 1859–1900* (Chapel Hill: University of North Carolina Press, 1989).

Cowles, Virginia. *The Kaiser* (New York: Harper & Row, 1963).

Davis, Arthur N. *The Kaiser as I Knew Him* (New York: Harper & Brothers, 1918).

Dorpalen, Andreas. "Empress Auguste Victoria and the Fall of the German Em-pire." *American Historical Review*, vol. 58, no. 1, October 1952, pp. 17–38.

Goerlitz, Walter, ed. *The Kaiser and His Court: The Diaries, Note Books and Letters of Admiral Georg Alexander von Müller, Chief of the Naval Cabinet, 1914–1918*. Trans. M. Savill (New York: Harcourt, Brace & World, 1964).

Hill, David J. *Impressions of the Kaiser* (New York: Harper & Brothers, 1918).

Hull, Isabel. *The Entourage of Kaiser Wilhelm II, 1888–1918* (Cambridge: Cam-bridge University Press, 1982).

Kohut, Thomas A. *Wilhelm II and the Germans: A Study in Leadership* (New York: Oxford University Press, 1991).

Kürenberg, Joachim von. *The Kaiser: A Life of Wilhelm II, Last Emperor of Germany*. Trans. H. T. Russell and H. Hagen (New York: Simon & Schuster, 1955).

Louise Sophie. *H.R.H. Princess Friedrich Leopold of Prussia: Behind the Scenes at the Prussian Court.* Ed. Desmond Chapman Huston (London: J. Murray, 1939).

Ludwig, Emil. *Wilhelm Hohenzollern* (New York: G. P. Putnam's Sons, 1926).

Pakula, Hannah. *An Uncommon Woman: The Empress Frederick, Daughter of Queen Victoria, Wife of the Crown Prince of Prussia, Mother of Kaiser Wilhelm* (New York: Simon & Schuster, 1995).

Palmer, Alan. *The Kaiser: Warlord of the Second Reich* (New York: Scribner's, 1978).

Röhl, John C. G. *The Kaiser and His Court: Wilhelm II and the Government of Germany.* Trans. T. K. Cole (Cambridge: Cambridge University Press, 1994).

*Röhl, John C. G., and Nicolaus Sombart, eds. *Kaiser Wilhelm II, New Interpretations: The Corfu Papers* (Cambridge: Cambridge University Press, 1982).

Topham, Anne. *Memories of the Kaiser's Court* (New York: Dodd, Mead, 1914).

Tuchman, Barbara W. *The Proud Tower: A Portrait of the World Before the War, 1890–1914* (New York: Macmillan, 1966).

Wheeler-Bennett, John. *Knaves, Fools and Heroes: In Europe Between the Wars* (New York: St. Martin's Press, 1974).

Whittle, Tyler. *The Last Kaiser: A Biography of Wilhelm II, German Emperor and King of Prussia* (New York: Times Books, 1977).

Wilhelm II. *The Kaiser's Memoirs.* Trans. T. R. Ybarra (New York: Harper and Brothers, 1922).

_____. *My Early Life* (New York: Doran, 1926).

Zedlitz-Trutzschler, Robert von. *Twelve Years at the Imperial Court.* Trans. A. Kalisch (New York: Doran, 1924).

## On Eastern Front Campaigns and Principal Figures

Asprey, Robert B. *The German High Command at War: Hindenburg and Ludendorff Conduct World War I* (New York: William Morrow, 1991).

Barnett, Correlli. *The Swordbearers: Supreme Command in the First World War* (New York: William Morrow, 1964).

Cameron, James. *1914* (Westport, Conn.: Greenwood Press, 1975).

Churchill, Winston. *The Unknown War: The Eastern Front* (New York: Scribner's, 1931).

Dallin, Alexander. *Russian Diplomacy and Eastern Europe: 1914–17* (New York: King's Crown Press, 1963).

Dreher, William C. "Von Hindenburg, General and Man." *Atlantic Monthly,* August 1915, pp. 254–265.

*Evans, Geoffrey. *Tannenberg, 1410–1914* (Harrisburg, Penn.: Stackpole, 1971), pp. 51–163.

Eyck, Erich. "The Generals and the Downfall of the German Monarchy: 1917–1918." *Transactions of the Royal Historical Society,* vol. 2, fifth series 1952, pp. 47–68.

Falkenhayn, Erich von. *General Headquarters and Its Critical Decisions—1914–1916* (London: Hutchinson, 1920).

Führungsakademie der Bundeswehr. *Die Tannenberg-Feldzeichen in der Führungsakademie* (Hamburg: Führungsakademie der Bundeswehr, n.d.).

Gardiner, A. G. *Portraits and Portents* (New York: Harper and Brothers, 1926), pp. 165–171.

Gies, Joseph. *Crisis 1918: The Leading Actors, Strategies, and Events in the German Gamble for Total Victory on the Western Front* (New York: Norton, 1974).

Goldsmith, Margaret, and Voigt, Frederick. *Hindenburg: The Man and the Legend* (New York: Morrow, 1930).

Golovin, Nicholai N. *The Russian Army in the World War* (New Haven, Conn.: Yale University Press, 1931).

_____. *The Russian Campaign of 1914: The Beginning of the War and Operations in East Prussia*. Trans. A. G. S. Muntz (Fort Leavenworth, Kans.: Command and General Staff School Press, 1933).

Goodspeed, D. J. *The German Wars: 1914–1945* (Boston: Houghton Mifflin, 1977), pp. 161–181.

_____. *Ludendorff, Genius of World War I* (Boston: Houghton Mifflin, 1966).

Harden, Maximilian. *I Meet My Contemporaries*. Trans. W. Lawton (New York: Holt, 1925).

Henderson, Ernest F. *Germany's Fighting Machine* (Indianapolis: Bobbs-Merrill, 1914).

Hillgruber, Andreas. *Germany and the Two World Wars*. Trans. W. C. Kirby (Cambridge: Harvard University Press, 1981).

Hindenburg, Helene Nostitz von. *Hindenburg at Home: An Intimate Biography* (New York: Duffield & Green, 1931).

Hindenburg, Paul von. *Out of My Life*. Trans. F. A. Holt (London: Cassell, 1920).

Hoffmann, Max. *The War of Lost Opportunities* (New York: International Publishers, 1925).

_____. "The Truth About Tannenberg." *War Diaries and Other Papers*, vol. 2. Trans. E. Sutton (London: Secker, 1929).

Ironside, Edmund. *Tannenberg: The First Thirty Days in East Prussia* (London: W. Blackwood and Sons, 1925).

Keegan, John. *The Mask of Command* (New York: Viking, 1987).

Kitchen, Martin. *The Silent Dictatorship: The Politics of the German High Command Under Hindenburg and Ludendorff, 1916–1918* (London: Croom Helm, 1976). The entire book is of great interest.

Kluck, Alexander von. *The March on Paris and Battle of the Marne* (London: Edward Arnold, 1920).

Knox, Alfred. *With the Russian Army, 1914–1917: Being Chiefly Extracts from the Diary of a Military Attaché*. 2 vols. (London: Hutchinson, 1921).

Liddell Hart, B. H. *The Real War* (London: Faber & Faber, 1930), pp. 15–130.

_____. *Reputations Ten Years After* (Boston: Little, Brown, 1928), pp. 181–208.

_____. *Strategy* (New York: Praeger, 1960), pp. 167–189, 202–219.

_____. *Through the Fog of War* (New York: Random House, 1938), pp. 116–119, 137–140, 213–228.

Lincoln, W. B. *Passage Through Armageddon: The Russians in War and Revolution, 1914–1918* (New York: Simon & Schuster, 1986), pp. 17–113.

Ludendorff, Erich. *The General Staff and Its Problems.* Trans. F. A. Holt (London: Hutchinson, 1920).

_____. *Ludendorff's Own Story: August 1914–November 1918.* 2 vols. (New York: Harper and Brothers, 1920).

Ludendorff, Margarethe. *My Married Life with Ludendorff.* Trans. R. Somerset (London: Hutchinson, 1930).

Ludwig, Emil. *Hindenburg.* Trans. E. Paul and C. Paul (Philadelphia: John C. Winston, 1935).

Maurice, Frederick. *The Last Four Months: How the War Was Won* (Boston: Little, Brown, 1919).

Menken, H. L. "Ludendorff." *Atlantic Monthly,* June 1917, pp. 823–832.

Parkinson, Roger. *Tormented Warrior: Ludendorff and the Supreme Command* (New York: Stein and Day, 1979).

Pitt, Barrie. *1918: The Last Act* (New York: Norton, 1963).

Ritter, Gerard. *The Schlieffen Plan: Critique of a Myth.* Trans. A. Wilson and E. Wilson (London: Oswald Wolff, 1958).

Schultze-Pfaelzer, Gerhard. *Hindenburg: Peace—War—Aftermath.* Trans. C. R. Turner (New York: G. P.. Putnam's Sons, 1932).

Silberstein, Gerard E. *The Troubled Alliance: German-Austrian Relations: 1914–1917* (Lexington: University Press of Kentucky, 1970), pp. 251–274.

Snyder, Jack L. *The Ideology of the Offensive: Military Decision Making and the Disasters of 1914* (Ithaca, N.Y.: Cornell University Press, 1984), pp. 107–198, 203–205.

Stone, Norman. *The Eastern Front: 1914–1917* (New York: Scribner's, 1975).

_____. "Hindenburg" and "Ludendorff." In *The War Lords: Military Commanders of the Twentieth Century,* ed. Michael Carver (London: Weidenfeld and Nicolson, 1976), pp. 44–54, 73–83.

Sulzberger, G. L. *The Fall of Eagles* (New York: Crown, 1977).

Taylor, Edmond. *The Fall of the Dynasties: The Collapse of the Old Order, 1905–1922* (New York: Doubleday, 1963).

Toland, John. *No Man's Land: 1918, The Last Year of the Great War* (New York: Doubleday, 1980).

Tschuppik, Karl. *Ludendorff: The Tragedy of a Military Mind* (Boston: Houghton Mifflin, 1932).

Tuchman, Barbara. *The Guns of August* (New York: Macmillan, 1962).

Turner, L. C. F. "The Significance of the Schlieffen Plan." In *The War Plans of the Great Powers: 1880–1914,* ed. Paul Kennedy (London: George Allen & Unwin, 1979), pp. 199–221.

Wheeler-Bennett, John. *Brest-Litovsk: The Forgotten Peace, March 1918* (London: Macmillan, 1938).

_____. "Hindenburg." In *Great Contemporaries* (London: Cassell, 1935).

_____. *Hindenburg: The Wooden Titan* (New York: St. Martin's Press, 1936).

\_\_\_\_\_. "Ludendorff, the Soldier and the Politician." *Virginia Quarterly*, vol. 14, no. 2 (spring 1938), pp. 187–202.

Wilson, Edmund. *To the Finland Station* (New York: Doubleday, 1940).


## On the Interwar Years

Bessel, Richard. *Germany After the First World War* (Oxford: Clarendon Press, 1993).

Burleigh, Michael. *Germany Turns Eastwards: A Study of "Ostforschung" in the Third Reich* (Cambridge: Cambridge University Press, 1988). Fascinating specialist study of prewar and early war attitudes.

Carsten, F. L. *The Reichswehr and Politics, 1918–1933* (Berkeley: University of California Press, 1973).

*Dorpalen, Andreas. *Hindenburg and the Weimar Republic* (Princeton, N.J.: Princeton University Press, 1964).

Feuchtwanger, E. J. *From Weimar to Hitler: Germany, 1918–33* (New York: St. Martin's Press, 1995).

Flood, Charles Bracelen. *Hitler: The Path to Power* (Boston: Houghton Mifflin, 1989).

Friedrich, Otto. *Before the Deluge: A Portrait of Berlin in the 1920s* (New York: Harper & Row, 1972).

Gay, Peter. *Weimar Culture* (New York: Harper & Row, 1970).

Gilbert, Martin. *Britain and Germany Between the Wars* (London: Longmans, 1966).

Gordon, Harold J. *Hitler and the Beer Hall Putsch* (Princeton, N.J.: Princeton University Press, 1972).

Hiden, John W. "The 'Baltic Problem' in Weimar's *Ostpolitik*, 1923–1932." In *Germany in the Age of Total War*, eds. V. Berghahn and M. Kitchen (London: Croom Helm, 1981), pp. 147–169.

Mayer, Milton. *They Thought They Were Free* (Chicago: University of Chicago Press, 1955).

Mee, Charles L. *The End of Order: Versailles 1919* (New York: E. P. Dutton, 1980).

Morrow, Ian F. D. *The Peace Settlement in the German Polish Borderlands: A Study of Conditions To-day in the Pre-war Prussian Provinces of East and West Prussia* (London: Oxford University Press, 1936).

Mosley, Leonard. *On Borrowed Time: How World War II Began* (New York: Random House, 1969).

Müller, Klaus-Jürgen. *The Army, Politics and Society in Germany, 1933–1945* (New York: St. Martin's Press, 1987).

*O'Neill, Robert J. *The German Army and the Nazi Party, 1933–1939* (London: Cassell, 1966).

Orlow, Dietrich. *Weimar Prussia, 1918–1925* (Pittsburgh: University of Pittsburgh Press, 1986).

Park, Bert Edward. "Hindenburg, MacDonald, and Pilsudski: The Interwar Years." In *The Impact of Illness on World Leaders* (Philadelphia: University of Pennsylvania Press, 1986), pp. 77–92.

Rauch, Georg von. *The Baltic States, the Years of Independence: Estonia, Latvia, Lithuania, 1917–1940.* Trans. G. Onn (Berkeley: University of California Press, 1974).

Reddaway, W. F. *Problems of the Baltic* (Cambridge: Cambridge University Press, 1940).

Shirer, William. *Berlin Diary: The Journal of a Foreign Correspondent, 1934–1941* (New York: Knopf, 1941).

_____. *The Rise and Fall of the Third Reich: A History of Nazi Germany* (New York: Simon & Schuster, 1960).

_____. *20th Century Journey, a Memoir of a Life and the Times: The Nightmare Years, 1930–1940* (Boston: Little, Brown, 1984).

Taylor, Telford. *Sword and Swastika: Generals and Nazis in the Third Reich* (Chicago: Quadrangle Books, 1969).

Tucker, Robert C. *Stalin in Power: The Revolution from Above, 1928–1941* (New York: Norton, 1990).

_____, ed. *The Great Purge Trial* (New York: Grosset & Dunlap, 1965).

Watt, Richard M. *Bitter Glory: Poland and Its Fate, 1918 to 1939* (New York: Simon & Schuster, 1979).

_____. *The Kings Depart; the Tragedy of Germany: Versailles and the German Revolution* (New York: Simon & Schuster, 1968).

Wheeler-Bennett, John. *The Nemesis of Power: The German Army in Politics, 1918–1945* (New York: St. Martin's Press, 1954).

Wiles, Timothy, ed. *Poland Between the Wars: 1918–1939* (Bloomington: Indiana University Polish Studies Center, 1989).

Winter, Jay. *Sites of Memory, Sites of Mourning: The Great War in European Cultural History* (Cambridge: Cambridge University Press, 1995).

## Part Four: Extinction

### General

Fischer, Klaus. *Nazi Germany: A New History* (New York: Continuum, 1995).

Keegan, John. *The Second World War* (New York: Viking, 1990).

Weinberg, Gerhard L. *A World at Arms: A Global History of World War II* (Cambridge: Cambridge University Press, 1994).

### On Adolf Hitler

Binion, Rudolph. *Hitler Among the Germans* (New York: Elsevier, 1976).

Bullock, Alan. *Hitler: A Study in Tyranny* (New York: Harper & Row, 1962).

_____. *Hitler and Stalin: Parallel Lives* (New York: Knopf, 1992).

Craig, Gordon A. "The Political Leader as Strategist." In *Makers of Modern Strategy from Machiavelli to the Nuclear Age,* ed. P. Paret (Princeton, N.J.: Princeton University Press, 1986), pp. 491–497.

Fest, Joachim C. *The Face of the Third Reich.* Trans. M. Bullock (New York: Pantheon, 1970).

Heston, Leonard L., and Renate Heston. *The Medical Casebook of Adolf Hitler: His Illnesses, Doctors and Drugs* (New York: Stein and Day, 1979).

Payne, Robert. *The Life and Death of Adolf Hitler* (New York: Praeger, 1973).

Rauschning, Hermann. *The Voice of Destruction* (New York: G. P. Putnam's Sons, 1940).

Schramm, Percy E. *Hitler: The Man and the Military Leader* (Chicago: Quadrangle Books, 1971).

Speer, Albert. *Inside the Third Reich: Memoirs*. Trans. R. Winston and C. Winston (New York: Macmillan, 1970).

______. *Spandau: The Secret Diaries*. Trans. R. Winston and C. Winston (New York: Macmillan, 1976).

Trevor-Roper, H. R., ed. *Hitler's Secret Conversations: 1941–1944*. Trans. N. Cameron and R. H. Stevens (New York: Octagon, 1953).

## On Eastern Front Campaigns and Principal Figures

Bartov, Omer. *The Eastern Front, 1941–45: German Troops and the Barbarization of Warfare* (New York: St. Martin's Press, 1985).

______. *Hitler's Army: Soldiers, Nazis, and War in the Third Reich* (New York: Oxford University Press, 1991).

______. "Savage War." In *Confronting the Nazi Past: New Debates on Modern German History*, ed. M. Burleigh (New York: St. Martin's Press, 1996), pp. 125–139.

Bialer, Seweryn, ed. *Stalin and His Generals: Soviet Military Memoirs of World War Two* (New York: Pegasus, 1969), pp. 179–339, 459–549.

Carell, Paul. *Hitler Moves East: 1941–1943*. Trans. E. Osers (Boston: Little, Brown, 1963).

Chuikov, Vasili I. *The Battle for Stalingrad*. Trans. H. Silver (New York: Holt, Rinehart & Winston, 1964).

______. *The Fall of Berlin*. Trans. R. Kisch (New York: Holt, Rinehart & Winston, 1967).

Clark, Alan. *Barbarossa: The Russian-German Conflict, 1941–45* (New York: William Morrow, 1965).

Craig, William. *Enemy at the Gates: The Battle for Stalingrad* (E. P. Dutton, 1973).

Dupuy, Trevor N. *Great Battles on the Eastern Front: The Soviet-German War, 1941–1945* (Indianapolis: Bobbs-Merrill, 1982).

*Erickson, John. *The Road to Berlin* (Boulder, Colo.: Westview Press, 1983).

*______. *The Road to Stalingrad* (New York: Harper & Row, 1975).

Fritz, Stephen G. *Frontsoldaten: The German Soldier in World War II* (Lexington: University Press of Kentucky, 1995).

*Garrard, John, and Carol Garrard, eds. *World War II and the Soviet People: Selected Papers from the Fourth World Congress for Soviet and East European Studies, Harrogate, 1990* (New York: St. Martin's Press, 1993).

Gehlen, Reinhard. *The Service: Memoirs*. Trans. D. Irving (New York: World Publishing, 1972).

Gilbert, Felix, ed. *Hitler Directs His War* (Oxford: Oxford University Press, 1950).

Glantz, David M., and Jonathan M. House. *When Titans Clashed: How the Red Army Stopped Hitler* (Lawrence: University Press of Kansas, 1995).

Goodspeed, D. J. *The German Wars: 1914–1945* (Boston: Houghton Mifflin, 1977).

*Guderian, Heinz. *Panzer Leader*. Trans. C. Fitzgibbon (New York: E. P. Dutton, 1952).

*Halder, Franz. *The War Diary 1939–1942*. Eds. Charles Burdick and Hans-Adolf Jacobsen (Novato, Calif.: Presidio Press, 1988).

Higgins, Trumbull. *Hitler and Russia: The Third Reich in a Two-Front War, 1937–1943* (New York: Macmillan, 1966).

Keegan, John. *Guderian* (New York: Ballantine, 1973).

Leonhardt, Hans L. *Nazi Conquest of Danzig* (Chicago: University of Chicago Press, 1942).

Liddell Hart, B. H. *The German Generals Talk* (New York: William Morrow, 1948).

_____. *Strategy* (New York: Praeger, 1960).

Lucas, James. *Last Days of the Third Reich: The Collapse of Nazi Germany, May 1945* (New York: William Morrow, 1986).

_____. *The Last Year of the German Army* (London: Cassell, 1996).

_____. *War on the Eastern Front, 1941–1945* (New York: Stein & Day, 1980).

Lukacs, John. *The Last European War, September 1939–December 1941* (Garden City, N.Y.: Anchor Press/Doubleday, 1976).

*Manstein, Erich von. *Lost Victories*. Trans. A. G. Powell (Chicago: Henry Regency, 1958).

O'Donnell, James P. *The Bunker: The History of the Reich Chancellery Group* (Boston: Houghton Mifflin, 1978).

Payne, Robert. *The Rise and Fall of Stalin* (New York: Avon, 1965).

Ryan, Cornelius. *The Last Battle* (New York: Simon & Schuster, 1966).

Seaton, Albert. "Field-Marshal Erich von Manstein." In *The War Lords: Military Commanders of the Twentieth Century*, ed. Michael Carver (London: Weidenfeld and Nicolson, 1976), pp. 231–243.

Shukman, Harold, ed. *Stalin's Generals* (New York: Grove Press, 1993).

Steinhoff, Johannes, Peter Pechel, and Dennis Showalter. *Voices from the Third Reich: An Oral History* (Washington, D.C.: Regnery Gateway, 1989).

Strawson, John. "Guderian." In *The War Lords: Military Commanders of the Twentieth Century*, ed. Michael Carver (London: Weidenfeld and Nicolson, 1976), pp. 298–315.

_____. *Hitler as Military Commander* (London: B. T. Batsford, 1971).

*Tighe, Carl. *Gdańsk, National Identity in the Polish-German Borderlands* (London: Pluto Press, 1990).

Trevor-Roper, H. R. *Blitzkrieg to Defeat: Hitler War Directives, 1939–1945* (New York: Holt, Rinehart & Winston, 1971).

_____. *The Last Days of Hitler* (New York: Macmillan, 1947).

Tully, Andrew. *Berlin: Story of a Battle* (New York: Simon & Schuster, 1963).

Warlimont, Walter. *Inside Hitler's Headquarters, 1939–45*. Trans. R. Barry (New York: Praeger, 1964).

Werth, Alexander. *Russia at War: 1941–1945* (New York: E. P. Dutton, 1964).

Whiting, Charles. *The End of the War, Europe: April 15–May 23, 1945* (New York: Stein and Day, 1972).

Zhukov, Georgi K. *Marshal Zhukov's Greatest Battles*. Trans. T. Shabad (New York: Harper & Row, 1969).

Ziemke, Earl F. *Stalingrad to Berlin: The German Defeat in the East* (New York: Military Heritage Press, 1985).

## On the Assassination Attempt on Hitler

Balfour, Michael. *Withstanding Hitler in Germany 1933–45* (London: Routledge, 1988).

Deutsch, Harold C. *The Conspiracy Against Hitler in the Twilight War* (Minneapolis: University of Minnesota Press, 1968).

Duffy, James P., and Vincent L. Ricci. *Target Hitler: The Plots to Kill Adolf Hitler* (New York: Praeger, 1992).

Fest, Joachim. *Plotting Hitler's Death: The Story of the German Resistance*. Trans. B. Little (New York: Holt, 1996).

Fitzgibbon, Constantine. *20 July* (New York: Norton, 1956).

Galante, Pierre. *Operation Valkyrie: The German Generals' Plot Against Hitler*. Trans. M. Howson and C. Ryan (New York: Harper & Row, 1981).

Hoffmann, Peter. *German Resistance to Hitler* (Cambridge: Harvard University Press, 1988).

_____. *Stauffenberg: A Family History, 1905–1944* (Cambridge: Cambridge University Press, 1995).

Noakes, Jeremy. "Nazism and High Society." In *Confronting the Nazi Past: New Debates on Modern German History*, ed. M. Burleigh (New York: St. Martin's Press, 1996), pp. 51–65.

Reynolds, Nicholas. *Treason Was No Crime: Ludwig Beck, Chief of the German General Staff* (London: William Kimber, 1976).

Royce, Hans, Erich Zimmermann, and Hans-Adolf Jacobsen. *Germans Against Hitler, July 20, 1944* (Bonn: Press and Information Office of the Federal Government of Germany, 1964).

Schlabrendorff, Fabian von. *The Secret War Against Hitler* (New York: Pitman, 1965).

Vassiltchikov, Marie. *Berlin Diaries, 1940–1945* (New York: Knopf, 1987).

Wolf, Ernst. "Political and Moral Motives Behind the Resistance." In Hermann Graml, Hans Mommsen, Hans-Joachim Reichhardt, and Ernst Wolf, *The German Resistance to Hitler* (Berkeley: University of California Press, 1970), pp. 193–234.

## On Matters Relating to Stutthof Camp and the Holocaust

*Abramsky, S., Ariel, Y. Berelson, B. Kahan, S. Savitt-Zavozhnitzky, and L. Sherer, *Jewish Community Book: Suwalk and Vicinity* (N.p.: Yair-Abraham Stern-Publishing House, n.d.).

Bauer, Yehuda. "The Death Marches, January–May, 1945." In *The Nazi Holocaust: Historical Articles on the Destruction of European Jews*, ed. Michael R. Marrus (Westport, Conn.: Meckler, 1989), vol. 9, pp. 491–511.

Central Commission for Investigation of German Crimes in Poland. *German Crimes in Poland* (New York: Howard Fertig, 1982), pp. 105–124.

Dimsdale, Joel E., ed. *Survivors, Victims, and Perpetrators: Essays on the Nazi Holocaust* (New York: Hemisphere, 1980).

Feig, Konnilyn, G. *Hitler's Death Camps: The Sanity of Madness* (New York: Holmes & Meier, 1981), pp. 191–203.

Gilbert, Martin. *The Holocaust: A Story of the Jews of Europe During the Second World War* (New York: Holt, Rinehart & Winston, 1985).

Goldhagen, Daniel Jonah. *Hitler's Willing Executioners: Ordinary Germans and the Holocaust* (New York: Knopf, 1996).

Gutman, Israel. *Encyclopedia of the Holocaust* (New York: Macmillan, 1990), vol. 1, pp. 348–354; vol. 4, pp. 1421–1423.

Gutman, Israel, and Shmuel Krakowski. *Unequal Victims: Poles and Jews During World War Two*. Trans. T. Gorelick and W. Jedlicki (New York: Holocaust Library, 1986).

Gutman, Israel, Ezra Mendelsohn, Jehuda Reinharz, and Chone Shmeruk, eds. *The Jews of Poland Between Two World Wars* (Hanover, N.H.: University Press of New England, 1989).

Heller, Celia S. *On the Edge of Destruction: Jews of Poland Between the Two World Wars* (New York: Columbia University Press, 1977).

Hertz, Aleksander. *The Jews in Polish Culture*. Trans. R. Lourie (Evanston, Ill.: Northwestern University Press, 1988).

Hoffman, Eva. *Shtetl: The Life and Death of a Small Town and the World of Polish Jews* (Boston: Houghton Mifflin, 1997).

Klee, Ernst, W. Dressen, and V. Riess, eds. *The Holocaust as Seen by Its Perpetrators and Bystanders*. Trans. D. Burnstone (New York: Free Press, 1988).

Krakowski, Shmuel. "The Death Marches in the Period of the Evacuation of the Camps." In *The Nazi Concentration Camps: Structure and Aims, the Image of the Prisoner, the Jews in the Camps—Proceedings of the Fourth Yad Vashem International Historical Conference*, Yisrael Gutman and Avital Saf, eds. (Jerusalem: Yad Vashem, 1984), pp. 475–489.

Mendelsohn, Ezra. "Interwar Poland: Good for the Jews or Bad for the Jews?" In *The Jews in Poland*, eds. Chimen Abramsky, Maciej Jachimczyk, and Antony Polosky (London: Basil Blackwell, 1986), pp. 130–139.

Rothkirchen, Livia. "The Final Solution in Its Last Stages." *Yad Vashem Studies*, vol. 8, 1970, pp. 7–29.

Segev, Tom. *Soldiers of Evil: The Commandants of the Nazi Concentration Camps*. Trans. H. Watzman (New York: McGraw-Hill, 1987), pp. 167–176.

Sofsky, Wolfgang. *The Order of Terror: The Concentration Camp*. Trans. W. Templer (Princeton, N.J.: Princeton University Press, 1997).

Steinlauf, Michael C. *Bondage to the Dead: Poland and the Memory of the Holocaust* (Syracuse, N.Y.: Syracuse University Press, 1997).

Warhaftig, Zorach. *Uprooted: Jewish Refugees and Displaced Persons After Liberation* (New York: Institute of Jewish Affairs, 1946).

## Literature Specific to East Prussia and Treks

*Dönhoff, Marion. *Before the Storm: Memories of My Youth in Old Prussia*. Trans. J. Steinberg (New York: Knopf, 1990). The German edition, *Bilder, die langsam verblassen* (Berlin: Siedler Verlag, 1988), is more fulsomely illustrated.

Kabus, Ronny. *Ruinen von Königsberg: Bilder eines Kaliningrader Architekten* (Husum: Husum Druck- und Verlagsgesellschaft, 1992).

*Lehndorff, Hans. *Token of a Covenant: Diary of an East Prussian Surgeon, 1945–47*. Trans. E. Mayer (Chicago: Henry Regnery, 1964).

*Schieder, Theodor, ed. *The Expulsion of the German Population from the Territories East of the Oder-Neisse-Line*. Trans. V. Stranders (Bonn: Federal Ministry for Expellees, Refugees and War Victims, 1958). A collection of eyewitness accounts.

Tighe, Carl. "1945: The Last Days of Danzig." *Gdańsk, National Identity in the Polish-German Borderlands* (London: Pluto Press, 1990), pp. 178–201.

## On Postwar Germany and Poland

Alter, Reinhard, and Peter Monteath, eds. *Rewriting the German Past: History and Identity in the New Germany* (Atlantic Highlands, N.J.: Humanities Press, 1997).

Annan, Noel. *Changing Enemies: The Defeat and Regeneration of Germany* (New York: Norton, 1996).

Baldwin, Peter, ed. *Reworking the Past: Hitler, the Holocaust, and the Historians' Debate* (Boston: Beacon Press, 1990).

Buruma, Ian. *The Wages of Guilt: Memories of War in Germany and Japan* (New York: Farrar, Straus, and Giroux, 1994).

Evans, Richard J. *In Hitler's Shadow: West German Historians and the Attempt to Escape from the Nazi Past* (New York: Pantheon, 1989).

Garton Ash, Timothy. *In Europe's Name: Germany and the Divided Continent* (New York: Random House, 1993).

Habermas, Jürgen. *The Past as Future*. Trans. M. Pensky (Lincoln: University of Nebraska Press, 1994).

Heurlin, Bertel, ed. *Germany in Europe in the Nineties* (London: Macmillan, 1996).

Jarausch, Konrad H. *The Rush to German Unity* (New York: Oxford University Press, 1994).

Kramer, Jane. *The Politics of Memory* (New York: Random House, 1996).

Lieven, Anatol. *The Baltic Revolution: Estonia, Latvia, Lithuania and the Path to Independence* (New Haven, Conn.: Yale University Press, 1993).

Machray, Robert. *East Prussia: Menace to Poland and Peace* (Chicago: American Polish Council, 1944).

Maier, Charles S. *The Unmasterable Past: History, Holocaust, and German National Identity* (Cambridge: Harvard University Press, 1988), pp. 19–25.

Mee, Charles L. *Meeting at Potsdam* (New York: M. Evans, 1975).

Newhouse, John. *Europe Adrift* (New York: Pantheon, 1997).

Rice, Condoleezza, and Philip Zelikow. *Germany Unified and Europe Transformed: A Study in Statecraft* (Cambridge: Harvard University Press, 1995).

Szabo, Stephen F. *The Diplomacy of German Unification* (New York: St. Martin's Press, 1992).

Vachon, John. *Poland, 1946: The Photographs and Letters of John Vachon* (Washington, D.C.: Smithsonian Institution Press, 1995).

# A Note on the
# Geography of East Prussia

In its long history the territory known to Germans as Ostpreussen has been subjected to many alterations, both physical and ideological. The most mundane and yet crucial for today's traveler involves signposts, maps, the simple task of asking directions. This can never be an easy proposition when various peoples have sought, many times with success, to erase every hint of a presence concerning their predecessors, those who may have lorded the land in previous generations. I hasten to say that this is the prerogative not simply of the present-day inhabitants, the Poles and Russians who inhabit the confines of the former Ostpreussen. In many ways they have simply copied what the German population themselves strove to achieve for hundreds of years. The result, unfortunately, is confusion. The central river of the region, for instance, is referred to by English speakers as the Vistula. Germans, however, call it the Weichsel, and Poles the Wisla.

For simplicity's sake, therefore, I used a single reference system. As this is primarily a book on German history, I have chosen to use German topographical names for villages, cities, and regions. This will no doubt irritate readers of a Polish persuasion, and for this I apologize. In the spirit of facilitation, I offer a short list of geographical equivalencies for those who may wish someday to visit any of the sites discussed in this book.

| | |
|---|---|
| Allenstein = Olsztyn | Heilsberg = Lidzbark Warminski |
| Cadinen = Kadyny | Königsberg = Kaliningrad |
| Danzig = Gdańsk | Kulm = Chelmno |
| Elbing = Elblag | Marienburg = Malbork |
| Finckenstein = Kamieniec | Marienwerder = Kwidzyn |
| Frauenburg = Frombork | Pillau = Baltijsk |
| Frisches Haff = Zalew Wiślany | Rastenburg = Ketrzyn |
| Gnewin = Gniew | Stutthof = Sztutowo |
| Graudenz = Grudziadz | Thorn = Toruń |

# Credits

# Acknowledgments

I was inspired to write this book after reading "The Nowhere City" by Amos Elon. My thanks to him for his advice and encouragement.

For a variety of reasons, many people interviewed in this book insisted that their names not be used. A host of others who helped with introductions, logistics, advice, and actual tromping about various sites wished anonymity as well, particularly in Kaliningrad. As one who depended on the expertise and generosity of so many, it pains me not to recognize their help more openly. I can only say that I know, and I hope they know, that this book could not have been written without them.

To those who submitted to interviews and constant follow-ups for clarification, my deepest appreciation. In particular Klaus von Holleben and Aronek Kierszkowski (Arnold Kerr) deserve my special thanks for their patience.

The following assisted me in Germany, many through the good graces of John Toland: Hein Ruck, the late Michael von Clemm, Oberstleutnant Norbert Richter of the Führungsakademie der Bundeswehr in Hamburg, Dorothee Bauer, Jeffrey Scott, Karola Gillich, and Dr. Ernst Aichner of the Bayerisches Armeemuseum. In matters of German phraseology and translation, Valeska Nygren was most helpful.

In Poland and Kaliningrad, my thanks to Vladimir Bayer, chief of police in Kaliningrad City; Lieutenant Sergey Romanov; Vladimir Rakov; Vladimir Beregovoje; Professor Vera Zabotkina of Kaliningrad State University; archivist Anatoly Bachtin of Ostpreussenclub; Helena Penkina, director of the history and art museum of Kaliningrad; and Pawel Zajdler of the Suwalki Regional Development Agency.

For help in translations of Polish material, my thanks to Marek Lesniewski-Laas and Edward Stapinski; for help in translations of Russian material, Ned Quigley, Vladimir Sarykov, and Michael Lurye.

Dr. Nechama Tec of the University of Connecticut at Stamford and the author of four books on the Holocaust provided me with key contacts. My appreciation as well to the Helena Preston Holocaust Education Committee of Yale University.

Friends in Ireland proved their worth by arranging several introductions to German émigrés now living in that country. The late Godfrey Skrine and his wife, Billie, along with Madelaine Jay were especially active on my behalf.

In the United States, the following were indispensable: Susan Bailey, Ralph Brown, Kay Cassidy, Jeannie and Sheldon Cooperman, Christopher Jeffrey, Julie Roy Jeffrey, Sophia Jeffrey, Bill Lane, Sana Morrow, Marcia Penrod-Hitch, Ned Quigley, Peter and Margaret Quigley, the late Marian Rudy, and John Ryan.

Laura Henderson and Elizabeth Welch were almost co-collaborators on this project in a variety of ways. They saved the manuscript from innumerable errors mechanical and perceptional. My greatest thanks to them both. An unsung hero for this writer was copy editor Alice Colwell, whose detection of mistakes, malapropisms, and grammatical foolishness proved a humbling experience. My particular gratitude as well to Wendy Oppel, whose design sensibilities have left their superior impact on all my books.

The unrivaled assemblage of libraries in the greater Boston area proved an invaluable resource. My particular thanks to the staffs of the Boston Public Library, the Boston Athenaeum, and the collections of Brandeis, Boston College, Tufts, MIT, and Harvard, as well as the Merrimack Valley Library Consortium.

Finally, as every writer knows, there exist three reserves of calm to which flight is possible in the stormy and uncertain world of publishing. The first is the domain of agents. Fergal Tobin, my longtime friend and editor in Dublin, was courteous enough to recommend the services of an able agent, Jonathan Williams. My sincere appreciation to each.

Even more valuable was my editor at Westview Press, Rob Williams. It is not often that editors smooth a path—indeed, their job description often seems very much the reverse—but my thanks to Rob for his helpfulness.

Looming largest, of course, is home and hearth, the people who share the ups and downs of creative life, which at times approach Armageddon-like proportions, however artificial the crisis of the moment may appear (luckily, the next day, things never seem so bad). To my children, Alix and Dana, my apologies when dinnertime did not go smoothly or when bedtime reading seemed less than convincing. And to my wife, Jan, my regret for distracted airs and general gloominess. At times I could, with conviction, blame the subject matter, but the Catholic in me confesses to a larger than usual dose of self-centeredness as the culprit. Unfortunately, my wife unerringly knows the difference. My heartfelt appreciation to her.

*JCR*
*November 1998*
Newburyport, Massachusetts

# Index

*fn refers to footnote on page indicated. (notes) refers to page indicated in Notes section.

Acre, 24(table), 49, 62
Adelson, Naum, 213, 225–226, 228–229, 229(photo). See also Kiersztowski, Aronek (Walter Kerr), childhood; Suwalki
AEG (Allgemeine Elektrizitaetgesellschaft, electrical firm), 169
Aizenberg family (Issac, Dodzik, Rose), 249, 250. See also Kiersztowski, Aronek (Walter Kerr), as concentration camp inmate
AK. See Armia Krajowa
Albania, 123
Albert I, (the Bear), Margrave of Brandenburg, 32, 48
Albert Frederick of Prussia, 108, 109(table)
Albrecht of Brandenburg-Anspach (Hohenzollern), duke of Prussia, 24(table), 98–101, 108. See also East Prussia (Ostpreussen), union with Brandenburg; Hohenzollern dynasty; Teutonic Knights, Order of, secularization
Alexander I, Tsar of Russia, 154, 232
Alexander Nevsky (film). See Eisenstein, Sergei
Alexander Nevsky, Saint, prince of Novgorod, 60
All Quiet on the Western Front. See Remarque, Erich Maria
Allenstein (Olsztyn), 16, 17(photo), 63(photo), 99, 179, 189, 214fn

Amber, 55, 55fn, 67. See also Amber Room; Hohenzollern Dynasty; Teutonic Knights, Order of, amber trade
Amber Room, 55fn, 122fn, 292fn. See also Amber; Koch, Gauleiter Erich; St. Petersburg (Leningrad)
American army, 266fn, 274, 287, 302, 303, 306
American army units, Third Army Group, 170
American Society of Mechanical Engineers, 214
Anatomy of the World, The. See Donne, John
Anna of Prussia, 109(table)
Arctic Sea, 5, 6
Arendt, Hannah (writer), 20fn, 247fn
Aristotle, 96
Armia Krajowa, 69, 227. See also Poland, anti-Semitism
Arnim, Hans Georg von, 107
Auerstädt, Battle of (1806). See Battles, in passing, Auerstädt (1806)
Augereau, Pierre, Duke of Castiglione, 150, 155
August 1914. See Solzhenitsyn, Aleksandr
Augusta Victoria of Schleswig-Holstein, Empress of Prussia, 172. See also Wilhelm II, Emperor of Germany
Auschwitz concentration camp, 54, 223–224, 242, 244, 247, 247fn, 251, 252, 322
  fiftieth anniversary of liberation, 213–214
"Auschwitz lie," 37, 246, 322
Austen Jane (writer), 65
Austerlitz, Battle of (1805). See Battles, in passing, Austerlitz (1805)

Austria, 113, 114, 128, 160(table), 168, 208(table), 262, 292fn
Austrian army, 104(table), 126, 146, 191
Austro-Prussian War (1866). See Wars, in passing, Austro-Prussian (1866)
Avery, Milton (painter), 214, 215(photo)

Bad Crenz (Zelednogradsk), 14
Baltic Sea, 6, 21, 33, 49, 51, 55, 66, 78, 106, 111, 129, 163, 251, 286, 299fn
Baltic States, 9, 25, 267
Baltijsk. See Pillau
Balt Oil (oil production company), 248
Bamberg, 278
Battle of Grünwald, The (painting). See Matejko, Jan
Battles, in passing
    Arcole, bridge of (1796), 126, 330(notes)
    Auerstädt (1806), 104(table), 142, 146fn, 147. See also Battles, in passing, Jena (1806)
    Austerlitz (1805), 104(table), 145, 155fn
    Cannae (216 B. C.), 145, 177, 185, 187. See also Schlieffen, Count Alfred von; Tannenberg, Battle of (1914)
    Crécy (1346), 86
    D day (1944), 209(table), 265, 266fn
    Dunkirk (1940), 287
    Gettysburg (1863), 189
    Gumbinnen (1914), 160(table), 175, 180, 184. See also Tannenberg, Battle of (1914)
    Jena (1806), 104(table), 142, 145, 145fn, 146, 146fn, 147, 155fn. See also Battles, in passing, Auerstädt (1806)
    Könnigrattz (1866), 160(table), 168
    Kursk (1943), 276
    Lützen (1632), 104(table), 110
    Marengo (1800), 155fn
    Marne, First Battle of (1914), 161(table), 190
    Masurian Lakes (1914), 161(table). See also Tannenberg, Battle of (1914)
    Mollwitz (1741), 91
    Mons (1914), 160(table)
    Operation Michael (1918), 192, 192fn. See also Ludendorff, General Erich Friedrich, military ability
    Passchendaele (1917), 190
    Sedan (1870), 160(table), 177
    Somme (1916), 190, 204
    Verdun (1916–1917), 58, 177, 189, 190, 266

Waterloo (1815), 104(table), 126, 147, 154, 166
Ypres (1914, 1915), 190, 254
Zorndorf (1758), 126
Bavaria, 99, 108
Bavarian Alps, 31
Bayer (Bayer Leverkusen, pharmaceutical firm), 169
Bechstein, Helen, 254. See also Hitler, Adolf, psychiatric studies
Beck, Colonel-General Ludwig, 262, 281
Beethoven, Ludwig, 77fn, 275
Before the Storm (memoirs). See Dönhoff, Countess Marion
Belarus, 4
Belgium, 147, 160(table), 174, 262, 285
Belsen concentration camp, 242
Bendlerblock. See German army (after 1871), Bendlerblock (army headquarters)
Benedicta, Teresia of the Cross. See Stein, Edith (Teresia Benedicta of the Cross)
Bennett, Alan, (playwright), 122
Bennigsen, Count Levin von, 149–152, 152–155
Berchtesgaden, 254
Berlin, 4, 13, 15, 17, 22, 29, 31–33, 38, 95, 110, 112, 114, 124, 127, 131, 142, 146, 153, 169, 172, 175, 184, 193, 194, 209(table), 214, 254, 271, 277–284, 310, 315, 324. See also German army (after 1871), Bendlerblock (army headquarters)
Berlin, Isaiah, 335(notes)
Berlin Wall. See Germany, Reunification; Iron Curtain
Bernard of Clairvaux, Saint, 48. See also Crusades
Bethlehem, 53
Bialystok, 218, 227
Bielenberg, Christabel (writer), 274fn
Bismarck, Prince Otto von, 15, 38–39, 53, 88, 119, 160(table), 165, 167–169, 172–173, 258
Black Sea, 111, 191
Blomberg, Field Marshal Werner von, 208(table), 260–261
Blücher, Field Marshal G. L. von, 104(table), 147–148, 181
Bohemia, 108, 145
Böll, Heinrich (writer), 275–276
Bolshevikism. See Communism

Bormann, Martin, 255, 269, 269(photo), 277

Bormann notes (*Bormann-Vermerke*), 269–272. *See also* Hitler, Adolf, character

Boston (American city), 209

Boston (English seaport), 73

Boyer, Charles (actor), 154fn

Brahms, Johannes (composer), 270

Brandenburg, 33, 36, 104(table), 109(table), 110, 112, 119, 130, 234. *See also* East Prussia (Ostpreussen), union with Brandenburg; Hohenzollern dynasty

Braniewe. *See* Braunsberg

Brauchitsch, Field Marshal Walther von, 261fn

Braun, Eva, 349(notes). *See also* Fegelein, SS Captain Hermann; Hitler, Adolf, assassination attempts on

Braunsberg (Braniewe), 133, 158

Braunschweig, 31

Bremen, 73

Brest-Litovsk, Treaty of (1918). *See* Treaties, in passing, Brest-Litovsk (1918)

Brezhnev, Leonid, 15

Bristol (England), 316

British air force, 305, 306. *See also* Great Britain

British army, 40, 204, 245, 266fn, 287, 292fn, 315. *See also* Great Britain

Brussels, 160(table)

Buchenwald concentration camp, 242

Bulganin, Nikolai, 271fn

Burma, 123

Buruma, Ian (writer), 276

Butcher, Captain Harry C. (naval aide), 284fn


Cadinen (Kadyny), 163–164

Caesar, Julius, 71, 145

Calvin, John, 100fn, 108

Canada, 129

Canadian army, 266fn

Cannae, Battle of (216 B. C.). *See* Battles, in passing, Cannae (216 B. C.)

*Canterbury Tales. See* Chaucer

Carmelite order, 244, 247, 247fn. *See also* Auschwitz concentration camp, fiftieth anniversary of liberation; Stein, Edith (Teresia Benedicta of the Cross)

Carthage, 4

Casimir III, (the Great), King of Poland, 217

Catherine II, (the Great), Tsarina of Russia, 126, 128

Catherine Palace (St. Petersburg), 122fn, 292fn

Caucasus Mountains, 111

Chamberlain, Prime Minister Neville, 263

Chaplin, Charles (actor), 140

Charles V, Holy Roman emperor, 99

Charles XII, King of Sweden, 111, 265

Chaucer, 69–70, 77. *See also* Henry, earl of Derby (Henry IV, King of England); Teutonic Knights, Order of, *reyse*

Chelmno. *See* Kulm

Chernobyl, 6

Chernyakhovst. *See* Insterburg

China, 123

Christian IV, King of Denmark, 107

Christians, Friedrich (banker), 21

Christiansen, Eric (historian), 75

Churchill, Prime Minister Winston Spencer, 164, 174, 192fn, 266, 271, 274fn

Cistercian order, 33, 140. *See also* Germany, early history

Clausewitz, Lieutenant-Colonel von, 124–125, 150, 170, 262, 264, 265. *See also* Prussian army (before 1871)

Columbus, Christopher, 137

Communism, 1, 16, 20, 32, 97, 139, 234, 257, 258, 270, 271

*Conquest* (film). *See* Boyer, Charles; Garbo, Greta

Conrad of Mazovia, Duke, 24(table), 51–52

Constant, First Valet de Chambre of the Emperor Napoleon, 153. *See also* Napoleon Bonapart, Emperor of France, affairs

Copenhagen, 55fn

Copernicus, Nicolaus (Mikolaj Kopernik), 94, 96–100, 129, 163. *See also* Fauenburg

Corfu, 90–91

Courland. *See* Kurland

Crimea, 208(table)

*Critique of Pure Reason (Kritik des Reinen Vernunft). See* Kant, Emmanuel

*Crowning of a King, The. See* Zweig,
    Arnold (writer)
Crusades, 34, 46–53, 71–77
    decline, 50
    Eighth, 50
    finances, 49
    First, 47–48
    in Holy Land, 47, 76–77
    Iberian, 49–50
    justification, 48, 329(notes)
    Second, 47–48
    Seventh, 47
    Slavic, 51, 71–72–77. *See also* Teutonic
        Knights, Order of
Curaçao, 219fn
Czechoslovakia, 41, 86–87, 262, 292fn

Dachau concentration camp, 242, 314
Danish Straits, 9
Danish War (1864). *See* Wars, in passing,
    Danish (1864)
Danzig, 19, 24(table), 36, 65–69,
    68(photo), 71, 73, 74(photo), 77–78,
    87, 94, 108, 111, 128, 129, 201,
    208(table), 209(table), 241, 242, 251,
    287, 304, 305, 321, 326. *See also*
    Westerplatte garrison
*Das Rheingold. See* Wagner, Richard
    (composer)
Davout, Louis-Nicolas, Duke of
    Auerstädt, 146, 155
D day, Battle of (1944*). See* Battles, in
    passing, D day (1944)
Debina, p. 45
*Decline and Fall of the Roman Empire.*
    *See* Gibbon, Edward (historian)
de Gaulle, Charles, 14, 276fn
de Joinville, Jean (French crusader), 77
de Molay, Grand Master Jacques (Knights
    Templar), 63–64. *See also* Crusades;
    Philip IV, (the Fair), King of France
Denmark, xiv, 108, 160(table), 168, 252
Derby, Henry of (King Henry IV of
    England). *See* Henry, earl of Derby
    (King Henry IV of England). *See also*
    Chaucer; Shakespeare, William;
    Teutonic Knights, Order of, *reyse*
*De revolutionibus orbium coelestium*
    (*On the Revolution of the Heavenly*
    *Spheres*). *See* Copernicus, Nicolaus
*Der Spiegel* (magazine), vii
Deutsche Bank, 21, 88
Dickens, Charles (writer), 65
*Die Loreley. See* Heine, Heinrich (writer)

*Die Walküre. See* Wagner, Richard
    (composer)
*Die Zeit* (newspaper), 18, 322
Dominican order, 54, 72
*Don Quixote*, 65
Dönhoff, Countess Marion, 11, 18, 19, 37,
    88, 254, 287, 288, 319, 322–325,
    323(photo). *See also* East Prussia
    (Ostpreussen), flight of German
    population,
    W .W. II; Friedrichstein (estate);
    Prussia, perception of
Dönitz, Admiral Karl, 282, 292fn
Donne, John (poet), 93
Dostoyevsky, Fyodor (writer), 6
*Drang nach Osten* ("drive to the east"),
    33. *See also* Teutonic Knights, Order
    of, aggressiveness
Dresden, 145, 155
Dunkirk, Battle of (1940). *See* Battles, in
    passing, Dunkirk (1940)
Düsseldorf, 16, 17
Dvina River, 34

East Prussia (Ostpreussen), 16, 17(photo),
    33–38, 61, 118, 124, 127, 150,
    238(photo), 285
    destruction, W. W. II, 29, 45, 95, 99,
        120, 286–287, 308(photo)
    economy, 9, 43, 196, 201
    flight of German population, W. W. II,
        17–18, 289(photo), 292–299,
        296(photo), 299fn, 304–305
    geography, xiv, 16, 17(photo), 34, 44,
        54, 56, 121fn, 129, 167
    military tradition, 3, 61, 117–118, 169
    Napoleonic wars, 149–154
    nostalgia for, 36, 37, 41–42, 198,
        316–318, 324–325
    poverty of, 100, 112, 119, 131, 166,
        168, 200, 319
    relationship between German
        landlords and Polish workers, 101,
        129, 167
    union with Brandenburg, 108–114,
        109(table), 129, 130
    W. W. I, 175, 179–191
    W. W. II, 232, 235, 238(photo), 286–299,
        304–305–306, 308(photo)
    *See also* German army (after 1871);
        Hohenzollern dynasty; Königsberg;
        Prussia; Prussian army (before 1871);
        Teutonic Knights, Order of; West
        Prussia

Ehrenburg, Ilya (journalist), 285
Eichmann, Karl Adolf, Supreme group
    Fuährer, 247, 247fn
Einsatzkommando (SS), 250, 302
Einstein, Albert, 77fn
Eisenhower, General Dwight, 284fn, 310
Eisenstein, Sergei (film maker), 58–60,
    58fn, 330(notes)
Elbe River, 33, 48, 209(table), 287, 305,
    307, 310, 315
Elbing (Elblag), 96(photo), 105, 209(table),
    304
Elblag. See Elbing
Elizabeth, (Petrovna), Tsarina of Russia,
    14
Elizabeth Christine of Brunswick-
    Wolfenbüttel, Queen of Prussia, 125.
    See also Frederick II, (the Great),
    King of Prussia
Elizabethschrein (Marburg), 28–29
Engels, Friedrich, 201
Ereda concentration camp, 248, 250
Erfurt, 316
Estonia, 33, 71, 223, 248–250, 326
    Estonians as concentration camp
        guards, 250
Eylau, 140, 143
Eylau, Battle of (1807), 104(table), 133,
    141, 150–152, 151(photo), 154. See
    also Napoleon Bonapart, Emperor of
    France

Fainsod, Merle (historian), 270
Federal Republic of Germany (West
    Germany), 14, 17, 18, 31, 195, 214,
    317, 324
Fegelein, SS Captain Hermann,
    349(notes). See also Braun, Eva;
    Hitler, Adolf, assassination attempts
    on
Fellgiebel, General Erich, 255, 279
Ferdinand, Prince Louis of Prussia, 128
Ferdinand II, Holy Roman emperor, 107
Feuchtwanger, Siegfried von (grand
    master), 99
Final and Eternal Being. See Stein, Edith
    (Teresia Benedicta of the Cross)
Finckenstein (Kamieniec), 120,
    121(photo), 128, 129, 152,
    153(photo), 154, 154fn. See also
    Napoleon Bonapart, affairs
Finland, 110, 267
France, 34, 61, 108, 113, 114, 117, 124fn
    revolution of 1789, 87, 143

revolution of 1848, 166
war of 1870, 160(table), 168
W. W. I, 170, 174, 190
W. W. II, 233, 285
See also French army; French army
    units
François, General Hermann von, 183,
    185, 187, 188
Franco-Prussian War (1870). See Wars, in
    passing, Franco-Prussian (1870)
Frankfurt, 25, 271, 325, 326
Frauenburg (Frombork), 93–98, 94(photo),
    163
Frederick I (Barbarossa), Holy Roman
    emperor, 50
Frederick I, King of Prussia, 55fn,
    104(table), 109(table), 120–121,
    292fn
Frederick I, (the Winter King), King of
    Bohemia, 107
Frederick II, Holy Roman emperor, 50, 53
Frederick II , (the Great), King of Prussia,
    36, 39, 91, 95, 104(table), 109(table),
    113, 115, 118, 120–132, 124fn,
    128fn, 131(photo), 142, 143, 258,
    267, 276, 334–335(notes)
    character of, 124–126
    homosexuality, 125
    love of French literature and culture,
        124, 127
    managerial qualities, 128–129, 148
    military genius, 124–126, 132, 145
    relationship with Voltaire, 124, 124fn
    reliance on Junkers, 120, 125, 146, 258
    tomb, 14, 127(photo), 142
    See also East Prussia (Ostpreussen),
        military tradition; Prussia; Prussian
        army (before 1871)
Frederick III, Emperor of Germany,
    172
Frederick William, (the Great Elector),
    104(table), 109(table), 112–114,
    113(photo), 119, 130. See also
    Hohenzollern dynasty
Frederick William I, King of Prussia,
    109(table), 118fn, 120–123, 122fn.
    See also Prussian army (before 1871)
Frederick William II, King of Prussia,
    145
Frederick William III, 145fn, 146,
    155
Frederick William IV, King of Prussia, 10,
    160(table), 166

Freikorps. *See* German army (after 1871),
　　Freikorps
French army, 126, 143, 144, 146, 174, 204,
　　290, 315, 323
French army units
　　Grand Armée, 148, 150
　　V Corps, Grande Armée, 149fn
Freud, Sigmund, 193fn
Friedland, Battle of (1807), 104(table),
　　154–155. *See also* Napoleon
　　Bonapart, Emperor of France
Friedrichstein (estate), 18, 88, 287,
　　324–325. *See also* Dönhoff,
　　Countess Marion
Frisches Haff (Zalew Wisálany), 55fn, 93,
　　163, 209(table), 244, 299, 304, 326
Frisches Nehrung (Mierzeja Wisálana),
　　241, 248, 304
Fritsch, Colonel-General Werner Freiherr
　　von, 208(table), 260–262
Frombork. *See* Frauenburg
Fromm, General Friedrich, 279, 281
Furtwängler, Wilhelm (conductor),
　　27
Galicia, 190
Galileo, 98
Garbo, Greta (actress), 154fn
Garrison Church (Potsdam), 39–41,
　　42(photo). *See also* Potsdam
Gay, Peter (writer), 201
GDR. *See* German Democratic Republic
Gehlen, Reinhard, General, 268
George III, King of England, 122
George William, Elector of Brandenburg,
　　109(table), 112
Georgia (Russia), 4
German air force, 155, 156(photo), 243,
　　282
German army (after 1871), 12, 37, 41,
　　41(photo), 46, 78–80, 88, 95, 166,
　　238–239(photos), 259fn, 259–263,
　　305–308, 308(photo)
　　Bendlerblock (army headquarters), 278,
　　　281, 282(photo), 284
　　Freikorps, 233
　　general staff, 62, 147–148, 148fn,
　　　169–170, 174, 180, 191, 262, 264,
　　　272
　　Landwehr (reserve army), 169, 186
　　oath, 258, 261–262, 262fn, 287
　　officer corps, 166–167
　　opinion of Weimar Republic, 203
　　preventative war as theory, 34, 53,
　　　266–268

rearmament, 261
two-front war, 132, 170, 174–175, 194,
　　220, 266fn
W. W. I, 173–175, 179–194
W. W. II, 232–240, 264–268, 271–277,
　　288–299, 301–312
*See also* Hitler, Adolf: attitude towards
　　officer corps, effect on aristocrats,
　　effect on army officers, obstinacy;
　　Panzer veteran (anonymous);
　　Prussia, perception of; Prussian
　　army (before 1871); Teutonic
　　Knights, Order of, effect on later
　　generations
German army (before 1871). *See* Prussian
　　army (before 1871)
German army units
　　Eighth Army (1918), 175, 180, 182,
　　　183, 186
　　First Tank Division (1941), 232, 234
　　Fusilier Regiment von Bülow (1758),
　　　126
　　I Corps (1914), 183
　　Leibstandarte Adolf Hitler (LAH,
　　　1945), 307–308
　　Sixth Army (1943), 272, 273, 275, 276
　　Sixth Panzer Division (1945), 311
　　XX Corps (1914), 180, 186
German Democratic Republic (GDR), 31,
　　38–41, 90, 95, 171, 193, 284, 318,
　　318fn, 319, 320
*Germania* (statue), 26, 27(photo)
German Imperial Bank, 197
German navy, 172, 243, 287, 312, 316
German parliament (Reichstag), 40, 169,
　　208(table), 254, 320
German-Soviet Nonaggression Pact
　　(1939). *See* Treaties, in passing,
　　German-Soviet Nonaggression Pact
　　(1939)
Germany, vii, 9, 18, 31, 35, 49, 87, 91, 99,
　　107–108, 117–118, 133, 168–169,
　　182, 313, 317
　　anti-Semitism, 246, 274, 317
　　early history, 33, 48, 51, 53
　　expansionist tendencies, 5, 33, 38, 51,
　　　53
　　extremist groups, 37, 38
　　immigrant workers, 27, 38, 322–323
　　Napoleonic wars, effect on, 146–147
　　reunification, 17, 36, 318, 324
　　revival of nationalism, 15
　　revolutions of 1848, 166
　　Second Reich, 166–168

Third Reich, 40, 46
Weimar Republic, 200–203, 204,
208(table), 321–323
Gestapo, 281
Ghent, 70
Gibbon, Edward (historian), 266
Glasnost, 6
Gnewin (Gniew), 56
Gniew. *See* Gnewin
Goebbels, Josef, 40, 124, 255, 258, 267,
271fn, 276, 278, 290, 310
Goerlitz, Walter (historian), 193, 261
Goethe, Johann Wolfgang von (writer), 21,
155, 184
Goltz, Field Marshal Colmar von der, 167
Gorbachev, Mikhail, 20
Göring, Hermann, 255, 258, 260, 275,
276, 277, 282
Grass, Günter (writer), vii, 42, 65, 67,
67fn, 242, 267, 275
Graudenz (Grudziadz), 54–55
Great Britain, 61, 66, 69, 71, 117, 142,
154, 166, 267–268. *See also* British
air force; British army
Great Elector, The. *See* Frederick
William, (the Great Elector)
Grodno, 218
Gros, Antoine (painter), 141, 151(photo)
Gross Pötzdorf (estate), 195–200,
200(photo)
Grosse Werder, 105–107, 110–111
Grote, Count Otto Friedrich Wilhelm,
204–205, 267, 305–312, 315–319,
325–326, 326(photo). *See also* East
Prussia (Ostpreussen), flight of
German population, W. W. II; Hitler,
Adolf: effect on common people,
oratory; Jungvolk; Varchentine
(estate)
Grudziadz. *See* Graudenz
Gruhn, Erna (second wife of Werner von
Blomberg), 260
Grünwald, 81–82, 85–86
Grünwald, Battle of (1410), 24(table),
81–84, 82(photo), 85(photo), 86, 99,
167, 190. *See also* Lithuania,
conflicts with Teutonic Knights;
Poland, conflicts with Teutonic
Knights; Teutonic Knights, Order of,
order falters
Grzegorczyk, Józef (politician), 214fn
Guderian, Colonel-General Heinz, 233,
236, 263, 264, 265, 266, 271, 272,
276, 276fn, 277, 311

Gulag Archipelago, The. *See*
Solzhenitsyn, Aleksandr
Gulf of Finland, 33, 53
Gulyga, Arsenij (professor), 4, 14
Gumbinnen, Battle of (1914). *See* Battles,
in passing, Gumbinnen (1914)
Gustavus II, Adolphus, King of Sweden,
104(table), 107–112
Gypsies, 243

Habermas, Jürgen (historian), 38
Hadrian's Wall, 34
Halder, General Franz, 256, 261fn, 263,
283
Hamburg, xiv, 18, 145, 321–322
Hannibal, 145, 185
Hanover, 17, 72, 122, 182, 183
Hanseatic League, 10, 32, 55, 67, 73. *See
also* Teutonic Knights, Order of:
amber trade, as businessmen
Hart, Liddell (historian), 183
Havel River, 274
Hecht, Ben (writer), 38
Heilsberg (Lidzbark Warmináski),
98(photo), 101(photo)
*Heimat*, 15–16, 18, 21
Heine, Heinrich (writer), 27
Heinrich, Willi (writer), 275
Heirl, A. (painter), 308(photo)
Henry, earl of Derby (King Henry IV of
England), 24(table), 69–77, 76(photo),
83
*Henry IV. See* Shakespeare, William
Henry IV, King of England. *See* Henry,
earl of Derby (King Henry IV of
England)
Henry VIII, King of England, 100
Henry of Saxony, (the Lion), 48, 307
Herder, Johan Gottfried (philosopher), 2
Hess, Rudolf, 257, 258
Hesse, 31
Heydrich, Reinhard, 247
Himmler, Heinrich, 62, 242, 247, 255,
259, 259fn, 260, 271, 276. *See also*
Schutzstaffel (SS)
Hindenburg, Field Marshal Paul von, 40,
115–116, 118–119, 161(table), 165,
181, 188, 194(photo), 208(table), 258,
259, 260
character, 30, 186, 187, 192
early career, 182
funeral, 29, 198
military ability, 182–183, 185, 192,
340(notes)

opinion of Hitler, 202
opinion of Kaiser Wilhelm II , 118–119,
    193, 260
senility, 192, 202
tombs, 29–30, 30(photo), 177
*See also* German army (after 1871);
    Hitler, Adolf; Ludendorff, General
    Erich Friedrich; Tannenberg, Battle
    of (1914)
Hindenburg, Oskar von, 116fn, 202
Hitler, Adolf, 12, 16, 25, 36, 40, 63, 88,
    124–125, 148, 171, 173, 177, 202,
    204, 213, 216, 231, 234, 253, 292fn,
    309, 319, 323, 324
    anti-Semitism of, 173, 247, 270,
    assassination attempts on, 3, 15, 256,
        277–283, 209(table), 280(photo),
        349(notes)
    attitude towards officer corps, 258–261,
        272
    attitude toward Stalin and Russia,
        263fn, 270
    beer hall putsch, 202
    character, 257, 269–271, 276, 276fn
    drug addiction, 275, 282
    early career, 253–254, 258, 271
    effect on aristocrats, 205, 206fn
    effect on army officers, 205, 261, 261fn
    effect on common people, 204–205
    headquarters, in passing:
        Wolfsschlucht (Wolf's Gorge), 254;
        Werwolf (Werewolf), 254
    invasion of Russia, 142, 263
    irresolution of, 264, 271, 276
    *Mein Kampf*, 256, 257
    nerves, 258, 263, 345(notes)
    obstinacy, 264, 276, 286
    oratory, 205–206, 206fn, 258,
    psychiatric studies of, 254, 254fn
    as strategist, 263- 265, 276; 286–287
    temper tantrums, 256, 263, 275, 277,
        282–283
    vegetarianism, 270, 275
    von Hindenburg funeral, 28–29, 198
    Wolfsschanze (Wolf's Lair), 209(table),
        254–256, 264, 266, 268–272,
        269(photo), 273, 275–283,
        278(photo), 280(photo)
    *See also* German army (after 1871);
        Grote, Count Otto Friedrich
        Wilhelm; Stalingrad, Battle of
        (1943); Panzer veteran (anonymous),
        effect of Hitler's oratory
Hitler (Schicklgruber), Alois, 253

Hitler Youth, 320
Hoechst (Hoechst Dyeworks AG,
    chemical firm), 169
Hofbräuhaus (munich), 254
Hoffmann, General Max von, 180–186,
    192, 192fn, 340(notes). *See also*
    Tannenberg, Battle of (1914); Zweig,
    Arnold (writer)
Hohenzollern dynasty, 30, 55fn, 99, 101,
    108, 109(table), 108–114, 118–121,
    121fn, 128, 166, 168, 173, 182, 260.
    *See also* Albrecht of Brandenburg-
    Anspach (Hohenzollern), duke of
    Prussia; East Prussia (Ostpreussen),
    union with Brandenburg
Hohoenloe, Prince Frederick Ludwig,
    145fn
Holbein, Hans the Younger (painter),
    74(photo)
Holleben, Klaus von, 170–172, 171(photo)
Holocaust, in passing, 221, 244, 246, 248,
    274, 323
Holy Roman Empire, 108, 110, 110(table),
    121, 121fn, 126
Hospital of St. John, Order of, 49, 50. *See
    also* Crusades
Huelle, Pawel (writer), 67fn
Hull (English seaport), 73
Hungary, 41, 251, 265

India, 257
Innocent IV, Pope, 24(table)
Insterburg (Chernyakhovst), 19, 180
Ireland, 105, 107, 117–118, 166, 178,
    229fn
Iron Curtain, 36, 41, 86, 129, 318, 324
Italy, 265, 324
Itkutsk, 11
Ivanov, Yuri (writer), 18, 20, 20fn
Jadwiga, Queen of Poland, 83
Jagiello, Wladyslaw, Grand Duke of
    Lithuania, 24(table), 83–84
James, William (philosopher), 62
Japan, 219fn
Jaspers, Karl (philosopher), 246, 262fn
Jefferson, President Thomas, 320
Jena, Battle of (1806). *See* Battles, in
    passing, Jena (1806)
Jerusalem, 48, 50, 51, 53, 64, 66, 247fn
Jews, in passing, 54, 69, 87, 149, 185, 197,
    217, 218, 220–222, 221fn, 228,
    229(photo), 243, 244, 247–248, 252,
    258, 270, 271, 273–274, 301, 309.
    *See also* Auschwitz concentration

camp; Hitler, Adolf, anti-Semitism
of; Kiersztowski, Aronek (Walter
Kerr); Poland: anti-semitism, anti-
Semitism as quasi-official policy;
Stutthof concentration camp

Jodl, Field Marshal Alfred, 29, 253, 255,
263, 266, 276

John of Gaunt (English nobleman), 70–71

John XXII, Pope, 72

John Paul II, Pope, 165, 165(photo), 213,
228

Johnson, President Lyndon, 135

Jomini, Baron Antoine-Henri, 150

Jonestown, 309

Josephine, Empress of France, 146

Joyce, James (writer), 665

Jungvolk, 307, 311, 319

Junkers, Prussian, 30, 86, 289
   character of, 25,88, 117–120, 137, 152,
   155, 163, 166–167
   Hitler assassination attempt,
   15
   opinion of Bismarck, 168
   opinion of Nazis, 88, 148, 203–204,
   259–261
   oppression of Poles, 101, 167, 201
   origin of class, 87–88, 91
   perception of, 88, 201, 326
   role in Prussian army, 119–120, 123,
   144, 146, 147, 169, 258
   Weimar period, 200–201, 203
   See also East Prussia (Ostpreussen);
   German army (after 1871); Hitler,
   Adolf; Hohenzollern dynasty;
   Prussian army (before 1871);
   Teutonic Knights, Order of

Kadavergehorsam (cadaver obedience),
118

Kadyny. See Cadinen

Kalinin, Mikhail Ivanovich, 1, 15, 19

Kaliningrad. See Königsberg

Kaliningrad Cultural Foundation, 18

Kaliningrad Oblast, 4, 33, 321

Kaliningradskaya Pravda (newspaper), 21

Kalinnikov, Leonard (professor), 137–139,
138(photo)

Kamieniec. See Finckenstein

Kant, Immanuel, 2, 3, 4, 10, 11, 14, 15,
20, 77fn, 126, 127fn, 136–139, 167,
335(notes). See also Kalinnikov,
Leonard (professor); Königsberg

Kapp putsch, 202

Karajan, Herbert von (conductor), 27

Kazakhstan, 3, 19

Keitel, Field Marshal Wilhelm, 29, 255,
276, 279, 280

Kennan, George, 95

Kessler, Count Harry (diplomat), 202

Ketrzyn. See Rastenburg

Khrushchev, Nikita, 268, 270fn

Kielce, 227

Kiersztowski, Aronek (Walter Kerr), 211,
213–224, 215(photo), 220(photo),
241, 246(photo)
   after liberation, 227–228, 313–314
   attitude toward Poles, 213–214, 217,
   221, 227–228, 301–304
   childhood, 214–217
   as concentration camp inmate,
   248–258, 299–302
   death march, 299–304
   early days of W. W. II, 218–222
   parents, 214–216,218–224, 220(photo)
   siblings, 215, 218, 220 (photo),
   222–223, 248–250
   See also Poland, anti-semitism;
   Stutthof concentration camp;
   Suwalki

Kiev, 13, 208(table)

Klitzing family (Anta, Dorothee, Hans
von), 292–299. See also East Prussia
(Ostpreussen), flight of German
population, W. W. II

Klitzing, Hans Ulich von, 290–291, 299

Kluge, Field Marshal Günther von, 279,
283

Knox, Major Alfred, 184, 186–189. See
also Tannenberg, Battle of (1914)

Koch, Gauleiter Erich, 292fn. See also
Amber Room

Kohl, Chancellor Helmut, 5, 14

Kolbe, Maximilian, 54

Königsberg (Kaliningrad), vii, 1–22,
2(photo), 36, 52, 55fn, 73, 77, 77fn,
78, 87, 93, 98, 101, 110, 120, 121,
126, 133–136, 137(photo), 140, 146,
152, 155, 167, 169, 180, 184,
209(table), 214, 231, 235, 304, 311,
316, 321, 324, 326
   capture during W. W. II, 1, 3, 9, 10, 12,
   21, 134, 135(photo), 136, 287,
   288(photo), 289(photo), 292fn
   deportation of native Germans, 3, 10
   destruction of German artifacts by
   Russians, 10
   economic collapse, 6–8, 7(photo), 9,
   321

isolation, 4, 127, 133
lawlessness, 5, 6–8, 8(photo), 21,
135–136, 156–157, 158(photo),
321
missionaries in, 19, 155–156,
157(photo)
proposed free trade zone, 18, 19, 21
public places: cathedral, 3, 15, 20, 135,
139, 155, 156(photo); Friedrich
Engels Sports Center, 8; Gamal
Abdel Nasser Park, 8; Hansaring, 15;
Hermann-Göring Strasse, 15; House
of the Soviets, 11, 12(photo); Lenin
Prospekt, 5; Lutheran Kreuzkirche,
10; Mira Prospekt, 7; Moskwa Hotel,
7, 13–14; Neue Königsthor, 10,
11(photo); October Revolution
Housing Estates, 8, 11; Paradeplatz,
11, 12, 20; Ploshchad Pobedy (Adolf-
Hitler-Platz), 2, 15; Reichplatz, 15;
royal palace, 3, 11, 292fn;
Steindamm, 15
role as Soviet base, 1, 5, 9
tourists in, 13–18, 155, 156(photo)
Königgratz, Battle of (1866). See
Battles, in passing, Könnigratz
(1866)
Kosáciuszko, Thadeusz, 130
Kovno, 219fn, 232
Knights Templar, Order of, 24(table), 49,
63. See also Crusades
Knipode, Winrich von (grand master), 81,
99
Koblenz (Coblenz), 316
Kopernik, Mikolaj. See Copernicus,
Nicolaus
Kraj Zapuszczanski ("the territory behind
the virgin forest"), 212
Kraków, 100
Krasinski Palace (Warsaw), 130
Krawczynski brothers, 218, 220(photo),
221. See also Kiersztpwski, Aronek
(Walter Kerr), early days of W. W. II
Kritik des Reinen Vernunft (Critique of
Pure Reason). See Kant,
Emmanuel
Krolewiec. See Königsberg
Kulm (Chelmno), 54
Küng, Hans (theologian), 217fn
Kurland (Courland), 191, 286
Kursk, Battle of (1943). See Battles, in
passing, Kursk (1943)
Kutuzov, Prince Mikhail, 11
Kwidzyn. See Marienwerder

Landwehr (reserve army). See German
army (after 1871), Landwehr (reserve
army)
Lannes, Jean, Duke of Montebello, 154,
155
Latvia (Livonia), 4, 24(table), 33, 61, 99,
208(table), 110, 111, 286, 326
Lauenburg (Lebork), 304
Lawrence, D. H. (writer), 280
League of Nations, 201
Lebensraum (living space), 256, 283
Lebork. See Lauenburg
le Carré, John (writer), 32
Lehi (terrorist group), 229fn. See also
Stern, Avraham
Lehndorff, Heini, 254
Leipzig, 215
Leipzig affair (1936), 78
Lenin, Vladimir Ilich, 1, 281
Leningrad. See St. Petersburg
Lidzbark Warminski. See Heilsberg
Liège, 160(table), 174, 181
Linz, 253
Lithuania, 4, 6, 19, 24(table), 110, 133
conflicts with Teutonic Knights, 33,
35, 52, 69, 71–77, 83–84, 142, 169,
212
Lithuanians as concentration camp
guards, 220, 222–223
"Little Lithuania", 4–5
W. W. II, 31, 219, 219fn, 220, 228, 250
Livländische Reimchronik (medieval
chronicle), 43, 61, 62. See also
Teutonic Knights, Order of
Livonia. See Latvia
London, 142, 215
Lorelei, Rock of (Rhine), 26–27
Louis X, King of France, 48
Louis XIV, King of France, 120
Louise of Mecklenburg-Strelitz, Queen of
Prussia, 146. See also Frederick
William III, King of Prussia
Lübeck, 33, 49, 56, 73, 148
Ludendorff, General Erich Friedrich, vii,
119, 161(table), 194(photo),
108(table)
character, 181–183, 276fn
beer hall putsch, 202
Eastern Front, 181–191
funeral, 29
later career, 202–203
military ability, 181–182, 191–192,
192fn
opinion of Hindenburg, 192

opinion of Hitler, 202
resignation and flight, 193
Tannenberg, Battle of (1914), 186–189,
    192
Western Front, 191–194, 340(notes)
See also German army (after 1871);
    Hindenburg, Field Marshal Paul von;
    Hitler, Adolf; Junkers, Prussian,
    character of; Tannenberg, Battle of
    (1914)
Ludendorff, Margarethe, 183, 202
Lufthansa (airline), 321
Luftwaffe. See German air force
Luther, Martin, 33, 98, 100, 100fn
Lützen, Battle of (1632). See Battles, in
    passing, Lützen (1632)
Luxembourg, 285
Lynn (English seaport), 73

Maastricht, Treaty of (1991). See Treaties,
    in passing, Maastricht (1991)
Macaulay, Thomas (historian), 124fn
McCarthyism (USA), 246
Magdeburg, 32–33, 38, 108
Malbork. See Marienburg
Malchin, 308
Mann, Golo, 195
Mann, Thomas (writer), 14
Mansfeld, Count Ernest von, 107
Manstein, Field Marshal Erich von, 231,
    232, 234, 256, 263–265, 274fn,
    275fn, 276
Marburg, 28–31
Maria Theresa, archduchess of Austria,
    128n
Marienburg (Malbork), 24(table), 56,
    59(photo), 64, 67, 73, 83, 84, 99,
    161(table), 181, 183, 209(table)
    damage in W. W. II, 57, 99
    loss to Poland (1466), 57, 86–87
    restoration after W. W. II, 10, 56–57, 62
    siege after Grünwald, 84
Marienwerder (Kwidzyn), 54
Mar La Plata (ship), 250
Marne, First Battle of (1914). See Battles,
    in passing, Marne, First Battle of
    (1914)
Marshall, General George C., 265
Marx, Karl, 20
Massalki, Bishop Ignacy, 130
Masuria, 17, 180, 211
Masurian Lakes, Battle of (1914). See
    Battles, in passing, Masurian Lakes
    (1914)

Matejko, Jan (painter), 83–84, 85(photo),
    96
Matutshkin, Vladimir (administrator), 21
Maximilian I, Duke and Elector of
    Bavaria, 107
Mazuw, SS officer, 310
Medvedev, N. A., (administrator), 20
Mein Kampf. See Hitler, Adolf, Mein
    Kampf
Meisel, SS concentration camp officer,
    300–304
Meissner, Otto von, 202
Memelland, 208(table), 209(table), 262,
    265
Memel River (Niemen River), 34, 35, 52,
    71, 126, 154, 167, 170, 174, 218, 231
Mendelssohn, Felix (composer), 318fn
Mendelssohn, Moses (philosopher), 137,
    318fn
Metternich, Prince Clemens von,
    160(table), 166
Meuse River,. 311
Mierzeja Wisálana. See Frisches Nehrung
Milton, John (poet), 65, 330(notes)
Molière, (Jean-Baptiste Poquelin, called),
    127
Mollwitz, Battle of (1741). See Battles, in
    passing, Mollwitz (1741)
Moltke, Field Marshal J. L. Count von
    (Moltke the Younger), 174, 182, 183,
    190
Moltke, General Field Marshal Helmuth
    Count von (Moltke the Elder), 169,
    175, 264, 268
Mons, Battle of (1914). See Battles, in
    passing, Mons (1914)
Moravia, 87
Morell, Dr. Theo, 256, 275, 282
Moscow, 4, 111, 128, 139, 143, 184, 213,
    232, 233, 236, 237, 272, 276, 292fn
Moscow News (newspaper), 9
Munich, 16, 219, 254, 271
Murat, Marshal Joachim, 151
Muschaken (Muszaki), 188
Mussolini, Benito, 281, 283
Muszaki. See Muschaken

Napoleon III, Emperor of France, 153fn,
    160(table), 168
Napoleon Bonapart, Emperor of France,
    104(table), 123, 126, 141–155, 218,
    231, 232, 237, 240, 272

affairs, 152–154. *See also* Finckenstein (Kamieniec); Walewska, Countess Marie
character, 141–144, 146fn
coronation, 144
Eylau, Battle of, 150–152, 151(photo)
Friedland, Battle of, 154–155
invasion of Russia, 141, 265
literature on, 143, 143fn
military genius, 143–144, 150
youth, 123, 143
Narody Kommissariat Vnutrennikh (NKVD), 304
National Democratic Party (National Populist Party), Poland, 217
National Museum (Warsaw), 83
NATO. *See* North Atlantic Treaty Orgnization
Neckar River, 31
Negenborn, Katharina von, 289–290, 291(photos),313, 314(photo). *See also* East Prussia (Ostpreussen), flight of German population
Neidenburg ( Nidzica), 47(photo), 180, 187
Nero, 173, 270
Netherlands, 161(table), 203fn, 245, 262, 285
Neubrandenburg, 307
Neudeck, 115–116, 117(photo), 120, 128, 202, 208(table). *See also* Hindenburg, Field Marshal Paul von
*New Times* (newspaper), 5
Newton, Issac (scientist), 217
New York City, 32
Ney, Marshal Michel, 149, 151, 152, 155
Nicholas II, Tsar of Russia, 172, 184, 191, 194
Nicolaievich, Nicholas, Grand Duke of Russia, 184, 190
Nidzica. *See* Neidenburg
Niemen River. *See* Memel River
Nietzsche, Friedrich, 61, 127fn, 148fn, 270
Night Watch. *See* Rembrandt, Harmenszoon van Rijn
Nile River, 106
NKVD. *See* Narody Kommissariat Vnutrennikh
Nogat River, 56, 62, 93, 105–106
Nordenburg, 140
Normans, 34, 118
North Atlantic Treaty Organization (NATO), 130
North Korea, 123

North Sea, 31, 191, 245
Notre Dame Cathedral (Paris), 63, 144
Nuremberg, 99, 270
Nuremberg War Crimes Tribunal, 148, 201, 247fn, 262fn, 266, 268. *See also* German army (after 1871), preventative war as theory
Oder River, 33, 34, 41, 51, 174, 307
*Odessa File, The* (film), 250
Olsztyn. *See* Allenstein
Operation Barbarossa (1941), 264, 266
Operation Michael (1918). *See* Battles, in passing, Operation Michael (1918)
Operation Valkyrie (1944), 254
*Ordensstaat*, 52
Orlau (Ortowo), 186
Ortowo. *See* Orlau
Orwell, George (writer), 299
Osiander, Andreas, 99, 101
Osterode (Ostróda), 294
*Ostkrieg* (war in the East), 118
Ostpreussen. *See* East Prussia (Ostpreussen)
Ostróda. *See* Osterode
Otto I, (the Great), Holy Roman emperor, 32
Oxenstierna, Count Axel Greve, 107
Oxford (England), 316

Palatinate, 28. *See also* Rhineland
Palestine, 219fn, 229fn
Paneriai execution site, Lithuania, 221
Pan-German nationalism, 2
Panzer veteran (anonymous), 205–206, 232–240, 234(photo), 238–239(photos), 259
advance into Russia, 233, 235–237, 240
background, 233
effect of Hitler's oratory, 205–206
fate of Russian prisoners, 233–235
opinion of Hitler, 259, 273, 279
as prisoner of war, 315–316
Stalingrad, Battle of, 238–239(photos), 240, 272–273
tactics, 234–236
Pappenheim, Count Gottfried Heinrich, 107
*Paradise Lost. See* Milton, John (poet)
Paris, 66, 142, 152, 175, 213, 215, 279
Passchendaele, Battle of (1917). *See* Battles, in passing, Passchendaele (1917)
*Patriotic Gore. See* Wilson, Edmund

Patton, General George, 170, 315
Paulus, Field Marshal Friedrich, 273
Perestroika, 6
Persia, 154
Peter I, (the Great), Tsar of Russia, 122fn
Peter III, Tsar of Russia, 14, 125, 126
Philip IV, (the Fair), King of France,
    24(table), 50, 63–64
Pilate, Pontius, 245
Pillau (Baltijsk), 9, 20, 93
Pilsudski, Marshal Jósef Kiemens, 216
Plato, 137
Plievier, Theodor (writer), 275
Poland, 9, 18, 22, 24(table), 31, 33, 35–38,
    41, 52, 54, 66, 105, 129–130, 133,
    142, 157, 177, 184, 190, 208(table),
    211, 228, 233, 244, 262, 267, 299fn,
    321, 326
  anti-Semitism, 216–218, 226–228, 247,
    292fn, 317
  anti-Semitism as quasi-official policy,
    1930s, 216–217
  casualty figures, W. W. II, 79
  conflicts with Teutonic Knights,
    83–85, 95, 98
  conflict with Sweden, 111
  economy, 27–28, 31–32, 128, 224,
    317–318
  kingdom of, 217
  Napoleonic wars, 148–149, 149fn
  nobles of, 128
  Partitions, 36, 217: First (1772), 95,
    104(table), 128, 128fn, 130; Second
    (1793), 104(table), 129; Third (1795),
    104(table), 129, 146
  Polish Corridor, 36, 79, 128, 195, 201,
    290, 300
  pollution, 56, 211
  program of historic renovations, 10, 56,
    62
  Reformation, 98
  relations with Germany, 124–125, 130
  relations with Russia, 128–130
  resettlement policies towards Germans
    after W. W. II, 95
  treatment of German territories after
    W. W. II, 10, 36, 95, 163, 179
Polish army, 69, 70(photo), 78–80, 149fn,
    218. See also Westerplatte garrison
    (Danzig)
Polish Corridor. See Poland, Polish
    Corridor
Polityka (newspaper), 38

Pomerania, 36, 71, 87, 119, 209(table),
    290, 300
Porphyria (disease), 122
Porsche, Ferdinand (engineer), 89
Portugal, 87
Potsdam, 14, 39, 41(photo), 124fn, 142,
    233, 239(photo), 260, 313. See also
    Garrison Church (Potsdam)
Pregel River (Pregolya River), 2, 135, 140
Pregolya River. See Pregel River
Prittwitz, General Maximilian von,
    160(table), 174, 180–181. See also
    Tannenberg, Battle of (1914)
Prokofiev, Sergey (composer), 58
Prussia
  crisis of 1848, 166
  decline of Frederician army and
    kingship, 142–143, 144–146
  defeat by Napoleon, 142
  ethos created by Order of Teutonic
    Knights, 34–35, 117–118
  Frederician Prussia 120–132
  parliamentary disputes, 1860s, 169
  perception of, 30–31, 88, 122, 130–132,
    171, 201, 234, 318, 324
  reactionary Metternichian period, 166
  reform 1807–1813, 146–148
  revival of interest in, 14–15, 317
  Second Reich (unification of Germany
    under Prussian kingship), 166, 168
  tradition of public service, discipline,
    117–118, 169
  union of Brandenburg and East Prussia,
    108–110, 109(table)
  See also East Prussia (Ostpreussen);
    German army (after 1871);
    Hohenzollern dynasty; Prussian
    army (before 1871); Teutonic
    Knights, Order of; West Prussia
Prussian army (before 1871), 118–120,
    123, 125–132, 126fn, 142, 144–149,
    169
  genesis of general staff, 62, 147–148,
    169
  See also Frederick II, (the Great), King
    of Prussia; German army (after
    1871); Teutonic Knights, Order of
Prussians (clan, Balts), 46, 52–53
Pushkin, Aleksandr (writer), 11

Radzyn Chelminski. See Rehden
Rangsdorf aerodrome (Berlin), 279
Rastenburg (Ketrzyn), 23–254
Rauschen (Svetlogorsk), 14

*Reclining Woman. See* Avery, Milton
Red Cross, The, 306
Reformation, The, 98, 99
Rehden (Radzyn Chelminski), 54, 55(photo)
Reichstag. *See* German parliament
Remarque, Erich Maria (writer), 193fn
Rembrandt, Harmenszoon van Rijn, 83
Rennenkampf, General Pavel, 160(table), 180–181, 184–186, 188–190. *See also* Tannenberg, Battle of (1914)
REP. *See* Republikaner (REP, political party)
Republikaner (REP, political party), 320
*Reyse. See* Teutonic Knights, Order of, reyse
Rhineland, 17, 46, 72, 262. *See also* Palatinate
Rhine River, xiv, 25, 26, 31, 146, 315, 316
Ribbentrop, Foreign Minister Joachim von, 255, 282
Richard I, (the Lion-Heart), King of England, 50
*Richard II. See* Shakespeare, William
Richard II, King of England, 75
Richelieu, Cardinal Armand-Jean du Plessis, 107
Richthofen, Baron Manfred von, 280
Rieben concentration camp, 300, 302
Riefenstahl, Leni (film maker), 205, 270
Riga, 111, 191, 208(table), 321
Riga River, 235
*Rise and Fall of the Third Reich, The. See* Shirer, William (writer)
Roehm, Ernst, 283, 283fn. *See also* Sturmabteilung (SA)
Romania, 265
Rome, 53, 87, 173, 270
Rommel, Field Marshal Erwin, 264, 279, 279fn, 283, 311
Roon, Count Theodor Albrecht von, 170
Roosevelt, President Franklin D., 271
Rosenberg, Alfred, 258
Rüdesheim, 25–26
Ruhr, 168, 323
Rundstedt, Field Marshal Gerd von, 279
Russia, 8, 9, 10, 21, 31, 35, 69, 170, 208(table), 219, 265, 299fn, 321, 326
conflicts, seventeenth century, 110, 113
partitions of Poland, 128–130
relations with Poland, 79, 218–219
W. W. I, 174, 180–191

W. W. II, 79, 218–219, 232–240, 264–268, 271–277, 286–299, 301–312
Russian army (before 1916), 126, 150–152, 154–155, 174–175. *See also* Eylau, Battle of (1807); Freidland, Battle of (1807)
Russian army (Red), 1, 3, 5, 9, 10, 13, 13(photo), 18, 36, 95, 97, 99, 196, 209(table), 235–236, 237fn, 243, 255, 265, 270fn, 285–287, 292–299, 303, 304fn, 310. *See also* Stalingrad, Battle of (1943)
Russian army units
    Eleventh Army of the Guards (1993), 9
    First Army (1914), 180, 185, 190
    Second Army (1914), 180–189
Russian navy, 5, 6, 9, 14, 21, 22, 93
Russian navy units, Baltic Fleet (1993), 6, 9
Russian Orthodoxy, revival of, 155–156, 157(photo)

SA. *See* Sturmabteilung
Saalfeld, 290
Saar, 168
St. Mary's Cathedral (Danzig), 69, 70(photo)
St. Mary's Hospital (Acre), 50
St. Petersburg (Leningrad), 4, 15, 18, 19, 55fn, 122fn, 209 (table), 213, 233, 235, 236, 237, 248, 250, 272, 292fn
Salza, Hermann von (grand master), 50, 99
Samland, 24(table)
Samsanov, General Aleksandr, 180–189. *See also* Tannenberg, Battle of (1914)
Sans Souci Palace (Potsdam), 14, 39, 127(photo), 127fn, 130
Sardinia, 276
Saxony, 31, 72
Scharfeter, SS concentration camp officer, 249
Scharnhorst, Gerhard Johann David von, 104(table), 147–148, 151, 169, 181. *See also* German army (after 1871), general staff; Prussian army (before 1871), gensis of general staff
Schiller, Friedrich (writer), 10, 31, 327(notes)
*Schindler's List* (movie), 58, 228, 322
*Schleswig-Holstein* (battleship), 78, 79(photo)

Schleswig-Holstein (province), xiv, 108, 160(table), 168, 270
Schlieffen, Count Alfred von, 148fn, 170, 174, 175, 180–181, 185, 187, 192, 264, 267. See also Schlieffen Plan
Schlieffen Plan, 160(table), 161(table), 174, 181, 190. See also Schlieffen, Count Alfred von
Schlobitten (Stobity), 44(photo)
Schmidt, Chancellor Helmut, 18
Schmidt, Hans (missionary), 19
Schönhausen (estate), 38
Schopenhauer, Arthur (philosopher), 270
Schubert, Franz (composer), 27
Schulenburg, Count von, 89–92, 318–319
Schulenburg, Field Marshal Adolf Friedrich von der, 91
Schutzstaffel (SS), 37, 62, 242, 243, 247, 247fn, 248, 256, 260, 261, 273, 274–275, 275fn, 279, 288, 293, 299–304, 308, 311–312, 348(notes). See also Einsatzkommando (SS)
Schwarzkopf, General H. Norman, 273
Sedan, Battle of (1870). See Battles, in passing, Sedan (1870)
Semenovich, Youain Mikolai, 286, 286(photo)
Semigallia, 24(table)
Sesupe, 71
Seven Years' War (1756–1763). See Wars, in passing, Seven Years' War (1756–1763)
Shakespeare, William, 70, 127
Shamir, Prime Minister Yitzhak, 229fn
Shawe-Taylor, Desmond (critic), 58
Shipov, Vitaly V., (politician), 20fn
Shirer, William (writer), 201, 242, 260
Shoshnikov, Colonel Viktor (police chief), 6, 8, 21
Siberia, 95, 219, 220, 224, 227, 228, 240, 304
Siemens (Siemens & Halske, electrical and telegraph firm), 169
Sigismund I, King of Poland, 101
Sigismund, John, Elector of Brandenburg, 108, 109(table), 110, 112, 114
Silesia, 10, 168, 211
Sokólka, 218, 219, 228
Soldau, 149
Solidarity (labor movement), 69
Solzhenitsyn, Aleksandr (writer), 6, 178, 185, 186, 287
Somme, Battle of (1916). See Battles, in passing, Somme (1916)

Spa, 193
Spain, 143, 252, 265, 266
Spartacists, 272
Speer, Albert, 269, 275
SS. See Schutzstaffel
Stalin, Joseph 3, 4, 8, 19, 133, 173, 246, 313
    invasion of Lithuania, 220
    invasion of Poland, 218
    purge of Red army, 59fn, 270, 270fn
    W. W. II, 257, 258, 262, 263fn, 265, 267, 268, 272, 276fn, 304
Stalingrad, Battle of (1942–1943), 208–209(tables), 238–239 (photos), 240, 268, 272–273, 275, 276, 287, 310, 315. See also Hitler, Adolf: obstinacy, as strategist; Panzer veteran (anonymous), Stalingrad, Battle of
Stauffenberg, Colonel Claus Philip Schenk von, 209(table), 253, 254, 255, 262, 277–283, 349(notes). See also German army (after 1871), Bendlerblock (army headquarters); Hitler, Adolf: assassination attempts on, Wolfsschanze (Wolf's Lair)
Stauffenberg, Countess Nina von, 283
Stein, Edith (Teresia Benedicta of the Cross), 247fn. See also Auschwitz concentration camp, fiftieth anniversary of liberation; Carmelite order
Steinort (estate), 254
Stern, Avraham (terrorist), 229fn
Stern Gang. See Stern, Avraham
Stettin, 197
Stobity. See Schlobitten
Stockholm, 274
Streicher, Julius, 258, 268
Stülpnagel, General Karl Heinrich von, 279, 283
Sturmabteilung (SA), 260, 271, 283
Stuttgart, 315
Stutthof concentration camp, 241–248, 246(photo), 251–252, 299–300, 326. See also Kiersztowski, Aronek (Walter Kerr), as concentration camp inmate
Südauen ("the southern fiields"), 212
Sugihara, Sempo (diplomat), 219fn
Sulalszczyna Province, 212
Sussi Vilki ("land of the vicious wolves"), 212

Suwalki, 211–219, 223–226, 228–229,
    229fn. *See also* Kiersztowski,
    Aronek (Walter Kerr)
Svetlogorsk. *See* Rauschen
Swabia, 315
Sweden, 10, 35, 97, 107–114, 142, 202
Swift, Jonathan (writer), 137

Tallin, 248, 250, 321
Tannenberg, Battle of (1410). *See*
    Grünwald, Battle of (1410)
Tannenberg, Battle of (1914), 175, 176,
    178(photo), 179–191. *See also*
    German army (after 1871);
    Hindenburg, Field Marshal Paul von;
    Hoffman, General Max von;
    Ludendorff, General Erich Friedrich;
    Eastern Front; Samsanov, General
    Aleksandr; Wilhelm II, Emperor of
    Germany
Tannenberg League, 203
Taylor, Telford (lawyer), 266
Tel Aviv, 229fn
Teutonic Knights, Order of, 2, 10, 20,
    24(table), 33, 36, 37, 39, 41, 52, 58,
    67–68, 82, 84, 86–87, 95, 98, 118,
    125, 131, 189, 201, 212, 256, 258,
    267
  aggressiveness, 53, 60, 71, 131, 142,
    287
  amber trade, 34, 55, 71, 88–89
  breeding of falcons, 75
  as businessmen, 34, 54, 56, 67, 76, 88
  character, 60–61
  chivalry, 60, 77
  conflict with merchant class and
    Junkers, 67, 119
  connections with Rome, 52, 53, 87
  connections with Venice, 87, 99
  conquest of East Prussia, 51–54
  effect on later generations, 167, 256
  grand masters, 49, 51, 52, 56, 64,
    75–77, 82
  heritage of, 61–62
  holdings in Western Europe, 53, 72
  later decadence, 60–61, 85, 87
  membership, 53, 72, 85
  order falters, 35, 57
  *reyse*, 69, 71–77, 83, 84, 77, 99. *See* also
    Henry, earl of Derby (King Henry IV
    of England)
  secularization, 99–101
  as soldiers, 34, 71, 88–89
  tenantry, 52, 87–88

Virgin Mary, patroness of Order, 61
  *See* also Albrecht of Brandenburg-
    Anspach (Hohenzollern), duke of
    Prussia; Crusades; East Prussia
    (Ostpreussen), military tradition;
    Lithuania, conflicts with Teutonic
    Knights; Poland, conflicts with
    Teutonic Knights
Thal, Elisa (refugee), 298
Thatcher, Prime Minster Margaret, 38
*The Train Was on Time. See* Böll,
    Heinrich (writer)
Thorn (Toruná), 33, 129, 209(table)
*Thoughts and Adventures. See* Churchill,
    Prime Minister Winston Spencer
Thuringia, 31, 72
Tiergarten (Berlin), 278
Tilly, Count Johann Tserclaes von, 107
Tilsit, Treaty of (1807). *See* Treaties, in
    passing, Tilsit (1807)
*Tin Drum, The. See* Grass, Günter
    (writer)
*Titanic* (ship), 325
Toruná. *See* Thorn
Tourism, 13–18, 26–27, 39, 44, 68–69, 86,
    94, 115, 179, 211, 231, 241–242
Toynbee, Arnold (historian), vii
Transylvania, 111
Trawniki execution site, Poland, 219
Treaties, in passing
  Brest-Litovsk (1918), 192
  German-Soviet Nonaggression Pact
    (1939), 58fn, 218, 268
  Maastricht (1991), 38
  Tilsit (1807), 104(table), 154, 232
  Versailles (1919), 204, 257, 261
  Westphalia (1648), 107
Treblinka concentration camp, 242
Treitschke, Heinrich von, 33, 96
Trevor-Roper, Hugh (historian), 206fn,
    257
*Tristan und Isolde. See* Wagner, Richard
    (composer)
*Triumph of the Will. See* Riefenstahl,
    Leni (film maker)
Truman, President Harry S., 267
Tuchman, Barbara (historian), 75
Turenne, Vicount Henri de La Tour
    d'Auvergne, 107
Turkey, 154

Ukraine, 4, 228
  Ukrainians as concentration camp
    guards, 219, 251, 300–304

*Ulysses. See* Joyce, James (writer)
UN. *See* United Nations
UNESCO. *See* United Nations
  Educational, Scientific, and Cultural
  Organization
Union of Propertied Noblemen (Verband
  des Besitzenden Adels), 16
United Nations (UN), 139
United Nations Educational, Scientific,
  and Cultural Organization
  (UNESCO), 138
United States of America, 5, 219, 219fn,
  267, 271, 320. *See also* American
  army
*Untermenschen* (subhuman), 228, 247
Ural Mountains, 272

Varchentin (estate), 305, 309, 311, 325
*Varieties of Religious Experience, The.*
  *See* James, Williams (philosopher)
Venice, 24fn, 64, 91, 211
Verband des Besitzenden Adels. *See*
  Union of Propertied Noblemen
Verdun, Battles of (1916–1917). *See*
  Battles, in passing, Verdun
  (1916–1917)
Versailles, 118, 124, 160(table), 168
Versailles, Treaty of (1919). *See* Treaties,
  in passing, Versailles (1919)
Victoria Louise, Princess Royal of Great
  Britain and Empress of Germany,
  172. *See* also Wilhelm II, Emperor of
  Germany
Vienna, 87, 128, 142, 168, 209(table), 213,
  228, 253, 326
Vilnius (Wilno), 4, 74, 77, 83, 208(table),
  218, 220–223, 248, 321
Vistula River, 24(table), 33, 34, 43, 46, 52,
  54, 56, 66, 93, 106, 125, 126, 128,
  129, 174, 175, 180.
*Vogue* (magazine), 135
Volga River, 19
Volkswagen (VW), 35, 89–90
Volprecht, Bernd, 195–199, 199(photo)
Voltaire (Françoise-Marie Arouet), 39,
  124, 124fn, 127, 129, 138,
  334–335(notes). *See also* Frederick
  II, (the Great), King of Prussia
*Vom Kriege (On War). See* Clausewitz,
  Lieutenant-Colonel von
VW. *See* Volkswagen

Wagner, Richard (composer), 26, 169, 254
Walesa, President Lech, 213, 214, 244

Walewska, Countess Marie, 152–154,
  153fn. *See also* Finckenstein
  (Kamieniec); Napoleon Bonapart,
  Emperor of France, affairs
Walewski, Alexandre, 153fn
Wallenstein, Albrecht Wenzel Eusebius
  von, , 107, 143
*Wall Street Journal* (newspaper), 77
Walser, Martin, vii
Wars, in passing
  Austro-Prussian (1866), 38, 160(table),
    168
  Danish (1864), 160(table), 168
  First Silesian (1740–1742), 91
  Franco-Prussian (1870), 26, 95,
    160(table), 168
  Gulf War (1991), 321
  of Liberation (1813), 104(table)
  Second Punic (218–201 B. C.), 185
  Seven Years' (1756–1763), 10, 14,
    104(table), 125, 126
  Spanish Civil (1936–1939), 252
  Spanish Succession (1702–1714), 90–91
  Vietnam (1955–1975), 273
  World War I (1914–1918), 36, 58
  World War II (1939–1945), 1, 3, 8–10,
    18, 46
Warsaw, 4 ,31, 54, 66, 130, 140, 148, 149,
  152, 180, 183, 184, 209(table), 213,
  219, 224, 227, 247, 321, 326
Wars of Liberation (1813). *See* Wars, in
  passing, of Liberation (1813)
Warweiden (Wirwajdy), 294
Waterloo, Battle of (1815). *See* Battles, in
  passing, Waterloo (1815)
Wedgwood, C. V. (historian), 107
Weekley, Frieda, (von Richthofen), 280
Weichel River, 290
Weinrowski, Lieutenant, 265
Wellington, Arthur Wellesley, first Duke
  of, 143
Welter, Mieczyslaw (sculptor), 97
Westerplatte garrison (Danzig), 78–80, 242
West Germany. *See* Federal Republic of
  Germany
Westphalia, Treaty of (1648). *See* Treaties,
  in passing, Westphalia (1648)
West Prussia, 36, 121fn, 129, 300. *See also*
  East Prussia (Ostpreussen); Prussia
Wheeler-Bennett, John (writer),
  203fn
*Wicher* incident (1932), 78
Wielbark. *See* Willenberg
Wiesel, Elie, 326

Wilhelm II, Emperor of Germany, 15,
   41(photo), 57–58, 91, 119, 160(table),
   163–164, 171–173, 175, 190,
   194(photo), 203fn, 233, 258, 319
   abdication, 193–194
   character, 172–173, 193, 330(notes)
   dismissal of Bismarck, 160(table), 164,
      173
   at maneuvers, 165, 165(photo)
   opinion of Hindenburg and Ludendorff,
      193
   opinion of Hitler, 203fn
   youth, 164, 172
   See also Cadinen (Kadyny); German
      army (after 1871); Hindenburg, Field
      Marshal Paul von; Ludendorff,
      General Erich Friedrich; Prussian
      army (before 1871); Tannenberg,
      Battle of (1914)
Willenberg (Wielbark), 188, 189
William I, Emperor of Germany,
   160(table), 168
Wilno. See Vilnius
Wilson, President Woodrow, 204
Wirwajdy. See Warweiden
Wittenburg, 100

Witzleben, Field Marshal Erwin von, 262,
   281
Wolfsburg, 89–90
Wolfsschanze (Wolf's Lair). See Hitler,
   Adolf, Wolfsschanze (Wolf's Lair)
Wrangel, Field Marshal Friedrich von,
   166, 172
Wuppertal, 19
Wyszynáski, Cardinal Stefan, 54

Yegorov, Admiral Vladimir, 6, 9, 21–22
Yeltsin, President Boris, 5, 20,
   37
Ypres, Battles of (1914, 1915). See Battles,
   in passing, Ypres (1914, 1915)
Yugoslavia, 321, 322

Zalew Wisálany. See Frisches Haff
Zelednogradsk. See Bad Crenz
Zhirinovsky, Vladimir (politician), 37, 322
Ziesenis, G. (painter), 131(photo)
Zorndorf, Battle of (1758). See Battles, in
   passing, Zorndorf (1758)
Zweig, Arnold (writer), 192, 192fn. See
   also Hoffman, General Max von